CW00566297

DEFENDING THE EMPIRE

Frontispiece: Portrait photograph of A.J. Balfour, *c.* 1900, outside House of Commons.

DEFENDING THE EMPIRE

The Conservative Party and British Defence Policy 1899–1915

Rhodri Williams

YALE UNIVERSITY PRESS
NEW HAVEN AND LONDON · 1991

Copyright © 1991 by Rhodri Williams

All rights reserved. This book may not be reproduced, in whole or in part, in any form (beyond that copying permitted by Sections 107 and 108 of the US Copyright Law and except by reviewers for the public press), without written permission from the publishers.

Set in Goudy Old Style by Excel Typesetters Co., Hong Kong

Printed and bound in Great Britain by Bell and Bain Ltd., Glasgow

Library of Congress Cataloging-in-Publication Data

Williams, Rhodri, 1959–
    Defending the empire: the Conservative Party and British Defence Policy, 1899–1915 / Rhodri Williams.
        p.   cm.
    Includes bibliographical references and index.
    ISBN 0–300–05048–8
    1. Great Britain—Politics and government—1901–1936.   2. Great Britain—Colonies—Administration—History—20th century.   3. Conservative Party (Great Britain)—History—20th century.   4. Great Britain—Military policy—History—20th century.   5. Great Britain—Defenses—History—20th century.   I. Title.
DA570.W53   1991
320.941—dc20   90–50944
                                                                                      CIP

For my parents

CONTENTS

LIST OF ILLUSTRATIONS

ACKNOWLEDGEMENTS

Writing this book has absorbed my interest and energies for the best part of a decade. I began researching the Edwardian defence debate in the autumn of 1981, when a graduate student at Balliol College, Oxford, and finished writing the book just a few months before leaving the academic world in the autumn of 1990. Nine years on the subject continues to fascinate me. I am delighted to see the book finally reach print; but I also feel that I am parting from an old friend.

In the course of my research and writing I have benefited from the help and advice of a host of people and I am pleased to have this opportunity of expressing my appreciation to them.

I would like to acknowledge with thanks the assistance of the staffs of the numerous libraries and record offices who kindly allowed me access to documents in their keeping.

I am most grateful to the following individuals and institutions for granting me permission to quote from materials of which they hold the copyright: the Warden and Fellows of All Souls College, Oxford (Wilkinson Papers); the Earl of Balfour (Balfour Papers); the Earl Bathurst (Glenesk-Bathurst Papers); the University of Birmingham (Chamberlain Papers); Lord Bonham-Carter (Asquith Papers); the Trustees of the British Library (Balfour, Arnold-Forster, Marker, North-cliffe, Long and Sydenham Papers); the Master, Fellows and Scholars of Churchill College in the University of Cambridge ((Fisher, Chandos and Spring-Rice Papers); the Earl of Cawdor (Cawdor Papers); Lord Esher (Esher Papers); Faber and Faber Limited; the Duke of Hamilton (Fisher Papers); the Controller of HMSO; Vice-Admiral Sir Ian Hogg (Gwynne Papers); the House of Lords Record Office (Wargrave, Blumenfeld and Bonar Law Papers); the Trustees of the Imperial War Museum (Wilson Papers); Sir Hector Monro, MP (Ewart Papers); A.J. Maxse and Mrs Patricia Gill, West Sussex County Archivist (Maxse Papers); the Trustees of the National Army Museum (Roberts Papers); the Trustees of the National Library of Scotland (Haldane, Rosebery and Haig Papers);

the Trustees of the National Maritime Museum (Corbett, Noel and Thursfield Papers); the Warden and Fellows of New College, Oxford (Milner Papers); the Marquess of Salisbury (Salisbury Papers); the Earl of Selborne (Selborne Papers); the Editor of the *Spectator* (St Loe Strachey Papers); Times Newspapers Limited; Walker Martineau & Co. (Harcourt Papers).

For permission to reproduce photographs of which they hold copyright I am grateful to the Marquess of Salisbury, the National Army Museum, the Imperial War Museum and the National Portrait Gallery.

I would like to thank Prof. A.J.A. Morris for kindly making available to me his transcripts of material in the Garvin Papers at the University of Texas, Austin, and the Rt. Hon. Earl Lloyd George of Dwyfor for allowing me to consult the papers of his grandfather, David Lloyd George, at The Hall, Freshford, Avon.

I owe numerous more personal debts of gratitude: to Dr Agatha Ramm, for inspiring my interest in early twentieth-century diplomatic history; to Sir Michael Howard, who supervised my doctoral thesis and from whom I have received innumerable kindnesses; to Colin Lucas, my former undergraduate tutor at Balliol, for his encouragement and support; to Michael Brock CBE, formerly Warden of Nuffield College, from whose interest in my career and knowledge of my subject I have profited greatly; to Gerry Webber and Alvin Jackson, fellow historians at Nuffield, for their ideas and company; to Henry Mayr-Harting, my colleague at St Peter's from 1985 to 1990, from whose example as both scholar and tutor I learned much; and to my many pupils during eight years' teaching at Oxford, whose humour and irreverence kept me from irredeemable donnishness.

John Darwin, Ewen Green and Robert Gooren did me the immense service of reading my manuscript in draft. I am very grateful to them all for the time and care they devoted to the task; their constructive advice improved the book in many ways and their good judgement saved me from a number of errors.

I would also like to thank John Nicoll and his colleagues at Yale University Press for making my first experience of authorship both pleasurable and uncomplicated.

My last and biggest thank you is to Hilary, my wife and best friend, who for six years has cheerfully put up with Balfour's presence in our lives.

Finally, I dedicate this book to my parents with love and gratitude.

CHAPTER 1

Introduction

This is not a book which tilts at historiographical windmills. Its pages contain no thunderous cannonades against fellow historians and even waspish footnotes are few and far between. The reader will not be deafened by the sound of axes being ground. This restraint will disappoint those who like their history 'red in tooth and claw', but there is a very good reason for it. Despite its interest and importance (which I intend to prove), the subject of the book is not one on which much has been written. The purpose of the book therefore is not so much to challenge scholarship as to make good its absence. This makes the role of the author less gladiator than pioneer. In fact, *Defending the Empire* treks into three distinct but contiguous areas of historiographical wilderness; the Edwardian Unionist party; British defence policy before the First World War; and the career of Arthur James Balfour. On each of these subjects it will leave subsequent travellers with a clearer idea of the historical terrain. The point of this introduction is to explain why pioneering metaphors are appropriate.

During the 1970s the foreground of Edwardian historiography was occupied by the struggle of the post-Gladstonian Liberal party to preserve its hegemony on the Left in the face of an increasingly class-conscious electorate, an organized labour movement and growing pressure for greater state intervention. The policy, organization and electoral base of the Liberal party came under intense scrutiny from scholars, as did the relationship between the Liberal and Labour parties at both the constituency and the parliamentary levels, and on all these issues a substantial literature came into being.[1] Debate focused (and continues to focus) on the vexed question of whether the Edwardian Liberal party had shown itself able to survive in an era of class-based politics.[2]

While the Liberal party enjoyed this historical limelight, the Unionist party was relegated to the wings.[3] Apart from a number of general works covering a longer period of party history, and a handful of significant monographs and articles, remarkably little was written during the 1970s on the Liberal party's chief electoral rival between 1900 and 1914.[4] Among scholars working on Edwardian Unionism, the focus of attention continued to be the Tariff Reform controversy which dogged the party throughout the pre-war period.[5] Although it is tempting to suggest some causal connection with the election of Margaret Thatcher as Prime Minister, it is probably coincidence that this imbalance began to be rectified in 1979. It was in that year that the concept of a 'crisis of Conservatism' first began to rival the 'strange death of Liberal England' as a subject of serious scholarly interest.[6]

Put simply, this posits the growth of acute ideological and political tensions on the British Right before 1914, as individual Unionists reacted differently to the threat posed to the party of property by the growth of socialism and the widening of the working-class electorate, and to the Empire by Britain's relative economic and naval decline.[7] Ideological fragmentation, it is argued, received institutional expression as leagues and pressure groups proliferated on the Right. The existence of the 'legion of leagues' constituted a serious threat to the cohesion of the Unionist party and a challenge to the authority of its leadership. The chief role in this drama is assigned to a group commonly referred to as the 'Radical Right', activists convinced that the interests of property and the interests of the Empire could only be safeguarded if the Unionist party adapted its policy and style to meet the demands of mass politics.[8] Recent research has subdivided the 'Radical Right' into various strands and tendencies, with fine distinctions being drawn between the ideas and aspirations of 'tory radicals', 'radical conservatives' and 'social imperialists' among others.[9] The political aims, organization and social basis of right-wing activism in Edwardian Britain have also been analysed in detail.[10]

Unfortunately, the expansion of research into the Radical Right has not been accompanied by a comparable improvement in our knowledge of what one scholar, writing in 1981, termed 'the most neglected aspect of the pre-war Right' in Britain, namely the formal Unionist party itself.[11] The impact on the Unionist party structure and programme of surging grass-roots militancy has been reconnoitred but no great advances have been made.[12] The assumptions, objectives and methods of the party leadership, those whom the Radical Right contemptuously denounced as 'mandarins', have also escaped serious reassessment. Historians of the Edwardian Right have found the wild men of the Unionist party, operating on its margins, more interesting than the party elite, who dominated its counsels.

This historiographical imbalance is nowhere more evident than in the field of defence policy. It is a commonplace of writing on the Radical Right that it was nationalistic, Germanophobic and committed to a strengthening of Britain's military and naval forces in preparation for the

European war which many of its number thought not only inevitable but also (in a Darwinian sense) desirable. Interesting comparisons have been made between the Radical Right in Edwardian Britain and *volkisch* nationalist groups in Wilhelmine Germany such as the Pan-German League and the Agrarian League.[13] Prominent among British counter-parts of the German *Verbande* are the Navy League and the National Service League, organizations which campaigned for increased naval construction and conscription respectively and which bitterly criticized governments of both parties for reacting with insufficient urgency to the German 'threat' in the years after 1900. Both the Navy League and the National Service League have attracted historians and their critique of Unionist party policy on defence has been adequately explained.[14] What we lack, however, is a corresponding understanding of the views of those whose policy they denounced. In existing literature on the attitudes of the Radical Right towards issues of national security the outlook of the 'mandarins' receives brief and simplistic treatment; the traditional party elite are seen merely as targets in the shooting gallery of Radical Right politics. It is not that historians have failed to acknowledge the salience of disputes over defence issues in the politics of the Right before 1914, rather that their perspective on those disputes has been very one-sided. Any light shed on the activities of the party leaders is refracted and dim. No serious effort has been made to understand the assumptions underpinning the policies of which militants were so critical; to explain the objectives which the Unionist party leadership pursued in the pre-war decade; or to analyse the reasons why their assessment of defence problems and their policy prescriptions so differed from those of their radical supporters.

The present work puts this situation to rights, providing the first comprehensive account of the defence policy of the official Unionist party between the outbreak of the South African War in 1899 and the coming of the First World War in 1914. My concern is with the Unionist leadership, those on the front bench at Westminster who decided official party policy. I examine the ideas of the party elite on defence issues between 1899 and 1914, concentrating on three broad areas of policy – military organization, naval construction and naval reform. The strategic assumptions on which Unionist policy rested are analysed, and the extent to which these changed between 1899 and 1914 assessed. The book also examines the way in which Unionist policy was made in and out of office, and sheds light on the role of successive party leaders. Since the book is about 'mandarins' and Westminster politics rather than militants in editorial offices and the constituencies it is not intended to add significantly to existing interpretations of the Radical Right. On the other hand, it should make it easier to understand why the influence of Radical Right pressure groups and agitations proved so limited in the field of defence. The reader wishing to master the arcana of army organization or Dreadnought construction before 1914 will definitely find this book disappointing because I have deliberately chosen not to follow my Unionist subjects into the 'Serbonian bog' of defence policy minutiae. Unlike many debates on defence policy in Edwardian parliaments, this is not an aridly technical book; it will give no one cause to echo the complaint of one Unionist spokesman on army affairs, 'my mind is grinding at the Army question'.[15] What it offers instead is an exploration of the matrix of 'political' factors which influenced defence policy outcomes within the Unionist party, including party pressures, electoral realities, parliamentary constraints, tactical opportunities and plain individual preferences. For this reason the debate over defence issues is constantly set against the general political background of the period and arguments over Dreadnoughts or conscription related to contemporary controversies over Free Trade, House of Lords reform and Irish Home Rule. In its coverage of the years 1899 to 1905, when the Unionist party was in power, the book builds on existing works by scholars of British defence policy who, despite approaching the subject from a less 'political' angle than the present author, have to some extent illuminated the political context in which the defence policy of the Salisbury and Balfour governments was made. In its coverage of the years 1906 to 1914, however, when the Unionist party was in Opposition, there are no scholarly footprints to map the way and the book breaks virgin historical ground. The relationship between the two periods is a crucial theme since the response of the Unionist Opposition to the policy of the Liberal governments of 1906–14 was largely determined by the party's own experience and achievement in office.

The second historiographical purpose of this book is to explain the party political context in which British defence policy was made in the Edwardian period.

A considerable body of scholarship exists on British defence policy in the years of Liberal government from 1906 to 1914. The machinery of policy-making has been comprehensively covered.[16] So has the organizational and technological development of the Army and Navy.[17] Inevitably, much interest has been devoted to the question of how far both services were 'prepared' for the European war that broke out in the summer of 1914.[18] Biographical studies of key policy-makers have also contributed to our understanding of the steps by which the British government readied the defensive forces of the country for the test of war.[19] In so far as scholars have shown interest in the political framework of defence policy-making after 1906, this interest has naturally centred on the ruling Liberal party and on its internal debate over armaments expenditure and foreign policy. The difficulties of the Campbell-Bannerman and Asquith governments in reconciling defence priorities with pressures from their backbench and constituency rank and file have been well treated.[20]

Remarkably little notice has been taken however, of the parallel *inter*-party debate on defence between the Liberal government and its Unionist Opposition. Many otherwise excellent accounts of British defence policy before 1914 neglect the context of two-party adversarial politics in which policy was made. Preoccupied with decision-making by ministers and experts in the quiet and shadowy corridors of Whitehall, they seldom acknowledge the fact that policy had then to emerge into the noise and glare of Westminster and the hustings where it was subject to the tough criteria of party politics. Existing studies of Liberal policy either leave the Opposition out of the picture altogether, or they cast them as a kind of gloomy Chorus looking on at the drama of the Liberal faction fight and periodically interjecting, in Cassandra-like tones, to warn of the German 'menace'. Their arguments on the issues of the day are sketched lightly, often cartooned. No thought is given to assessing what influence, if any, the Unionists might have exercised upon the direction of Liberal policy. As the present work will make clear, this is a crucial and distorting omission. By explaining the response of the Unionist Opposition to Liberal defence policy, and the ways in which they sought (and were often able) to influence its direction, I hope to restore a neglected but vital political dimension of British defence policy in the decade or so before 1914.

The final historiographical wilderness to be tamed here is biographical. One individual dominates the following pages: Arthur James Balfour. As Prime Minister from 1902 to 1905, and leader of the Opposition from 1905 to 1911, Balfour's was the single most important voice in determining Unionist defence policy throughout the period covered by this study. Balfour has had numerous biographers, all of whom have identified and discussed his career-long interest in defence issues.[21] Their approach has been, however, to emphasize Balfour's non-party activities in the field of defence, notably his involvement in the creation and early development of the Committee of Imperial Defence.[22] Of Balfour's partisan activities in the defence field, notably his handling of defence issues as Unionist leader from 1902 to 1911, next to nothing has been written. In view of Balfour's consuming interest in defence matters and their central importance in Edwardian politics, this is an astonishing gap in our knowledge. That gap is now filled; the present work provides a detailed account of Balfour's party leadership in what was a vital area of Edwardian political debate. In doing so it lodges a third and last claim to historiographical importance.

CHAPTER 2

The South African War and Army Reform
1899–1903

The Thin Red Line

The product of 'a vast yet casual imperialism', the British Empire at the close of the nineteenth century comprised a complex pattern of overlapping spheres of formal and informal influence.[1] Britain's formal possessions, including India, Canada, Australia and New Zealand, covered approximately a quarter of the world's surface; their land frontiers extended for 20,000 miles. But in addition to these authentically pink patches on the world map there were vast areas in Africa, the Far East and Pacific in which Britain had important strategic or economic interests; here imperial influence was exercised by means which fell short of outright annexation and direct control. Binding these areas of formal and informal influence together was the web of sea lanes along which the commercial life-blood of the Empire flowed. Those sea lanes in turn depended on a network of scattered naval bases and coaling stations, what Lord Curzon called the 'tollgates and barbicans of Empire'.

Whereas the extent of this Empire 'on which the sun never set' was a source of complacent pride in the schoolrooms and music-halls of late Victorian England, to British governments it was 'the greatest example of strategical over-extension in history' and presented nightmarish challenges.[2] In the mid-nineteenth century, Britain, in Palmerstonian costume, had swaggered alone on the world stage as the energies of the major European powers were absorbed by the transforming effects on the Continent of the powerful currents of liberalism and nationalism. By the 1890s, however, moving from nation- to empire-building, the European powers had turned outward; Russia to the Far East and Central Asia, France to Africa and South-East Asia, Germany to Africa and the Near East. Across the globe Britain's interests threatened to collide with those of rival powers whose governments were under domestic pressures, both economic and political, to secure a 'place in the sun'. For a small island nation, whose once-dominant economy was experiencing the first pains of relative decline, the vulnerability of the Empire, that 'Weary Titan', imposed a growing strain.[3] As the gap between Britain's commitments and her resources widened through the 1890s, her governments pursued a fundamentally defensive foreign policy, seeking to preserve the status quo in areas of vital interest to Britain such as the Ottoman Empire and China. This policy, which would eventually lead Britain to abandon her stance of diplomatic non-alignment, so-called 'Splendid Isolation', has been superbly covered by diplomatic historians such as J.A.S. Grenville and George Monger.[4] It forms the backdrop to the evolution of British defence policy described in the present study.

Whereas adroit diplomacy could neutralize potential threats, it could not eliminate the need for effective defences. The changing balance of global power at the close of the nineteenth-century placed increasingly heavy demands on the military resources of the Empire. These were severely limited. For the 'immense business of providing for the defence of the Empire' late Victorian governments had fewer than a quarter of a million men under arms.[5] Of this total some 75,000 were stationed in the subcontinent of India, where they supplemented the native Indian army.[6] Alone among the major European powers of the period, Britain had not adopted conscription as a solution to its military manpower needs. The British would 'sooner throw over Imperialism than accept the military system of foreign countries', wrote Sir Edward Hamilton of the Treasury in February 1900.[7] By the middle of the nineteenth century an historic distrust of large standing armies had been reinforced by the emergence of a 'liberal laisser-faire ideology which rendered the notion of enforced service to the state unacceptable to most British citizens'.[8] The consequence of this loyalty to the voluntary principle was that, as the Director-General of Ordnance, Sir Henry Brackenbury, observed in 1899, late Victorian and Edwardian Britain attempted to maintain the largest Empire the world had ever seen with the military resources of a 'third class military power'.[9]

What made this possible was the supremacy of the Royal Navy; its command of the seas protected Britain's weak garrisons – the 'thin red line' – from overseas attack and allowed them to be reinforced in an emergency. It was for this reason that the Colonial Defence Committee declared in 1896 that sea supremacy was 'the basis of the system of Imperial defence' and the 'determining factor in shaping the whole defensive policy of the Empire'.[10] But naval supremacy was not in itself sufficient; the security of the Empire also depended on the rapid expansion of the Regular Army in a great crisis. For this governments looked to India, 'that English barrack in the Oriental seas', the dominions, and the Auxiliary forces. Between the Mutiny of 1857 and 1914 'Indian troops served in over a dozen different campaigns in places as far apart as China and Egypt'.[11] However, as well as inflaming the sensitivities of Liberal opinion in Britain, the use of Indian troops beyond India's borders was a source of friction between the governments in

London and Delhi. The nub of the argument was financial rather than constitutional, with each government trying to pass on to the other the cost of sending Gurkhas or Sikhs to fight in imperial wars. Dominion troops played a less conspicuous role in imperial armies in the later nineteenth-century, although Canadians and Australians served in the Sudanese expedition of 1884–5. It was in the naval, rather than the military, sphere that Britain was most successful in securing dominion contributions to imperial defence. Other than Indian and dominion troops, British governments could look for the expansion of the Regular Army to the three irregular or 'Auxiliary' forces of the Crown; the Militia, an infantry force descended from the county trained bands of the Elizabethan era; the Yeomanry, a cavalry force raised from gentry and farmers in the counties; and the Volunteers, a force of infantry established at a time of Anglo-French tension in the 1850s and raised from the urban middle classes.[12] However, the Auxiliary forces were deficient in numbers and equipment and their value as a means of expanding the Regular Army was limited, since they were under no obligation to serve abroad. The government could only trust to their patriotism and sense of duty in a national emergency.

Such an emergency occurred in South Africa in the autumn of 1899. Friction between Britain and the Boer Republics of the Transvaal and Orange Free State had been increasing steadily since the Jameson Raid of 1896. Negotiations had foundered on the unwillingnesss of the two sides to compromise; Britain's strategic interests in the Cape and her economic interests in the Rand proved irreconcilable with the Boers' desire for autonomy. Crisis point having been reached over the rights of the 'Uitlanders' or foreigners in the Transvaal, war broke out in early October 1899.[13] The Unionist government in London, headed by the sixty-nine-year-old Marquess of Salisbury, expected a small war and a quick victory. Instead they got a big war and a string of bloody reverses which demoralized a jingoistic public used to easy laurels. 'The skill of Sir Garnet at thrashing the cannibal' proved inadequate in a conflict against a skilled, well-armed and resourceful 'European' opponent; 'the British have lost all skill in fighting', wrote an American observer, 'and the whole world knows it'.[14] The Army's failures culminated in the 'Black Week' of December 1899 when, within seven days, at Stormberg, Magersfontein and Colenso, the gilt was knocked off the Victorian age. Deficiencies in training, leadership and the quality of recruits were matched by administrative and logistical failures. Experienced in mounting small-scale expeditions, the War Office was severely tested by the task of mobilizing the largest force Britain had ever dispatched overseas; the resulting abuses, errors and shortages were a further source of public and political dismay and brought opprobrium on the government.

Even though the tide of war on the veld turned in the spring of

1900, restoring British military and public morale and delivering Salisbury's government a 'khaki election' victory in October, the pacification of the Boers took a further two years to achieve, two years during which the scale of Britain's military effort in South Africa steadily grew. Throughout the war the military resources of the Empire were committed to breaking the resistance of the Boer commandos, to which end troops were withdrawn from India, Egypt and other colonial garrisons. Never had the 'thin red line' along the Khyber Pass and the Nile been stretched quite so thin, a fact which explains the anxiety of the British government to avoid a quarrel with France or Russia while the war lasted.[15] Even the United Kingdom itself was denuded of Regular troops to the point where its defence depended upon the inadequately trained and equipped Auxiliary forces.[16] The resulting sense of public insecurity was to fuel a surge of invasion scares and stories which persisted for a decade.[17] More serious still, the war had glaringly revealed the absence of any real power of expansion in Britain's military system. A system which had strained even to maintain the peacetime garrisons in India and the Colonies and to mount expeditions to imperial trouble spots was inevitably stretched to breaking point by the manpower demands of a major war. When, in February 1900, the newly appointed Commander-in-Chief in South Africa, Lord Roberts, asked the government for substantial reinforcements, he had to be informed that none were available.[18] In the event, Roberts' requirements were only met by strenuous efforts at recruitment, the mobilization of Volunteer, Militia and Yeomanry units, and the dispatch of unprecedentedly large contingents of Dominion troops. Salisbury's nephew, Arthur James Balfour, then First Lord of the Treasury, later described this as 'the lowest point reached during the whole of the war'.[19]

If the war against the Dutch Republics proved the inelasticity of Britain's military system, it also sent its cost spiralling upwards. The Treasury's expectation of a cheap war on the pattern of the Zulu wars of the 1870s proved less justified than Joseph Chamberlain's prediction that the bill for the war would be 'something tremendous'.[20] In 1898–99 total defence expenditure had been £44 million; in 1900–1 ordinary spending on the Army alone exceeded £30 million. When the actual cost of the war was taken into account military spending rose to a figure in excess of £95 million.[21] Given the necessity for a continuing military commitment in South Africa, and in view of a menacing international climate, the prospects for post-war economy were bleak. Yet economies there had to be; in February 1903 the Chancellor warned the Cabinet against the risk of provoking a violent public reaction to the costs of imperial defence.[22] The possibility of savings depended entirely on the creation of a more elastic military organization. Only by reverting to a small and economical peacetime army could retrenchment be effected and only if coupled with some new system of expansion could such a peacetime army be justified.

Mr Brodrick's Army Corpses

'From Marlborough to Wellington, the Crimea, the Mutiny, Egypt and South Africa, the story is the same. Belated preparation; frantic effort; disappointment; recrimination; scapegoats; followed by inertia'.[23] This assessment of the British response to military disaster in the nineteenth century can be made to fit the facts of the South African war in all but one respect. Far from being characterized by inertia, the post-war period saw two governments make a determined effort to reform the British Army.[24] The Salisbury government embarked upon the course of army reform even before the war had ended. During the 'khaki election' of October 1900 ministers acknowledged the necessity of reform, and the removal of the Secretary of State for War, Lord Lansdowne, in the ensuing Cabinet reshuffle signified a readiness for change as well as releasing Lansdowne from what he called his 'hard spell of W.O. servitude'.[25] His successor, the Under-Secretary at the Foreign Office, William St John Brodrick, had recently spoken out against any serious attempt at army reform being made while the war was in progress, a stance similar to that adopted by the Chancellor, Sir Michael Hicks Beach, who was determined to resist further financial strain.[26] Within weeks of taking office, however, Brodrick had changed his mind and was busy with plans for military reorganization.[27] His conversion to immediate action, and the Cabinet's decision to back him and to overrule Beach, owed to both military and political considerations. On the one hand, Brodrick persuaded Salisbury and his colleagues that, in view of the tension between Britain and her imperial rivals, France and Russia, it would be dangerous to delay what would necessarily be a protracted and debilitating process of reform until the end of the war, by which time the Army would be exhausted and the Empire militarily vulnerable.[28] On the other hand, ministers were under no illusion that reform was vital to placate a public opinion highly critical of the government's handling of the war; 'the feeling is by no means confined to the Press that we have blundered terribly and that Gt Britain could not be in its present position if we had shown reasonable foresight', wrote Brodrick in January 1900.[29] A vigorous and successful attempt at army reform could restore the government's tarnished image and, with it, public confidence. Moreover, there was also a strong political case for trying to absorb the cost of army reform, which ministers expected to be high, while the war had still to be won and public opinion was still committed to securing victory, rather than after a peace, when the public would be weary and resistant to further sacrifices.[30] Even Hicks Beach acknowledged a 'universal feeling of present day in favour of increased expenditure'.[31]

The major constraint on Brodrick's freedom of action, other than the imperative need for economy, was the impossibility of conscription. There were political and military obstacles to compulsory military service. The political obstacle has already been identified; no party was prepared to challenge that 'exemption from responsibility for his own defence' which had come to seem 'an Englishman's constitutional birthright'.[32] Even to moot the idea was deemed electoral suicide. The military objection to compulsion rested on the peculiar requirements of imperial defence. Maintaining overseas garrisons called for a steady flow of long-term volunteer recruits; to send conscripts would be wasteful and inefficient since, by the time they had been trained and dispatched, too short a period of their service would remain for them to be be useful. So, although Brodrick declared in Parliament in March 1901 that his adhesion to the voluntary principle was strictly limited by its ability to deliver sufficient forces, the obvious alternative was not a political or practical possibility.[33] The traditional model of a small professional army reinforced in war by voluntary enlistment was thus reinforced. This meant that, like its predecessors, the Salisbury government had to rely on popular patriotism in an emergency. It also confirmed the potential importance in any reform scheme of the Auxiliary forces which, for all their deficiencies, constituted a reservoir of partly trained manpower by which the Regular Army could be expanded.

Able and hardworking, Brodrick was commonly regarded in official circles as one of the few bright young prospects in a greying Cabinet.[34] He was a personal friend of Balfour's and a fellow member of the Souls, that gilded late Victorian social circle whose ethos John Morley described as 'delightful, but most blighting to one's democracy'.[35] Brodrick had previously served at the War Office, as Financial Secretary in 1886–92 and as Parliamentary Secretary in 1895–8, and his new appointment satisfied a long-standing ambition.[36] The reform scheme which he introduced in the House of Commons on 8 March 1901 was the fruit of personal knowledge and experience, as well as of consultation with Lord Roberts, the recently appointed Commander-in-Chief. The scheme was conservative in retaining the principle of pairing battalions at home and abroad introduced by Edward Cardwell in 1870, the purpose of which was to ensure a parity between battalions deployed abroad and battalions retained at home. It was innovative in reorganizing that portion of the Regular Army stationed in the UK into six self-contained army corps on the German model, each based on a territorial military district to increase decentralization.[37] Three of these corps were to be composed entirely of Regular battalions and to constitute a 'striking force'; three were to include both Regular and Auxiliary units and to be allocated a

'War', cartoon of W.F. St John Brodrick by
'Spy', *Vanity Fair*, 18 July 1901.

primarily home defence role. Brodrick's scheme was intended to provide
that means of military expansion which had been lacking in 1899 and
simultaneously to strengthen the defence of the British Isles themselves.
In both respects it reflected its author's conviction that the Empire had
been dangerously vulnerable during 1899 and 1900 and a concern that
the antagonism felt towards Britain by the other European powers might
be leading to war. It not only made available at home a strong force
ready for immediate dispatch abroad in any future crisis, but by inte-
grating the Auxiliary forces with the Regular Army in peacetime, it
also facilitated their expansion of the Regulars in war. Since Brodrick
believed it possible that the British Army might have to fight in Europe,
he sought to construct it on a European scale; hence the unprecedented
size of the striking force.[38] The home defence provisions of the scheme
were a direct response to the threat of invasion which recent diplomatic
tension had revived and to the public's patent lack of confidence in the
Auxiliary forces. Brodrick proposed not only to increase the number
of Regular troops allocated to home defence, but also to improve the
efficiency of the Auxiliaries by lengthening their period of training and
reducing inefficient units. Such steps would also better fit the Auxiliaries
to play an expansionary role if called upon in a future national emergency. Given his preoccupation with the European situation Brodrick's

army scheme made sense, and according to his assessment of Britain's needs it possessed distinct merits. However, if it was to become a military reality two conditions had to be met. First, the War Office had to find, and Parliament to pay for, an additional 11,500 Regular recruits annually.[39] Second, the Auxiliary forces had to be persuaded to acquiesce in their own reform. It was his failure to meet both these conditions which explains the frustration of Brodrick's reform hopes and his ignominious departure from the War Office in the autumn of 1903.

Though initially sanguine, by June 1901 Brodrick was convinced of the difficulty of improving recruitment.[40] Many battalions were already well below their nominal establishment, victims of the perennial struggle to produce drafts for India and the other imperial garrisons.[41] Brodrick's solution was to make service more attractive by reducing its length from six years in the Colours followed by six in the Reserve, to three in the Colours followed by nine in the Reserve. At the same time pay would be increased.[42] However, this policy created the problem of how to reconcile such short enlistments with the demands of service in distant corners of the Empire. It could only be justified, and an inefficient and disruptive rotation of short-term troops avoided, if some means could be found to induce a large enough number of three-year men to extend their Colour service for a further period of years. This inducement Brodrick offered in the form of still higher rates of daily pay but even this failed to sustain an adequate supply of recruits, as well as setting the War Minister at loggerheads with Hicks Beach.[43] Brodrick's hopes that 75 per cent of three-year men would re-enlist for a further term proved groundless; the actual figure was closer to 20 per cent and by 1903 posed a grave threat to the supply of drafts to garrisons abroad. As the recruiting crisis deepened through 1902, the drain of men from the Militia into the Regular Army quickened. This further undermined the scheme since the continuing debilitation of the Militia rendered it even less fit than before to play a role in the corps structure; it sank further below establishment and the poor quality of its rank and file became ever more glaring. Brodrick's projected increase of 50,000 in the Militia Reserve came to seem fanciful.

While the result of three-year enlistments was calling into question the military feasibility of Brodrick's scheme, and prompting talk of 'Army corpses', his proposals for reforming the Volunteers were undermining the Secretary of State's political position.[44]

The home defence aspects of the scheme depended upon the correction of those deficiencies in the Volunteers which the South African War had both exposed and exacerbated. However, in tackling those deficiencies Brodrick faced two major difficulties. The more fundamental was that, by necessitating a more exacting standard of training and service for the Volunteers, any effective reform would risk deterring recruits; indeed, existing Volunteers might choose to leave the force, or be compelled to leave by their employers, rather than submit to increased demands on their time.[45] Brodrick's second difficulty was that any meaningful reform was certain to arouse the determined opposition of the Volunteer colonels, whose sensitivity to War Office encroachment on their 'fiefs' would provide another motive for resistance. The colonels regarded the best possible reform as an increase in the capitation grants they received from the War Office, not a set of onerous regulations which would demoralize the force and jeopardize its future. Their attitude was the more immediate of Brodrick's problems because many of them sat in Parliament, and of these the great majority were Unionist. In the wake of the khaki election there were over forty 'Volunteer MPs', constituting a well-organized group on the government back benches. Additional recruits were to be found among the large number of 'country gentlemen' on the Unionist benches who, while no longer actively soldiering, preserved 'picquant memories of their annual training'.[46] On several occasions during the 1880s and 1890s the Volunteer MPs and their allies had shown a willingness to defy the government of the day over issues touching the interests of the force.[47] Though the social basis of the Volunteer force was relatively narrow, and although its numbers were electorally insignificant, the strength of its parliamentary representation gave it an influence which no Secretary of State could ignore, least of all a Unionist one.

Anticipating trouble and wishing to avoid a parliamentary discussion, Brodrick chose to introduce his first measure of Volunteer reform – a new set of camp regulations – by Order-in-Council during the autumn recess of 1901.[48] However, when Parliament met early in 1902 there was a vigorous protest against the new regulations from the Volunteer MPs.[49] Brodrick was forced to placate them by promising a revision of the regulations and by appointing a committee of Volunteer commanding officers to examine problems arising locally from their implementation. Though intended by the Secretary of State to channel criticism, the second of these measures was politically damaging because it recognized the claims of the more active and militant colonels to speak for the Volunteers as a whole. The significant body of moderate Volunteer opinion which was prepared to accept the regulations was thus denied expression. Nor did Brodrick's concessions stem complaints from the Volunteers in Parliament, led by the Unionist Member for Sheffield, Sir Howard Vincent. Discontent grew during 1902 as a sharp drop in the number of active Volunteers seemed to confirm the case against Brodrick's policy; by the spring of 1903 the force was 100,000 men below establishment. The Secretary of State was unconcerned by this development since he saw, rightly, that reduction was prerequisite for greater efficiency. The government whips, by contrast, were far from content and feared an adverse vote when Parliament discussed the Army Estimates in March.[50] Their anxiety stemmed from the increasingly broad-based opposition to Brodrick's policy within the Unionist party.

In November 1900 the Unionist chief whip reported that his backbenchers were determined on a 'thorough overhaul' of the War Office administration; feeling in favour of army reform was less marked.[51] Nevertheless, Brodrick's scheme received widespread approval among Unionist MPs when introduced in March 1901 and thus a secure passage through Parliament. There emerged, however, a critical and highly vocal minority whose opposition to the reforms would continue until Brodrick moved to the India Office in September 1903. This group of around twenty centred on the so-called 'Hughligans', Winston Churchill, Lord Hugh Cecil (from whom the group took its name), Arthur Stanley and Lord Percy, whose attacks on 'Mr Brodrick's Army' between 1901 and 1903 must be seen as part of their self-conscious attempt to recreate the 'Fourth Party' of the 1880s.[52] The rather stiff and touchy Brodrick, with his grandiose plans, proved an irresistible target for a group of young, able and ambitious backbenchers seeking to 'ginger' up a party and Cabinet grown tired and unenterprising in office. But it would be misleading to depict the Hughligan group as motivated by political mischief alone. They, and Churchill in particular, developed a consistent and coherent case against Brodrick's corps scheme, arguing that it was unsuited to Britain's real military needs. They arrived at this conclusion because, in contrast to the Secretary of State, their assessment of those needs was not shaped by concern about Britain's poor relations with the European powers; neither the prospect of a British army fighting in Europe nor the likelihood of an invasion from the Continent seemed to them to justify distraction from the traditional demands of imperial defence. 'We must be prepared to deal with all the little wars which occur continually on the frontiers of the Empire', said Churchill (who had served in several himself); 'We cannot expect to meet great [i.e. European] wars; we can only assure ourselves that ultimately we shall be able to realise the entire forces of the Empire . . . '.[53] Paradoxically therefore, Brodrick's striking force was both too large *and* too small; while one corps was 'quite enough to fight savages', three were 'not enough even to begin to fight Europeans'.[54] What Britain wanted was a better army, not a bigger one. Churchill and others also condemned the home defence corps as unnecessary, this time on the grounds that the Navy, not the Army, was the guarantor of Britain's insular security. The enormous cost of the Brodrick scheme would be better spent on the Navy, in accordance with what Churchill suggested was 'the first and main principle which should animate British statecraft in the realm of imperial defence', namely 'the promotion of a steady transfer of expenditure from military to marine'.[55]

By resting their indictment on the scheme's allusions to European 'militarism' the Hughligan group created common ground between themselves and the Liberals. Their view of the right balance between the military and naval elements in British defence policy, and their warning that Brodrick's 'costly, trumpery, military playthings' would divert resources from the Navy, won them sympathy within their own party. Since many of the Hughligan group had some connection with the Auxiliary forces they readily made common cause with the Volunteers. [56] However, it was their rejection of any increase in military spending which won the Hughligan group most influence; it not only appealed to opinion on both sides of Parliament but also captured the mood of the country. From the summer of 1901, and particularly after the Peace of Vereeniging in May 1902, public opinion rapidly hardened against further financial sacrifice. Unfortunately for Brodrick, that same period saw military expenditure rise inexorably as the price was paid for the introduction of three-year enlistments.

By the close of 1902, therefore, the Secretary of State was on a collision course with public and parliamentary opinion; 'Never before has his stock been quoted so low', wrote Balfour to Lady Elcho. [57] The problem was compounded by Brodrick's unfortunate parliamentary manner, which one MP described as 'hectoring pomposity stiffened with pipe clay'; often critics seemed to find it easier to lambast the Secretary of State than to coordinate their differences of view on his policy. [58] His sensitivity to criticism deepened with the appointment in the summer of 1902 of a Royal Commission under the Earl of Elgin to examine the preparations for and conduct of the war in South Africa. [59] The work of the Commission, which spent fifty-five days taking expert testimony, exposed both glaring maladministration and serious organizational weaknesses within the War Office. Although its report was not published until August 1903, the activities of the Commission were a constant strain upon the Secretary of State. [60]

Under constant bombardment in Parliament and in the press, and with his position being sapped by the Elgin Commissioners, Brodrick depended heavily on the support of the Cabinet. On going to the War Office, he had been well aware that 'the success of any reforming Minister must depend on the confidence his colleagues show him'. [61] In the event, while his proposals received markedly little criticism from anyone but the Chancellor, Hicks Beach, there was conspicuously little interest or enthusiasm shown either. Undoubtedly the preoccupation of Salisbury and Balfour with winning the war, and their instinct that tangible reform was politically expedient, help explain why they appeared 'apathetic'. [62] Although a majority of the Cabinet sided with Brodrick against Beach in January 1902 when the Chancellor attempted to force the abandonment of the expensive three-year system, the narrowness of the vote did not indicate a strong commitment to the scheme as a whole.[63] The consistent public and parliamentary criticism of the scheme during 1902 did nothing to increase his colleagues' confidence in Brodrick's policy and when Beach's successor, C.T. Ritchie, launched a fresh attack on the cost of the scheme in February 1903 he found the Cabinet receptive.[64] Three days later, on 24 February, the parliamentary crisis broke when the Unionist MP Ernest Beckett moved an amendment to the address critical of Brodrick's policy and the government suffered a significant backbench revolt; nineteen of its supporters voted against it, fourteen walked out, and a further thirty supported it with grave misgivings.[65] The rebellion was the more serious because it coincided with an onslaught from a reviving Liberal Opposition. During 1901 and much of 1902 the Liberals had been too badly divided over the war to offer serious resistance to the government and thus the dissident Unionists had been easier for the whips to deal with. But by the spring of 1903 the rift between 'pro-Boers' and 'Liberal Imperialists' was healing and the Liberal party was regaining strength and unity in response to the government's education bill of 1902 which had outraged nonconformist sentiment.[66]

On 1 March 1903 Hood commented sombrely that 'if we persist in sticking to Brodrick's scheme . . . it will end in disaster in the House, and we shall have the country and the Press against us'.[67] The coming session would present Brodrick's various critics with ample opportunity to coalesce against the government, and Hood was convinced that the whips could only hope to preserve the government's majority by draconian measures which would severely test party loyalty and damage party discipline.[68] In a confidential memorandum for Arthur James Balfour, who had succeeded his uncle Lord Salisbury as Prime Minister in July 1902, he suggested four possible lines of action to deal with the 'very grave situation'.[69] The first was that Brodrick should be forced to resign; this Hood rejected on the grounds that 'sacrificing' a Minister to 'the youngest and most turbulent section of the party' would not only create a bad precedent but also offend party stalwarts, even those who disliked Brodrick personally. A second option was for the government to defy its critics and run the risk of unfavourable divisions in the House; this Hood rejected because it would advertise the depth of feeling against Brodrick within the party and might bring the government down. Hood favoured a combination of two further options. First, he recommended that the government should exploit the fact that Churchill and some of his associates were known to be keen on a political realignment which would link them with the Liberal Lord Rosebery and his supporters; Unionist loyalists might be less inclined to join the attack on Brodrick if they suspected it to be part of a covert plot to create a new centre party.[70] Second, the government should submit the home defence portion of the Brodrick scheme to the recently reformed Committee of Imperial

Defence. A pretext was to hand in that the Cabinet had recently decided to construct a new naval base at Rosyth on the east coast; it could easily be argued that this made necessary some reconsideration of the case for maintaining three home defence corps.

The major drawback of Hood's plan lay in its admission that 'the Cabinet of 1900 allowed a gigantic scheme of reform to go through without full consideration, and committed the country to a vast expenditure without sufficient foresight'. On the other hand, the whips' firm view was that the government's supporters would be more tolerant of such a confession than they would of any attempt to persist with Brodrick's policy. The beauty of the plan was that it would divide the Secretary of State's critics; in particular, it would divide the Volunteers, whose opposition was concentrated on the home defence portion of the Brodrick scheme, from the Hughligan group whose chief grievance was the striking force.

Hood's strategy had obvious appeal for the new Prime Minister. Aged fifty-five in 1903, Balfour had entered Parliament in 1874. Though his Cecil connection had provided him with powerful political patronage, 'Prince Arthur' earned his political reputation and title to the party leadership; first as Chief Secretary in Ireland from 1887 to 1891 when he displayed Cromwellian toughness in suppressing the Nationalist 'Plan of Campaign' (and earned the new soubriquet 'Bloody Balfour'), and second as Leader of the House of Commons from 1895 to 1902 when he displayed formidable parliamentary and debating skills. Balfour's intellectual eminence, together with a taste for philosophy and metaphysics, gave him a reputation for remoteness, scepticism and indecision – the *Pall Mall Gazette* once pictured him 'shivering in philosophic doubt on the steps of a metaphysical bathing machine' – but he was a keen-witted political animal with more than a streak of steel in his character.[71] As Winston Churchill wrote memorably of him: 'Had his life been cast amid the labyrinthine intrigues of the Italian Renaissance, he would not have required to study the works of Machiavelli'.[72]

Balfour's interest in questions of imperial and national defence had emerged in the 1870s. As private secretary to Lord Salisbury, then Secretary of State for India, he had attended the historic Congress of Berlin in 1878 – convened in the wake of a Russo-Turkish war to seek an answer to the vexed Eastern Question – and so had witnessed the encounter between two of the most remarkable statesmen of the age, Bismarck and Disraeli.[73] This experience quickened an interest in India and the Near East which Balfour had inherited from Salisbury, his political patron and mentor. His long-standing concern for the defence of India against Russian aggression through Afghanistan – a salient theme of this book – was due to the fact that his earliest and formative ministerial experience was in Cabinets preoccupied with the threat posed to India by the southward expansion of late Tsarist Russia. It was from the 1870s and 1880s – perhaps the heyday of 'the Great Game' – that one can date that sense of India's military vulnerability which was to shape Balfour's conduct when, as Prime Minister, he became responsible for the military policy of the Empire.[74] As far as naval policy was concerned, Balfour's views were utterly conventional. Like most of his countrymen he was an instinctive 'navalist', convinced that Britain's security and prosperity were inextricably linked with her naval supremacy. That supremacy was, for him, 'the very basis of [the] whole national and Imperial structure'.[75] There was, he once said, 'no subject dearer to his heart' than the Navy.[76] He could demonstrate a 'considerable knowledge of naval history' and was a keen reader of the works of the naval historian Sir Julian Corbett.[77] In all this Balfour was a man of the age; 'The vastly increased interest in and knowledge of naval affairs by Englishmen was one of the most striking aspects of English history in the 90s', writes Professor Marder.[78] As this book will show, Balfour's navalist convictions were to deepen during the years to 1914, and his expression of them to become more outspoken, as the same period saw Britain's naval primacy seriously called into question. His interest in what he referred to as 'the conditions of Modern Naval Warfare' would also become a more pronounced facet of his political character after 1900, as technological and geopolitical changes upset the old orthodoxies of naval policy and demanded new thinking on ship design and naval strategy; the complexities of the 'modern science of naval warfare' excited Balfour's intellectual interest as much as did the strategic and logistical challenges of Indian defence. His accession to the premiership in 1902 thus brought to the making of defence policy a mind not only attuned to the problems of imperial defence but also drawn naturally to them. 'We cannot pay too much attention', he told the Commons in 1902, 'to the larger problem of strategy, partly military, partly naval, which the defence of the Empire involves'.[79] It was for this reason that since 1895 Balfour had actively supported efforts to improve the coordination of policy between Admiralty and War Office.[80] The culmination of these efforts was the Committee of Imperial Defence, established under his aegis in December 1902, about which more will be said later.

The new Prime Minister had no wish to sacrifice his premiership to a scheme of army reform for which he had never felt enthusiasm. He recognized that the unpopularity of the Secretary of State for War and his policy constituted 'a most serious menace to the Government'.[81] On the Beckett motion he had been forced to appeal personally for loyalty to his own backbenchers; together with the reluctant support of the Irish MPs, anxious not to lose an important Land Bill which was pending, this had been vital in saving the ministry from defeat.[82] However, Balfour preferred another approach to the situation, though one faithful to

Hood's principle of 'divide and rule'. He decided to establish a Royal Commission, on the model of the Elgin Commission, to investigate the condition and future of the Auxiliary forces. The advantages of this course were twofold; first, it was a more direct and far-reaching response to the grievances of the Volunteers, and second, it would be easier to sell to Brodrick than Hood's plan. Balfour recognized that Brodrick had to be induced rather than compelled to give ground. He did not consider dismissing the Secretary of State, or risking his resignation by forcing on him a revised scheme 'involving fewer regulars and less hard and fast treatment of the Volunteers', because either action would further harm the prestige of the government.[83] Given the short life of his ministry Balfour's caution is understandable; his personal ties to Brodrick were possibly another factor.[84] However, how was Brodrick to be reconciled to concession? The embattled Secretary of State had become increasingly hostile to the Volunteers' defence of their vested interest, and increasingly convinced of the wholesale inefficiency of the force. Anxious to undermine the position of the Volunteers, in early March 1903 he sought Cabinet permission to publish a damning memorandum on the state of the force signed by Roberts.[85] Permission was denied; the Cabinet had no wish to aggravate an already perilous parliamentary situation. Coming so soon after the Beckett motion, Brodrick's proposal reveals the extent to which his misfortunes had clouded, rather than cleared, his political vision. The deftness of Balfour's Royal Commission idea was that it offered Brodrick a way of authoritatively and conclusively demonstrating the inadequacies of the Volunteers. As important to him was the fact that such an enquiry could be justified as a response to the shrinkage of the force since 1901, and need entail no admission that the corps scheme had failed. The Secretary of State did not see, or chose not to see, that the very establishment of a Royal Commission into the Auxiliary forces *implied* a suspension of the corps scheme in so far as it concerned home defence and that its findings would inevitably determine the scheme's future. In this respect the Royal Commission, which was to be chaired by the Duke of Norfolk, marked a definite defeat for Brodrick. On the other hand, Balfour too had given a hostage to fortune; the Norfolk Commission might undermine Brodrick's scheme, but there was no guarantee that any alternative solution it offered to the problem of the Volunteers would be politically or financially acceptable.

The Commission's brief was to 'enquire into the organization, numbers and terms of service of our Militia and Volunteer Forces; and to report whether any, and if any, what, changes are required in order to secure that these forces shall be maintained in a condition of military efficiency and at an adequate strength'.[86] Its announcement did not prevent the government suffering a further parliamentary battering on the Army Estimates, but it did draw the teeth of the Volunteer MPs and so eased the pressure on ministers.[87] However, any sense of relief which Balfour and his colleagues may have enjoyed was shattered six weeks later when, in a speech at Birmingham on 15 May, the Colonial Secretary Joseph Chamberlain launched his Tariff Reform campaign.[88] 'The Birmingham speech', writes Leo Amery, 'was a challenge to free trade as direct and provocative as the theses which Luther nailed to the church door at Wittenberg'.[89] Chamberlain's vision of an Empire united by preferential trading agreements appealed to a wide range of groups and interests from supporters of imperial consolidation to manufacturers and farmers suffering foreign competition. The raising of the banner of protection for the first time since the 1840s had a dramatic impact on British political life. The Unionist party split, and for the remainder of his premiership Balfour had to struggle to preserve party unity and his own power by holding a precarious balance between Chamberlainites and Unionist free traders; that struggle is the backdrop to the defence debates which the present work describes.[90] The Liberal party, on the other hand, was galvanized into unity by the assault on Free Trade; the bitter schism of 1899–1902 was overshadowed by the crusade against 'food taxes'.

One definite beneficiary of Chamberlain's initiative was St John Brodrick. Public and press attention was powerfully diverted from army matters, and with the disintegration of the government in prospect, the stillborn army corps scheme and the recruiting crisis also slipped from the parliamentary limelight. For the Secretary of State for War, however, this was but a temporary reprieve since in August the report of the Elgin Commission was published. The report contained much damning evidence of negligence in the preparation for the war in South Africa and of inefficiency in its conduct.[91] It also echoed the findings of a Select Committee of 1901 in criticizing the overcentralized, heavily bureaucratic organisation of the War Office itself, singling out the undue concentration of responsibility on the office of Commander-in-Chief.[92] The government's failure to coordinate its military preparations with its policy in South Africa also emerged clearly in the Commission's published evidence. As Secretary of State on the outbreak of hostilities, Lansdowne bore the brunt of criticism: but Brodrick's record also received its fair measure. Revelations of friction between the Secretary of State and his advisers over a range of issues were grist to the already overheated mill of Brodrick's enemies, and were lapped up by the press. Brodrick reacted more calmly than Lord Roberts to the wave of hostile comment and was slow to see that his credibility and authority had received a devastating blow.[93]

It was to be the Tariff Reform controversy which dealt the *coup de grâce*. Within weeks of the Elgin Report the tensions in the Cabinet on the fiscal issue came to a head; Chamberlain and three other ministers resigned, forcing Balfour to reconstitute his government.[94] The Prime

Minister grasped the opportunity thus provided and moved Brodrick to the India Office, thereby earning jibes about the promotion of failure. Brodrick's fate confirmed the War Office as a graveyard of reputations.[95] It also seemed to mark the bankruptcy of Conservative policy, but this was not entirely true.

The Watch on the Himalayas

Though Brodrick's mounting troubles have been in the forefront of this account of events in 1903, there were other developments in the background which qualify the sorry appearance of Conservative policy. These developments centred on the CID, established in December 1902 as (in Balfour's words) 'an advisory body summoned by the Prime Minister of the day to aid him in the consideration of the wider problems of Imperial defence'.[96] Though the initial idea belonged to others, it was Balfour's commitment which brought it to fruition and he has generally received the credit from historians.[97] The prospect of introducing greater rationality and method into British defence policy-making appealed greatly to his constructive instincts. He also saw greater rationality in defence policy as a route to economy. Here, too, one can detect the influence of Salisbury, whose 'concern for the careful co-ordination of foreign policy with defence planning, and for the economical use of resources, was an enduring one'.[98] The CID was intended to improve coordination between the Admiralty and War Office, bringing the civilian heads of both departments together with their respective expert advisers. The addition of a permanent secretariat was intended to provide stability and continuity. The administrative evolution of the CID after 1902 is a study in its own right; our interest here lies rather in the influence its earliest discussions had on the government's attempt at army reform.

When Brodrick undertook to reform the Army in 1900, the most recent statement of the strategic purposes for which the British Army was maintained was the Stanhope Memorandum of 1888.[99] This gave highest priority to imperial commitments, followed by home defence and, third, possible military involvement in Europe. During the 1890s a public and political consensus emerged in support of this imperial strategy. Numerous works on the subject, such as *Imperial Defence* by Sir Charles Dilke and Spenser Wilkinson published in 1892, asserted that the Army's principal role was to defend India and the colonies; the Navy could ensure the security of the UK itself.[100] This so-called 'Blue Water' thinking mirrored the reality of British defence policy in the 1890s. The reason why Brodrick's scheme provoked such a storm in 1901 was that it represented a distinct break with this orthodoxy. With its onus on home defence and on readiness for continental war, it plainly departed from the strategic assumptions adumbrated by Stanhope and hardened by a decade of writing by publicists and journalists. In the parliamentary debates of 1901 and 1902, it fell to the Hughligans and their allies to champion the traditional imperial strategy against a Secretary of State whose strategic vision was focused on north-west Europe rather than the Himalayas or the Nile. For eighteen months Brodrick's strategic innovation escaped challenge in the Cabinet; once again, the preoccupation of ministers with waging war offers the likeliest explanation for seeming indifference. With victory secured, however, Balfour was freed to pursue the goal of devising some means of coordinating military and naval policy and so placing them on a cost-effective footing.[101] The establishment of the CID in December 1902 was ominous for Brodrick because it had the effect of concentrating Balfour's attention on the hitherto neglected strategic premises of his scheme. The first subject given by the Prime Minister to the CID for consideration, and one to which it would revert in 50 of its more than 80 meetings between 1902 and 1905, was the defence of India.[102]

As far as imperial defence was concerned, India was less the jewel in the imperial crown than a crown of thorns. It constituted the single most important defence policy concern of British governments in the later nineteenth century. The defence of the subcontinent was regarded as 'second only in importance to that of the British Isles, and throughout the Salisbury era India's security was thought to be in jeopardy'.[103] The quest for that security dominated the foreign and defence policy agenda of the Cabinets in which Balfour and other leading Unionists of the Edwardian period had their formative governmental experience, and its influence on them is an underlying theme of the present study. The military problem of containing Russia's presence on India's extended frontiers in Persia and Afghanistan was one of unequalled scale and complexity.[104]

> To take the offensive against Russia . . . seemed out of the question. . . . To allow Russia to advance towards the frontier of India through Afghanistan without counter-action would convince the Indian people that the British could not tackle the Russians, and fatally undermine their prestige as rulers. To establish a defence line inside Afghanistan between Kabul and Kandahar . . . would tie up troops in difficult, mountainous country amid a doubtfully friendly population . . . . In any warfare beyond the Indian frontier, Russia would have great numerical superiority, while the forces sent against her could be withdrawn safely from India itself only if adequate reinforcements arrived from Britain and in the event of war no reinforcements at all could be guaranteed.[105]

Faced with so discouraging a military outlook, Salisbury had opted for a diplomatic solution to the problem, seeking to create political deterrents to Russian aggrandizement in central Asia; the creation of 'buffer states' in Persia and Afghanistan and the improvement of relations between Britain and Russia's European rivals can be seen in this light.[106] As Prime Minister Balfour proved to be even more preoccupied with the Indian defence problem than his uncle had been.[107] But his approach to it differed markedly. Where Salisbury had looked to diplomacy, Balfour looked to a military solution. He was generally more sceptical than his uncle, a master diplomatist, about the efficacy of diplomacy and warier of regarding diplomatic arrangements as a substitute for military and naval strength. A further reason for the difference of approach between the two lies in the fact that, unlike Salisbury, Balfour had an appetite for constructive administration. He embarked on his premiership keen to reorganize the defences of the Empire; inevitably, this meant accepting the challenge of finding a military answer to the Empire's greatest military problem.

The new Prime Minister dominated the CID's discussions of Indian defence. He relished the opportunity to give practical expression to his long-standing interest in the strategic issues involved. The subject would continue to exercise its spell throughout his period in office; years later, Balfour's political secretary, Jack Sandars, recalled that his last work as Prime Minister – 'as we were packing up boxes and papers at Downing Street' – was to complete yet another in a long line of papers on Indian defence.[108] His first two papers on the subject were adopted by the CID as a provisional report on 11 June 1903.[109] The dominant factor in the situation facing the British government in 1902–3 was the relentless advance of Russian railway construction towards the Indian frontier. The re-evaluation of British strategy after 1902 was profoundly influenced by the progress of work on the Orenburg–Tashkent line, the final stage of Count Witte's plan to connect European Russia with Afghanistan.[110] It was this, above all, which accounts for the divergent approaches to Indian defence of Balfour and Salisbury. 'In seeking to counter a possible Russian ascendancy over Afghanistan, Salisbury did not fear an invasion of India by the Tsar's armies from that quarter'; he believed that logistics, and financial weakness, precluded it.[111] Balfour, by contrast, believed that the new Russian railways had made invasion a real threat; he told Lord Roberts in November 1905 that they had 'rendered war with a great Power a military possibility'.[112] Balfour's examination of the question brought home to him the difficulties of defending India; one historian even suggests that he was 'overawed' by Russia's growing military might in Central Asia.[113] More significant was his deepened awareness of the relationship between the defence of India and imperial military policy as a whole. 'The number of troops required by India is in my view the central element in the whole problem of Imperial Defence so far as this depends upon the Army', he wrote to Lord George Hamilton, Secretary of State for India, in March 1903.[114] Pending receipt of figures from the government of India, the CID estimated that India would need 100,000 reinforcements during the first year of an Anglo-Russian conflict on the North-West Frontier; 30,000 men would have to be dispatched immediately on the outbreak of war, the remainder sent later. This calculation was to dominate Balfour's approach to army reform until he left office in December 1905. The logic of the CID discussions was that Britain's imperial commitments must determine her military policy. By envisaging the reinforcing of India in stages, the Committee also made the case for a small peacetime army readily expansible in time of war. During the South African War Balfour had written a memorandum arguing that increasing the Militia would be an effective, as well as the cheapest, means of expanding the Regular Army.[115] This idea was now urged on him again by the First Lord of the Admiralty, Lord Selborne who wrote in April that:

> the cheapest way of finding 100,000 men to reinforce the North West Frontier is to provide 100,000 Militia which can relieve and so set free obligatory garrisons of regulars in India and the colonies.[116]

The CID's conclusions on the subject of Indian defence thus diverged sharply from the strategic basis of Brodrick's army reform scheme. The gap widened when, following a brief examination of the defences of Egypt in June 1903, the Committee turned in July to the question of home defence. Balfour again undertook to draft a paper summarizing progress. Completed in November 1903, this paper has been described as 'a landmark in the history of British defence policy'.[117] It gave a ringing endorsement to the Blue Water theory. Maintaining that a surprise attack was out of the question in modern conditions, Balfour went on to argue that Britain's naval superiority in home waters would prevent an invader coming with a force larger than 70,000. In other words, it was for the contingency of raids rather than an invasion that Britain's land defences had to be prepared. The paper suggested a minimum home defence force of one Regular division supplemented by adequately organized and trained Auxiliary forces; this Regular division was to be additional to the 100,000 troops required as reinforcements for India. Balfour made public the CID's conclusions on home defence in the Commons on 11 May 1905.[118] 'Serious invasion of these islands is not an eventuality which we need seriously consider', he announced.

Balfour's Home Defence paper, taken with its predecessor on Indian defence, marked his commitment to a strategic vision focused on the Empire rather than mainland Europe. His ideas on strategy, as they developed during 1903, were sharply different to those underlying

Brodrick's scheme of army reform; in a word, they were more *traditional*. Brodrick's flirtation with Europe had briefly shunted British defence policy off the Indian mainline and into an unfamiliar siding; in 1903–4 Balfour switched the points and policy resumed its traditional direction. In terms of army organization, Balfour's ideas pointed to a smaller Regular Army at home and a greater emphasis on the role of reformed Auxiliary forces, both in home defence (the Volunteers) and as a means of expanding the Regular Army in war (the Militia). In a memorandum of late 1904, the Prime Minister argued that Britain required a total of 209,000 troops; 27,000 for home defence, 30,000 for colonial garrisons, 52,000 for Indian garrisons, and 100,000 to reinforce India in war.[119] The importance of that reinforcing power, the lack of which had deepened the crisis of 1899–1900, was further fixed in his mind by the Elgin Commissioners, whose report included the warning that 'no military system will be satisfactory which does not contain powers of expansion outside the limit of the Regular Forces, whatever that limit might be'.[120] Thus, by the time that Brodrick quit the War Office, Balfour had clearly established through the CID the strategic parameters for a very different policy of military reform than that to which his government had been publicly committed since the spring of 1901. Selborne described Balfour's statement of imperial strategy in May 1905 as 'epoch-making'.[121] George Wyndham, who had recently resigned as Chief Secretary for Ireland, believed that it had set a new mould for defence policy and debate, and would 'dictate the lines of successful reply and by degrees attain to universal and axiomatic acceptance'.[122] Similarly, the Prime Minister's argument that 'the Indian frontier is our first military difficulty' had become the focal point of a Cabinet consensus on military policy. The activities of the CID had given ministers a 'fuller sense of Britain's liability in the event of war with Russia and the magnitude of the military assistance which India would undoubtedly require'.[123] So, if Brodrick's removal rid the government of a serious political liability, it also opened the way for a fresh attempt to reconcile Britain's limited military resources with her responsibilities as a military power in Asia.[124]

CHAPTER 3

The Politics of Naval Reform 1900-3

Avoiding a Naval Colenso

The Spithead Review of June 1897 had given the world and posterity a dramatic image of British naval power at the zenith of the Victorian age. The ranks of assembled warships stretched for miles, a mass of guns, funnels and wireless masts, gleaming paintwork and fluttering pennants. In boasting that the Royal Navy was 'the most powerful and far-reaching weapon which the world has ever seen', *The Times* reflected the surge of patriotic pride that this imposing spectacle aroused in the public, both those who came by the trainload to see for themselves and those thrilled by pictures in newspapers and magazines.[1] In September 1898, when a small French force under Captain Marchand defied Lord Kitchener's Egyptian Army at Fashoda and brought Britain and France to the verge of war, British sea power seemed to reach as far as the wastes of southern Sudan.[2] In the eyes of John Bull, it was fear of the Royal Navy that made the French government climb down ignominiously rather than run the risk of war.[3] The Prime Minister himself reflected this faith in Britannia's ability to rule the waves when he claimed in a speech of May 1898 that the Empire could maintain itself against 'all comers'.[4]

Yet within a year events in South Africa had made such confidence seem like hubris. If the tough struggle against the Boers destroyed the reputation of the British army, it also shattered that mid-Victorian complacency about sea power which long decades of peace had hardened into dogma. 'They told us that our navy was our all in all', wrote one veteran, 'but we thought differently when we got to the Drakensberg'.[5] The war stretched the naval, as well as the military, resources of the Empire past the point of safety. Protecting the passage of troop ships from the colonies and guarding the long sea lanes to the Cape forced the Admiralty to disperse the fleet, with cruisers being particularly thinly spread. As a result, across the globe, the margins of Britain's naval superiority narrowed as the strain on its resources deprived the Admiralty of that flexibility which had been the basis of British naval policy since the eighteenth century. In the western Atlantic and in the Far East, the

challenge posed to the Royal Navy's local superiority by the growing
fleets of the USA and Japan became more obvious than before. In home
waters, naval defence devolved, in part, on to the Reserve fleet, brought
almost out of mothballs for the purpose. As with the Army, what made
this strategic overextension more worrying was the coincidence of acute
tension between Britain and the Dual Alliance in several areas of the
world where their interests collided – in China, Persia and Morocco.
During 1900 and 1901 public and press opinion was intermittently
excited by a fear that the French would take advantage of Britain's
embarrassments on the veld to send an invasion fleet across the
Channel.[6] It was this anxiety which helps explain the priority that the
newly appointed Brodrick gave to the matter of home defence. However,
loss of confidence in the Navy went beyond a mere concern that it was
over-committed. 'For the first time since the eve of the Naval Defence
Act [of 1889] the quality of the fleet was seriously called into question.'[7]
The devastating exposure of Britain's military unpreparedness and
inefficiency in the autumn of 1899 led to questions being asked about the
Navy's fitness for war. Could Britain survive 'a naval Colenso'? If put to
the surprise test of a major conflict, would the Navy fare any better than
the Army? To many, the answer to this question was no. Doubts were
raised about the strength of the fleet, about its materiel, about the
sufficiency of its stores and the standard of its gunnery. Before six months
of the war had passed, an agitation was under way to force the Salisbury
government to address itself to the war readiness of the Navy.

The vehicle of this agitation was the Navy League. Established in
1895, the League was the institutional focal point of a movement of
naval evangelism which had been steadily gathering strength since 1884
when W.T. Stead launched his sensational 'Truth about the Navy'
campaign in the *Pall Mall Gazette*.[8] Its primary purpose was to 'secure as
the primary object of the national policy the command of the sea'. With
its journal and other publications, and its promotion of events such as
the Trafalgar Day anniversary, the Navy League encouraged and helped
sustain the efforts of a generation of journalists, publicists, naval officers
and politicians who put their energies into educating the late Victorian
public into greater awareness of the vital contribution that sea power
made to the security and prosperity of the British Empire. The explosion
of pride over naval reviews such as that of 1897 was one index of the
success achieved, as was the theatrical vogue for 'choruses of mimic tars
capering on the boards, and tenors or baritones in uniforms of blue
singing braggart songs'; but a more significant index was public acquiescence in the rising Naval Estimates of the decade after 1889. 'It is
perfectly clear', writes Professor Marder, 'that by the turn of the century
the country was naval-minded as never before since Trafalgar'.[9]

The South African War transformed the nature of this popular navalism. The jingo complacency of the late Victorian age vanished almost overnight, to be replaced by an Edwardian insecurity and defensiveness which would last until the outbreak of war in 1914. This profound change was mirrored in the policy of the Navy League. From 1895 to 1900 it had been broadly supportive of government policy. During 1900, however, it became increasingly critical and in October issued a manifesto challenging the adequacy of British naval policy in the face of the Franco-Russian menace. This demanded an increase in Britain's relative naval strength, and called for the Channel and Mediterranean fleets to be placed on a permanent and enhanced war footing.[10] The publication of the manifesto to coincide with the 'khaki' election was an obvious ploy to bring public pressure to bear on the Salisbury government.[11] Already in the pillory for their military policy, ministers were naturally dismayed to find controversy descending on the Admiralty. They were aware that the influence of the Navy League lay not in its actual membership – a mere 15,000 by 1900 – but in its ability to generate a climate of public concern through newspapers, public meetings and other means of propaganda.[12] Because the overwhelming majority of its members were Unionist in their politics, and because Navy issues struck such a chord with the Unionist electorate, the disfavour of the League was particularly unwelcome to a Unionist government.[13] The problem had a parliamentary dimension, too, since the League claimed support among Unionist MPs as well as among their constituents; the President of the League, Robert Yerburgh was MP for Chester, and other backbench members included Ian Malcolm and Sir John Dickson-Poynder. The fact that the League claimed fewer MPs than belonged to the Volunteer lobby is not a good indicator of its influence at the parliamentary level; if a commitment to naval supremacy was standard political baggage for all Unionist MPs, most were committed to it in principle, and thus the potential catchment area for a serious Navy League campaign was significant.[14]

In public the government put a brave face on this unwelcome development. Joseph Chamberlain reassured an audience at the Fishmongers' Hall that there was no cause for concern; 'Britannia still rules the sea', he declared, 'and, with humble excuses to the Navy League [laughter], I think that she will continue to do so [cheers]'.[15] Such statements brought accusations of complacency from the naval lobby.[16] Privately, however, ministers were far from complacent, acknowledging that the emergency had revealed deficiencies in the Navy and that significant remedial expenditure was called for.[17] Less political concern was shown about naval affairs than about the question of army reform, but nevertheless the need for action was recognized. When the First Lord of the Admiralty, G.J. Goschen, chose the opportunity of the election to retire, it was widely thought that his departure was intended to spare the government and himself embarrassment. The need to find a new First Lord gave the Prime Minister an opportunity to meet the government's critics head on. His choice fell upon William Waldegrave Palmer, second Earl of Selborne, Under-Secretary to Joseph Chamberlain at the Colonial Office since 1895. The promotion of Selborne to the Admiralty and Brodrick to the War Office was an obvious attempt to infuse new blood and talent into the Cabinet and to defuse the row over the country's readiness for war in 1899. To many outsiders, on the other hand, Selborne's appointment smacked of nepotism; the forty-one-year-old peer was the Prime Minister's son-in-law and Balfour's cousin.[18] But, as we shall see, Selborne went on to justify his appointment by proving himself a competent and constructive administrator and was to exercise an important influence over Unionist defence policy until the First World War. His contribution to a new course in British naval policy after 1900 has never been sufficiently recognized.[19] The most obvious sign of the government's openness to naval reform was the appointment of H.O. Arnold-Forster as Parliamentary Secretary to the Admiralty. A noted expert on defence issues and a long-standing advocate of Admiralty reform, Arnold-Forster's appointment to a position which made him Selborne's deputy and chief government spokesman in the House of Commons was a signal that in naval affairs, as in military, the Salisbury government intended to respond constructively to its loss of public confidence.

The intention was carried through; between 1900 and 1903 measures were taken which greatly enhanced the Navy's fitness for war.[20] To strengthen Britain's position relative to the Dual Alliance – as well as to hedge against the emergence of other naval powers – the two-power standard was revised upwards.[21] From October 1902 the Admiralty adopted the formula of 'equality plus a margin' over the two next strongest naval powers.[22] Soon after taking office, Selborne had informed the Cabinet that Britain had only a bare lead over the combined forces of France and Russia and that, assuming the completion by both of their published programmes, by 1906 the situation would be one of parity.[23] From 1901, arrears of construction which had built up under Goschen (and been the target of Navy League criticism) were made good, and fresh construction sanctioned, so that by March 1903 Britain had a total of 42 first-class battleships in commission as against the 32 of France and Russia combined. When the figures for battleships under construction or projected were included, the totals increased to 57 and 47 respectively.[24] The issue of war readiness, central to the Navy League agitation, was addressed by augmenting the Reserve fleet and improving mobilization arrangements generally. The Mediterranean fleet, which Arnold-Forster described as 'just strong enough and big enough to be a terrible loss to us if defeated, and just small enough and weak enough to invite the French

'Admiralty', cartoon of 2nd Earl Selborne by 'Spy', *Vanity Fair*, 3 October 1901.

and Russians to take the initiative against us', was strengthened in 1901.[25] The aim was not only to deter attack, but also to relieve the Mediterranean fleet of the need to await reinforcement before taking the offensive against the French Toulon fleet; the success of British naval strategy in the Mediterranean depended on the destruction of the French fleet before Russia's Black Sea fleet could slip through the Dardanelles to its rescue.

The constructive work undertaken by the Unionist government in the wake of the South African War went beyond simply improving the Navy's immediate readiness for war, although this was an important aim.[26] Marder calls the period from 1900 to 1903 'a great reform era' because it began the vital task of freeing the Navy from the shackles of its own past.[27] In the crisis of 1899 the Navy seemed to many to be paying the penalty for a century of peace; it appeared 'weary with inaction'. The war lent credence to the charge, current in informed naval circles during the 1890s, that many of the Service's attitudes and practices were relics of the Nelsonic era and profoundly unsuited to the demands of naval warfare in the technological age. It also focused the allegation that the Navy had lost sight of its rationale as an instrument of war, and had become dangerously preoccupied with the enervating routines of peacetime; spit and polish seemed to absorb more time and effort than did gunnery and tactics. To fit the Navy for modern warfare required a change of attitude and approach. It required imagination and a determination to measure every aspect of naval policy against the prospect of war. It meant, in the circumstances of 1900, a willingness to break with tradition. It is in these terms that Selborne and Arnold-Forster construed the need for reform and in these terms that their record must be assessed.

Their major reforming effort was in the field of naval education and training, which had remained little changed for more than half a century and had failed to keep pace with the increasingly complex technology of war at sea. The lore and craft of the yard-arm continued to prevail; the study of gunnery and tactics was hardly known. Selborne grasped that the best way to modernize the Navy was through its classrooms; a reform of naval education would be a stimulus to progressive change in every aspect of the thinking and practice of the service. 'Important as is the materiel of the navy, the personnel is much more important', he declared in his first parliamentary statement of February 1901.[28] In July 1901 he publicly indicated his intention to reform.[29] Selborne's highlighting of the education issue was to have an unintended but momentous consequence: it brought about a partnership between the Unionist party and one of the Navy's most celebrated and controversial admirals, 'Jacky' Fisher.

Enter Sir John Fisher

Admiral Sir John Arbuthnot Fisher was the dominant figure in the Royal Navy during the period covered by this study and has a good claim to be regarded one of the most interesting and significant men of the Edwardian age.[30] He was to exercise a profound influence over the development of the Royal Navy and the fleet that went to war in 1914 bore the hallmarks of his unique naval vision. For this reason his policy and personality have been examined in considerable detail by biographers and naval historians.[31] If the scholarly assessments of Professors Marder and Mackay offer detailed guides to Fisher's achievements in office, his published correspondence (selected and edited by Marder) offers the most vivid picture of the man himself.[32] Fisher's personality matters because much of the controversy that surrounded his policy – a controversy to be examined here – was, at bottom, a struggle between those who admired him and those who detested him and his ways. He won affection and hatred in equal and generous measure; 'having been able to claim one King of England as his best friend, he would be judged worthy of hanging from the yard-arm by that same King's son and successor'.[33] Much has been written of Fisher's extraordinary qualities.[34] Tough, cunning, ruthless and vindictive, he was an intriguer, a braggart and a bully. But he also possessed enormous charm, a devastatingly persuasive tongue, an ebullient wit, a soft heart, and irrepressible gaiety. One astute observer described him as 'a mixture of Machiavelli and a child'.[35] Perhaps his dominant characteristic was energy, unbounded and infectious. He was once told by a doctor that he had so much vitality he 'ought to have been twins'.[36] Fisher's energy was evident in his every activity, from Admiralty administration to his favourite pastime of dancing, and it pulsates through his correspondence. He was dubbed 'a tornado with a nib on the end', and anyone who has known a gloomy afternoon in an archive brightened by the discovery of a letter written in Fisher's large, clear hand will testify to the allure of his sparkling phrases, blood-curdling invective and valedictory remarks such as 'Yours till we play harps!' Historians are as easily captivated by Fisher as were contemporaries.

In 1899 Sir John Fisher was an angry and disappointed man. The Salisbury government's choice of Lord Walter Kerr to be First Sea Lord in place of the retiring Sir Frederick Richards had dashed his hopes of succeeding to the Navy's highest post.[37] When Kerr's period in office ended, Fisher would be sixty-three and with a mere two years of active service remaining could hardly hope for preferment. Instead of going to Whitehall, he was forced to content himself with Malta, where he went

Postcard photograph of Admiral of the Fleet Lord Fisher, *c.* 1910.

to become Commander-in-Chief of the Mediterranean fleet, the Navy's most prestigious command and the mainstay of Britain's maritime defence against the Dual Alliance. As it turned out, however, Fisher's career was not to draw to a gentle close against a backdrop of glowing Mediterranean sunsets; instead it received a powerful new impetus. At Malta he sealed his reputation as a dynamic and innovative naval administrator. Within two years he had changed beyond recognition the ethos of what was Britain's premier fleet. A traditional tendency to regard 'brass and paintwork' as the touchstones of efficiency gave way to the new criteria of speed of manoeuvre and accuracy of firepower. Fisher proclaimed a gospel of immediate war readiness which came to dominate the thinking and action of the fleet; manoeuvres were conducted frequently and at a fierce pace. An atmosphere of 'hustle' and prepared-ness prevailed in which comfortable but inefficient practices perished. The outlook of officers, especially junior officers, was transformed as Fisher demanded that they air their views and think creatively and critically about tactics, gunnery and the use of torpedoes. The result was an exhilarating sense of innovation and reform, what the later Lord Hankey, then a Marine officer with the Mediterranean fleet, remem-bered as 'a veritable renaissance'.[38]

There were those who deplored Fisher's radicalism and his aggressive, hectoring methods; 'his was not the method of leading smoothly', wrote an officer of the day, 'but of driving relentlessly and remorselessly'.[39] Resentment born of Fisher's brutal treatment of incompetents, critics and doubters mixed with the hostility felt towards him by those whose habits, sense of tradition or vested interests he assaulted. But to others, Fisher's activities and priorities signposted the way for the Navy to escape the mental and moral rut in which it found itself in 1900. Among these was Lord Selborne. On taking office he had invited Fisher to write to him on naval topics and the Admiral took full advantage of the invitation. Their correspondence survived both a bruising and protracted row between Fisher and the Board over the strength of his fleet in 1901 and Fisher's increasing outspokenness about what he saw as the lack of "ginger' and enthusiasm' characteristic of Kerr and the other Sea Lords.[40] 'There is no doubt about my being 'tabooed' by the whole Admiralty', wrote Fisher to his wife in July 1901, 'except I think Lord Selborne, as his two letters were very cordial, and he has done two or three things I have telegraphed to him about!'[41] Fisher's enthusiasm for reform had great appeal to Selborne, a shrewd and intelligent politician with strongly constructive instincts, anxious to justify his appointment by delivering naval reform.[42] Fisher's emphasis on putting readiness for war above all other considerations struck an obvious chord with Selborne and his colleagues, Arnold-Forster and the Civil Lord, Ernest Pretyman, mem-bers of a government reeling from the disasters of 1899–1900. From their earliest contact in 1900, their appreciation of Fisher's philosophy and administrative gifts outweighed (although it never dispelled) their awareness of his faults of character and method. Selborne's realization that Fisher's 'intellectual flaws [were] on the same great scale as his intellectual virtues' did not shake his conviction that the man was touched by genius.[43] Writing as a septuagenarian in 1932, Selborne would describe Fisher as 'the best intellect with which I ever worked in close combination', tribute indeed from a man who had been a Cabinet colleague of both Balfour and Asquith.[44]

It was plain to Selborne in 1902 that enormous advantage could be gained from harnessing Fisher's creativity and drive to the reform of naval training and education. In the spring he invited the Admiral to become Second Sea Lord, a post with special responsibility for all personnel matters. 'I much hope that you will come', wrote Selborne, 'because I believe there is a great deal to be done in connection with the personnel, and that we can do much together for the good of the Navy'.[45] Fisher accepted the appointment with alacrity; he was being presented with an opportunity to shape the *mentalité* of the future Navy, and to do so in accordance with his own principles. On his arrival at the Admiralty in June he set to work on a scheme whose underlying object was to adapt the training of naval officers to the increasingly technological nature of warfare at sea. 'The existence of the Navy depends on machinery, and . . . therefore, all combatant officers must be Engineers'.[46] Naval officers were to be given an education appropriate for an age of wireless telegraphy, steam engines, and torpedoes. The 'Selborne Scheme' introduced on Christmas Day 1902 established a common entry for naval officers at the age of twelve and common training until the rank of lieutenant at nineteen. Specialization between the executive, marine and engineer branches of the profession had hitherto been enforced from entry; in future it would be delayed until all midshipman entrants had undergone a common training geared towards the skills required in an increasingly mechanized Navy.[47] As Selborne had intended, the scheme absorbed much of Fisher's time and energy during his fourteen months in Whitehall; 'Reform after reform connected with the personnel of the Navy was brought about . . . with bewildering rapidity'.[48] But the influence of the Second Sea Lord was also felt more widely. Though measures had been in hand before his arrival, he lent a new momentum to the process of reform in numerous areas of policy. Gunnery is a good example; in 1901 Selborne had begun the attempt to improve the deplorable state of naval gunnery – for years annual tests had produced an excess of misses over hits – but Fisher's enthusiastic support for the pioneering work of Captain Percy Scott greatly quickened the rate of change.[49]

The reforms of 1902–3, of which the Selborne Scheme was the most far-reaching, brought the Unionist government political dividends. By 1903 public confidence in the Admiralty and in the government's handling of naval policy had been restored. There was widespread recognition of the new businesslike atmosphere in Whitehall.

> In every branch of the British service, a new energetic spirit is apparent, and the confident and almost careless attitude handed down from the hard-fought battle of Trafalgar is being banished now that the truth is being realized that victory in the hour of battle will go to the men who win it by constant and thorough training in time of peace.[50]

Commiserating with Selborne on the ministry's military and tariff troubles in May 1903, Lord Milner expressed pleasure that 'in all the hubbub . . . the Admiralty not only comes in for comparatively little criticism, but, by its success, substantially strengthens the position of the Govt. as a whole'.[51] The contrast between the Admiralty and the War Office could not have been more striking. Where Brodrick's attempt at reform brought the wrath of the back benches upon his head, those responsible for the naval reforms of 1900–3 found Parliament docile and appreciative. The Admiralty's 'immunity' from criticism was much remarked upon.[52] Outside Westminster, the picture was similar. The Navy League's annual report for 1902, issued in April 1903, confessed to finding 'little to criticize, and very much to approve, in Admiralty policy'.[53] Selborne's admission to an audience at St Pancras in February 1903 that the country had been 'shamefully unbusinesslike' in matters of national defence was a mark of his confidence that the charge was no longer valid.[54]

However, to those involved, the reforms of 1900–3 amounted to more than just a successful attempt to restore the government's credibility in naval affairs. 'The fact is that we are going to make a great revolution', Arnold-Forster wrote in November 1902, '. . . a revolution which will leave its mark on the Naval service for many a year to come'.[55] In September 1903, when it was mooted that he should replace the embattled Brodrick at the War Office, Selborne appealed to Balfour to be left at the Admiralty to superintend the 'very big reforms, almost a revolution' which he felt had been started.[56] The Prime Minister thought the claim just.[57] The experience of 1902–3 bound Selborne and Arnold-Forster more closely to Fisher. When inviting him to become Second Sea Lord, Selborne had made it plain to Fisher that the post did not carry the right of succession to Kerr.[58] However, it seems that by the spring of 1903 the First Lord had decided that Fisher should indeed replace Kerr when the latter retired in 1904. Selborne's exhilaration at the pace of reform had persuaded him to give the Admiral a mandate to pursue change on a broader front. He took this route in the certain knowledge that to do so was to risk controversy within the Navy.

Fisher was already a controversial figure when he became Second Sea Lord; the cutting edge of his reforms in the Mediterranean had left many casualties. During 1902–3, however, there had begun to emerge a polarization of naval opinion on pro- and anti-Fisher lines which was to characterize the service until into the First World War. 'The "Band of Brothers" tradition which Nelson had handed down was for the time discarded, and behind the open hostility of chieftains flourished the venomous intrigues of their followers.'[59] From this point on, one was either in or out of the 'Fishpond', as Fisher's faction was called. The source of this division was the Selborne Scheme, which challenged the Navy both as a professional organization and as a social institution. To ensure that naval officers knew about engines involved breaking down the traditional barriers between the engineer and executive branches of the naval officers' corps.[60] Two kinds of criticism were heard. The more public was criticism of a technical, practical kind, from those who asserted the need for specialized rather than general training and warned of the dangers of producing 'composite' naval officers with superficial skills. The second type of criticism, less public, was of a social kind. Despite their growing number and the increasing importance of their function in the late Victorian Navy, the predominantly middle-class engineer officers – 'greasers' or 'plumbers' as they were disdainfully known – were looked down on as social inferiors by executive officers, and their expertise despised. The status and privileges of the executive branch, including its monopoly of the Navy's higher ranks, were most jealously guarded by those who regarded the narrow social basis of the Navy as its greatest strength. 'The argument', writes Marder, 'was that a naval officer must be a gentleman, and that a gentleman was born and not made, and, as a rule, he could be born only of gentle parents'.[61] By insisting on all officers 'going down in the coal-hole', the Selborne Scheme struck at not only the professional but also the social distinction between the two branches. This was Fisher's aim; as a self-made outsider who had lacked any advantages of wealth or connection, he despised the Navy's social exclusivity and its internal snobberies. The howls of protest which the Selborne Scheme aroused were a sign that the first shots in his fight for the *carriere ouverte aux talents* had been on target.

So, just as Selborne was reaping the political fruits of naval reform, he was instrumental in precipitating a new era of inter-service dissension. His enlistment of Fisher in 1902 had inevitably soured the atmosphere among the existing naval members of the Admiralty Board. 'My colleagues look on me as a sort of combined Robespierre and Gambetta', Fisher wrote to his son in November 1902.[62] Fisher treated his naval colleagues as adversaries and acrimony followed. Their resentment of his brusque, pugnacious manner mingled with genuine distrust of his proposals. It was only the weight of his political backers which ensured the acquiescence of the Board in the Selborne Scheme. Somewhat disingenuously Arnold-Forster praised Kerr for 'loyally' falling into line behind plans of which he did not approve; 'a smaller man would have simply set his face against the whole thing . . .'.[63] Outside the Admiralty, the opposition proved less tractable. Criticism of Fisher's 'revolutionary' scheme emanated from respected serving officers such as Captains Berkeley Milne, Hedworth Lambton and Reginald Custance, as well as from retired Admirals such as Penrose Fitzgerald, Vesey Hamilton and the widely respected Sir Frederick Richards. There was considerable apprehension among such men at the prospect of Fisher becoming First Sea Lord.[64] But Selborne's awareness of 'the very conflicting streams of opinion' to which the scheme had given rise did not cause him to waver.[65] Like Fisher, he had an obstinate streak, and now set his jaw against opposition to a scheme with whose underlying philosophy he was in complete agreement. He was ready, in effect, to put his political weight behind Fisher and to build his policy, and that of the government, upon the Admiral's brand of radical reform. As we shall see, the Unionist party would live with the consequences of that decision for a decade.

It was agreed between Selborne and Fisher that the latter should not remain at the Admiralty pending Kerr's retirement in 1904, but should go instead to Portsmouth as Commander-in-Chief. Fisher's poor relations with Kerr were a factor in this, but more important was the view that at Portsmouth he would be well placed to supervise the implementation of the Selborne Scheme and, at the same time, would be accessible to Whitehall. The year would serve to consolidate what had already been accomplished and to prepare the next phase of reform.

From 1902 Fisher's prospects of power rested on his ability to retain the patronage of Selborne and, through him, the Unionist government. His return to the Admiralty as First Sea Lord was not yet guaranteed. During his year at Portsmouth two factors strengthened his hand in this respect. The first was his selection by the Prime Minister as a member of the War Office Reconstitution Committee. When the idea of a small committee to carry out a reform of the War Office was mooted by the King in the spring of 1903, Fisher's name was mentioned as a possible member.[66] When the idea was eventually taken up by Balfour in September 1903, in the context of Brodrick's transfer to the India Office, Fisher was formally nominated to serve with Lord Esher and Sir George Clarke, the former Governor of Victoria.[67] Since Balfour's object in creating the Committee was to remodel the War Office on Admiralty Board lines, and at the same time to meet public expectations of a thorough reform, the inclusion of Fisher made good sense. His reforming credentials were impeccable, and he was a well-known and popular figure with the public. Arnold-Forster, who had been chosen to replace Brodrick and would thus work closely with the troika, argued forcefully that Fisher was 'much the best man' for the job and that 'no name will command as much confidence with the public as Sir John's'.[68] Balfour concurred, and to allay Selborne's fears that Fisher's new task would distract him from his vital naval work, instructed that the so-called 'Esher' committee should convene at Portsmouth.[69] While Fisher's actual contribution to the Committee's reports, published in February 1904, may have been 'comparatively small', in political terms the episode had a considerable significance in that the Cabinet's acceptance of the Committee's recommendations further identified him with the government of the day.[70]

The reaction of senior Unionists to the choice of Fisher for the Committee showed that he was already known and respected by men who had no direct personal experience of him, such as Joseph Chamberlain.[71] But in 1903–4 his profile was further raised as he was 'afforded opportunities for impressing leading politicians, as well as the King'.[72] There can be no doubt that Fisher's 'breezy, picturesque and always positive language' and his ability to hold his own in argument impressed politicians unused to such treatment. The contacts he obtained at this time can be seen as a further stage in Fisher's effort to build political support for his controversial naval reforms. Most important in this respect was the access to Balfour which he came to enjoy. In September 1903, the Prime Minister knew of Fisher by reputation only. He could not but be struck by the evident admiration for Fisher of both Selborne and Arnold-Forster. 'He is not infallible', wrote Selborne, 'but he *is* clever and as full of fiery energy as Joe [Chamberlain]'.[73] Arnold-Forster praised Fisher's 'experience and great force of character'.[74] By May 1904 Fisher was counting Balfour among his patrons; 'the present Prime Minister has stood by me against "all hands"', he wrote.[75] What had brought Balfour and Fisher together was not only the Esher Committee but also the simultaneous investigation of the invasion issue by the CID.[76] While at Portsmouth Fisher pursued his long-standing interest in submarines, conducting sea trials and manoeuvres, and experimenting with torpedo tubes. On 29 December 1904 he sent the Prime Minister a paper entitled 'Invasion and Submarines', which expanded on the proposition that naval science had not yet discovered a weapon to counter the submarine. Accordingly, the presence of 'absolutely unattackable' submarines must be a formidable deterrent to seaborne invasion. 'Fancy 100,000 helpless, huddled up troops afloat in frightened transports with these invisible demons known to be near. Death near – sudden – awful – invisible – unavoidable! Nothing conceivable more demoralizing!' By the same token, bombardment of British ports and coastal towns by an enemy fleet would be impossible if submarines were present, or even suspected to be. Though his paper for Balfour was marked 'private and secret', Fisher's views on the invasion issue were public knowledge; he had broadcast them, for instance, in a speech to the Royal Academy dinner earlier in the year.[77] But his dispatch of a forceful paper to Balfour at this juncture reflects his awareness that a rationalization of British strategy was currently in hand. He had already seen Balfour's paper on invasion and plainly wished to reinforce its conclusions. He took care also to draw the attention of the reader to the fact that the growing potential of the submarine was a further reason for reducing expenditure on the home Army and transferring it to the Navy.

> the Submarine Boat has made Invasion impracticable, and this being so . . . it follows the Army requires to be reconstituted because Invasion has apparently been hitherto a governing condition in arranging its strength.[78]

Unsurprisingly, Fisher's argument found a receptive audience in Balfour. 'It is unnecessary to tell you how heartily I am in sympathy with your observations', the Prime Minister replied on 3 January: 'indeed, my paper on Home Defence, which I think was shewn you, is largely based upon the considerations to which you refer'.[79] A few days later Balfour sought information about Fisher's experiments with transports and troop landings in the Mediterranean as additional material for the CID's deliberations.[80] In April Fisher delightedly reported to Balfour, via Sandars, the result of a recent naval exercise in which 'six slow 'pre-adamite' periscope-less submarines here at Portsmouth foiled the great Home Fleet and 3 Flotillas of destroyers and sent millions of money to the bottom!'[81] Balfour's correspondence with Fisher on submarines was to continue intermittently for over a decade. At this early stage it was useful in obtaining for Fisher a direct line of communication to the Prime Minister; he was no longer dependent upon the First Lord to act as intermediary. It also identified him in Balfour's mind as an adherent to the Blue Water doctrine. However, it must be added that there were limits to Fisher's support for the new framework of defence policy which was slowly emerging in 1903–4. If he agreed that the Army was not required for home defence, he disagreed with Balfour over what it should do instead. In Fisher's view, the Army should be reorganized as a small, mobile expeditionary force to act as the striking arm of the Navy.[82] What was wanted, he told the King in September 1903, was 'an Army and Navy Co-Operative Society by which the Army would be a Reserve for the Navy – like Nelson had the 69th Regiment on board at the Battle of Cape St Vincent'.[83] Fisher showed no sympathy for Balfour's 'Indocentric' views. 'That damned North West Frontier is what your master is suffering from!' he suggested to Sandars in June 1904; 'For God's sake ask him to drop it.'[84] As the next chapter shows, such an argument fell on deaf ears.

CHAPTER 4

Army Reform and the Militia Issue 1903–5

The Heritage of Woe

During the second half of September 1903 Balfour was preoccupied with the task of finding a new Secretary of State for War. His deliberations proceeded against a background of ministerial concern about the damaging effect of the Elgin report on the government's standing. The main target of public criticism was the unreformed War Office, whose organization the Commissioners had roundly condemned. The departing Joseph Chamberlain regarded the government's ability to 'meet the overwhelming public demand for a reform of the War Office' as the key to its survival.[1] Selborne warned Balfour that 'unless you can satisfy the strained & irrational public sentiments of the moment about the W.O. we stand a good chance of being beaten on some division in the House'.[2] Jack Sandars, a man of acute political instincts, agreed that the government would suffer in Parliament if it failed to offer 'tangible evidence' that it had recognized the gravity of the Commissioners' indictment. 'Our real chance of salvation is to make a splash', he observed, a view in which the Home Secretary, Akers-Douglas, concurred.[3] A prompt and effective response to the Elgin Report would not only protect 'the future fate of the party at the polls', but also promised to restore its morale, battered by the defections on the tariff issue; 'the one thing which will pull us together more than anything else', suggested Hood, 'is a change at the War Office'.[4]

Balfour's choice of successor to Brodrick fell upon Arnold-Forster, Parliamentary Under-Secretary of the Admiralty since 1900. Arnold-Forster's reputation as an expert extended to military as well as naval affairs; he had written extensively on military topics, had published a well-received book on *The War Office, The Army and The Empire* in 1900, and was proud of having 'tramped with troops in every sort of uniform'.[5] Existing accounts of his appointment suggest that he was only given the War Office because a number of preferred candidates could not be persuaded to accept it, and that this fact undermined his authority in office.[6] Evidence in the collected papers of Jack Sandars, who was at the centre of the week-long deliberations between Balfour and his colleagues, calls this view into question. Arnold-Forster had been considered for the War Office in July 1902, when Balfour's accession to the premiership prompted talk of a Cabinet shuffle in which Brodrick would be replaced.[7] In the event, Brodrick survived, but when his ouster came fourteen months later Arnold-Forster's name was the first to be put forward. There was a general recognition among ministers consulted by Balfour that the public would regard his appointment as 'a symbol of thorough-going reform'.[8] Arnold-Forster was 'not tarred with the brush of having been in the Cabinet of 1895 & therefore as "particeps criminis" with Lansdowne'.[9] It was thought that his experience of the Admiralty Board system would aid the desired 'assimilation of method' between the two service departments.[10] As was seen in the last chapter, he had also acquitted himself well as one of an Admiralty Board which had introduced a number of very well-received reforms. Joseph Chamberlain believed his appointment would 'spike the guns of the opposition before they have well opened fire' and serve to contain the damaging impact of the Elgin report.[11] (Arnold-Forster's support for Tariff Reform gave Chamberlain an ulterior motive in pressing for his promotion to the Cabinet.) Selborne urged Arnold-Forster's parliamentary strengths, an important consideration in the light of Brodrick's fate in the House of Commons; 'the House believes in him in these military & naval questions', he wrote: 'The Press also believes in him & would give him a longer & better chance than anyone else.'[12]

It is ironic, in the light of later developments, that Balfour did not share the enthusiasm of his colleagues for Arnold-Forster's appointment. 'I personally view his appointment with doubt', wrote the Prime Minister, 'because he is not merely a reformer, which we want, but has publicly committed himself in detail to large numbers of particular reforms, which would only be embarrassing'.[13] Balfour's caution was reinforced by two further obstacles. The first was the insecurity of Arnold-Forster's parliamentary seat in West Belfast. If promoted to the Cabinet, he would, as a matter of convention, have to face a by-election, but there were divisions within the local Unionist camp and recent reports indicated that the seat might be lost to the Nationalists, who had made much progress in the constituency.[14] With its parliamentary majority attenuated by the tariff controversy, this was a risk the government could not afford to run. The second obstacle to Arnold-Forster's appointment was the attitude of the King. The King had a strong personal dislike of Arnold-Forster, whom he regarded as 'a prig & "another St John"'.[15] He insisted that Arnold-Forster's well-known *idées fixes* on military topics, coupled with his brusque and dogmatic manner, were a recipe for friction with the soldiers and so disqualified him for the task of War Office reform, which required tact and diplomacy.[16] The

constitutional role of the Crown in army matters, including appointments, necessitated good relations between the King and his Secretary of
State; this was particularly true in the case of Edward VII, who took a
close interest in military affairs. Balfour believed that one reason for
Brodrick's failure had been his lack of royal confidence, which had led to
'perpetual intrigues' between the King and high-ranking soldiers behind
the Secretary of State's back, and he was anxious to avoid a recurrence of
the problem with Brodrick's successor.[17] The King's resistance to
Arnold-Forster on personal grounds was thus a decisive consideration. It
was for this reason, and on account of the electoral difficulty, that
Balfour insisted on considering alternative candidates for the War Office.
In the event, no acceptable alternative could be found. Five Cabinet
ministers were considered – Selborne, Wyndham, Austen Chamberlain,
Douglas and Walter Long – but for various reasons they declined or were
ruled out; Selborne, for example, successfully argued that his naval
reforms would be jeopardized if he were moved from the Admiralty.[18]
Attention then turned to the possibility of recruiting 'an able indepen-
dent non-party outsider', an idea which Sandars was pressing on Balfour.[19]
Here again, of six names discussed those approached – the proconsuls
Lords Cromer and Milner, and Lord Esher, a member of the Elgin
Commission – declined what they must have regarded, justly, as a
poisoned chalice.[20] The elimination of eleven alternative candidates left
Balfour no option but to swallow his own doubts about Arnold-Forster
and to prevail upon the King to acquiesce in the appointment, the
by-election fear having meanwhile been allayed by reassuring news from
Belfast.[21] The pill was sweetened for the King by the promise of a small
committee under Esher to 'assist' Arnold-Forster in devising a scheme of
War Office reform.[22]

If Arnold-Forster was appointed to cleanse the Augean stables at the
War Office, he had also to make a fresh start in the vexing matter of
army reform. As in 1900, the necessity for such an attempt was as much
financial as political or military. By the autumn of 1903 the Balfour
government faced the prospect of budgetary deficit in the coming year.[23]
With Selborne's shipbuilding programme making significant Admiralty
economies impossible, the burden of retrenchment was placed squarely
on the War Office. The problem of army reconstruction thus dovetailed
with that wider crisis of public finance with which the Balfour government had to contend. To avoid exacerbating the crisis, the War Office
had to deliver substantial economies. However, a large reduction in the
Army Estimates could only be obtained by a reduction in the number of
troops with the colours. Since the Army was already overstretched, the
abolition of Regular battalions for economy purposes would only exacerbate the problem of supporting scattered imperial garrisons. As in 1900,
the solution to a difficult equation was expansion. The possibility of

'The Heritage of Woe', cartoon of H.O.
Arnold-Forster by 'Spy', *Vanity Fair*, 24
August 1904.

reductions on a financially meaningful scale depended on the provision
of some means of rapidly expanding the Regular Army in any future
emergency. In pursuing this goal, Arnold-Forster, like Brodrick before
him, would have to tackle the question of the Auxiliary forces, the
existing expansionary element in Britain's military system. Unfortunately, he had also to confront the mistrust and suspicion which were the
legacy of his predecessor's quarrel with the Volunteers.

In a memorandum sent to the King in December 1903 Balfour
explained his approach to the question of army reform:

> What are, in Mr Balfour's opinion, the objects to be aimed at may be
> roughly summarised as follows: we want an army which shall give us
> sufficient force for at least any immediate needs of Indian defence;
> and, in conjunction with the auxiliary forces, for Home defence;
> which shall be capable of expansion in times of national emergency
> . . . and which shall throw a smaller burden on the taxpayer. This
> last is of peculiar importance, not merely because of the present
> condition of our finances, but because the demands of the navy are so
> great and so inevitable that the total cost of imperial defence threatens
> to become prohibitive.[24]

It is striking how closely Arnold-Forster's views on army reform accorded with those of the Prime Minister and the CID. His 'Blue Water' credentials were impeccable and predated the CID's inquiries. He held that the responsibility for home defence against invasion lay with the Navy, backed by the Auxiliary forces, and that the aim of military policy was therefore to organize the Regular Army for service overseas, 'primarily India'.[25] His remark in the House of Commons in March 1903 that 'India is our only possible place of contact with a great European Army' reflected a strategic outlook founded, like that of Balfour, on imperial priorities and a concern for the Russian threat in Central Asia.[26] Arnold-Forster was also in step with Balfour in his desire to see a contraction of defence expenditure, and within it a shift away from the Army and towards the Navy; 'the country demands & is entitled to receive [substantial cuts]', he wrote.[27]

The scheme of reform which the new Secretary of State revealed to his Cabinet colleagues in February 1904 was based on ideas to which he had long been publicly committed.[28] The crux of the scheme was the abolition of the Cardwellian system of linked battalions. Believing it to have been 'completely vindicated' by the war, Brodrick had retained the linkage of battalions.[29] Arnold-Forster took the different view that with Britain's overseas responsibilities increasing, and with the demands made upon the Regular Army for home defence diminishing, linkage had become an obstacle to the efficient allocation of military resources to imperial needs. Instead he proposed to divide Regular battalions between two separate armies; a 'General Service' army of 112 battalions whose function would be to garrison India and the colonies and provide a striking force, and a 'Home Service' army of 30 battalions based in the UK whose function would be to expand the General Service Army in wartime.[30] The two armies were to be differentiated by their period of enlistment, as well as by function, with recruits to the General Service Army serving nine years with the Colours and their counterparts in the Home Service Army serving two years. While the General Service Army matched the manpower needs of the imperial garrisons, the Home Service Army was a solution to the problem of an Army Reserve badly depleted since 1901; thus one historian has argued that militarily the scheme 'made a great deal of sense'.[31]

Arnold-Forster's thinking differed as markedly from that of Brodrick when it came to the crucial issue of the Auxiliary forces. Because his strategic outlook led him to emphasize the strengthening of Britain's home defences rather than the expansion of imperial garrisons, Brodrick had concentrated on remedying the deficiencies of the Volunteer force, and had not squarely confronted the need for Militia reform. For Arnold-Forster, the priorities were reversed; his own strategic views, together with the political imperative of Regular Army reductions, led him to focus on the question of expansion. Accordingly, while adopting Brodrick's formula for reform of the Volunteers – reduction plus increased efficiency – he devoted his attention and energies to reforming the Militia, the traditional source of expansion for the Regular Army. As indicated earlier, by 1903 the Militia was deep in crisis.[32] Drained by the manpower needs of the Regular Army and deprived of officers of 'the country gentleman class' by rural depopulation, it lacked artillery and any organization above the brigade level.[33] Moreover, despite Brodrick's efforts to the contrary, it continued to be exempt from any liability for service overseas, a serious obstacle to efficiency. Arnold-Forster was not alone in regarding the condition of the Militia as 'profoundly unsatisfactory' but he went further than other critics in denying not only the possibility, but also the desirability, of its successful reform. He was deeply sceptical about the value of non-Regular troops under conditions of modern warfare.[34] He believed that the South African War had clearly shown the terrible cost levied by modern weapons upon 'raw heroism and amateurism'.[35] Britain's 'sham armies' had been hard pressed by ragged Boer farmers; to pit them against well-trained and disciplined European conscripts was a recipe for national disaster. He could draw support for his views from the report of the Norfolk Commission into the Auxiliary Forces, set up by Balfour to disarm the Volunteers in 1903; the Commissioners concluded in April 1904 that the Militia and Volunteers had neither 'the strength or the military efficiency required to enable them to fulfil the functions for which they exist'.[36] Arnold-Forster determined, therefore, that the existing Militia should be abolished. He proposed that its best sixty battalions be converted into short-service Regular units liable for overseas service and thus become part of the Home Service army. The remaining sixty-four battalions of Militia were either to be disbanded, if beyond renovation, or reformed to serve a purely home defence role alongside the Volunteers and Yeomanry.

Arnold-Forster presented his proposals to a Cabinet more acutely aware of the politically charged nature of the army reform issue than its predecessor of 1900 had been. It is not surprising, in view of the fact that the Chancellor of the Exchequer was facing 'the worst possible outlook', that the Cabinet's reaction focused initially on the scheme's financial implications.[37] 'Although Mr Forster's scheme appears . . . a great improvement on the linked battalion system', wrote Balfour, 'it does not seem likely to be very much cheaper'.[38] The lack of any provision for reducing the number of Regular battalions would keep the Army Estimates above £29 million in 1904–5, a level which would necessitate the raising of fresh taxation. This the Cabinet determined to avoid; it promised not only electoral disaster, but also a heightening of the party's internal fiscal controversy.[39] A Treasury Committee was therefore set up in February to examine the Arnold-Forster scheme; it was chaired by the

Chancellor, Austen Chamberlain, who described the slim savings offered by Arnold-Forster as 'wholly inadequate, both to the expectation of the public and to the real necessities of the situation'.[40] The Chancellor's goal was Estimates of £25 million by 1907. Pending the Committee's report a frustrated Arnold-Forster was pressed to defer any Parliamentary statement on his proposals until the summer.[41]

Further reason for caution was provided by the Parliamentary situation. The Cabinet recognized immediately that Arnold-Forster's scheme would bring the government 'considerable parliamentary difficulty' at the hands of an alliance of Militia and Volunteer MPs.[42] Even before details of the scheme had been made public, a series of leaks from the War Office had caused a hardening of backbench opinion; on 14 May a hostile deputation from the Unionist-dominated Service Members' Committee called on Balfour to protest against the rumoured abolition of the Militia. During the week prior to Arnold-Forster's long-awaited Commons statement on 14 July further press speculation brought discontent among Unionists to a head.[43] Badly frightened, the Cabinet insisted that Arnold-Forster couch his statement in the most general terms, so as to 'make retreat possible without discredit'.[44] Though he did express his private view that the Militia should be absorbed into the Home Service Army, the Secretary of State was forced to pledge that the government would take no action in the matter without parliamentary consent.[45] The Liberal Opposition gloated over 'the collapse of the Army Reform balloon'.[46] Two weeks later the government was fiercely attacked in the House of Lords by a group of Militia peers including Lord Wemyss, who denounced the idea of abolition as 'contrary to sound policy destroying as it does the ancient constitutional foundation of our existing military system'.[47]

By this stage Arnold-Forster was encountering resistance to his plans for the Militia within the Cabinet itself. The Volunteer force lacked patronage at the highest levels of the Unionist party and had been championed against Brodrick by backbench MPs. For the most part these spokesmen were urban and middle class, reflecting the social composition of the force itself. The Militia, on the other hand, was rooted in the English counties and this gave it a very different political profile.[48] Its spokesmen tended to be landed, often aristocratic, and concentrated in the House of Lords rather than the Commons. Arnold-Forster denounced the Militia colonels as 'old women who look upon their regiments as a sort of honorary addition to their positions as County Magnates or as leading figures in some dull, ineffective society'.[49] However, unlike the Volunteers, the Militia enjoyed support among the predominantly landed Unionist elite. As a result, whereas Brodrick's attempt to reform the Volunteers had encountered Cabinet resistance only when its damaging parliamentary implications had become clear,

Arnold-Forster's planned abolition of the Militia met such resistance almost immediately. It was led by Lord Selborne and the 4th Marquess of Salisbury, son and successor of the late Prime Minister, both of whom were active colonels of Militia regiments.[50] 'Jim Cranborne and Selborne are good fellows and good Militiamen', noted Arnold-Forster, 'and naturally stick up for a force they have worked so hard to save from decay'.[51] Esher offers a vivid picture of Salisbury 'under the shadow of his perfect Elizabethan place [Hatfield] . . . drilling and training seven or eight hundred fine young Englishmen, quite as stalwart as any who fought for the Tudors'.[52] The involvement of Salisbury and Selborne in the Militia was one facet of their presence in the county communities of Bedfordshire and Hampshire respectively; Selborne saw the relationship between the colonel and his regiment in consciously paternalist terms.[53] The commitment of both men to the history and tradition of the force precluded their ready acquiescence in Arnold-Forster's plans. 'The Militia is one of the very oldest institutions of the country . . .', wrote Selborne, 'the oldest except the Church and the Monarchy. The history of my regiment goes back without interruption for five hundred years. Now is it wise or is it possible for the Unionist Party to abolish a national institution such as this?'[54]

If underpinned by a firm layer of sentiment, however, the case made for the Militia by Selborne and Salisbury turned less on principle than on practicality. While, like their colleagues, they welcomed the dual army concept, they argued for the substitution of a reformed Militia in place of the proposed Home Service Army as a means of removing the financial and political dangers attending the original scheme. 'The road to further economy is through the Militia', wrote Selborne.[55] Arnold-Forster's insistence on using Regular units, albeit short-service ones, in a Home Service role precluded a financially significant reduction in the Regular Army. Abolishing the Militia would indeed save money, as Arnold-Forster claimed, but not as much as would be saved if the Militia were retained and half the projected short-service Regular battalions disbanded. If the aim was 'the most economical form of Home Army which would produce the necessary number of reservists', then the Militia could serve this purpose *and* a parliamentary storm be averted. His opponents thus rejected Arnold-Forster's view that the Militia was beyond renovation; they warned him not to judge the Militia of the future by the Militia of the present. They envisaged major changes in the character and organization of the force; the elimination of weaker units, the imposition of a liability for overseas service on the remainder, longer periods of training, and an increased allocation of Regular officers.[56] They thus wished to narrow the gap between the Militia and the Regular Army to a lesser extent than the Secretary of State, but to a greater extent than other Militia leaders such as the Duke of Bedford.[57] During the spring and summer of 1904 they drafted a series of proposals whose common object was to show the feasibility of preserving the Militia as the second line of imperial defence.[58]

The case for the Militia alternative gained force from the summer of 1904 onwards as, on the one hand, the government's budgetary strait-jacket tightened, and, on the other, the Army's recruiting crisis deepened.[59] 'The British Infantry as a fighting force is in danger of dissolution', moaned Arnold-Forster in October.[60] The system of three-year enlistments, still in operation, together with a continuing drop in the rate of re-engagements, was making the provision of drafts to India and other imperial garrisons steadily more difficult.[61] The government had already been criticized on this score in the Commons at the end of June.[62] The Secretary of State regarded the crisis as an indictment of the Cabinet's refusal to back his scheme of reform with its adoption of seven-year enlistments. He did not, however, see it as a reason for dropping the plan to convert some Regular battalions to a two-year enlistment, an attitude which cost him the backing of the Army Council. His expert advisers now withdrew their earlier consent to the experiment with short-service Regular recruiting on the grounds that it would negate the beneficial effect of seven-year enlistments and so compound the Army's shortage of drafts.[63]

By the end of 1904 Arnold-Forster was struggling against opposition within the War Office, in Parliament and in the Cabinet; to this extent, his position resembled that occupied by Brodrick in mid-1903. However, unlike Brodrick at the comparable stage, Arnold-Forster had yet to announce his reform policy, let alone implement it. As the Balfour government wearily approached the session of 1905, the only credit it could claim in military affairs was the successful reform of the War Office by the Esher Committee; as far as army reform went, the record and outlook were unremittingly bleak. It was at this critical juncture that Balfour chose to intervene against his Secretary of State.

The Prime Minister had welcomed the innovation of a two-line Army in place of the Cardwell system, but he disliked the outright abolition of the Militia with its long history and proud tradition, and was in no doubt as to the political and financial hazards attending such a step.[64] For these reasons he responded positively to the arguments of Selborne, one of his closer colleagues, and Salisbury, his cousin, and attempted to persuade Arnold-Forster to rethink. He was also being prodded in this direction by Sir George Clarke, the recently appointed secretary of the CID, who believed that 'the virtual destruction of the Militia [would be] a grave mistake', and that the force was capable of regeneration; like the dissenting ministers, Clarke produced his own draft scheme for utilizing a reformed Militia as the second line Army.[65] After a visit from Balfour and George Wyndham, another Militia sympathizer, in June 1904,

Arnold-Forster recorded that the Prime Minister had 'tried to persuade me that my scheme was wrong . . . that we have too many men, and should remedy the evil by retaining the Militia instead of the thirty-five line battalions'.[66] Arnold-Forster was highly critical of Balfour's habit of 'talking about the Militia and the Line as if they were interchangeable counters', which he deemed a sign of wishful indifference to the deficiencies of non-Regular troops. He dismissed as horrific the prospect of 'a battalion of Militia boys, as I have seen them, being sent out within four months of the commencement of a war to keep the peace in an Indian city in midsummer, or to protect communications against Afridis or Pathan tribes'.[67] The substitution of the Militia for the Home Service Army, as sketched out by Salisbury, Selborne and Wyndham, was 'a plan which would give us chaff for grain'.[68]

Balfour's commitment to the Militia alternative was meanwhile being strengthened by the CID's continuing examination of the Indian defence issue.[69] As was emphasized in Chapter 3, by 1905 the Prime Minister was convinced that, as he put it, 'the main purpose for which the Army exists is not the defence of these shores, but the protection of the outlying portions of the Empire, and notably of India'.[70] It was for this reason that he welcomed Arnold-Forster's break with the Cardwell system which emancipated the Regular Army for its imperial role. But Balfour's belief that India was 'the true measure' of Britain's military needs also influenced him in senses unfavourable to Arnold-Forster.[71] First, he regretted the extent to which the Secretary of State's scheme, by converting over thirty Regular battalions to Home Service, prevented full advantage being taken of the ending of Cardwellian linkage. Second, and more important, his 'Indian' strategy had the effect of distancing him from Arnold-Forster's thinking on the Militia issue. The CID's preoccupation with 'the power of Russia to concentrate upon the Afghan frontier' led to protracted discussions in 1904 between London, the government of India and the Commander-in-Chief of the Army in India, Kitchener, of the number of reinforcements that India would need during the first year of an Anglo-Russian war.[72] It was continuing Russian railway construction in Transcaucasia which kept the issue on the agenda. Balfour told the Commons in May 1905 that 'the construction of railways abutting or closely adjoining the Afghan frontier, which we can only regard as strategic railways, place[d] the whole military situation in the East on a totally different footing'.[73] It had, he explained to Roberts in a letter of November 1905, 'rendered war with a great Power a military possibility'.[74] Between January 1904 and the beginning of 1905 the government of India progressively revised its estimated need for reinforcements, from 107,092 to 143,145.[75] This uncertainty affected the debate in London over the future composition of the Army. 'The present crux is the Indian demand', wrote Sandars in December 1904; 'K. (à la Oliver Twist) keeps asking for more'.[76] The CID, however, continued to work on the figure of 100,000 at which it had arrived in 1903, taking the view that broad considerations of 'Imperial policy' precluded any firm commitment to larger numbers.[77] This decision reflected a reluctance on the part of ministers to commit an even greater proportion of Britain's military resources to India; Balfour did not demur at this caution even though, as Monger notes, his 'theories of imperial strategy made it difficult for him to resist Indian pressure'.[78] At a relatively early point in its deliberations, the Committee reached the important conclusion that, 'having regard to the magnitude of the obligatory garrisons of India, which might be relieved by the reinforcements, it is not necessary that the whole of the 100,000 men should be immediately fit to be put in the fighting line'.[79] To Balfour, this contention had a direct bearing on the Militia controversy, because it confirmed Selborne's point that 'the cheapest way of finding 100,000 men to reinforce the North West Frontier [was] to provide 100,000 Militia which [could] relieve and so set free obligatory garrisons of Regulars in India and the colonies'.[80] To this extent, the Militia and the Line *were* 'interchangeable counters', notwithstanding Arnold-Forster's protests. Moreover, if the Militia were allocated such an ancillary role behind the fighting line, then the relative lack of training of the force compared to Regular units became less urgent. Balfour took the point a step further:

> There is one fundamental fact which ought never to be forgotten in considering the possibility of using the Militia as our second army, namely, that there will almost certainly be a very considerable interval between the outbreak of any war in which they are likely to be engaged and the moment at which they will be called upon to take an active part in it.[81]

Given the geographical context of an Anglo-Russian war, and the logistical difficulties both sides would confront in Afghanistan, it would be eight months or a year before 'any large bodies of troops would come into collision'. During such a period, Balfour was persuaded, the Militia could not only play an ancillary role, but might also be readied for a combat role. Again, Arnold-Forster's fears of 'shipping thousands of immature boys to India' seemed exaggerated.[82] Imperial strategy, there-fore, as well as domestic economy and party politics led Balfour to reject the abolition of the Militia.

When it became clear in the summer of 1904 that Arnold-Forster's original plan for the Militia did not enjoy Cabinet backing and would harm the government in Parliament, Balfour had been tempted briefly to draft an alternative scheme of reform which would attempt to reconcile the conflicting views on the 'heart-breaking' Militia question.[83] In the event, no such scheme materialized, Balfour looking instead to the recess to defuse the parliamentary situation and bring the contending ministers

to an accommodation. But the Prime Minister did circulate to the
Cabinet on 24 June a paper entitled 'A Note on Army Reform and the
Military Needs of the Empire', which reflected the opinion of the CID
that the particular circumstances of Indian defence permitted the
employment of a non-Regular 'reinforcing army'.[84] This made no impact
on the Secretary of State, and the Cabinet impasse persisted throughout
the autumn. While the strength of the opposition to Arnold-Forster lay
in the antagonism of Parliament to his proposals, the strength of his
position lay in Balfour's inability either to overrule him or to dismiss him.
The Prime Minister judged that the frail political health of the Ministry
could not survive such a blow, and was thus prevented from riding
roughshod over Arnold-Forster's objections. In January 1905, in a fresh
attempt to break the stalemate, Balfour persuaded a by now much
embittered Arnold-Forster to agree to a subcommittee of the CID whose
object would be to 'harmonize' his scheme with the retention of the
Militia.[85] Its outcome was a draft reform scheme, drawn up by Balfour
with the assistance of Esher and Clarke, who was lobbying simultaneously for a Militia scheme of his own.[86] Balfour proposed the substitution of
'the Militia in an improved state' for the Home Service Army.[87] The
improvements envisaged were similar to those mooted months earlier by
Selborne and Salisbury. An accompanying memorandum for the Cabinet
set the case for the Militia squarely in the strategic context of Indian
defence. In this respect, Balfour's scheme of army reform of March 1905
must be seen as the logical culmination of the prolonged process of
strategic analysis on which he had launched the CID in 1903. It gives the
lie to the suggestion that he was more interested in strategic theory than
in military administration; the one was important as a means to efficiency
and economy in the other.[88] 'We must have a long-service army, because
a short service army gives us no security that we shall be able to maintain
the necessary peace garrisons in India and the Colonies', Balfour wrote.
'On the other hand, we must have some cheaper force to supplement the
long-service army, because no Exchequer is rich enough to maintain, in
addition to our peace requirements, the number of long-service soldiers
necessary to carry on a prolonged war with a great military Power.'[89]
Clarke estimated that the Balfour scheme could save some £3.75
million.[90] If the scheme meshed strategic with economic considerations,
it also reflected political realities. Regarding tradition and vested interest
as obstacles to progress, Arnold-Forster was prepared to defy the consensus in favour of the Militia within the Cabinet and the parliamentary
Unionist party, a consensus which reflected the continuing importance
of the landed element within the Unionist alliance. Balfour, acknowledging the deep political roots of the Militia, would have made that
consensus the foundation of his government's military policy.

By the early summer of 1905, Arnold-Forster felt himself to be at 'the centre of a conspiracy of intrigue', his paranoia fuelled by the efforts of Clarke and Esher to win over senior War Office officials to the Militia scheme.[91] The Secretary of State dug in his heels; 'I do not regard the solution of Army difficulties which you have proposed as a possible one', he wrote to Balfour.[92] He reiterated that any modification of his scheme would compel him to resign.[93] He was only prepared to acquiesce in the use of the Militia in place of the Home Service Army on the unacceptable condition that the force would not be utilized for foreign service 'unless and until they have been brought up to the standard of the Line'. Selborne was of opinion that 'if A.J.B. is firm, A.F. will not resign' but, as he had when confronted with Arnold-Forster's periodic resignation threats, Balfour chose not to run the risk.[94] The 'alarming declension' of the government's parliamentary majority during the spring of 1905 – it enjoyed narrower escapes over the Army than over fiscal policy or Ireland – imposed severe limits on the Prime Minister's room for manoeuvre.[95] His hand had already been weakened by the simultaneous departure from the Cabinet in March of two of the Militia's staunchest advocates – Selborne, who left to replace Milner as High Commissioner in South Africa, and Wyndham, who had resigned under a cloud following an outcry among Irish Unionists over allegations that he was contemplating a scheme of devolution for Ireland.[96] Notwithstanding the fact that Selborne's replacement, Cawdor, was a Militia officer of nearly forty years' service, Arnold-Forster was much helped by this thinning of the Opposition ranks. A further handicap for Balfour was the fact that the House of Lords had recently shown itself hostile, not merely to the abolition of the Militia, but also to any alteration in its terms of service.[97] This seemed to preclude the force being made liable for service overseas, the precondition of the various Militia schemes put forward in the Cabinet since 1903. By driving the parliamentary representatives of the force to adopt an extreme position, Arnold-Forster's radicalism on the Militia issue had apparently blocked the route to a compromise solution on Balfourian lines. As if things were not grim enough, in June the issue of Volunteer reform was exploded once more. The Volunteers had rather slipped from the limelight during 1904 as Arnold-Forster 'tackled' the Militia, but in the summer of 1905 their hackles were raised by a tentative but clumsily worded circular from the War Office which was interpreted as a portent of draconian change. A furious parliamentary row in July worried the government whips and brought Arnold-Forster under new Cabinet pressure to stay his hand; the Volunteers had repelled yet another reforming minister.[98] In August a sketch by 'Spy' of a grim-faced Arnold-Forster at the dispatch box appeared in Vanity Fair magazine with the cruelly appropriate caption 'The Heritage of Woe'.

The situation with regard to the full scheme of army reform was thus one of absolute deadlock. 'The moment must come when patriotism will demand a solution', was Salisbury's sombre comment.[99] However, there was to be movement on a narrower front.[100] Balfour's sensitivity to the dangers of losing his Secretary of State was shown when, in June, Arnold-Forster threatened to resign unless given permission to 'experiment' with the conversion of eight Regular battalions to short-service enlistments.[101] 'The P.M. said frankly that it was a case of political exigency', recorded Clarke of a conversation with Balfour on 23 June, 'and that he could not just now shed Arnold-Forster or find anyone to take his place'.[102] Since the autumn of 1903 changing circumstances had undermined the Secretary of State's military arguments; but during the same period his political position had become increasingly strong as the Unionists' hold on office weakened.

Balfour had avoided the political problems that abolishing the Militia would have created: but, by the same token, he had been denied the political credit that a successful reform of the Militia would have brought. Far from binding the Cabinet together as had been hoped in September 1903, the army reform issue had been deeply divisive. Far from reviving an ailing ministry, it had further debilitated it. In August 1905, when a second recess intervened to spare the government further parliamentary embarrassment, Balfour confided to Lord Roberts that 'one of the greatest disappointments' of his premiership had been 'the failure to find, *or to get adopted*, some new organisation which would give greater military expansion in time of war, and, if possible, bring with it greater economies in time of peace'.[103] Thus the problem which had faced Salisbury's government in 1900 remained unsolved in December 1905 when Balfour resigned and the Unionists returned to Opposition. This performance aroused sharp criticism from all quarters. The defence expert Spenser Wilkinson depicted the three Unionist war ministers since 1899 as 'a series of amateur vivisectors . . . each of whom surpassed his predecessor in ignorance of the organism which he has had in his hands, and therefore in the ruthless use of the scalpel'.[104] Winston Churchill suggested to the government that the Army was not 'an inanimate thing, like a house, to be pulled down or enlarged or structurally altered at the caprice of the tenant or owner'.[105] But the oscillations of policy to which such barbs were directed, and the trials and tribulations of both Brodrick and Arnold-Forster masked the evolution in 1904–5 of a distinctive policy of army reform, a policy of reorganization based on the Militia, which united the strategic vision of the CID with Unionist politics and the financial necessities of the government. Intended to match Britain's limited military resources to the needs of imperial defence, for political reasons this policy had never been adopted officially by the Balfour government; in the very different circumstances of Opposition, however, it would acquire new significance. Far from vanishing in 1905, what one historian refers to dismissively as their 'heady enthusiasm for the Militia' survived, and would determine the Unionists' response to the policy of Arnold-Forster's Liberal successor.[106]

Enter Lord Roberts

While the Unionist government struggled to find solutions to Britain's military problems, there were those who believed that it was looking in entirely the wrong place. The three years of Balfour's premiership were marked by the emergence of a body of public opinion convinced that no successful and durable policy of army reform would be forthcoming until Britain abandoned the voluntary principle and compelled its citizens to bear arms in their own defence. The vehicle of this opinion was the National Service League (NSL), an organization which has attracted the interest of several historians.[107] The League has been seen as both a symptom and an agent of militarism in Edwardian society, and taken to characterize a new brand of radical political activism on the Right of British politics before 1914. Existing accounts of the League pay considerable attention to its relationship with the Unionist party; inevitably, they tend to examine the relationship somewhat narrowly, from the perspective of the League rather than that of the party. In this account, however, the emphasis will be placed on the attitude towards that relationship of the party leadership. The aim is to explain the response of the Unionist elite to one of the most significant pressure groups to emerge on the Right during the so-called 'crisis of Conservatism'. The rest of this chapter describes the encounter between the party and the League in its early stages.

The formation of the National Service League in February 1902 was one product of that late Victorian anxiety about Britain's national efficiency of which the South African War was a major catalyst.[108] The League's goals were never to be clearly or lastingly defined; 'the emphasis was constantly changing as new arguments were assimilated into what was always an unwieldy and contradictory corpus'.[109] At different stages in the League's history 'national service' meant conscription by ballot, compulsory service for all males, and compulsory training only; around these three broad variants a multitude of more or less detailed, more or less overlapping schemes emerged. By 1905 the League's formal demand was two months' compulsory training for males aged eighteen to twenty-two, to be supplemented by two weeks' annual training thereafter.[110] This would ensure a reserve of trained manpower available in any future imperial crisis and would help fortify the nation for struggle (economic and military) by raising the physical standard of the male population and instilling the values of patriotism, duty and sacrifice. 'Whatever happens & whoever may be the ultimate enemy,' wrote Lord

Milner in 1907, 'a people which can fight will prevail in the long run over a people that can't'.[111] Although its object was only attainable through legislation, the League disavowed party political affiliation, insisting that the cause of compulsion transcended party, as well as class and religious, boundaries. This claim to be above politics was defensive; the League's leaders realized that public opinion was unfavourable to their cause, and that any party which adopted compulsory service as part of its programme would suffer heavily at the polls. Insisting on the non-partisan status of the issue, and seeking to mobilize support across party lines, was the League's pragmatic response to the fact that no party leader could be expected to risk electoral eclipse by unilaterally repudiating the voluntary principle.[112]

Historians have been deeply sceptical about the League's claim to be above politics, pointing out that from its early days the majority of its members were Unionist in political allegiance.[113] The same evidence has led them to treat the Unionist party as a hotbed of compulsionist sympathy. But the membership profile of the NSL is misleading in this respect. It has tended to divert attention from two important facts, the truth of which will become evident in the course of this and subsequent chapters. The first is that there always existed serious obstacles to the growth of support for the League within the Edwardian Unionist party. The second is that the League was never able to translate its support among Unionists into meaningful influence over the policy of the party.

Resistance to military compulsion in Edwardian Britain is commonly attributed to some deep-rooted cultural bias towards voluntarism.[114] Contemporaries spoke of 'the sentiment that to be compulsorily trained would be an infringement of the rights of a free-born Briton'.[115] However, any such sentiment is invariably grounded in and fostered by real institutions; thus military voluntarism in the Victorian and Edwardian periods was grounded in and fostered by the historic institutional framework of the Auxiliary forces. The extensive connections between Unionists and those forces created a thick hedge of tradition, loyalty and vested interest which obstructed the process of conversion to the principle of compulsion. The Unionist party, it could be argued, was in fact highly unfavourable ground for the NSL. The contrast between the three MPs whose support the NSL claimed in 1904 and the strength of the Volunteers' parliamentary lobby is most revealing.[116] Despite the findings of the Norfolk Commission, between 1902 and the end of 1905 the attention and energies of Unionists at every level focused on the issue of reforming, not replacing, the Auxiliary forces. The fact that there was no clear consensus within the League on exactly what it meant by 'compulsion' hampered its progress further. Its ill-defined and contradictory proposals inevitably failed to displace the government's highly detailed and specific plans from the political centre-stage. Although this

Postcard photograph of Field Marshal
Earl Roberts, *c.* 1904.

would later change, to 1905 the League's activities and concerns were
never more than marginal to the internal Unionist party debate over
defence.

But in November 1905 the League did win a propaganda victory over
the Balfour government when the late Commander-in-Chief, Lord
Roberts ('Bobs'), the septuagenarian hero of Kabul, Kandahar and South
Africa, resigned his membership of the CID to assume the League's
presidency.[117] During 1905 Roberts had been finding it increasingly
difficult to reconcile his position as a military adviser to the government
with his growing conviction that only the adoption of compulsion could
remedy what he perceived to be Britain's condition of military unfitness
and unpreparedness. He had earned Balfour's displeasure with a number
of public speeches critical of current policy and sympathetic to the NSL's
case; one of these, at the Mansion House in August, was deplored by
Balfour as 'sure to be misunderstood by the general public, and to be used
by partisans as a political weapon'.[118] Later in August, Roberts, a patron
of the Miniature Rifle Clubs movement, tried unsuccessfully to persuade
the government to give official support to the introduction of rifle
shooting in schools; the War Office expressed modest interest, but a
circular to other departments elicited strong opposition.[119] Undeterred,
at a CID meeting at the beginning of November, Roberts formally

presented proposals for both rifle shooting in schools and universal training for 18–19-year-olds. On being turned down, he broke his link with the government and, two weeks later, became President of the NSL. His resignation correspondence with the Prime Minister was subsequently published, and is of interest because it revealed publicly Balfour's considered opposition to the cause of compulsion. In a polite but frosty and hard-edged letter of 18 November, Balfour indicated his personal distaste for what he referred to as 'the yoke of compulsory military service' and the 'system of Government inquisition into the movements of families and individuals' which it must entail; the introduction of conscription into Britain would, he argued, constitute a 'social revolution' which the country was unlikely to accept.[120] But the thrust of Balfour's case was strategic and military, rather than personal and political. 'The reason that I am content to adhere to the voluntary system is based upon the long discussions upon Indian frontier defence, in which you [Roberts] have given such notable aid to the Committee of Imperial Defence', he explained. India was 'the true measure' of Britain's military needs, and India required steady reinforcements of trained men over a period of a year or more, not a mass of 'imperfectly trained soldiers' on the outbreak of war.[121] While expressing interest in seeing 'something done at secondary schools and at the Universities in order to encourage such training', Balfour made it plain to Roberts and others that the twin objectives of government policy would continue to be a sufficient machinery for training recruits and an improved Militia.[122] The connection between the imperial strategic vision of the Balfour government and its adherence to voluntary service was put more pithily by George Wyndham in a letter of October 1905. 'Conscription at home – by whatever name you like to call it – is insular', he wrote; 'Our Empire is Oceanic.'[123] Wyndham's vision extended to 'a Militia in all parts of the Empire, receiving a small Imperial retainer and all coming on to a uniform rate of Imperial pay in the hour of Imperial emergency'.

By December 1905 the Unionist party had two military policies. One, Arnold-Forster's, was in the public domain yet a hollow sham; the other, Balfour's, though not yet in the public domain due to Arnold-Forster's intransigence and the Prime Minister's political timidity, represented the authentic direction of Unionist policy. Both were set on lines of thought fundamentally different to those of the National Service League. Arnold-Forster and Balfour differed over much, but were alike in seeing in their policies a means of making the voluntary system work to meet the needs of imperial defence.

Within a month, however, the Unionists were out of office and the future of British defence policy plunged into uncertainty. Like the new Opposition, Roberts and the NSL trained their sights upon Arnold-Forster's Liberal successor, Richard Burdon Haldane.

CHAPTER 5

The Politics of Naval Reform 1903–5

Cutting the Gordian Knot

The reformation of the Navy had not come cheap. In 1895–6 the Navy Estimates had been £19,613,821; by 1901–2, inflated by the war, they had risen to £31,964,973. Writing to Curzon in January 1903, Selborne observed that it was 'a terrific task to remain the greatest naval Power when naval Powers are year by year increasing in numbers and in naval strength and at the same time to be a military Power strong enough to meet the greatest military Power in Asia'.[1] The upward path of spending continued inexorably, despite the best efforts of Hicks Beach and his successors, C.T. Ritchie (July 1902–October 1903) and Austen Chamberlain (October 1903–December 1905). By the beginning of 1903 it was clear that the government was heading towards a major budgetary crisis. In a memorandum of 21 February Ritchie pointed out that since 1899 government expenditure – excluding the costs of the war – had increased from £120 million to £150 million.[2] During the same period revenue had grown from £120.5 million to £163 million. However, the appearance of prosperity was deceptive since £34 million of the £42.5 million revenue increase was accounted for by non-recurrent war taxation, and so it was obvious that only retrenchment could spare the government fresh borrowing or new taxation. However, rather than bringing retrenchment, 1903 saw naval spending continue to rise sharply. The Navy Estimates for 1904–5 reached the unprecedented figure of £36.8 million an increase of more than £2 million over 1903–4. Much of the increase was due to shipbuilding; Selborne informed Balfour in October 1903 that 'those accursed Russians' had accelerated their battleship construction programme, and that the Admiralty had no option but to respond in kind if the two-power standard was to be maintained.[3] To an extent the upward shift in spending from 1902 reflects Balfour's succession to Salisbury, for where Salisbury had regarded service expenditure with ethical distaste and deplored 'the "jingo" spirit which is driving us to financial ruin', the new Prime Minister was more pragmatic in his approach and immune to financial purism of the kind represented by Beach.[4] The Cabinet's acquiescence is primarily to be explained in terms of the international context. While the ending of the South African War had taken some of the strain off the Empire's defences, tension between Britain and the Dual Alliance persisted. The Balfour Cabinet did not regard the gradual diplomatic rapprochement with France during 1903 as a pretext for defence economies, and in the winter of 1903–4 the outbreak of the Russo-Japanese conflict threatened to draw Britain into war with France and Russia on a global scale.[5] Against this menacing canvas, Selborne's requests for expenditure on construction, however unpalatable, were hard to resist. 'We cannot afford to relax, presently or prospectively, our efforts to strengthen the Empire by land or sea', argued Lansdowne in February 1904.[6] In 1903 the Cabinet sanctioned an additional expenditure of £1.75 million for the purchase of three Chilean battleships which, it was feared, could fall into Russian hands and so tilt the naval balance in favour of the Dual Alliance.[7] A keen sense of the dangers of entanglement in the Far Eastern war explains why the Cabinet did not demur at the massive 1904–5 Estimates. Ministers did not need reminding by the Foreign Secretary that 'the Govt. of 1899 [would] never be forgiven because it refused to spend in timely preparations a sum which looked large at the time, but which bulked very small when the floodgates were once opened'.[8] With the Navy largely exempt, the brunt of Cabinet pressure for economy fell upon the War Office. Writing to the King in December 1903, Balfour justified the Cabinet's search for military cut-backs on the grounds that 'the demands of the navy are so great and so inevitable that the total cost of imperial defence threatens to become prohibitive'.[9] It seems clear that, at this stage, the Prime Minister did not regard the costs of the Navy as being open to significant reductions. Other ministers took a similar line. In his memorandum of February 1903 Ritchie pointed to cuts in the Army Estimates as the best source of financial relief, and early in his period of office Austen Chamberlain devoted himself to that same cause.[10] A similar disposition to concentrate fire upon the Army rather than the Navy can be seen in the parliamentary debate over defence spending. The economy-minded sections of the Unionist party devoted their energies to battering Brodrick into abandoning his costly army corps scheme. As we saw, the cost of that scheme was a rallying ground for the Secretary of State for War's many critics throughout the House of Commons. The Admiralty also profited by Brodrick's misfortunes in that the Hughligan case against military profligacy was often couched as a case for increased spending on the Navy.[11] Strictures against naval expenditure were never marked by the same force or conviction. The general acquiescence in high estimates which had characterized the 1895 Parliament continued, leading the Liberal Sir Henry Campbell-Bannerman to observe in February 1904 that 'a tendency to increase expenditure was more likely to meet with approval in respect of the Navy than in respect of almost any other department of the public service'.[12]

During 1904, however, circumstances changed to the Admiralty's disadvantage. Government expenditure came under insistent parliamentary attack from a fast reviving Liberal Opposition as Campbell-Bannerman found the issue of Unionist profligacy a useful rallying point for his fractious party.[13] At the same time the chance of any further cut in the Army Estimates disappeared.[14] By September Chamberlain knew that he would have his work cut out to prevent an actual increase in 1905–6.[15] The Admiralty could no longer count on the War Office to decoy the financial guns of the Treasury; Selborne now found himself in the Chancellor's sights. Chamberlain warned both service ministers that 'however reluctant we may be to face the fact, the time has come when we must frankly admit that the financial resources of the U.K. are inadequate to do all that we should desire in the matter of Imperial Defence'.[16] In March 1904, anxious to get Chamberlain's assent to the 1904–5 Estimates, Selborne had pledged that he would 'consider it [his] first duty, even at a further sacrifice of programme, to ensure that there is no increase in the Navy Estimates of 1905–6'.[17] By the autumn of 1904 even this was no longer adequate to the situation. Chamberlain made it plain that the character of the 1905 Budget, 'vile or passable', depended on the ability of the Admiralty to deliver reductions and that those reductions must be on a scale commensurate with the crisis:

I should have to look to you for a reduction of not less than 2.5 millions in navy estimates in order to avoid new taxation; for a reduction of 3 millions to make me feel comfortable; & for a reduction of 3.5 millions if I am to carry my head high and face the world without reproach.[18]

The financial issue was inextricably bound up with the precarious political position in which the Unionist government found itself by late 1904. The twelve months leading up to Balfour's decision to resign in December 1905 saw continuous speculation about the future of the ministry. Enfeebled by its fiscal divisions, hard pressed to maintain its parliamentary majority and harrassed by an Opposition scenting office, the government seemed unlikely to survive the 1905 session. Against this background, ministers calculated their every action with care. The immediate political consequences were obviously of greatest concern; thus Chamberlain's discussions with Selborne centred on the parliamentary risks of a bad Budget in 1905. But almost as important was speculation about the fate of the Navy under any incoming Liberal government. Jack Sandars argued that 'a reasonable reduction settled by us appears to me more prudent than leaving our large Estimates to be cut down recklessly by our successors'.[19] Ironically, it was Chamberlain who spelled out most clearly the dangers of pushing economy too far.

> I do not think *we* ought to starve the Navy or allow our Naval strength to fall below what *we* consider to be its proper standard [he wrote to Selborne]. Others may, & probably will, do that. Let our hands be clean in office that we may be merciless critics of such practises [sic] when we are in opposition. I would not for the sake of momentary advantage sacrifice the result of our own labours in the last 9 years, or weaken our position as champions of a strong Navy, or shake the confidence which our countrymen have in us on this point.[20]

The challenge facing Selborne, as he contemplated the Estimates for 1905–6, was a daunting one and made him 'wince horribly'.[21] How to reverse the historic trend of rising Navy Estimates without in any way compromising the strength or efficiency of the Navy? As it turned out, his anxiety was unnecessary; the Board of Admiralty accomplished the miracle demanded of it. Within months the Estimates were to be slashed by £3.5 million; the Chancellor could, after all, carry his head high. What made this possible was the launching in late 1904 of a new phase of naval reform which would dramatically increase the efficiency of the service. The signal for this development was Fisher's return to the Admiralty as First Sea Lord.

In June 1904 Admiral Sir Charles Drury, Fisher's successor as Second Sea Lord, told a friend that Selborne was 'not so very keen about *new* schemes as he was and that the Cabinet are setting their face against expenditure at the rate of the last few years'.[22] This interpretation is confirmed by a memorandum sent to Fisher in May in which Selborne unequivocally raised the flag of economy.

> It is quite certain that the Navy Estimates have for the present reached their maximum in the present year. In 1905–1906 not only can there be no possible increase, but it is necessary, for the influence of the Admiralty over the House of Commons and for the stability of the national finances, that we should have a substantial decrease.[23]

This memorandum accompanied Selborne's formal invitation to Fisher to become First Sea Lord. By October, when the Admiral arrived back in Whitehall, the political and financial parameters of naval policy were yet more sharply defined. Within days of taking office, Fisher chaired a new Navy Estimates Committee whose task was to scrutinize Admiralty expenditure 'in order to see what economies, if any, can be effected consistent with the fighting efficiency of the Fleet and its instant readiness for war'.[24] He was entirely at ease with this brief, having spent much of the preceding year assiduously cultivating an image as a champion of economy in Admiralty administration. He was acute enough to see that this was the surest way to the heart of a government whose fate depended on an improvement in its finances. 'We can't go on with such increasing Navy Estimates', he had written as early as July 1903, 'and I see my way very clearly to a *very great reduction* WITH INCREASED EFFICIENCY!'[25] His virtues as an 'economist' were pressed by the King, who had become an admirer in 1903 and would remain a staunch friend; 'The King told Selborne *straight* I would save them millions', Fisher reported to Esher in May.[26] The irony is that Fisher had reacted to news of Selborne's appointment in 1900 by doubting the capacity of the young minister to uphold the Navy's financial claims against the Treasury and its then head, the 'unmitigated cold-blooded rude brute Hicks Beach'.[27] Once it became apparent to him that the Cabinet were not proposing to drop 'the Indian Frontier Bogey and the 100,000 men wanted', and that the Navy could not expect to benefit at the Army's expense, Fisher pressed the case for naval economies still more forcefully.[28] In mid-August, in a meeting at Portsmouth, he spelled out to the First Lord his plans for slashing the Estimates; they amounted to an integrated 'scheme', the main elements of which were a redistribution of the fleet, the scrapping of obsolete vessels and the reorganization of the Reserve fleet on the basis of a system of nucleus crews.[29] Fisher cleverly argued that the promised economies could only be effected if his scheme of reform were to be introduced in its entirety; 'it is all so interlaced that any tampering will be fatal'. That Fisher hoped to exploit the government's financial crisis to win a free hand for himself at the Admiralty can be deduced from his deliberate briefing of both the Prime Minister and the Chancellor. During his discussions with Balfour and Chamberlain in November, Selborne found both men preoccupied with the connection between the bleak financial situation and Fisher's reform programme. 'If, as I understand, there are large reductions which you can make without danger to our naval supremacy, make them . . . ', Chamberlain urged; 'what could be worse for us than that the public should come to learn that we had produced naval Estimates of (say) 35 millions when the necessary strength & efficiency could have been obtained . . . for 33 or 34 millions?'[30] Writing to Selborne from Hatfield in late November, Balfour was more explicit.

> I gather that you have in contemplation far-reaching schemes of reform which, partly by improved distribution of our squadrons, partly by the . . . abandonment of all ships not really valuable for fighting purposes, partly by an improved method of dealing with ships in reserve, will greatly add to the efficiency of our fleets, and at the same time greatly conduce to economy.[31]

The source of Balfour's information was transparent. His sensitivity to the government's political difficulties showed in his anxiety that, if practicable, such action should be taken quickly and made public as soon as possible. In September, Sandars had cautioned his chief that Fisher's cooperation in the economy drive might depend upon acceptance of his 'revolutionary schemes'.[32] Balfour, it appears, was excited, rather than deterred, by the prospect and had evidently accepted Fisher's point that the scheme must be introduced whole. So Fisher's tactic of presenting himself and his policy as the keys to retrenchment had achieved its purpose; having secured the succession to Lord Walter Kerr, he had managed to persuade the Prime Minister, the Chancellor and the First Lord to endorse in advance his programme of sweeping reforms. Balfour also agreed to a reorganization of Admiralty business which Fisher had first proposed in January 1904 with the object of strengthening the position of the First Sea Lord relative to the other members of the Board.[33] While ostensibly an attempt to rationalize the distribution of business within the Admiralty, there is little doubt that Fisher's ulterior motive was to prevent obstruction of his schemes by the other Sea Lords By assenting to the change, Balfour and Selborne gave him unprecedented powers to carry his policies. It would be wrong to suggest that they were prepared to go to such lengths solely for reasons of political economy – as we shall see, Balfour was a firm believer in the positive naval benefits of Fisher's policy. But it remains true that it was the self-interest of the Unionist government which created the opportunity for Fisher to launch reforms on a historic scale.

Those reforms can be briefly described.[34] The peacetime distribution of the Royal Navy had changed little since the era of Don Pacifico and Palmerstonian gunboat diplomacy. Britain maintained a large number of vessels on scattered stations across the globe, flying the flag, 'keeping the police of the seas and protecting semi-barbarous and barbarous men against kidnapping and various forms of outrage'.[35] This state of affairs was much to the liking of the Foreign and Colonial Offices, keen on 'showing the flag', and pleased the daughters of HM consuls who were regularly supplied with tennis and dancing partners, but it ignored the realities of naval technology. Advances in communications had given the Admiralty a new capacity for responding rapidly and flexibly to a local crisis, and so removed the need for a permanent presence. At the same time, many of these naval outriders of Empire were antiquated, slow and lacking armour. They were highly vulnerable, neither strong enough to engage an enemy nor fast enough to run away from him. Fisher's solution was to abolish several stations – South Atlantic, North America, Pacific and China – and scrap the obsolete vessels thus freed. Though the size of Britain's fleets in non-European waters had been reduced before – notably by 40 per cent between the mid-1860s and 1872 – this was the largest single reduction to be enacted at any one time.[36] Hence Balfour's later reference to a 'courageous stroke of the pen'. The culling process was extended to the seagoing fleet as a whole, the aim being to eliminate all unarmoured cruisers slower than 25.5 knots. Fisher preached 'the necessity for the Admiralty to have the fleet strong, efficient and reliable, instead of retaining it as a floating museum of the varying types of usefulness of bygone ages . . . '.[37] This policy led to the scrapping of 154 ships in 1904–5, resulting in a major saving in one of the Navy's largest areas of expenditure, repair and refit costs and dockyard work. The saving was increased by Fisher's use of the personnel of scrapped ships to reorganize the naval reserve. Fighting ships in reserve were re-manned with two-fifths of their complement; this 'nucleus crew' was to include all the technical specialists and officers required to ensure a vessel's immediate readiness for sea in a crisis. The new system, experimented with in 1903 but stalled since for lack of men, was described by Fisher as 'the keystone of our preparedness for war'.[38] In removing inefficiency while cutting costs – ships under nucleus crews were far better maintained than before – this reform was similar in kind to the others. The three together produced a dramatic fall in the Navy Estimates for 1905–6: down from £36.8 million to £33.3 million. The government was spared the necessity for fresh taxation and Chamberlain's Budget proved 'passable' rather than 'vile'. When the government eventually resigned in December 1905, financial considerations were not of decisive importance.

If Fisher had severed the Gordian knot of high Navy Estimates, he had also renewed the sense of achievement which his political colleagues at the Admiralty had enjoyed in 1902–3. Pretyman, who had filled Arnold-Forster's position, and Arthur Lee, who had replaced Pretyman as Civil Lord, were both Fisher enthusiasts. Lee expressed his 'genuine admiration' for the First Sea Lord whom he thought an 'undoubted genius'.[39] He described the fruits of Fisher's policy as 'a Navy . . . greater in strength and efficiency, better manned and equipped, better trained and educated in every way, and more ready for instant service' than ever before.[40] Until his departure from the Admiralty in the spring of 1905 to become High Commissioner in South Africa, Selborne remained a firm supporter of Fisher's policy. His successor was the 3rd Earl of Cawdor, a prominent Unionist peer who was then chairman of the Great Western Railway. Cawdor, recently recommended to Joseph Chamberlain as 'the best chairman now living', had been Walter Long's suggestion for the War Office in September 1903, and it was Long, acting for Balfour, who persuaded him to take over at the Admiralty.[41] His appointment was a shrewd one, in that his business acumen and experience were ideally suited to an institution preoccupied with the search for efficiency and economy. Fisher was delighted since, as a peer, Cawdor would not have the House of Commons to distract him from the task of administration. His delight must have owed something to Cawdor's lack of a naval background, a distinct advantage to Fisher in bringing the new First Lord to his point of view. Cawdor had no strong preconceptions on naval matters, few links with the Navy, and as open a mind as Fisher could have wished. Yet it would be wrong to see Cawdor as Fisher's uncritical dupe; he was hard-headed, sceptical and independently minded, and his confidence had to be earned. Nevertheless, he proved to be one of Fisher's strongest supporters.

By now, however, Fisher's most important supporter was the Prime Minister. In a memorandum of December 1905 Balfour recorded that he had been in 'the closest touch' with the Admiralty since Fisher's return in October 1904, and had been kept informed of policy.[42] Balfour made no secret of his faith in Fisher's vision of naval modernization. He described the linked reforms of 1904–5 as a 'beneficent revolution' and, speaking in Glasgow in January 1905, claimed that they had increased the fighting power of the Navy 'not once, or twice, but threefold'.[43] Of Fisher himself, Balfour wrote: 'at the very moment when the changed conditions of naval sea power rendered administrative revolution necessary, in Sir John Fisher was found a man of genius peculiarly fitted to aid in its execution'.[44] Balfour's conviction that he was participating in 'a period of great naval reform' quickly superseded political self-interest as his main bond with Fisher, and was to be of immense

Portrait photograph of 3rd Earl Cawdor, *c.* 1905.

importance to both men during the Unionist party's impending period of Opposition. It is clear that his connection with Fisher and involvement in his reforms deepened Balfour's interest in and knowledge of naval policy.[45] But it is also clear that Fisher's handiwork appealed to another side of him which Dr Mackay's valuable study highlights, namely his appetite for constructive administration. It was this which led Fisher to describe the Prime Minister as 'a splendid man to work with'.[46] Like reorganization of the Army and the development of the CID, radical reform of the Navy should be seen as evidence of the positive and creative character which Balfour tried hard to give to his ministry, a character often overshadowed by the wearying and negative controversy over tariffs. Contemporary observers rarely acknowledged his efforts in this respect; even Beatrice Webb, a decided admirer of the Unionist leader, alleged that there was 'no determinate result from the combination of his reason with his knowledge of facts'.[47] Balfour's activity in the sphere of defence – a subject not much in the eye of the Fabians – highlights just that 'organic quality' for which Mrs Webb was looking.

There were Cabinet members unconnected with the Admiralty or unacquainted with Fisher who did not share their colleagues' enthusiasm. Brodrick was sceptical about what he termed Fisher's 'prognostications', and Salisbury distrusted his 'reckless imagination', but those responsible for the making of naval policy were united behind the First Sea Lord.[48] However, as it had during the first phase of his reform career in 1902–3, their support for Fisher ranged the government against a significant body of hostile naval opinion. Fisher had advertised his return to the Whitehall as 'a case of Athanasius contra Mundum. Very sorry for Mundum', he wrote to Arthur Lee, 'as Athanasius is going to win!'[49] His opponents had regarded Fisher's accession as First Sea Lord with as much dread as he felt glee, and events after October 1904 brought many new recruits into their ranks.[50] The redistribution and scrapping policies evoked loud protest from naval officers such as Sir Gerard Noel, Commander-in-Chief China station, whose commands were summarily axed.[51] The adoption of the Dreadnought design – of which more will be said later – heightened alarm at the sudden diminution in the size of the seagoing fleet. Sir Frederick Richards, having an angry and far from tranquil retirement, charged that the whole Navy had been 'morally scrapped and labelled obsolete at the moment when it was at the zenith of its efficiency'.[52] The scrapping and Dreadnought policies also infuriated those, such as Sir William White the naval architect, whose own work on naval construction and design had become an item of history overnight.

In May 1905 a journalist friend of Fisher's had noted that 'the reformed Admiralty is now the object of a chorus of praise from an enchanted and adoring press', and six weeks later Pretyman had cause to remark complacently on the quiet parliamentary outlook for the Admiralty; 'I wish other political matters were as smooth', he wrote to Selborne.[53] Ironically, it was at just this time that the base of the struggle against Fisher's policy started to broaden significantly. What had been, for the most part, an internal naval dispute was moving increasingly into the public domain. As was indicated earlier, the Senior Service was an innately 'aristocratic' institution; if the Church of England was the aristocracy at prayer, the Navy was 'Society' afloat. This meant, in practice, that indignation over Fisher's actions and his 'tyrannical' methods quickly spread to the dining, drawing and smoking rooms of London; for example, the *salon* of the marchioness of Londonderry became a focal point of anti-Fisher sentiment. Those social milieux in which naval officers moved, and found sympathy for their complaints, tended – like the officers themselves – to be Unionist in politics. Lady Londonderry's husband, the 6th marquess, was a minister in Balfour's government.[54] 1905 also saw a growing anti-Fisher voice in the metropolitan press, once again concentrated in publications of a Unionist persuasion such as the *Daily Mail, Morning Post*, and *Standard*; in each of these cases, the agent was a naval correspondent in touch with dissident naval officers, H.W. Wilson of the *Mail*, Spenser Wilkinson of the *Post* and Leslie Cope-Cornford of the *Standard*. Their efforts in print were starting to carry critical comment on Admiralty policy to public opinion in general, and Unionist opinion in particular. On the other hand, this process was paralleled by the emergence of a strong body of opinion supportive of Fisher. He had always enjoyed a loyal following in the Navy, and had (in many instances) rewarded that loyalty with preferment.[55] Both the major service journals, the *Army and Navy Gazette* and the *Naval and Military Record*, backed him. Fisher could also count on the *Daily Telegraph* and *The Times* – both Unionist papers – whose naval correspondents, Archibald Hurd and J.R. Thursfield respectively, were devoted admirers. Other journalistic allies included Julian Corbett, the naval historian, Arnold White and John Leyland. The pro-Fisher lobby was thus a mirror image of the 'Syndicate of Discontent' in that it was composed of a similar mix of people and had the same party political complexion. This created the danger that the intensifying row over Fisher's policy could spill over into internecine friction within the Unionist party itself.

It is instructive to draw a parallel between Fisher's situation and that of Arnold-Forster. Both men aroused animosity on account of their methods and personality – Arnold-Forster matching Fisher's violence and bluster with monumental tactlessness, dogmatism and a repellent over-earnestness. Both were Establishment outsiders, shouldering comparably large chips, who sought to introduce reforms which brought them directly into collision with vested interests concentrated within the

Unionist party. Their separate experience reveals the politically and socially charged nature of defence issues within the Unionist party. The predominance of Unionists within both services greatly complicated the task of reform for a Unionist government. Arnold-Forster was right to argue that the task of army reform was particularly difficult for a Unionist War Minister who had to contend with 'social influences, class influences and other detestable sources of confusion' as well as with the obvious parliamentary and financial difficulties.[56] Fisher could have made a similar complaint – and justly so.

The government acknowledged, but chose deliberately to discount, the groundswell of criticism of Admiralty policy. They regarded it as the predictable but misguided response to progress, and believed that the Navy's 'good will and power of adaptation would eventually prevail'.[57] A period of resolute administration was needed during which time the reforms would prove their lasting value. Such a policy was signalled in a document entitled A Statement of Admiralty Policy, published on December 1905 within hours of the government's resignation.[58] Known as the 'Cawdor Memorandum', this made it crystal clear that the Unionist Board was committed to consolidating the Fisher 'revolution'. That commitment was underscored by a crucial decision which Balfour took at this time. Although it was no longer customary for the Sea Lords to resign on a change of ministry, Fisher's tenure of office was due to end in January 1906 when his commission would expire. This prospect alarmed Cawdor, who believed that no one else could steer his policies through the shoals and banks of naval reaction.[59] Balfour agreed, and to allow Fisher to remain in office to safeguard his achievement, approved his promotion to Admiral of the Fleet, a rank carrying no age restriction. Selborne and Pretyman were delighted by the assurance of continuity, the latter expressing relief that 'the policy of the Board would be maintained whatever may happen about the new Cabinet'.[60]

The Kaiser Rattles The Trident

In 1889 when the two-power standard was adopted officially as the measure of British naval strength, the two next strongest navies were those of Republican France and Tsarist Russia. The alliance of those powers in 1893–4 was as serious a blow to Britain as her own rapprochement with France and Russia would be to Germany a decade later since it converted what had been a hypothetical measure of naval strength into a desperate imperative.[61] To late Victorian governments and public opinion the two-power standard became the tangible and necessary guarantee of Britain's ability to defend her imperial interests wherever they might be threatened – in the Mediterranean, the Persian Gulf or the Pacific. Since France and Russia constituted the world's most powerful naval combination, the two-power standard was thought to secure Britain against any contingency. As a matter of sober fact, in January 1901 that dominance amounted to no more than a superiority of two battleships over the actual combined strength of France and Russia; Admiralty arithmetic gave Britain a total of 45 battleships in commission or reserve, as against the 43 of France and Russia.[62]

Selborne arrived at the Admiralty at a turning point in British naval history. In the absence of significant extra-European navies, Britain's late nineteenth-century control of the 'narrow seas' around Europe had automatically conferred on her a dominance of the world's other oceans; accordingly, as the measure of Britain's supremacy in home waters, the two-power standard was also her guarantee of global command and was seen as such by the public.[63] By the turn of the century however, this advantageous position had been undermined by the emergence of 'new' naval powers, particularly the USA, Japan and Germany. The proliferation of sea power made the two-power standard, 'exacting as it was, a less efficient guarantee of safety' than before.[64] A firm grip on home waters was no longer a guarantee of global command. The growth of the American and Japanese navies deprived Britain of local superiority in the Caribbean and Far Eastern waters and thus of her ability to protect imperial interests in those regions. A quarrel with either power would force the Admiralty to divert forces from other stations, and so weaken Britain's defences against the Dual Alliance; if either power chose to throw in its lot with the Dual Alliance, Britain would be placed in a position of local inferiority and the problem of deploying stretched resources made much worse. To meet this situation, the Admiralty and government had three main options. To build more ships; to divert existing resources to the Far East and Caribbean, thus entertaining risks elsewhere; or to neutralize the potential threat by other than naval means. The first option was impossible for financial reasons. The second was ruled out by the threatening disposition of Russia and France, described by the Secretary to the Admiralty, H.O. Arnold-Forster, in June 1901 as 'our probable and most formidable enemy in maritime war'.[65] The third option was the one taken. In the case of Japan, an alliance was signed in January 1902 which ensured Britain's interests in the Far East while obviating the need for an increased British naval presence.[66] In the case of the USA there was no alliance, but instead a deliberate decision by the government to base its policy in the region on the assumption that a war between the two great 'Anglo-Saxon' powers was inconceivable. This assumption, which was used to justify the progressive reduction of Britain's military and naval presence in the Caribbean and Canada after 1901, glossed over an uncomfortable truth which Balfour and his colleagues recognized all too clearly; if the Americans determined on naval pre-eminence, and directed their enormous economic and technological resources to that purpose, Britain could not hope to compete.[67] Accordingly, the Cabinet acquiesced in Selborne's decision to opt out of the contest by excluding the US Navy from the two-power standard. This amounted to a major reinterpretation of a standard which, since its inception, had generally been treated as independent of diplomatic considerations.

The benefit to Britain of these important developments lay in the squaring of a vicious circle of limited resources, extended commitments, and simultaneous and multiplying dangers. They constituted not only a step away from diplomatic isolation, but also an admission that the Empire could no longer take on all comers. This was a fundamental shift away from the naval self-reliance of the preceding era, but its dimensions were obscured by the way in which politicians continued to talk of the two-power standard in traditional terms, that is as a naval guarantee of global interests. The fact that Britain's position outside European waters now depended on diplomatic understandings, both tacit and explicit, was never openly acknowledged. Nor was the fact that an element of political contingency had been inserted into the traditionally 'apolitical' standard. Friedberg argues with justice that British policy-makers were guilty of self-delusion; unwilling to acknowledge the erosion of Britain's relative naval strength, they continued to invoke 'the time-honoured symbols of British supremacy, even though their meaning had already begun to change'.[68]

The growing naval strength of Germany posed a different but no less distinctive challenge to British governments. The increased number of naval powers since 1889 had raised the spectre of the Royal Navy emerging victorious from a war with the two next strongest naval powers, France and Russia, only to find itself so weakened as to be unable to resist the aggression of a third. By the end of 1902 the likelihood of the USA and Japan playing *tertius gaudens* had receded due to Lansdowne's diplomacy and the Cabinet's commitment to friendship with the USA. By this stage, however, Germany had come to seem entirely convincing in the same sinister role. The publication of the German Navy Law (Amendment) of 1900, with its preamble spelling out the 'risk theory' of the celebrated Admiral Tirpitz, had given a clear indication that the purpose of the German fleet was to give the government in Berlin political leverage in its dealings with the 'strongest naval Power' of the day.[69] It fell to Selborne to respond to the Kaiser's rattling of the trident. In December 1900 he suggested to Hicks Beach that the obvious alternative to mounting Navy Estimates was an alliance with Germany against France and Russia.[70] But his interest in this idea lapsed with the fruitless Anglo-German negotiations of 1901, and during the next eighteen months his attitude towards Germany underwent a dramatic change.[71] By July 1902 he was writing to Balfour of his fear of 'the

German danger'.[72] Selborne set out his views in a sombre Cabinet memorandum of 10 October, in which he explained that since the autumn of 1901 he had made a close study of German naval policy.[73] 'The result of my study', he continued, 'is that I am convinced that the great new German navy is being carefully built up from the point of view of war with us'. This conviction stemmed in part from the reports of the Director of Naval Intelligence, Reginald Custance, who from late 1900 sought to draw the attention of the Board of Admiralty to 'the formidable German force . . . being rapidly developed in the North Sea'.[74] Further evidence gathered by Arnold-Forster on a visit to Wilhelmshaven in August 1902 showed that German battleships were designed for service in the North Sea; their cabins were too cramped and their cruising radius too limited for war in more distant waters.[75] The concentration of the fleet at Kiel and Wilhelmshaven afforded an excellent strategic position for intervention against Britain in any war in which the latter might be involved. Broader strategic considerations could be advanced in support of the Admiralty's interpretation. The German fleet could make no difference to the outcome of a war between Germany and the Franco-Russian alliance, which must be decided on land and by armies; indeed, the huge naval expenditure on which the German government had embarked in 1898 involved 'a deliberate diminution of the military strength which Germany might otherwise have attained in relation to France and Russia'. It was therefore plain to the First Lord and his advisers that Germany was sacrificing offensive power on the Vosges and in East Prussia to the goal of challenging Britain at sea.

In the spring of 1901, and again in the autumn, Selborne informed the Cabinet that, notwithstanding the existence of the three new navies, the Admiralty would continue to frame its construction policy with reference to the combined strength of the French and Russian fleets. 'If we make such provision as will offer us the reasonable certainty of success in a war with France and Russia we shall have fully provided for all contingencies', wrote Selborne, ignoring the fact that 'matching France and Russia . . . no longer guaranteed control of the world's oceans'.[76] On the other hand, the existence of the German Navy meant that Britain must not only win any war with the Dual Alliance, but win and remain capable of beating off a fresh assailant; in short, a mere numerical equality with France and Russia was no longer a sufficient measure of strength in home waters. Selborne aired this view in the Cabinet as early as January 1901, but it was not until October 1902 that he sought formal approval for a modification of the two-power standard. If, as seems likely, the pressures of the war and deference to the Treasury were responsible for the delay, it is clear that the Admiralty's new alertness to German naval ambitions lay behind his eventual action. His striking analysis of German policy in the memorandum of 10 October 1902 was accompanied by the proposal that

Britain should in future adopt a policy of 'equality plus a margin' over the two next strongest naval powers.[77] This formula was made public for the first time in March 1904.[78] In the autumn of that year, a special Admiralty committee quantified the margin as 10 per cent in battleships and 2:1 in armoured cruisers.[79]

The First Lord had also recommended that the government should commit itself to a five-year programme of construction designed to give Britain the desired margin of battleships over France and Russia by 31 December 1907.[80] He argued that the alternative method of 'only settling from year to year what ships shall be laid down [made] it impossible for the Admiralty to work on a definite policy or work out a reasoned programme or to regulate the expenditure except in a hand to mouth way'. The addition of a margin of six battleships above the two-power standard was approved by the Cabinet, a sign of the impression that Selborne's interpretation of German policy had made on his ministerial colleagues, but the idea of a fixed-term programme was rejected. While not prepared to see Britain's naval security eroded, the Cabinet had no desire to exacerbate a difficult financial situation by pledging revenues in advance. Hicks Beach had left the Cabinet in July 1902, but his spirit lingered on. By making the Admiralty adhere to its traditional method of following rather than anticipating foreign construction, the government kept its hands free to economize in the happy event that the building programmes of other powers were cancelled or disrupted.

In the event respite was to be provided by the Russo-Japanese war, which broke out in April 1904 following prolonged tension between the two powers over Manchuria and Korea. The war, which precipitated revolution in Russia in 1905, also crippled Russia as a naval power. In September 1904 Sandars suggested to Balfour that Russian losses offered 'ample justification' for relaxing Britain's construction effort.[81] This was also Fisher's view; in August he had urged Selborne 'not to take any step to lay down any fresh battleships, or that will in any way bind you to do so'.[82] Fisher set the case for taking advantage of Russia's troubles in the financial context of which ministers were so acutely aware. 'You will see the enormous effect on next year's Estimates if, with solid ground for so doing, we mark time a little bit on new construction!', he wrote.[83] Political circumstances made this an offer the government could not refuse. The 1905-6 Estimates contained provision for only a single battleship and four armoured cruisers, the smallest programme since 1895. In May 1905 an Admiralty committee under the Director of Naval Intelligence, Captain Charles Ottley, concluded that the recent Battle of Tsushima provided a clinching justification for the action taken. Togo's annihilation of the Russian fleet dramatically improved Britain's relative naval position. On the outbreak of the Russo-Japanese war, an

Admiralty comparison of the relative strength of the powers not only revealed that Britain had so far attained only a bare margin over France and Russia, but also that Germany and Russia were practically equal; the totals – of battleships built, building or projected – were Britain 65, France 35, Russia 29 and Germany 28.[84] By the summer of 1905, however, Britain enjoyed a 10 per cent margin over the combined strength of Russia, France and Germany.[85] 'Not for ten years has the naval outlook of Great Britain been as cheerful as at present', wrote one lay expert.[86]

The eclipse of Russian sea power in the Far East also facilitated Fisher's policy of concentrating the British fleet in home waters. But the further stage in this process reached in 1905 was also due to wider political developments. The first of these was the *entente cordiale*. The steady improvement in Anglo-French relations under way since 1902 led to the signing in 1904 of a diplomatic convention intended to remove all outstanding sources of friction; its centrepiece was the recognition by Britain of France's preponderant influence in Morocco in return for French recognition of Britain's pre-eminent position in Egypt.[87] Diminishing Anglo-French tension made possible a reduction in Britain's naval presence in the Mediterranean. The second development was the challenge launched by Germany to France's growing influence in Morocco. The Kaiser's provocative landing at Tangiers in March 1905 was designed as much to test the entente as to stake Germany's claim to a place in the Moroccan sun. It backfired since Britain chose to honour that clause in the Anglo-French agreement by which she was bound to provide France with diplomatic support, and the ensuing international conference at Algeciras in 1906 saw Germany rebuffed.[88] The episode produced a sharp increase in Anglo-German tension, against which backdrop the redistribution of the fleet acquired an anti-German character it had not originally possessed.[89]

Early Russian naval losses against the Japanese had led some Unionist ministers to speculate that the two-power standard might soon become obsolete. Selborne had put a stop to such reveries. 'It is an error to suppose that the two Power standard . . . has ever had reference only to France and Russia', he warned in February 1904, more than a year before the full extent of Russia's losses was known.[90] 'It has always referred to the two strongest naval Powers at any given moment, and has been identified in many minds with France and Russia only because France and Russia have for some years past possessed the two most powerful navies next to our own.' This definition of the two-power standard was inconsistent with that which the government had developed in response to the growth of American naval power; 'If the two-Power standard was once again to be considered an automatic, apolitical gauge of naval adequacy, then there could be no logical reason for excluding the United

States should that country's power continue to grow.'[91] Yet, contradictory though it was, this is exactly the line Britain took in 1905 when, as a result of her losses, Russia sank into fourth place among the naval powers as swiftly and abruptly as her fleet had gone down in the Straits of Tsushima. France and Germany were now the world's second and third strongest naval powers and the Admiralty promptly took their combined strength as the measure of the two Power standard. Unlike the goodwill of the USA, the amity of France was not to be taken for granted; 'Ententes may vanish', wrote Fisher, 'battleships remain'.[92] Where America was concerned the Admiralty and government had conveniently departed from that apolitical view of the two-power standard which had prevailed before 1900–2. Where France was concerned, the traditional standard was reasserted. What made the exclusion of the USA possible was the fact that, for all its potential, its navy was not yet among the world's second and third strongest; exempting the USA from the two-power standard in 1902 was a decision of long-term significance but it made no material difference to Britain's actual current naval strength, required no public explanation and allowed politicians to continue professing the traditional standard as though nothing had happened. In contrast, to have exempted France, the second strongest naval power of the day, would have destroyed the two-power standard at a stroke, necessitated an immediate reformulation of the basis of British policy and entailed a real diminution in British naval strength. Such a departure was too drastic for the Unionist government to contemplate.

As it was, even the decision to build only a single battleship in 1905–6 was heavily criticized. The Germanophobe *National Review* attributed Admiralty policy to the imminence of an election; ministers were 'making an electioneering raid on the Navy, so as to be able to pose as economists before the constituencies'.[93] H.W. Wilson, the naval writer, commented on the irony of a government committed to the Blue Water doctrine cutting back the Navy.[94] But more controversial than the size of the programme was its content. The battleship and three of the armoured cruisers were to be built to the revolutionary new 'Dreadnought' design. Little need be said here about a subject which has been covered extensively by Marder, Sumida and others.[95] The design was the product of years of inquiry and experimentation; technological change, particularly the development of long-range weaponry and heavy armour, had made a ship of the Dreadnought type inevitable. Fisher, an enthusiast for the cause since his Mediterranean days, gave it a high priority and an Admiralty Committee on Design was established whose work led to the original Dreadnought. The Russo-Japanese naval actions of 1904–5, particularly Tsushima, seemed to Selborne to confirm 'the wisdom and foresight' of the Admiralty's initiative.[96] An historic step had indeed been taken; the coming of the 'all big-gun ship', superior in firepower and speed to any vessel then afloat, transformed the basis of international naval competition to Britain's disadvantage; at a stroke, Britain's existing superiority in ships of all types was devalued. 'No numerical preponderance in types of warships that have ceased to be effective in the highest sense will justify a sense of security', the Ottley Committee concluded.[97] It was this aspect of the Dreadnought policy that aroused the most sustained and fierce condemnation. Critics argued that British naval supremacy had been wantonly thrown away for an unproven innovation and a new and costly naval race begun in which Britain and the other powers started as equals. The Admiralty countered that it had been left no option in the matter since other powers were busily planning similar ships. 'We were face to face', explained Lee, 'with the question of whether we would . . . run the risk of the British Navy dropping behind in this most vital matter'.[98] The first power to build a preponderance of Dreadnoughts would occupy an unassailable position. It was imperative, therefore, that Britain should be that power.

The introduction of the Dreadnought was arguably the most far-reaching aspect of the Fisher 'revolution'. Achieving a Dreadnought superiority was to be the cardinal goal of British naval policy until the outbreak of war in 1914. The Unionist government had a bare nine months remaining in office when that goal was adopted. Their acceptance of Fisher's case was shown in the Cawdor Memorandum of December 1905 which contained a commitment to build four Dreadnoughts annually in accordance with 'strategic requirements'.[99] It was stated that this programme would not be exceeded unless 'unforeseen contingencies' arose, but also that it might have to be enlarged once foreign admiralties determined on their response to the Dreadnought. But these statements had a hollow ring. At the time the Cawdor Memorandum was issued, Balfour's mind was hardening in favour of resignation. The fate of the policies to which it pledged the Unionists would soon be taken out of their hands.

CHAPTER 6

Into Opposition 1905–6

Since 1903 the Cabinet had settled for an uneasy compromise on the tariff issue. Meanwhile Chamberlain, who had resigned in September 1903 to evangelize his cause nationwide, and his opponents, the Unionist free traders led by the Duke of Devonshire, had waged war for the hearts and minds of the party rank and file. The years 1904–5 were marked by acrimonious party conferences, constituency infighting, and widespread demoralization among Unionists.[1] Balfour's strenuous efforts to preserve a semblance of unity made matters worse by estranging both factions. Ministerial resignations had taken their toll; by 1905 the Ship of State resembled 'a scratch crew on a raft'.[2] Unfortunately, the seas got rougher during 1904–5 as Unionist policy on a number of issues – alien immigration, education, and the use of indentured Chinese labour in the Transvaal – proved highly unpopular in the country. Having been in the wilderness of Opposition since 1895, the Liberals rejoiced to see their hour approaching. With its credibility in tatters, the government finally bowed out on 4 December, bringing ten years of Unionist administration to a lacklustre close. It surprised no one that Balfour chose not to stagger on into a new parliamentary session; rumours of an impending resignation had been circulating since October.[3]

For months beforehand ministers had been giving much private thought to the prospect of Opposition. As will be clear from earlier chapters, the activities of the Liberal party had not seriously influenced the defence policy of either the Salisbury or the Balfour government. Far more important as influences on Unionist policy-making had been the force of public opinion and the strength of various lobbies on the Unionists' back benches. 'I have received much more criticism from my own party than from yours', wrote Arnold-Forster to a Liberal correspondent in December 1905.[4] From 1899 to 1902 the Opposition had concentrated on condemning the government for leading the country into a war for which the Army had been patently unprepared: from 1902 to 1905 they had concentrated on denouncing the excessively high level of defence expenditure. Essentially negative, such an approach spared the Liberal leadership the need to address the issues of naval and military reform which were not only complex but also potentially divisive. In fact, most Liberals were profoundly uninterested in the details of military and naval policy, regarding defence issues as a distasteful distraction from the priorities of domestic reform.[5] The Liberal benches cleared magically when service debates were called and only a handful of recognized 'experts', such as Sir Charles Dilke and Carlyon Bellairs, kept a Liberal interest in the proceedings alive. On the other hand, because the services were soaking up resources urgently needed for domestic reform, and because 'wasteful' defence spending offended Cobdenite morality, the defence issue could not altogether be ignored.[6] Zeal for economy led Liberals to denounce Brodrick but to support Fisher's reforms.[7] Arnold-Forster's scheme was a more difficult target for the Opposition, not only because it was seldom on parliamentary view but also because it kept changing shape. On the strategic arguments underpinning the defence debate after 1903, however, the Liberals were fully in agreement with their opponents. Liberals of all stripes gave wholehearted support to the 'Blue Water' principle and its corollary, an imperial Army.

During 1905 it became increasingly clear that the Liberal party would fight the next election on a platform of a traditional Gladstonian stamp; 'the old creed and the old cries are rushing in', noted a dejected Beatrice Webb.[8] To the Unionists, unlike many historians, there was nothing 'new' about Liberalism in 1904–5. Campbell-Bannerman's talk of peace, retrenchment and reform in a speech at the Albert Hall on 21 December 1905 brought back memories of 1892–5, even of 1868–74.[9] It was for this reason that Unionists habitually referred to their opponents not as Liberals, but as 'Radicals'. They anticipated that a Liberal government would follow a path of doctrinaire Gladstonian economy, leading to a 'perilous diminution' of Britain's military strength.[10]

In naval policy, this implied the possible abandonment of the two-power standard; Selborne had detected a note of scepticism in Liberal pronouncements on the subject as early as 1904.[11] It would certainly mean cut-backs in construction, perhaps with a view to encouraging international disarmament. The Unionist government had been warned that its own reduced programme for 1905–6 offered 'an example to the Bannermans, the Bryces, and the Robertsons, which they [would] not be slow to follow'.[12] Apprehension about future Liberal policy had given Selborne and Balfour additional incentive to launch a second wave of Admiralty reform in the autumn of 1904. But there was a real danger that in proclaiming Fisher's gospel of efficiency through economy the Unionists had presented a serious hostage to fortune. What would stop the Liberals using Fisherite slogans to justify drastic cuts?

Balfour had tried to narrow his opponents' room for manoeuvre in military and foreign policy by delaying his resignation until the rearmament of the field artillery (with quick-firing 18 pounders) was complete and negotiations for the renewal of the Anglo-Japanese treaty of 1902 brought to a successful conclusion.[13] He tried a different gambit in regard to naval policy; the publication of the Cawdor Memorandum within hours of the Unionist government's resignation was rightly seen by the Liberals as a blatant attempt to saddle them with a long-term programme of Dreadnought construction.[14] With an early election anticipated, the document was also a useful propaganda vehicle for the Unionists; Asquith later denounced it as 'an electioneering pamphlet'.[15]

In military policy there was a different but comparable danger. Would any Liberal ministry be able to resist interpreting the new Blue Water doctrine as an invitation to reduce spending on the Army? Campbell-Bannerman had not only denounced the Unionists' costly 'experiments' in military policy but also indicated an appetite for reductions in the Army. It was for this reason that Balfour expressed a reservation about the proposed extension of the Anglo-Japanese treaty of 1902 to provide for Japanese assistance to Britain on the North-West Frontier in a war with Russia; he believed that the risk of drastic reductions would be 'greatly augmented' if a Radical government believed it could rely in war upon an unlimited supply of Japanese troops.[16] For his part, Arnold-Forster apprehended 'great reductions in the Army, tricks played with the Militia . . . and ill-judged additions to the Volunteer Force'.[17]

A reassuring element in the situation, from the Unionist point of view, was the brittle unity of the Liberal party. Fighting the good party fight over the tariff issue after 1903 had served to patch over, rather than to heal, the schism between the party's Gladstonian mainstream and its Liberal imperialist wing who, since the 1890s, had sought to remove the party's defence and foreign policy from the 'fly-blown phylacteries' of the Midlothian era.[18] Although the effective retirement of their leader, Rosebery, had also helped push the Liberal Imperialists back into the party fold in 1903–4, the internecine bitterness of 1899–1902, when the Liberal Imperialists' support for the South African War isolated them from the 'pro-Boer' majority, was slow to dissolve. Balfour's awareness of the internal divisions within the Liberal party had an influence on his decision to resign in December 1905, rather than seek a dissolution. It was widely held that the credibility of any Liberal government in defence matters (at least in the eyes of moderate public opinion) depended upon its inclusion of the three leading Liberal Imperialists, H.H. Asquith, Sir Edward Grey and Richard Haldane. In forcing Campbell-Bannerman to form a ministry before appealing to the country, the Unionist leader undoubtedly hoped to see his opponents 'parading a decade's soiled linen before the electorate', but he also intended to make it hazardous for

Campbell-Bannerman to exclude the Liberal Imperialists.[19] Had Campbell-Bannerman been permitted to fight and win the election before forming a government, he would have been able to dispense with them without risk. Balfour's tactic paid off in that Campbell-Bannerman sought, successfully, to induce the Liberal Imperialist *troika* to serve under him; Asquith became Chancellor, Grey Foreign Secretary and Haldane Secretary of State for War.[20] This outcome was very advantageous to the new Opposition; a strong brake had been fitted to the Radical charabanc. Together with a looser 'Whiggish' element in the Cabinet, represented by a trio of earls, Tweedmouth, Crewe and Elgin, the Liberal Imperialists would, so it was thought, constitute a strong barrier against extreme departures in policy. This seemed most certain in the field of defence, which had been an area of policy in which the Roseberyites' lack of sympathy for traditional Liberalism had been most evident; they preferred a new vocabulary of national efficiency to the formulaic shibboleths of 'Peace, Retrenchment and Reform'. The news that Tweedmouth was to be the new First Lord and Haldane the new Secretary of State for War was thus welcome indeed to Unionists apprehensive of major discontinuities in policy. A moderate Liberal with extensive Unionist connections and friendships, Tweedmouth's appointment greatly relieved his party's opponents. 'I cannot say how glad I am', wrote Brodrick to the new First Lord, 'that the Admiralty is to be in your hands when the pressure to reduce begins'.[21] Selborne and Cawdor reacted similarly.[22] Cawdor actually remained at the Admiralty for some two weeks after the Unionist government's resignation because, owing to Campbell-Bannerman's slowness in selecting a Civil Lord, a new Board could not be constituted.[23] During this period the outgoing First Lord was able to discuss the full range of policy with Tweedmouth and to impress on him the case for continuity.[24] The convention that outgoing ministers briefed their successors – 'a thoroughly English proceeding, showing the essential solidarity of the governing class' – also gave Arnold-Forster an opportunity to influence future events.[25] His successor Haldane was a rotund and genial lawyer with an appetite for good living and a penchant for philosophy (hence his nickname of 'Schopenhauer'). He had no military experience, and no track record of interest in army affairs.[26] Campbell-Bannerman had little fondness for Haldane, whom he rightly thought an intriguer, and took sly pleasure in appointing him to the politically inhospitable War Office; 'Let us see how Schopenhauer gets on in the Kailyard', he remarked sardonically.[27] Arnold-Forster saw his successor as a *tabula rasa* and hurried to make an early imprint. The two men met, and Haldane also received a stream of memoranda covering every conceivable aspect of military policy and War Office administration. Unlike Cawdor in his dealings with Tweedmouth, Arnold-Forster's main concern was not for continuity since there was no

policy in place to be continued! Instead his objective was to steer
Haldane away from the idea of basing army reorganization on the Militia.
'A policy of getting rid of real officers and men, in order to put
make-believe officers and men in their places' might win votes, he
warned, but it would be militarily disastrous since 'in the day of battle
make-believe goes to the wall'.[28] Arnold-Forster was deeply suspicious of
the influence that would be exerted upon Haldane by those shadowy
denizens of the CID, Clarke and Esher. He told Leo Maxse, the acidic
editor of the *National Review*, that he feared a conspiracy 'in which Esher
and Clarke are the principals, C.B. the accomplice and of which
Haldane . . . may be the dupe, to reduce the fighting Army and to put
playabout soldiers in the place of real ones'.[29]

Arnold-Forster would have been still more nervous had he known that
Balfour was in on the plot. On 10 December the ex-Prime Minister had
met the new Secretary of State for War at the CID in Whitehall
Gardens. Clarke, who was present, reported to Esher that 'Mr Balfour in
his charming manner told Haldane where the difficulties [in army reform]
lay, spoke fully of his scheme, and explained why it was not carried out,
and . . . indicated the direction in which he wished to move.'[30] Clarke
thought it likely that Haldane would adopt the Militia scheme shelved
nine months before; 'will it not be strange', he mused, 'if we got Mr

Portrait photograph of R. B. Haldane,
c. 1906.

Balfour's policy carried out by C.-B.?' Esher shared his optimism, predicting to Kitchener that the India-oriented scheme would now get a fair trial.[31] It must be noted that this was by no means Balfour's first contact with Haldane. The two men had known each other for some years and had collaborated across the party divide before, notably over the London University Bill in 1897.[32] The Unionist leader was thus favourably disposed when in the autumn of 1905 Esher and Clarke undertook to 'groom' Haldane for the role of War Minister in a future Liberal government.[33] Esher encouraged Balfour to regard Haldane as a potentially moderating influence on the policy of a Liberal government and to seek his views on the likely fate of the CID under a Campbell-Bannerman administration.[34] To Haldane, Esher stressed the political opportunities open at the War Office, encouraging him to believe that with his cooperation and Balfour's sympathy Haldane would be able to slash the Gordian knot of army reform. Haldane was temperamentally receptive to an appeal which played upon his constructive instincts as well as upon his considerable ambition. This is why, to the astonishment of many, he accepted an office which one of his colleagues compared to 'one of those caravan routes across the African desert, strewn with whitened bones which show the disasters of those who have passed that way before'.[35]

The passage of both service ministries as well as the Foreign Office into 'safe' hands thus partially redeemed the situation facing the new Opposition. The Unionists would have been further reassured to learn of the decision taken by Grey and Haldane in early January 1906 to sanction secret conversations between the French and British General Staffs with a view to concerted military action in the event of a Franco-German rupture over Morocco. In fact, these conversations had been initiated under the Balfour government and, following its resignation, had continued under the aegis of the CID.[36] Grey's attitude towards them was entirely consistent with his determination to maintain the *entente* as the keynote of British foreign policy. The military conversations marked a definite tightening of the link with France forged by Lansdowne in 1902–4. The Opposition's response to this development, unknown to them in 1906, will be examined later.[37]

The election of January 1906 dealt the Unionists a disastrous blow. Salisbury bemoaned a 'catastrophe . . . amazing in its completeness'.[38] A clutch of former ministers, including Balfour, lost their seats, and a mere 157 Unionist MPs were returned to Westminster. Confronting them were 376 Liberals, the bulk of whom were associated with the Radical wing of the party. With the votes of their 83 Irish Nationalist and 54 Labour allies, the government commanded a massive overall majority of 358.[39] It seemed that the Opposition would be powerless to prevent sweeping policy changes. 'We can object to what the Government does, we can criticise', said Joseph Chamberlain, 'but there is no possible combination we can form by which we can turn them out of office, and that is a very comfortable position for them'.[40]

The nature of those changes had been foreshadowed in the election campaign. Although many Liberals rubbed in the Unionists' lamentable military record and condemned 'costly and confused experiments' at the War Office, they devoted more time and energy to spelling out their own plans than to criticizing their opponents.[41] The Liberal leadership left the country in no doubt that, if elected, they would embark on a course of retrenchment and would pursue international agreement on disarmament. Campbell-Bannerman interpreted his party's huge majority as a clear mandate for such a departure.[42] The Unionists, on the other hand, rejected any such inference. They attributed their defeat to domestic causes, such as tariffs, education and labour issues, and did not regard defence matters as having played a significant part in the outcome.[43] This analysis was reassuring in that it allowed the Unionists to go on regarding themselves as 'natural' custodians of the nation's defences. This self-image had emerged in response to the Liberals' declaration of intent and much to their indignation.[44] Unionists depicted their opponents as irresponsible extremists willing to sacrifice national security to utopian dreams of world peace. They suggested that similar ideas entertained by a previous Liberal government had led to national humiliation at Majuba in 1881 and the loss of Gordon at Khartoum in 1885.[45] It was noticeable however, that while Unionists were quick to raise alarums and to sling historical mud, few chose to stand on the Balfour government's own record in defence. Only 33 per cent of Unionist candidates specifically raised defence questions in their election addresses.[46] If paid at all, attention was paid to naval policy and the party's claim to champion the cause of a strong Navy upheld. A deafening silence prevailed in the Unionist camp on the subject of army reform.

The emphatic size of the Liberal majority made the existence of potential allies for the Opposition within the government all the more significant. Powerless themselves, the Unionists had to trust to the willingness of Cabinet moderates such as Haldane and Grey to oppose reckless disarmament. Unfortunately, the preponderance of Radicals on the Liberal back benches greatly weakened the moderates' hand. Their Cabinet opponents would be able to appeal to a powerful parliamentary coalition of backbench Radicals, Labour and Irish MPs, a coalition bonded by a common commitment to retrenchment. In such circumstances the question was no longer what the 'sound' men in the Cabinet could do to help the Opposition, but what the Opposition might do to help them. Answering this new question would preoccupy Balfour during his almost six years as Opposition leader.

CHAPTER 7

Dreadnoughts and Politics 1906–8

Peace, Retrenchment and Reform

The Liberal government of 1906–14, which was to leave so significant a mark on the history of twentieth-century Britain, literally stumbled into office. On the day Campbell-Bannerman and his colleagues went to kiss the royal hand London was smothered by a fog of Dickensian density. Several of the new ministers got hopelessly lost on their journey to and from the Palace; having stepped from his brougham to try to identify landmarks, Haldane was unable to find it again and only reached the War Office by 'trudging through the mud and feeling the horses' heads' along the Horse Guards.[1]

Six weeks after this inauspicious beginning, however, the Liberals had secured their landslide election victory and with it the power to pursue the Gladstonian goals of peace, retrenchment and reform. For the next three years, the period covered by this chapter, the Liberals made substantial reductions in British naval expenditure. Between fiscal years 1906–7 and 1908–9 the Navy Estimates remained on average some 15 per cent below the peak reached in 1904–5. Along with surplus tax revenue, the savings achieved were used to liquidate debt which in turn released for spending on social reform funds which would otherwise have been needed for debt-servicing.[2] While these savings can be attributed in part to the deferral of various naval works and to a reduction in the number of ships in commission, they were mainly the result of a reduced construction programme. Expenditure on battleships and first-class cruisers fell from almost £8.5 million in 1905–6 to below £6 million in 1908–9.[3] Rather than building four Dreadnoughts per annum, as the Cawdor memorandum had foreshadowed, the Liberal government built three in 1906–7, three in 1907–8 and just two in 1908–9. Though they argued over detail, the Sea Lords of the Admiralty, led by Fisher, consistently endorsed the broad thrust of the government's policy.[4] What allowed the government to justify, and the Sea Lords to approve, this policy departure was the confusion and delay into which foreign shipbuilding plans were thrown by the arrival of the mould-shattering

Dreadnought. However, recognizing the temporary nature of the advantage won by the Dreadnought, the Liberal Cabinet sought other means of perpetuating the lower levels of naval expenditure on which the success of their domestic programme depended. They enthusiastically supported the Second Hague Peace Conference of 1907, hoping that it would produce an international accord on naval arms limitation. As an earnest of their sincerity, and as an example to the other powers, the government promised to drop one of the British Dreadnoughts of 1907–8 if the Conference proved fruitful. In the event it did not, and the vessel was built.[5] While pursuing the chimera of international disarmament, the Liberals also tried to redefine the traditional two-power standard. As explained in Chapter 5, the Unionist governments of 1900–5 had behaved inconsistently in this matter, applying an apolitical definition of the standard in the case of France but not in that of the USA. From the outset, the Liberals wished to abandon the apolitical standard altogether. They wished to forge a connection between naval policy and foreign policy and held that British naval policy should be based on actual diplomatic relationships rather than on hypothetical combinations of powers. The apolitical standard was unsatisfactory, they argued, because it took no account of the fact that Britain's relations with the two next strongest naval powers, France and Germany, were peaceful. Nor did it acknowledge the circumstances – notably Germany's possession of Alsace-Lorraine – which made a hostile combination between the next two strongest powers inconceivable.[6] Anxious to escape an onerous naval standard which they considered unrealistic and illogical, the Liberals had nevertheless to proceed cautiously due to the symbolic importance the two-power standard possessed in the public mind; as Haldane told the Kaiser in 1906, it was 'a way of expressing a deep national tradition, as sacred as the Gospel'.[7] Nevertheless, in parliamentary navy debates from the summer of 1906 Campbell-Bannerman and other leading Liberals argued for a redefined naval standard that would secure Britain not against *any* combination of powers, but against any *reasonable* combination. Such a concept was not officially adopted, but it shaped Liberal policy unofficially until 1912, when, in the light of changed circumstances, the two-power standard was dropped altogether.

From this brief sketch of Liberal policy it will be obvious that the hopes of continuity in naval policy which Unionists had entertained in December 1905 were to be comprehensively dashed. The rest of this chapter describes their response.

Keeping Watch

The Unionists' predictable hostility to the reduction of the Cawdor programme was defused by Fisher, who corroborated the government's claim that foreign shipbuilding programmes had been seriously delayed by the Dreadnought. In a conversation at the Travellers' Club in November 1906, the First Sea Lord impressed upon Balfour Britain's favourable position *vis-à-vis* her naval rivals and reminded him that his own government had trimmed the 1905–6 programme on the strength of slackened construction overseas.[8] Balfour was reassured, accepting that 'the actual ships we were building were enough to meet the actual ships of other people'.[9] Once informed, his colleagues responded similarly. Austen Chamberlain, who would take an active interest in naval affairs in Opposition, was persuaded that:

> we have without doubt a very good margin just now, because other Powers stopped their building programme to see what the Dreadnought was going to be and have not yet decided how to meet it.[10]

In briefing Balfour on Admiralty policy, Fisher was playing the early hands of a difficult double game. His active cooperation in the Liberal Cabinet's quest for naval retrenchment was wholly consistent with the cost-cutting reputation he had established during the last two years of Unionist administration. It is also to be explained by his need to retain ministerial support against critics of his reforms. However, as will be seen in Chapter 9, Fisher recognized that the survival of those reforms also depended on the continued support of Balfour and his colleagues, and they objected to the cut-backs in shipbuilding. His dilemma was to prevent his collaboration with the Liberals over shipbuilding damaging his 'auld alliance' with the Unionist front bench. To this end, Fisher played on Balfour's trust. 'I am sure you know I would not stop here one minute if anything were wrong', he wrote in November.[11] He maintained that reductions were not only justifiable on naval grounds, but also advisable on political grounds. By making safe and legitimate reductions now, the Admiralty would defuse the Radical agitation and prevent pressure building up for draconian cuts; it was a question of 'a moderate reduction in order to prevent a large one'.

What, in these circumstances, was the proper role for the Opposition? Fisher argued for a policy of restraint. The Unionists should eschew any attack on the government which would force the Admiralty, in self-defence, to disclose Britain's ample margin of security. If the true strength of the Navy became known to the Radicals, they would undoubtedly demand commensurate reductions.[12] As he trusted Fisher's assurances on the facts of the naval situation, so Balfour accepted his political logic, concluding that on 'purely public grounds' the Opposition must act cautiously.[13] At their leader's behest, during the winter Unionist spokesmen refrained from attacking government policy; 'we cannot make a strong attack here at present', Chamberlain admitted.[14] When George Wyndham stepped out of line with some aggressive remarks on the Navy in a speech in his Dover constituency in late 1906, Fisher hurriedly warned Balfour that his colleague had done the Navy 'a bad turn'.[15] It seems that Balfour subsequently issued a caution, for soon after Wyndham was writing that 'without further knowledge, it is not wise to attack the Government for not laying down more ships'.[16]

Just as the military policy of the Opposition after 1906 was to be strongly influenced by the relationship between Balfour and Haldane, so Opposition naval policy was shaped by the relationship which had developed between Balfour and Fisher in 1903–5.[17] In both cases Balfour's policy was agreed by his immediate colleagues but caused frustration among their supporters. Since July there had been calls from the back benches and in the press for a tough Opposition line on the Navy. There was some criticism of the Opposition's response to the announcement of cut-backs on 27 July; H.W. Wilson alleged in the *National Review* that 'the Unionist benches were empty, and, except for a vigorous speech by Mr Lee and a mild protest from Mr Balfour, there was no response to what is really a revolution in naval policy'.[18] During the autumn and winter of 1906 senior Unionists were lobbied to take the offensive against government policy. Wyndham, for example, was prompted by Leslie Cope-Cornford, naval correspondent of the *Standard*.[19] Responding to this pressure, Arnold-Forster suggested to Balfour that 'it would be to the advantage both of the country and of the Party' if the Opposition challenged the government over its shipbuilding policy.[20] But Balfour declined to move.

While prepared to accept that objective circumstances warranted a modification of the Cawdor programme, Balfour was far from complacent about the naval situation. He looked ahead to the inevitable moment when the activity of the other powers would be resumed and Britain compelled to renew large-scale shipbuilding. It was on this prospect that Opposition energies would focus during 1907. Maintaining his policy of not attacking the recent reductions, Balfour concentrated instead on extracting from the government a commitment that they would react promptly and substantively to the resumption of foreign construction. Growing mistrust of Liberal intentions made this a matter of urgency. 'I distrust C.-B.,' wrote Austen Chamberlain, 'and his party are ready to give away anything when the pinch comes'.[21] By the spring of 1907 it was a commonplace among Unionists that the Campbell-Bannerman ministry was in thrall to its large and unruly majority.[22] Like late nineteenth-century Liberal governments it seemed to have embarked on the path of 'log-rolling'; in 1906 and 1907 legislative gestures were made towards each of the major elements in the coalition – Labour, Irish, and Nonconformist – and a fresh campaign launched against the House of Lords. In these circumstances further concessions to the 'economists' seemed inescapable. 'There is no more chance of the Government adding an extra million to the Estimates in a particular year . . . than there is of their standing up to a Labour member, or protecting the Loyalists in Ireland', wrote Arnold-Forster.[23] The task to which Balfour directed the attention of the Opposition front bench in 1907 was finding a means of making it impossible for ministers to waver in their duty towards the Navy if – or, rather, when – confronted with a choice between renewed foreign construction and party political pressures.

The means chosen was the two-power standard. If the traditional formula of a margin of strength above the combined strength of the two next strongest powers remained official policy, then it would automatically dictate increased British construction once work in the naval yards of France, Russia and Germany quickened pace. The goal of Opposition policy was therefore to force the government into publicly affirming the traditional apolitical standard. The fact that their own party's attitude to the standard had been inconsistent and ambiguous did not stop them. From the spring of 1907 Unionist spokesmen responded aggressively to the ambiguities and qualifications which characterized ministerial statements on the subject. The Prime Minister's tentative redefinition of the standard in July 1906 and March 1907 was violently denounced by Balfour as 'most menacing to the country'.[24] During the Estimates debate of March 1907 the Unionist leader appeared to trap a 'blusterously angry' Campbell-Bannerman into recanting his heresy.[25] Cawdor, watching from the peers' gallery, was delighted 'at the way C.B. put his foot in it over the Two Power Standard, and at the way in which [Balfour] rolled the old thing up'.[26] Chamberlain wrote of 'an acceptance wrung from C.B. of the Two Power Standard as we have always understood it, i.e. a margin of security over any *two* other Powers at any time', conveniently forgetting the fact that when in office the Unionists had interpreted the standard selectively.[27] If Balfour's debating success was no substitute for beating the government in the division lobby, it nevertheless gave the Opposition leadership considerable satisfaction because it seemed to tie the government's hands in the matter of naval construction. However, by the end of the year the argument over the two-power standard, though by no means dead, had lost much of its significance as a result of the resumption and acceleration of German Dreadnought construction.

The German Navy Law amendment of November 1907, which shortened the statutory lifespan of German Dreadnoughts and thereby dictated a faster tempo of construction, marked the recovery of German naval policy from the disarming spell cast on it by the launch of HMS Dreadnought in 1906. It produced uproar in Unionist circles in Britain, where it was universally recognized as proof of Germany's ambition to dispute Britain's naval supremacy.[28] The excitement was intensified by the simultaneous revival of the controversy over invasion.[29] The new law merely confirmed many Unionist journalists, publicists and backbench politicians in a suspicion of Germany which dated from 1904, if not from 1898. In response to Selborne's annual assessments the members of Balfour's government had come to regard German naval policy similarly.[30] But they seldom expressed such views publicly, keeping references to the German challenge or 'menace' for private correspondence and conversation. A sense of ministerial responsibility deterred them from making statements which might inflame Anglo-German relations; when Arthur Lee adverted to the prospect of an Anglo-German naval war in a speech in his Eastleigh constituency in the spring of 1905 his incaution almost cost him his job as Civil Lord.[31] Unionist speeches in 1906 and early 1907 suggest that this inhibition survived the transition from office to Opposition. But the events of the autumn of 1907 produced a greater candour and trenchancy in the way in which frontbench spokesmen addressed the German question in public. 'There is no secret whatever', observed Lee in the Commons in March 1908, 'that Germany . . . is frankly and openly seeking to create a fleet of sufficient strength to imperil the supremacy at sea which we now possess'.[32] For the first time, in debating naval policy Unionists acknowledged that the axis of British naval strategy now lay, not in the Mediterranean and the Channel, but in the North Sea. 'There has been Orientation', argued Wyndham, 'and we have now to look East'.[33] Balfour was somewhat anxious about the risk of provoking Berlin, and seems to have counselled prudence on his colleagues.[34] The new sharpness of tone was unavoidable; the Navy Law amendment had made German ambitions the focal point of the British Navy debate.

At all levels of the Unionist party the news from Germany was taken to signal the end of the period of grace won for the Admiralty by the launching of the Dreadnought. The writing had been espied on the wall four months earlier, when the German, Austrian and Italian representatives to the Hague Conference had flatly refused to enter into a debate on disarmament.[35] Having repeatedly anticipated the renewal of the international naval arms race, the Unionists now expected the Liberal government to face facts and respond with a substantial construction programme which would secure Britain's position. In some quarters there was a demand that two British keels should be laid down for every one German.[36] Consequently, the appearance of the 1908–9 Estimates produced consternation on the Opposition benches. It was not merely the small size of the programme – just one Dreadnought battleship and one battle cruiser – that offended, but also the fact that only 10 per cent of the total cost of the vessels was provided in the Estimates for work in the coming year. By preventing the assembly in advance of vital components such as armour and gun-mountings, the ships' completion would be delayed. To the Unionists, preoccupied with the quickening rhythm of German shipbuilding, such delay was the opposite of what the situation required.

If the debate over the 1907–8 Estimates had turned on the different interpretation the two parties placed upon the two-power standard, the debate over the 1908–9 Estimates turned on their different assessments of the German 'challenge'. Two issues were in dispute; first, the likelihood of the German government fulfilling its new target of starting four Dreadnoughts each year, and second, the time each of those ships would take to complete. On the first point, ministers took the view that the German government would have difficulty extracting the necessary credits from a recalcitrant Reichstag.[37] On the second, they continued to believe that Britain retained a significant edge in shipbuilding capacity; Fisher had assured Tweedmouth, for Cabinet consumption, that the German dockyards still took 33 months to complete a Dreadnought, nine months longer than their British counterparts.[38] These favourable assumptions lay behind the government's decision to further limit Britain's construction effort in 1908–9. They also underpinned the forecast of comparative naval strengths which the Admiralty's spokesmen, Edmund Robertson and George Lambert, gave the House of Commons. They announced that Germany was expected to have six Dreadnoughts complete by early 1911 but admitted that, if 'certain possible alterations' occurred, she might have ten. Against this, Britain would have completed twelve Dreadnoughts. At worst, therefore, Britain would have a margin of superiority of two ships.[39]

In response, the Unionists argued that there was no reason to doubt the Germans' determination to carry out their programme in full. 'We cannot count on the German programme being cut down on the grounds of financial stringency', warned Lee; a sympathetic public and chauvinistic press would help overawe the Reichstag.[40] On the matter of relative shipbuilding speeds the Opposition were convinced by newspaper and other evidence that the Germans had greatly accelerated the construction of Dreadnoughts; the first German Dreadnought, *Nassau*, had recently been launched just eight months after laying down.[41] Since 1906 Balfour had followed the progress of German shipbuilding with interest and was in no doubt as to its potential; 'If the Germans think it worth their while, I do not think we can count upon building battleships quicker than they can', he had told the Commons as early as July 1906.[42] Now he and Lee publicly credited Tirpitz's claim that Germany's construction capacity was now 'practically . . . or largely identical' to Britain's. This development lent an ominous significance to the fact that in any given year, whereas work on new British vessels began in December, work on new German vessels began six months earlier, in June or July.[43] Given equal construction speeds, therefore, the Germans would complete their annual programme six months before the British programme of the same year.

Their different assumptions led the Unionists to offer a strikingly more pessimistic view of the naval outlook than that of the government. Balfour contended that:

> if German shipbuilding is now, or is going to be in the immediate future, as fast as our shipbuilding, whatever we may do next year [1909], Germany will be superior to us during the later months of 1911 in ships of capital importance.

He and his colleagues focused attention on the autumn of 1911, rather than the spring as Robertson had done. They pointed out that whereas Britain's position in spring 1911 (as depicted by Robertson) would be highly unsatisfactory, in the autumn it would be precarious. By then the German ships begun in June 1908 would have been finished, giving a total of thirteen German Dreadnoughts. By that stage, the British programme begun in December 1908 would still be some six months from completion, giving a total of only twelve British Dreadnoughts. This would leave Britain dependent for a bare margin of superiority over Germany on the two newest pre-Dreadnoughts the *Lord Nelson* and *Agamemnon*, ships which the Unionists refused to regard as equivalent to Dreadnoughts.[44]

So, as in 1906 and 1907, the argument between the parties was not over Britain's present but her future security. The dominating issue was Germany's shipbuilding capacity. The government doggedly defended its unhurried and cautious response to events in Germany and insisted on Britain's continuing productive superiority. The Opposition maintained that that superiority had been lost and argued that the mere possibility of Germany achieving a lead in Dreadnoughts by the end of 1911 demanded immediate precautionary action in the form of an increase in the Navy Estimates then before Parliament. For three days the Admiralty's spokesmen were harried by Balfour and Lee, backed up by Chamberlain and Wyndham. It was an unequal contest; one lobby correspondent described the Liberal duo as 'very much at sea and nervous about the floating mines of facts which were constantly blowing them up'.[45] Robertson often seemed close to tears as he struggled to master his complicated brief.[46] Yet, for all their debating ascendancy, the Opposition made no headway with their demands for further new construction. So Balfour changed tack, concentrating on the situation that would confront the country *if* events showed the government to have underestimated German potential and the Opposition's apprehensions to have been well founded. It would take a massive naval effort in 1909–10 if Britain was to have any chance of averting a crisis in 1911–12. Though Robertson and Lambert acknowledged as much,

Balfour wanted them to go further. As over the two-power standard in 1907, he hoped to commit the government in advance to taking the necessary action. This was plainly the most that the Opposition could now hope to achieve. On 10 March he succeeded in his aim when a series of direct and forceful questions brought Asquith to his feet. Deputizing for the mortally ill Campbell-Bannerman, the Chancellor dismissed the various assumptions about German construction speed and capacity on which the Unionist case rested. He also made it plain that he expected the German government to fall short of its published goals. But he also gave the House the vital assurance for which Balfour had been pressing:

> Without in any way forecasting the shipbuilding programme for next year, I will say this without the faintest hesitation, that if we find at that time [i.e. in 1909] there is a probability of the German programme being carried out in the way the paper figures suggest, we should deem it our duty to provide and we should provide not only for a sufficient number of ships, but for such a date for laying down those ships, that at the end of 1911 the superiority which the right hon. Gentleman foreshadows would not be an actual fact.[47]

'The event of the past few days', Esher observed on 14 March, 'has been the success of A.J.B. in drawing from Asquith a declaration about the Navy'.[48] The Opposition were undoubtedly helped by the revelation three days before that Tweedmouth had received and responded to a letter from the Kaiser on the subject of British naval policy; widely construed as an attempt to influence the Cabinet debate over the Navy Estimates, the so-called 'Tweedmouth Letter' agitated public opinion against Germany and fuelled suspicion of German policy. Though the official Opposition did nothing to embarrass the government, treating the matter with 'philosophic indifference', the public outcry strengthened their hand in Parliament.[49] Yet Balfour's tactics were probably the more important cause of Asquith's concession. By focusing debate on the single intelligible issue of construction schedules, and generating unease about the outlook for 1911, the Opposition leader drove the government into a corner. Unable to prove that the Unionists' assumptions about German shipbuilding speed, capacity and intent were ill founded, Asquith could only defuse public anxiety by pledging the government to vigilance and decisive action. Balfour was well pleased with the outcome of the debate; 'A.J.B. came out of the House radiant this afternoon', wrote Sandars on the 10th, 'exclaiming "we have had had a real Parl[iamentar]y triumph"'.[50] Cawdor subsequently referred to an 'undertaking' that the needs of the Navy would be met and Sandars wrote of 'an answer which dwarfs into insignificance everything that has yet been said on the subject of National Defence'.[51]

Looked at critically, the outcome of the debate was far less favourable to the Opposition than these grandiloquent claims suggest. The most striking thing about Asquith's declaration was its limited nature. It committed the government only to maintaining a one-power standard relative to Germany, not to maintaining a two-power standard relative to Germany and France. Opposition pressure on that issue had proved totally fruitless. The government would not be tied down to so exacting a measure of naval strength at a time when Britain's diplomatic relations were pacific and when the international naval race was regaining momentum; Germany's lead would soon be followed by the other powers, including the USA. The most that ministers would accept was Campbell-Bannerman's diluted version of the two-power standard – superiority over 'any reasonable combination' of powers.[52] Disappointing though this was to the Unionists, it would not deter them from continuing to hound ministers to clarify their attitude towards the traditional standard. The issue remained politically useful. It embarrassed the government, whose obvious reluctance to drop the two-power standard altogether reflected its perceived hold on the public imagination.

Balfour's delight at events on 10 March did not blind him to the unpalatable fact that he and his colleagues had failed to prevent a further suspension of the Cawdor programme. Nor did he underestimate the considerable political obstacles to a reversal of the trend of economy in naval policy, obstacles which solidified with each year that the resumption of large-scale construction was deferred. The first of these was finance. How would the government meet the cost of turning its policy around? Excluding the cost of any new naval programme, the Exchequer would be liable to some £8 million of new expenditure in 1909. The Budget of 1908 gave no indication of where even this sum was to be found. On the second reading of the Finance Bill on 2 June, Balfour protested that the country was 'face to face . . . with . . . vast expenditure for which no provision is made or foreshadowed by the Government'.[53] Winston Churchill poured fuel on the fire by confiding to the Unionist leader at a house party that the government were 'in an awful mess about next year's finances and at their wits' ends how to provide for their expenditure'.[54] Against this lowering financial horizon, with no sign yet of Lloyd George's fiscal lightning, Unionists naturally doubted the ability of the government to make good Asquith's recent undertaking on the Navy.[55] The second obstacle to effective government action in 1909 was the inevitable resistance from the Radical wing of the Liberal party; Balfour's concern in this respect will be explained in the next section.

Though Balfour stressed the need for 'the utmost vigilance', there was really nothing for the Unionists to do but wait on events in Germany.[56] The debate in March had won the government a period of grace. How could ministers be condemned for neglect when the current strength of the Navy exceeded a two-power standard and when the German danger existed only on paper? They could not be indicted on an hypothesis. Balfour concluded that for the Opposition to attack prematurely would not be in the interests of the Navy. They ran the risk of 'crying "Wolf"'. A premature attack in 1908 would greatly diminish their ability to rouse public opinion against the government if it reneged on its commitments in 1909. As in 1906 and 1907, therefore, for tactical reasons Balfour opted for a strategy of restraint. As in 1906 and 1907, his decision was influenced by Fisher. The First Sea Lord had anticipated the outcry over the 1908–9 Estimates. On the eve of the debate he wrote breezily to Balfour to express the hope that Lee and other Opposition spokesmen would not be too 'acrimonious' in the Commons; 'You yourself and Lord Cawdor have always set such a splendid example', he added.[57] Fisher again stressed the danger of the Opposition helping the 'economists' by exposing the fact that the strength of the Navy exceeded Britain's needs. As he had in 1906 and 1907, Balfour followed this counsel in the sense that the Opposition's case in March 1908 turned not on Britain's current security but on her possible future insecurity. On the other hand, he was unconvinced by Fisher's assurances about the outlook for 1911 and 1912 and would not be deflected from subjecting the government to intense pressure on that subject, with the results already described.[58] In general, however, Fisher's standing among senior Unionists was substantially unaffected by the row over shipbuilding. Like Balfour, they did not hold the First Sea Lord accountable for the government's decision to mark further time over construction. Believing Fisher to be 'very clever and even anxious for war with Germany', Austen Chamberlain for one found it 'hard to believe' that he would willingly sacrifice national security.[59]

Balfour's continuing restraint on the naval issue produced dissension on the Unionist back benches, where anger over Liberal policy was not tempered by a cautious appreciation of political realities. Cawdor acknowledged publicly that his apparent willingness to give the government the benefit of the doubt was unpopular among sections of his party.[60] One index of backbench frustration was a schism within the Navy League. Early in 1908 some of its more militant Unionist members, led by Edward Turnour and F.E. Smith, seceded to form a rival Imperial Maritime League, the avowed object of which was to 'put some ginger' into the Opposition's performance in the Navy debate.[61] The IML was also vigorously anti-Fisher; the animosity of its members towards the First Sea Lord had been fuelled by his evident acquiescence in a further round of naval cuts. 'The traitors at the Admiralty have consented to play the game of the Cobdenite cheeseparers and to endanger our Sea Power at the very time that we ought to be making a special shipbuilding effort', wrote Maxse.[62] In agitating for both a tougher Opposition line on the construction issue and an inquiry into Fisher's administration the predominantly Unionist IML was implicitly challenging Balfour's conduct of naval affairs. However, as in the winter of 1906–7 the challenge remained implicit and restricted to fairly narrow circles of opinion. The IML lacked frontbench patronage. Its activity certainly had no appreciable effect on Balfour, who stood by his strategy; 'I am by no means clear that the best policy is to attack them [the Government] before they have manifestly fallen short of their duties', he wrote to one IML member in March 1908.[63] Such remarks contained the promise that the Opposition leader would not be found wanting in aggression if future events showed the government to be neglectful of national security. This had always been the corollary of the strategy of restraint he had pursued since the first batch of Liberal cut-backs in the summer of 1906. In November 1906 Balfour had pledged to 'rouse the country' if convinced that government policy was leading to a serious erosion of Britain's comparative naval strength.[64]

Cockleshell Fleeters and Liberal Imperialists

During 1908 Balfour's approach to the Navy debate came increasingly to be dominated by a belief that the Cabinet was seriously divided on the shipbuilding issue.

As explained earlier, Unionists expected the Liberal ministry to be bullied into cutting defence expenditure by a coalition of Radical, Labour and Irish MPs. Events proved them correct. The 'economists', organized into a backbench Reduction of Armaments Committee, and strongly supported by Liberal newspapers such as the *Nation, Daily News* and *Manchester Guardian*, campaigned continuously after January 1906 for deeper cuts than the Liberal government was prepared to make.[65] They urged the government to promote the Gladstonian causes of reform at home and peace abroad by slashing Britain's 'bloated armaments'.[66] Their agitation conformed to a distinct annual pattern. A year-round series of meetings, speeches and delegations to the Prime Minister would reach its climax each autumn as the Admiralty and Cabinet argued over the following year's Estimates. When, in the spring, the outcome of that argument was known, the economists in Parliament would condemn the Estimates and construction programme alike as excessive and move resolutions for reduction. They also routinely demanded the formal abandonment of the two-power standard, fully matching their Unionist opponents in the zeal with which they scrutinized ministerial pronouncements on the issue. The parliamentary coalition of 'Cockleshell Fleeters' (as the Tory press dubbed them) was led by J.M. Robertson, J. Murray Macdonald and Sir John Brunner, each of whom became an established figure in the demonology of Unionist editors such as Maxse and H.A. Gwynne of the *Standard*.[67] The numerical strength of the economists –

fluctuating between 70 and 120 – was insufficient to prevent their resolutions being consistently defeated, but sufficient to force the government to take them very seriously. Forced on to the defensive, ministers were obliged to appease the back benches by sympathetic assurances of their earnest desire for peace and their determination to cut the cost of the Navy as far as safety allowed.

Annual Estimates debates thus saw ministers having simultaneously to justify their action against Unionist allegations that they were doing too little for the Navy, and against Radical accusations that they were doing too much. As *The Times* put it pithily in March 1908, ministers regularly found themselves 'playing the not very enviable part of Mr Facing-Both-Ways'.[68] The role of the Unionists in this intriguing piece of political theatre was a subtle one. The activity of the economists drew them into a form of tactical alliance with the government. While, as we have seen, they challenged the government aggressively over its reluctance to give guarantees about future naval policy, and while they roundly denounced the deference of ministers to Radical opinion, Balfour and his colleagues were compelled to prevent bad Estimates becoming worse by supporting the government in the division lobby against hostile Radical motions. In this way, the theme of containment underlying Balfour's conduct of naval affairs after 1906 was reinforced.

As we shall see, this tactical alliance with the government had its parallel after 1906 in Balfour's continuing support for the Board of Admiralty against the 'Sanhedrin of Admirals'.[69] Such behaviour was accompanied by frequent assertions that the Unionist party regarded the Navy as being, 'above politics'. Opposition spokesmen consistently denied that 'party spirit' lay behind their criticism of the government.[70] This rhetoric of non-partisanship, which was commonplace in front-bench speeches from 1907, won the Unionists no thanks from their opponents, but it had the important effect of reinforcing their consciousness of giving the government the benefit of the doubt over naval policy. The belief of Balfour and senior party figures that, in the national interest, they had exercised a disinterested restraint in naval affairs between 1906 and 1908 would be of explosive significance when, in 1909, the limits of that restraint were reached.

Balfour's appreciation of the government's difficulties with its own supporters was matched by his alertness to divisions within the Cabinet itself. It has been suggested that his decision to resign office in late 1905 was influenced by a wish to engineer the inclusion of the Liberal Imperialists in Campbell-Bannerman's government.[71] It was to the Liberal Imperialists, Haldane, Grey and Asquith, that the Opposition front bench looked for Cabinet resistance to Radical extremism. Faith in the judgement of the Liberal Imperialists underpinned Balfour's willingness to accept that the cut-backs of 1906 and 1907 were safe and legitimate; their acquiescence in the reductions corroborated Fisher's assurances on the point. Austen Chamberlain argued in January 1907 that 'Until and unless Asquith is proven false to his word, we ought to accept it and scout the idea that he will give way . . .'[72] This trusting attitude contrasted sharply with the response of more militant Unionists whose faith in the Liberal Imperialists was shattered by the opening round of defence economies in the summer of 1906:

> Remember always [wrote Gwynne of *The Standard*] that Haldane, Asquith, Grey, Elgin, Tweedmouth; all these men of whom we have said to ourselves, 'these at any rate will prevent an utter débacle', have made absolutely no resistance, and have allowed themselves to be swept off their feet by Little Englanders of the Lloyd George type.[73]

Not subscribing to this view, during 1907 the Unionist leadership confidently expected that the Liberal Imperialists would defend the Navy against reckless economies. Even after the 1908–9 Navy Estimates the Unionist leadership remained confident that the Liberal Imperialists had not yet sold the pass. However, they were irritated by the frequency with which Grey, Haldane and Asquith made statements sympathetic to Radical aspirations. The Unionist front bench was particularly infuriated by Asquith's response to a Radical motion for retrenchment moved in the Commons on 2 March 1908 by Murray Macdonald, a Scot of 'the cold, grey, dour Covenanter type'.[74] Asquith's speech echoed Campbell-Bannerman's line on the two-power standard and seemed to hold out the prospect of further savings on naval expenditure.[75] 'It sticks in my gizzard', wrote Wyndham, 'that a Chancellor of the Exchequer who has just "passed" the Estimates . . . shd. meet a motion challenging his estimates in this indirect and ambiguous manner'.[76] The Unionists thought the speech ambiguous because they were convinced that Asquith's true views were closer to theirs than to those of the Radicals. They believed that he was masking his true position in order to avoid straining his authority over those on the Liberal left who distrusted his Roseberyite past. Hence Balfour's attempt to force Asquith out into the open by proposing a sly amendment intended to expose Liberal differences on the two-power standard; 'he probed the wound', wrote Austen Chamberlain, 'and turned his knife round and round'.[77]

In fact, for all their subtlety, the Unionists – Balfour included – were badly deluding themselves. Remarks of Asquith's which they construed as a sop to Radical sentiment were, in fact, a genuine reflection of the Chancellor's commitment to the Radical cause of retrenchment. While the Unionists had regarded him as a friendly fifth-columnist within the Cabinet, Asquith had actually been in the van of the campaign for changes in naval policy both in 1906–7 and 1907–8.[78] 'Asquith at the Treasury acted not at all as a Liberal Imperialist', writes John Grigg, 'but as a Gladstonian "economist"'.[79] He had, for example, strongly favoured revising the two-power standard on the grounds that naval spending must be 'a question of policy, to be decided mainly by reference to the state of our relations with foreign powers'.[80] Though conspicuous in Asquith's public statements on naval affairs, such opinions were dismissed by the Opposition as disingenuous and tactical. They persisted in viewing him as the defiant Liberal Leaguer of 1899–1902 and were blind to the transformation of his political character since 1904–5. Their attitude smacks of wishful thinking. Powerless themselves, perhaps Balfour and his colleagues were too eager to believe in the existence of a Cabinet faction which would stem the rising tide of Radicalism. Anyway, in 1908 the gap between the real and the imagined Asquith widened. Following his succession to the premiership in April, Asquith swung further left on the shipbuilding issue. In early July, he told the newly appointed First Lord, Reginald McKenna, of his 'scepticism' about the entire Dreadnought policy.[81] 'There is much money in it,' he wrote, 'and more than money'; further economies would help consolidate his hold over the Liberal party; would release funds for social reform and so promise an improvement in the disappointing legislative record of the ministry; and would help sustain the process of fiscal reform which he had bequeathed to his successor at the Exchequer, David Lloyd George. For these reasons Asquith was now more than ever inclined to pare Britain's naval spending to a minimum.

To the Unionists the situation appeared very different. During the summer of 1908 they became convinced that a battle royal was raging within the Cabinet over defence expenditure, in which Asquith, Haldane and Grey were pitted against the Radical duo, Lloyd George and Winston Churchill. The Radicals seemed to them to have exploited Asquith's succession as leader to extend their influence within the government. A fierce Cabinet row over the Army Estimates in the summer was construed as early evidence of their new political muscle.[82] So was the Budget, with its lack of provision for new naval construction. This made the first serious dent in Asquith's reputation among senior Unionists. Selborne was led to wonder whether, after all, 'Asquith, not to mention Haldane and Grey, would consent to be responsible for running the awful risk of falling too low in Naval strength compared with Germany?'[83] Austen Chamberlain was dismayed by hints in Asquith's speech in defence of the Budget that he envisaged further reductions in naval spending. 'I cannot think what he is at,' wrote Chamberlain; '. . . I am loath to believe that he means to content himself with fine words and theatrical attitudes in such vital matters of national security'.[84] For all their indignation, however, Chamberlain and his colleagues continued to assume that Asquith was acting for reasons of political self-interest rather than out of conviction. He was believed to be under intense pressure to appease the Radicals. 'Asquith does not seem to me to be going strong', observed Lansdowne; 'Lloyd George must make him profoundly uncomfortable'.[85] This interpretation of Cabinet politics bore no relation to the facts of the Navy debate. It did, however, correspond to the facts in the Army debate since in July 1908 Asquith had backed Haldane against Lloyd George and Churchill. Unfortunately, Haldane's account of the dispute over the Army Estimates, which reached Balfour via Esher, had the effect of confirming the Opposition leader's mistaken assessment of Asquith's stance in the Navy debate.[86]

Against this backdrop, during the autumn of 1908 the Opposition mounted a campaign intended to strengthen Asquith's hand in what they took to be the 'great row going on in the Cabinet about the Navy'.[87] Given their misunderstanding of the situation, this made political sense. In previous years the Opposition had kept a low profile in the months preceding the publication of the new Estimates; their greater visibility on the naval issue in late 1908 reflects a growing apprehension about the ability of the Cabinet moderates to defy Lloyd George and the 'economists' on the back benches. On public platforms Opposition spokesmen deliberately acknowledged Asquith's credentials as a 'strong Navy' man. They loudly proclaimed their confidence in his determination to resist the siren voices of economy and propose a large construction programme for the year ahead; the *Daily Telegraph* commented on the Opposition's readiness 'to credit the Government with good intentions towards the Navy'.[88] Remarks made by the Prime Minister at the Lord Mayor's Banquet on 9 November, and his apparent affirmation of the two-power standard in Parliament three days later, were seized on by Balfour and Cawdor as tokens of his resolve. 'We may rest content', the Unionist leader told a meeting in South Wales on 19 November, 'that the present Government do really intend to carry out what has been the traditional policy of successive Governments in regard to the maintenance of the Navy'.[89] The point of all this was to create a climate of public expectation about the new Estimates which would both fortify Asquith against capitulation to Radical pressures and make capitulation politically hazardous. It was an intelligent strategy but one which led the Unionists deeper than ever into the error of investing hope in the Prime Minister. Disillusionment, sudden and bitter, was at hand.

CHAPTER 8

The Greatest Army Bill for Centuries

Schopenhauer in the Kailyard

The most striking aspect of the new Secretary of State for War's early public pronouncements was their acceptance of what *The Morning Post* referred to as 'Mr Balfour's naval strategy', namely the doctrine of reliance on the Navy for home defence and dedication of the Army to imperial defence.[1] Sandars thought Haldane's first Commons speech on 8 March 'very Blue Watery'.[2] Balfour's contact with Haldane since the previous autumn had clearly left an imprint.[3] There were also signs that Haldane, like Balfour, was moving from this strategy to a policy of army reform involving the revitalization of the Militia. On 8 March he spoke of ending the 'disastrous' situation in which the Militia was 'bled white' to feed the Line, and confirmed that he envisaged the force acting in support of the Regular Army.[4] This news delighted Selborne, but alarmed Arnold-Forster who retorted that it was 'an absolute fallacy to suppose that you could make war with scratch armies'.[5]

The debate on the Army Estimates in March focused on the question of economy rather than on reform, with the Opposition warning Haldane to resist the pressure from within his party for immediate reductions in the Regular Army. Any such reduction must be part of 'a general scheme for an expansible army', argued Balfour on 15 March.[6] On the same day the Opposition showed Haldane that he could count on their support against the 'economists' on his own benches by voting with the government to defeat a backbench Liberal motion in favour of reducing the Army by 10,000 men. With Unionist votes the government majority was 240. In suitably military parlance Haldane reported to his mother that 'we beat the enemy heavily by showing a firm front. Arthur Balfour & the Tories helped me all they could.'[7] Haldane's resistance to Radical pressure produced a sense of confidence in him among senior Unionists. Even when, in June, rumours began to circulate about imminent cuts, causing an outcry in the Unionist press, the official Opposition – in the person of Lansdowne, leader in the House of Lords – refused publicly to anticipate the issue.[8] It was precisely because they had come to trust Haldane that the Unionist front bench suffered such sharp disillusionment when, on 12 July, he announced plans to abolish ten Regular battalions (or 20,000 men).[9] Just as the decision to abandon the Cawdor programme strained the hitherto cooperative relationship between the two front benches over naval affairs, so Haldane's statement soured his relations with the Unionists. Balfour and his colleagues condemned the Secretary of State for 'beginning at the wrong end', cutting the Regular Army before producing a scheme which would provide 'that expansible power' which was 'the real necessity' of the country.[10] Balfour complained to Esher that the cuts made Britain 'less than ever able to meet possible Indian demands'.[11] The Unionists were angry at having been lulled into a false sense of security, and frustrated at being powerless to block Haldane's plans; unlike increases in the Army, reductions did not require parliamentary consent.[12]

Since January Haldane had been hard at work with his expert advisers on the framework of an army reform scheme. The progress of his thinking was marked by a series of memoranda which served as the basis of discussions with the Army Council and with unofficial advisers such as Clarke and Esher of the CID. The first of Haldane's six memoranda, dated 1 January 1906, stressed the need for a 'highly-organized and well-equipped striking force which can be transported, with the least possible delay, to any part of the world where it is required'.[13] The absence of any such force had become clear to Haldane as a result of the stock-taking exercise on which he and his officials had been engaged since the change of ministry. His attention was to be riveted on this problem by a conversation with Sir Edward Grey at Berwick on 8 January, in the course of which the Foreign Secretary explained the tense state of Franco-German relations and enquired of Haldane how large a force Britain could mobilize if, in the event of hostilities breaking out over the Moroccan issue, the government decided to assist the French.[14] Seeking an answer, Haldane discovered that the existing arrangements for mobilization were 'critically defective' and that a lack of transport, artillery and medical supports meant that Britain could field no more than 80,000 men in no shorter a period than two months.[15] From this point on, spurred by the Moroccan crisis, Haldane attached the highest priority to the reorganization of the Regular Army at home into a striking force.[16] He resolved that this force should be composed of divisions rather than corps, the smaller unit allowing greater flexibility. This policy reflected a concern on the part of his advisers to create a force fit to meet a range of military contingencies, ranging from a European war to uprisings in Egypt or Somaliland.[17] The size of the force, six divisions and a cavalry brigade (some 154,000 men), was determined by the number of Regular troops left at home under the existing distribution of battalions. Since Arnold-Forster's planned reorganization had not come about, the Regular Army was still distributed on Cardwellian lines, although the needs of imperial defence had upset the principle of parity between overseas and home battalions so that, by 1906, 85 Regular battalions abroad were fed by 71 at home.[18] Haldane decided to retain the Cardwell system (and, indeed, to restore the intended parity), not only because he thought it an efficient method of draft-producing, but also because the battalions thus retained at home could be organized into the six divisions of the desired striking force.[19]

Like Haldane, and for the same reason – concern for a fragile European peace – Brodrick had regarded the creation of a striking force as vitally important, and had allocated to it three of his six corps. However, the 'imperialist' Arnold-Forster, whose tenure of office was largely undisturbed by European complications, attached low priority to maintaining a striking force, and altered the emphasis of British policy in favour of a form of organization directed to the peacetime requirements of imperial defence.[20] Of Brodrick's grand concept only a single corps, based at Aldershot, survived. In a note of December 1904 Balfour lent his authority and that of the CID to this change; 'The Committee of Defence, were, and, I believe, are of opinion that to keep on foot in time of peace an expeditionary force for no other purpose than to capture some outlying colony . . . is not worth the cost which it must necessarily entail.'[21] The Aldershot corps was now earmarked, not for a striking role, but as the second wave of reinforcement (70,000 men) which India had been promised in war. In the first Commons army debate after the election, George Wyndham confirmed that the Unionists still regarded the provision of a striking force as a task of secondary importance; the role of the Army at home, he said, was to serve as 'a proper nursery and school for our Indian and Colonial garrisons'.[22]

Haldane's announcement on 12 July that he intended to create a six-division expeditionary force thus represented a marked shift of emphasis in military policy. Balfour was quick to probe the rationale of the new policy.[23] While admitting that so large an expeditionary force might be needed to deal with 'some Continental situation, the defence of Belgium for instance', he rejected the idea that such a contingency should be allowed to determine army organization. Britain's paramount concern must be the security of the Empire, particularly India, and this should dictate military policy. Balfour defined the goal of policy as 'the power of sending continuous reinforcements to India in a great emergency'. The debates of summer 1906 thus revealed that, whatever its impact on the new Liberal Cabinet, the Moroccan crisis of 1905–6 had done nothing to break the Indian mould of Balfour's strategic and military thought. A continuing preoccupation with the North-West Frontier, rather than any new sense of 'continental commitment', characterized the Unionist leader's response to Haldane's expeditionary force, just as it had his response to the reduction of the Regular Army.

Balfour's attention to the nature and timing of a war in Afghanistan had persuaded him that the Militia was an invaluable means of expanding the Regular Army by units. Haldane's concern with maintaining an expeditionary force fit for immediate deployment in Europe led him to a different conclusion. He recognized that the rapid mobilization of the expeditionary force would depend upon the advance provision of various ancillary services – transport, ordnance, medical, and clerical. He also concluded, on the basis of extensive War Office investigations, that the expeditionary force could not be maintained in the field unless provision were made for a supply of drafts to make good its losses; the rate of 'wastage', as the War Office termed it, was estimated at an appalling 75 per cent during the first six months of any war, a figure based on assessments of earlier conflicts, notably the Russo-Japanese war of 1904–5.[24] Since reasons of economy ruled out the possibility of the mobilization and drafting needs of the expeditionary force being met by Regular troops, Haldane naturally turned to the Militia as a potential source of trained but non-Regular manpower. He envisaged using a portion of the force, some 31,000 men, to support the expeditionary force on mobilization, and planned to organize the remainder into battalions, one per pair of Regular battalions, whose function would be to supply the Line with drafts. To this end, militiamen would receive longer training. In his sixth memorandum Haldane asserted that it was 'of greater relative importance to make certain of maintaining in a state of the highest efficiency whatever force we place in the field than to be in a position to indefinitely expand that force with new units or new formations'.[25] So, although his concept of a 'third' or Militia battalion behind each pair of Regular battalions resembled Balfour's plan of 1905, it had a vital difference; whereas Balfour had seen his Militia battalions as fighting units, Haldane saw them primarily as reservoirs of men. As for the Volunteers and Yeomanry, Haldane proposed that they should form a new 'Territorial Force', complete with artillery and non-combatant services and administered by part-elective 'county associations'.[26] The main role of this force would be home defence, but it might also supply units for overseas service during the course of a protracted war.

Haldane sketched his plans for the Militia in outline in the Commons on 12 July. By this stage he had already tried twice, and failed twice, to secure the Militia's acquiescence in them. The first attempt occurred in the context of the consultative 'Territorial Army Committee' convened in May, the second in late June at two bilateral meetings between War Office officials and representatives of the Militia.[27] On both occasions it was proposed to the Militia colonels present, headed by Bedford and Raglan, that the force should accept a liability for overseas service and become a 'second line of the Regular Army'. An undertaking was offered that it would be employed, whenever possible, in complete units. On the other hand, the colonels were asked to agree that, whenever necessary, Militia battalions should supply drafts for the Line battalions with which they were linked. Led by Bedford, who had decided in advance to take an uncompromising line, the colonels rejected the proposition.[28] They argued that 'any attempt to use the Militia as drafts . . . rendered service in the Militia highly unpopular with officers and men, and that, if these conditions were enforced it would be impossible to enlist Militiamen for service overseas'.[29] After the War Office meetings, which he had chaired, Esher described the difference of view between the Army Council and the Militia colonels as fundamental; 'while the latter desire that the Militia Infantry should be used only in battalion units for the purpose of expansion in time of war, the former, while not altogether precluding the use of the Militia in battalion units, desire to have the power of using them as an Army reserve for the purpose of finding drafts . . . '[30]

Though urged by Major-General Douglas Haig, the Director of Military Training, to reject the Militia's demands, Haldane determined to pursue agreement further.[31] He was not yet prepared to settle for the alternative plan of forcing the Militia into the new Territorial Force. (Forcing was the operative word since the colonels had also vetoed this idea, fearing the loss of their autonomy to the local associations). However, the failure of another mediation attempt in September, this time under the auspices of Lord Derby, convinced Haldane that the requirements of the new expeditionary force were irreconcilable with the Militia's desire for independence of the Line. He decided to integrate those Militia cadres which were efficient into the units of the new Territorial Force, 'restoring' them to their county place and snapping their close links with the Line; in future the Militia would play a home defence role.[32] This policy would free the 'professional substance' of the Militia, those men and boys who joined it for a military experience closer to that of the Regular Army than the Volunteers could offer, for absorption into a second new military organization, the Special Reserve. As its name implied, the rationale of the Special Reserve would be the production of drafts. It would consist of 74 battalions organized exclusively for training, not fighting, purposes, and would thus provide a 'reservoir' of some 80,000 non-Regular troops for the Line. Its recruits would be liable for overseas service, and would be trained for six months on enlistment and for two weeks annually thereafter.

Balfour knew from September onwards that the Secretary of State's plans for the Militia were changing, but there is no evidence that he or his colleagues knew in detail of the evolution of the Special Reserve scheme.[33] Under no conspicuous backbench or press pressure to do otherwise, they merely waited upon events.[34] Indeed, during the autumn the army issue was pushed from the centre stage of the defence debate by the row over the Home Fleet, while defence issues in general were overshadowed by the controversy over the government's Education bill. During this hiatus in army affairs Haldane and Balfour happened to meet while guests of the King at Windsor. The only surviving account of their conversation is Haldane's, written in 1916; 'I told him [Balfour] my plans and difficulties, and asked him if he would help me, in return for which I should endeavour to make the measure a non-party one, to be carried by co-operation. He generously agreed, and allowed me to intimate to my colleagues that the bill might be taken under the innovation of a timetable . . .'[35] In his memoirs, published in 1929, Haldane added to his earlier account a remark of Balfour's; 'He [Balfour] said that as the Unionist Government had not succeeded in disposing of the Army problem it was only right that we should have our chance.'[36] In a subsequent chapter something will be said about Haldane's motive for stressing Balfour's non-partisan approach to the army reform bill. Here it is sufficient to point out that there is absolutely no justification for inferring that the outcome of the Windsor conversation was a pledge by Balfour to refrain from opposing Haldane's bill.[37] Haldane did not seek such a pledge; his concern was merely to secure the assent of the Leader of the Opposition to a timetable. The Cabinet had a long legislative agenda on which army reform occupied a lowly place, and Haldane knew that his indifferent colleagues could only be persuaded to grant precious time to an army bill if that bill promised to be economical and manageable in parliamentary terms.[38] If Haldane's object in approaching Balfour was a narrow one, Balfour's response was no less limited. Any chance he was prepared to give Haldane extended only to seeing the latter's scheme put before Parliament for decision; how the Opposition would treat the scheme was in no way prejudged.

On 9 January 1907, at Haldane's request, Esher sent Balfour a copy of the report of the CID subcommittee which had recently scrutinized Haldane's proposals; Esher's covering letter strongly suggests that Balfour had no prior knowledge.[39] Referring to the Special Reserve, Esher observed that 'this was the A.J.B. scheme of two years ago', but such a comparison was misleading. Given his consistently held views on the issue, Balfour could hardly be expected to welcome the sacrifice of the Militia for purposes of draft production. Because Unionist thinking revolved around the expansion of an imperial army, and not around a striking force fit for war in Europe, the issue of drafting in wartime had not been as salient in the army debates within the late government; both Arnold-Forster and his Militia opponents had favoured a system of large depots feeding the Regular Army abroad. It is hardly surprising, therefore, in view of the entirely different approach to imperial defence which it reflected, that the Special Reserve proposal was regarded by the Opposition as the pivot of Haldane's scheme and that it absorbed the lion's share of their energy and attention during the bill's parliamentary life; they also criticized aspects of the new Territorial Force, such as its conditions of service and the creation of non-Regular artillery, but throughout these themes were secondary and will be treated as such here. Although the fact has entirely escaped the notice of previous historians, the Unionists' preoccupation with the Militia issue was to be of great significance in determining the outcome of Haldane's attempt at reform.

Mr Balfour's Army

The substance of the Haldane scheme was debated with the 1907–8 Army Estimates on 25, 27 and 28 February: the bill was given a first reading on 4 March and a second reading on 9, 10 and 23 April. The long debate gave Haldane ample opportunity to confirm his reputation for making dull, prolix and interminably long speeches. Austen Chamberlain characterized Haldane's gestures as 'penguin-like . . . elbows pressed in and fat hands splayed out with upturned palms'.[40] The arrival of the Secretary of State for War at the dispatch box was apt to trigger a stampede to the tea-room on the part of those not trapped by frontbench obligations and produced an amusing instance of cross-bench collusion on 25 February when, shortly before Haldane rose, the Unionist Alfred Lyttelton passed a scribbled note across the table to the Liberal, Loulou Harcourt; 'Submitted that the House is too hot or is it my inflammation of blood at the prospect of 3 hours from Schopenhauer?'[41] The burden of listening to Haldane and of Opposition spokesmanship was shared by Balfour, Wyndham and (despite his frequent absences through ill health) Arnold-Forster. Arthur Lee and Walter Long also contributed significantly. From the first Balfour appears to have coordinated the frontbench performance, and as Hansard shows he put in long hours of attendance at the Commons.[42] Of his interest in the subject, and the importance he attached to it, there could be no doubt. Given the extensive personal overlap between the parliamentary Unionist party and the Auxiliary forces, the debates over Haldane's bill also aroused considerable backbench interest and provoked a great many backbench speeches. These speeches scattered their shot widely, a reflection on the myriad vested interests disturbed by any attempt to reform the Auxiliary forces. By contrast, speeches from the Unionist front bench were strikingly coherent and consistent. In part this was due to Balfour's close supervision, but it owed more to the consensus among senior Unionists which had emerged in 1904–5.

The Unionist case was that, as Wyndham put it, 'there are no powers of expansion in this scheme'. Haldane's proposals ignored the fact that the defence of a distant empire required 'a continuous succession of waves to support the Regular Army'. The Special Reserve could not play an expansionary role because its battalions were glorified depots, not organized fighting units. Moreover, if Special Reserve battalions were sent abroad, 'the whole machinery for supplying drafts' would be 'smashed and destroyed'. The Territorial Force was no less unsuitable for expanding the Regular Army in the early stages of a conflict; Haldane had admitted that it would require six months' training after embodiment in war to become militarily efficient. Underpinning these criticisms was the 'Indian' strategy of the late Unionist government. 'The great military problem' confronting any government, Balfour declared on 28 February, was the defence of India. As in 1904–5, here lay the reason for reforming rather than abolishing the Militia. The Militia had served three purposes, Wyndham suggested on 9 April; 'It has given a stream of recruits to the Line, it has given us battalions to take the place of regular battalions at Colonial stations, and thus liberated those regular battalions to take their place in the fighting line.'[43] This fighting line was not envisaged in Europe. 'If we had, through some unhappy fate, to defend the North-West Frontier of India', remarked Balfour on 23 April, 'your Militia battalions would take the place of Regular battalions in garrisons in the Mediterranean, some of them might even take the place of Regular troops in the heart of India itself'.[44] *The Times*, commenting on the parliamentary debate, approvingly identified the crux and force of the Unionist case against Haldane's bill as 'the strategical issue'. 'The real argument against the destruction of the Militia is to be sought . . . in practical considerations of Imperial strategy', ran a leader on 25 April. 'Is a system which gives us the largest possible Regular Force on mobilisation and nothing else except an untrained skeleton of a Territorial Army better than one which has a smaller Regular Force, but interposes a second partially trained force between it and the raw national levies?'[45]

Haldane was swift to point out that the Unionists' defence of the Militia was inconsistent with their policy in office. 'The plan which was the plan of the Opposition when they sat upon this side of the House was a plan more sweeping . . . than anything I put forward', he claimed.[46] After all, Arnold-Forster had intended to abolish the Militia cadres themselves; the present bill proposed merely to integrate them into the Territorial Force. Balfour's response to the charge of inconsistency was candid. He admitted to having always personally favoured a policy of regenerating the Militia, and informed the Commons that there had been in 1905 'an alternative plan affecting the Militia which was never brought before the House, but with which, as there was a record of it, [Haldane] must be fully acquainted'.[47] That alternative plan, vetoed by Arnold-Forster in 1905, was now official Unionist policy and serving as the measure of Haldane's scheme. Balfour's admission of the disunity over army reform within his own government, with its clear implication that Arnold-Forster's policy had since been abandoned, symbolized the eclipse of Haldane's predecessor. In a real sense, Balfour's authority in army matters had grown out of office. No longer heading a fragile ministry vulnerable to threats of resignation, he was able to liberate his party's policy from the grip of Arnold-Forster's hostility to non-Regular forces. As for the luckless former Secretary of State, he conspicuously refused to join his leader and Wyndham in pressing the claims of the Militia, instead devoting his energies to attacking the shortcomings of the Special Reserve.

The Unionists argued that the innovation of the Special Reserve was 'notoriously the more precipitate result of a hitch and failure to arrive at a satisfactory agreement between the Army Council and the Militia Colonels'.[48] Their information had obviously improved since the autumn of 1906, perhaps thanks to Esher. Balfour alleged that 'if the Militia had consented not merely to serve abroad in units but to supply drafts to the Regular Army', then Haldane would have been content to retain and reform the force as an integral part of Britain's military system.[49] The Opposition urged Haldane to retrace his steps to July 1906 and consider a fresh attempt at negotiation. Wyndham said that there was 'every reason to believe that the Militia . . . dislike the scheme in its present state more than in its original shape'.[50] It was Salisbury, as a Militia colonel himself, who lent this appeal credibility. In the House of Lords on 21 March he distanced himself from Bedford and the other Militia 'spokesmen' by accepting the principle of drafting, and in a letter to *The Times* on 27 May went further in showing Haldane that he should not assume that the views of Bedford and his associates were representative of the Militia as a whole. Salisbury claimed that the question of 'whether the Militia could usefully continue if it were to be eviscerated by providing drafts for the Regular Army' was one on which opinions differed; he would not, he observed, subscribe to Bedford's dogmatic view.[51]

The Unionists' insistence on the amenability of the Militia to Haldane's original proposal found support in the press. The military correspondent of *The Times*, Colonel Repington, had been a close confidant of the Secretary of State since 1906 and had supported his early plan to convert the Militia into an effective second-line army. Following the July meetings he had taken a tough line towards the recalcitrant Militia colonels. 'From the Duke of Bedford downwards they seem to care for nothing but the interests of their wretched battalions', he wrote: 'One cannot form an army out of people who want to decide what they are to do in war.'[52] Repington backed Haldane's decision to reject the colonels' demands, but he retained a 'sneaking fondness' for the abandoned idea of a drafting Militia.[53] His commitment to the Militia, like Balfour's, stemmed from a preoccupying interest in the defence of India. He had written in *The Times* as early as October 1905 in favour of a regenerated Militia as an integral part of a military system geared to Indian needs.[54] He felt that the creation of the Expeditionary Force had made the Militia more relevant to Britain's needs than ever before by absorbing those Regular forces hitherto earmarked for expanding and replenishing the Indian garrison in war. 'Who would undertake to march into Afghanistan in those circumstances?' Repington asked Raymond Marker, Kitchener's secretary.[55] The journalist did not share the Secretary of State for War's lack of concern about the military threat to India; 'Haldane's idea is that we can let Russia run loose, which, in my humble opinion, is a piece of lunacy.'[56] Haldane's fault, Repington observed, was that he knew 'nothing whatever of the army of India & almost as little of the Empire'.[57] When the debates in Parliament revealed the depth of hostility to Haldane's bill on the Unionist front bench, as well as among the backbench Militia partisans, Repington began to use the columns of *The Times* in an attempt to persuade Haldane to rethink.[58] He undoubtedly inspired the editorials (already mentioned) which applauded the Opposition's stress on the relevance of the Militia to the problem of imperial defence. He also joined the Unionists in focusing attention on the 1906 War Office meetings – to which he had been privy – and in a long article on 29 March severely criticized Bedford's attitude.[59] Here, and in a second piece a week later, Repington depicted Haldane's creation of the Special Reserve as 'simply a plain business expedient forced upon us by the restricted vision and respectable intractability of the Duke and his following'.[60]

Repington and Balfour were thus working in the same direction, attempting to undermine Bedford's position and build a new bridge between the War Office and the Militia. But Haldane was not for turning. Balfour erred in supposing, as he did, that Haldane would still prefer, if possible, to preserve the Militia in place of the Special Reserve. The Opposition were not 'forcing an open door', in Wyndham's phrase, but battering against a firmly closed one.[61] Haldane dismissed the claim that his policy towards the Militia was 'political' in origin, and justified it instead in terms of practicability. He was adamant that the Militia could not combine the provision of drafts with service as units and offered the views of the Militia colonels in his defence. He said that he shared their conviction that the imposition of a drafting responsibility would 'ruin' the force.[62] The Militia could not survive if given two functions as the Opposition were urging. The evidence suggests that this opinion was genuine and had hardened in Haldane's mind during the autumn of 1906.[63] By January 1907 the Secretary of State seemed to have 'burned his boats' with the Militia and 'made retreat impossible'.[64] His legislative proposals represented his belief that there was no alternative but to divert the manpower of the Militia into the Special Reserve and to territorialize its shorn cadres. On 8 April, the eve of the Second Reading debate, he issued an uncompromising memorandum which made it brutally plain that 'the laudable ambition of the Militia to take the field in its own units, each under its own officers' could only be satisified within the Territorial Force.[65]

On 20 March *The Times* reported that 'in consequence of urgent representations which [had] been made during the last few days by members specially interested in the welfare of the Auxiliary Forces', a frontbench Opposition amendment could be expected on the Second Reading.[66] Balfour was anxious that a flurry of backbench amendments should not distract attention from the issue upon which he and his colleagues had tried to focus the debate thus far, namely the new willingness of the Militia to compromise. Accordingly, a shadow Cabinet on 18 March decided to maintain the initiative and keep the pressure upon Haldane to reconsider his Militia proposals, by means of an official Opposition amendment.[67] In the Second Reading debate on 9 April, Wyndham moved that:

> this House, though anxious to increase the capacity for expansion of the forces of the Crown in time of war, regrets that the Government should make proposals which, while destroying the Militia, discouraging the Yeomanry, and imposing new and uncertain liabilities on the Volunteers, would not, in a period of national peril, provide an adequate force for home defence, or prompt support for the Regular Army in the field.[68]

The Second Reading debate saw a dogged restatement of the positions held so far by both sides. Haldane was manifestly unimpressed by the Unionists' 'turning' strategy and denied point blank that his policy was the outcome of a 'temporary quarrel'; he gave not the slimmest hint of concession. Backed by a huge Commons majority, why should he? The Opposition amendment was beaten resoundingly and the bill given a second reading by 388 votes to 109. The Secretary of State was jubilant; 'A great day & only 14 months since I came to this office'.[69]

But, Haldane was far from home and dry. His bill still had to survive in committee and then to face its stiffest test in that bastion of Militia influence, the House of Lords. In view of Haldane's inflexibility, Balfour thought him 'over sanguine about getting his bill'.[70] Bedford, Raglan, Hardinge and other Militia peers were known to be concerting plans for opposition. Whether or not they were successful in frustrating the bill would depend upon the attitude adopted by the Unionist leader in the Upper House, Lansdowne. If Lansdowne chose to back the Militia resistance, the bill would inevitably be 'killed', much as Birrell's Education bill had been some six months earlier.[71] Haldane took comfort from an interview which Repington had with Lansdowne on 19 April, in

'Mr Haldane's Army Bill Second Reading. Mr G. Wyndham Opens The Attack', sketch by Ralph Cleaver, 1907.

which the latter indicated that he had no intention of 'wrecking' the bill and was not in collusion with Bedford.[72] On the other hand, Lansdowne expressed a desire that the Militia should go over 'bag & baggage' to fill the place of the Special Reserve, and complained that 'too much' had been made of the drafting question. It is clear that Lansdowne was speaking personally: he and Balfour had not yet agreed the line which the Opposition would take when the bill reached the Upper House. Balfour was preoccupied with its remaining stages in the Commons. Relations between the Unionists and Haldane had taken a sharp turn for the worse early in May, following the Secretary of State's announcement that a closure rule would be imposed on the committee stage. Balfour, no doubt mindful of his helpful response to Haldane's Windsor overture, reacted angrily to the 'wholly absurd' provision of a single day for discussing the vital clause dealing with the future of the Militia.[73] The proceedings in committee began in an acrimonious and confrontational atmosphere on 28 May. The Unionists resumed their strategy of focusing attention and criticism on the Militia proposals; Haldane rebutted their arguments and hammered home the 'iron logic of facts' as he saw it.[74] A reference to the 'deep sense of responsibility' he felt for his decision signalled Haldane's resolve and determination to press ahead in the teeth of criticism. Further fruitless debate, leading to conflict in the Lords, seemed inevitable.

Within minutes of Haldane resuming his seat, however, this bleak outlook was transformed.

At various times in the debate Haldane had answered Unionist criticism that the plan provided no force capable, as the Militia had been, of doing garrison and relief duty early in war, by pointing to the retention for this purpose of twelve battalions of Irish Militia. The absence of a Volunteer force in Ireland meant the exclusion of that country from the new Territorial Force framework; to meet the needs of home defence in Ireland, therefore, Haldane had no option but to allow the survival of the Irish Militia.[75] Together with six Regular battalions not required for the expeditionary force, these twelve units would, Haldane argued, be adequate for that expansionary role on which the Unionists, with their imperial outlook, placed such stress. Now, on 28 May, replying to a question from F.E. Smith, Haldane tried to minimize the significance of this anomaly in the bill's treatment of the Militia by pointing out that the conditions of service of Irish militiamen were to be modified so as to bring them into line with those of the new Special Reservists; in other words, they too would be liable to serve overseas and as drafts. The only difference between Irish Militia and English Special Reserve battalions, other than their name, was that the former would be units organized to fight but subject to drafting, while the latter would be units organized exclusively for drafting.

Balfour had been aware of the Irish 'flaw' in Haldane's design for the Militia since at least the beginning of March, when his attention had been drawn to it by Clarke.[76] Whether or not he realized its full implications earlier, it was not until this moment, on 28 May, that he attempted to exploit the issue. The Unionist leader seized upon Haldane's admission that the Irish Militia battalions were to be subjected to 'the double strain of providing drafts and doing work on the lines of communication'. What, then, became of the Secretary of State's repeated insistence that just such a strain would destroy the English Militia? 'If that could be done in Ireland,' demanded Balfour, 'why on earth could it not be done in England?'[77] Haldane's Irish Militia policy, he said, 'supplied the severest condemnation' of his policy of 'destroying the Militia' in England.

This intervention by Balfour would prove to be the turning point of the debate. It discredited Haldane's claim that an inexorable *military* logic told against the retention of the English Militia under drafting conditions and seemed to justify Unionist suspicions that his 'logic' was, in fact, an effort to rationalize a decision forced upon him by a political failure – his inability to 'square' the Militia colonels. The role allotted to the Irish Militia under the bill was, of course, that offered to the colonels in July 1906. Since the debate began the Opposition had been trying to persuade Haldane to retrace his steps to that point. Now, having undermined Haldane's stated reason for not doing so, Balfour had further eased the way by suggesting that the Secretary of State should merely extend the Irish Militia 'formula' to the English Militia. This gave Haldane, if he chose to change course, a way of covering his tracks; he need not seem to be bowing to pressure or accepting some new modification of the bill, but could rather claim simply to be bringing two sections of the bill into line.

If the evidence gives no indication that Balfour's intervention was premeditated, it also suggests that Haldane had not anticipated the sudden highlighting of the awkward Irish Militia question. On 30 May, following lengthy consultations with his military secretary Colonel Gerald Ellison, Haig, Repington and Esher, he decided to explore the possibility of meeting the Opposition's wish that the Militia should replace the proposed Special Reserve. This was a major climb-down. We can be sure that Haldane was encouraged in it by Repington, perhaps also by Esher who will have sensed the way the political breeze was blowing. Haig, whose political instincts were stunted – his diary shows that he had entirely missed the implication of the exchanges of 28 May – may have continued to advise against concession but, if he did, was ignored.[78] Haldane's reaction to events was determined by the political reality that his bill could not hope to pass through an Upper House bristling with Militia partisans unless the Unionist leadership withheld opposition. It is surprising that he seems not to have faced up to this fact hitherto and had maintained a steady course of defiance. Lansdowne's moderate comments to Repington on 19 April may have contributed to this by suggesting that the Unionists would shrink from destroying the bill. One must conclude that Haldane's rapid shift of ground after 28 May was due to Balfour's conjuring of the Irish Militia formula. The opening up of a politically innocuous line of retreat transformed Haldane's attitude towards his opponents. He had thus far rejected the idea of concession and insisted on the integrity of his scheme as a whole. Now, however, concession and the integrity of the scheme were reconcilable. Moreover, conceding the Irish Militia formula carried the promise of Unionist cooperation in the House of Lords and a much enhanced prospect of getting the bill on to the statute book. This was what mattered most to Haldane, bent on winning an historic reputation as the greatest army reformer since Cardwell. The obvious victim of his volte-face was his 'conviction', so often expressed, that a drafting Militia was not militarily viable. Two interpretations are possible; either that the Secretary of State had simply sacrificed a genuinely held opinion to political realism, or that the Unionists had accurately portrayed him as an unwilling convert to the abolition of the Militia. Whatever the reason, Haldane's next step was to put to the test Unionist assertions that the Militia would now accept the role rejected in July 1906.

It was Salisbury who would play the pivotal role in the events that followed. As a leader of Militia opinion and Lansdowne's lieutenant, and in view of his public statements during the debate, he was the natural recipient of Haldane's first conciliatory overture. On 3 June Salisbury lunched with the Secretary of State; Esher, Repington and Haig were also present.[79] Haldane offered to meet the Opposition by retaining the English Militia but he stipulated conditions. The Special Reserve would now consist of sixty-six battalions of Militia whose primary purpose would be to furnish drafts to the Regular Army in wartime, but which would also be available for deployment as units. A further twelve battalions of Militia were to be kept primarily for use as units, but were also to be liable to furnish drafts when called upon. According to Haig, Salisbury 'spoke in a statesmanlike way regarding the scheme, and was quite ready to make sweeping changes in order to make the Militia efficient'.[80] He acknowledged at once that Haldane was making 'great concessions' and, while expressing regret at the suggested drafting distinction between the new Special Reserve Militia units, responded positively. He was not able, of course, to commit his colleagues in any way. But, in fact, Balfour was delighted by developments, describing the survival of the Militia as 'an enormous relief' to him, and he indicated that the bill so revised would receive his assent.[81] Lansdowne was similarly enthusiastic; 'to my mind it will be a great achievement if we can get Haldane to give us some such terms', he wrote.[82] The Unionists' surprise and pleasure is testimony to the complete absence of any indication thus far in the debate that Haldane would consider any concession, let alone one of such magnitude.

Through Salisbury, Haldane secured the Unionists' complicity in an elaborate piece of parliamentary stage-management. He had only agreed to amend the bill because the change in question was capable of being disguised and would involve him in no loss of face or political credit. Beyond that, his main concern was to pre-empt any feeling on his own back benches that he was giving way under Unionist pressure; such a reaction would tie his hands and scupper the emergent Militia compromise. On 10 June, the last day in committee, Balfour formally asked Haldane to extend to the English Militia the same duties as were prescribed for the Irish Militia; this would not, he suggested, 'violate the fundamental lines of the scheme'. Replying, Haldane formally agreed to give the idea his 'careful consideration'.[83] The tone of this exchange was in sharp contrast to earlier tense clashes and reflected prearrangement. 'Mr Balfour was very helpful', wrote Haldane the next day, '& all went smoothly'.[84] Repington later wrote of 'the anamorphosis of the Government plan so cleverly executed by designers of debate'.[85] Balfour told Clarke that he had deliberately minimized the 'magnitude' of the concession to avoid provoking the Radicals, although it was the Irish Militia formula which had made the sleight of hand possible.[86] As yet, of course, the Unionists had their concession on trust only. Haldane did not bite the bullet until 17 June, at the report stage, when he announced the changes put to Salisbury exactly two weeks earlier but since concealed by frontbench agreement.[87] Now all but 23 of the 124 battalions of Militia were to be retained; 66 serving as 'third' Special Reserve battalions, 27 serving as 'fourth' battalions. The third and fourth battalions would be differentiated according to role, the former being primarily but not exclusively draft producing, the latter being primarily but not exclusively a source of units for relief work; this was the condition set by Haldane in his talks with Salisbury. Balfour thanked the Secretary of State: 'the scheme as regards the Militia (now) fits in with our ideas', he said.[88]

It had always been clear that, whatever the feeling of the *franc-tireurs* on the Unionist back benches, the attitude of the front bench towards the bill would rest upon the fate of the Militia. The criticisms which Balfour and his colleagues levelled against the Territorial Force (which will be explored in Chapter 9) were serious, but never decisive. As early as 11 June Haldane was writing privately that the Opposition had been 'squared'.[89] On 19 June George Wyndham confirmed the fact publicly, by explaining that the Opposition would now abstain on the third reading.[90] Their refusal to be more positive reflected both scepticism about the Territorial Force and the fact that the bill did nothing to redress their grievance against Haldane's 'reckless' reduction of the Regular Army. On the other hand, by the spirit, if not the terms, of their negotiations with Haldane, Balfour and Lansdowne were morally committed to assisting the passage of the bill in the Lords. When the recently ennobled Brodrick, now Lord Midleton, suggested to Cawdor on 17 June that the House of Lords 'should by some motion call attention to the general effect of the proceedings of the last eighteen months on the Military Policy of the country', he was advised that any such suggestion must be submitted to Lansdowne, who would judge whether it could be allowed 'without destroying the Second Reading of the Bill'.[91] At the same time, however, the Unionists had no compunction about exploiting the uncertainties inherent in the situation in the Upper House to draw Haldane into further concessions.[92] They sought a percentage from their role as honest brokers between the Secretary of State and the Militia peers. What they most wanted was the abolition of the distinction between third and fourth Militia battalions. They also wanted clarification of the mode of drafting from Militia units, being concerned that militiamen should always go abroad under their own officers; in practice, this meant drafting by companies. Lansdowne and

Salisbury pressed these demands in the Lords on 26 June, reminding Haldane that his scheme could not succeed without goodwill; 'unless the men of the Militia back you up, you are defeated on the very threshold of your scheme'.[93] The purchase of their arguments upon the Secretary of State was due to the evidence, which the debate provided, of the undiminished hostility towards the bill of Bedford and his associates. They rejected what Raglan called Salisbury's 'rose-coloured view' of the revised Militia proposals. Ampthill referred dismissively to 'an impression abroad that something in the nature of a compromise had been arrived at in regard to the Militia', and went on to warn that he and a 'good many' others would have nothing to do with it.[94] The colonels doggedly restated their opposition to drafting and made clear their desire for the independence of the Militia from the Line. Their speeches reflected frustration at the way in which their position as 'spokesmen' of the Militia had been undermined by Salisbury. It is ironic that, ahead of the debate, Bedford had counted on Salisbury for support.[95] As Selborne later commented, events would have turned out very differently – and the Militia avoided coming close to extinction – if Haldane had approached Salisbury and himself in July 1906, rather than Bedford and Raglan.[96] Nevertheless, despite their loss of advantage, Bedford and the other militants could still ruin the bill in committee so Haldane had no option but to seek to isolate them further by consolidating his hold on moderate Militia opinion.

On 2 July Esher called on Salisbury at his home in Arlington Street and 'settled with him, in writing, the main military points upon which the Militia officers lay stress'.[97] To these points, in particular the removal of the drafting distinction between Militia battalions, Esher was himself sympathetic.[98] At numerous meetings over the next five days the details were hammered out, with Esher acting as honest broker.[99] Haldane, who had slipped off to Scotland for a few days, was called back to sanction these further concessions to the Opposition.[100] He met Salisbury on 5 July and three days later the Under-Secretary of State at the War Office, Lord Portsmouth, revealed the latest revisions to the bill in the House of Lords, so formalizing the frontbench agreement.[101] Haldane was delighted by the 'excellent co-operation' which he had received from 'the responsible leaders of the Opposition', and praised Salisbury's 'large-minded' approach.[102] During the next few weeks the Secretary of State was in frequent touch with both Balfour and Salisbury, as all three worked hard to frustrate various attempts by Bedford to sabotage the bill, notably an attempt on 18 July to impose a moratorium of two years on the implementation of the Militia reforms.[103] This *démarche* had to be foiled by an official Unionist amendment, moved by Brodrick with Haldane's assent, substituting a delay of only one year.[104] *The Times*

Portrait photograph of 4th
Marquess of Salisbury, c. 1908.

commented on the cooperative spirit in which the two front benches
now dealt with the Militia question, a spirit which extended to other
aspects of the bill; the government made concessions, for example, on
the terms and conditions of enlistment into the Territorial Force.[105]
Collusion between Haldane and Balfour also helped to avert a potentially
damaging backbench row over the responsibilities of the new county
associations. With Balfour giving 'friendly help', the amended bill
returned to the Commons and was passed in the early hours of 31 July. 'It
is a heavy piece of work accomplished,' exulted a weary Haldane, 'the
greatest Army Bill for centuries'.[106]

The Territorial and Reserve Forces Act was the first major piece of
legislation to be carried by Campbell-Bannerman's government.[107] This
account casts fresh light upon Haldane's achievement. Achievement it
was, since he had succeeded where his two predecessors had failed, in
passing a comprehensive reorganization of Britain's Regular and Auxiliary forces. However, it was simply untrue, as Haldane would subsequently claim, that the bill reached the statute book 'substantially
unaltered'.[108] 'There was of course fighting', he wrote in 1929, 'but it
[the bill] was touched in no point that was material'.[109] But Haldane's
own Under-Secretary, Lord Portsmouth, had long since given the game

away; 'when the Bill was originally drafted' he admitted in the Upper House on 9 July 1907, 'the place of the Militia in the Government's scheme was really a very different one from that which it now occupie[s]'.[110] The Militia concession transformed 'the dominant feature' of the original scheme, the Special Reserve.[111] In Esher's words, the substitution of Militia battalions gave the reform 'an entirely new shape'.[112] It may be that Haldane's ingenious efforts to prevent his own party appreciating the significance of his climb-down were all too successful in that, in time, he himself came to mistake a carefully contrived appearance for reality. On the other hand, as historians have shown in other contexts, Haldane's recollections of his pre-war career were heavily influenced by a desire to defend his reputation against unscrupulous detractors.[113] To have revealed the full story of events in 1907 would have been to diminish his own credit by conceding the extent to which his great reform reflected not his, but Balfour's, views.

For Haldane's gloss has distracted attention from the fact that of the two central features of the Act – the creation of the Special Reserve and establishment of a Territorial Force – the former was the product of a highly effective piece of opposition. Balfour and his colleagues succeeded in keeping the focus of the debate on what they deemed the crucial issue and defined the area of eventual compromise. They patiently rebuilt the links between Haldane and the Militia. J.A. Spender recalled Balfour bringing 'all his dialectical gifts to bear on the scheme to discover dilemmas and inconsistencies', but this gives only a partial picture.[114] The main feature of the Unionist performance was its constructive nature. This is not to imply that the Unionists conducted 'an obligingly restrained opposition'; on the contrary, they fought very hard and tenaciously.[115] But it is nevertheless true that their emphasis throughout was on advancing a practicable alternative and on exploring ways to a compromise solution. It was Haldane, not the Unionists, whose behaviour (at least until 28 May) best fits the picture of negative resistance.[116]

The Unionists' approach is easily explained. Whereas the creation of the expeditionary force in 1906 had marked a break with Unionist policy and strategy, the reform of the Auxiliary forces in 1907 accorded well with both.[117] The key theme of Unionist policy since 1900 had been the addition of powers of expansion to Britain's military system. Since 1904, under Balfour's aegis and in keeping with the Blue Water doctrine, that policy had come to revolve around the fashioning of a new relationship between the Militia and the Regular Army. By casting the Militia in the role of 'an expanding & also a replenishing force', Haldane's scheme, as amended by Unionist pressure, gave material shape to ideas to which Balfour had been committed since 1904–5; in a real sense, the Special Reserve can be seen as 'Mr Balfour's Army'. When the Unionist leader sent Repington a memorandum on his 1905 scheme the latter immediately recognized in it 'the genesis of the Haldane plan'.[118] It is ironic that Balfour had been able to accomplish in Opposition what had eluded him in office.

CHAPTER 9

The Politics of Naval Reform 1906–10

The Syndicate of Discontent

Events after 1906 conspired to show that the confidence of the Balfour government in the future of Fisher's naval reforms had been dangerously premature.[1] For two and a half years following the Liberals' landslide election victory, the position of the First Sea Lord was to be permanently insecure and the maintenance of his policy continuously in doubt. During those years the shipbuilding controversy between the parties came to fuel the controversy over naval modernization and the ranks of Fisher's critics grew. That the First Sea Lord survived was due, above all, to his success in retaining the confidence of the Liberal government of the day, but an important factor in that success was the continuing loyalty to him and his policy of Balfour and the Opposition front bench. Had his original collaborators chosen to repudiate him and his works, Fisher's prestige would have crumbled and with it his ability to convince the government to defy the discontented. As the key to Fisher's political position after 1906, the attitude of the Opposition leader was to be a vital element in the calculations of all those locked in the struggle over naval modernization. Fisher made a strenuous effort to keep Balfour and other senior Unionists loyal, an effort documented by the presence in their papers of numerous letters and memoranda in Fisher's flamboyant script. 'I am storing up ammunition for you to fire away in the House of Lords', wrote Fisher to Cawdor on 23 January 1906, 'should any of [the] fossils get some noble Lord to speak'.[2] At the same time, Balfour and his colleagues were the recipients of desperate overtures by those bent on Fisher's downfall. Balfour's handling of this tricky situation is the subject of this chapter.

During 1906 the brunt of the opposition to Fisher fell upon the Selborne scheme of officer training, which for the first time gave engineer and executive officers a common training to the rank of lieutenant. Critics argued that the scheme ignored the importance of specialization and would produce naval officers who were proverbial 'jacks of all trades'.[3] They insisted on its unpopularity in the Navy and argued that the disturbed state of opinion made an inquiry necessary. Critics of other Fisher policies, such as the *Dreadnought*, rallied behind the inquiry demand, hoping to intimidate the newly installed Liberal ministry into suspending the further development of Fisher's schemes while a reappraisal took place. The inquiry idea had an ulterior appeal; not only would it abort the First Sea Lord's policies, but it would also be a mark of his failure to win the confidence of the government and as such would compel his resignation. But the agitation for an inquiry was fended off by the new Parliamentary Secretary to the Admiralty, Edmund Robertson. 'A lawyer, short and stout, and irritable', Robertson made it clear that the Selborne scheme was to be given a fair trial.[4] The announcement in July that three new Dreadnoughts were to be built in 1906–7 was a further sign of continuity. From the Opposition front bench meanwhile, pressure for an interruption of the recent changes was fiercely resisted. Early in the new Parliament Arthur Lee had made it plain that he and his colleagues wanted to see the government 'continue and maintain the broad lines of naval policy which had been handed over to them by their predecessors': if this happened, Lee promised, the Government would receive from the Opposition 'every possible support and assistance'.[5] This desire for the continuation of Fisher's policy was reflected in the stout defence which Unionist spokesmen put up on behalf of both the Selborne scheme and the Dreadnought type when they came under parliamentary attack in 1906. On 1 March, in a speech warmly commended by Fisher, Arnold-Forster defended the Selborne scheme as 'one of the greatest reforms' ever carried out for the Navy.[6] On 24 May Arnold-Forster and Lee strongly rebutted criticism of the new 'interchangeability' between executive and engineer officers, and praised the abolition of the invidious 'class distinctions' which had hitherto existed between the two branches.[7] Lee expressed the satisfaction of the Opposition that 'the present Board of Admiralty saw no reason to disapprove of or depart from the policy of its predecessor in this matter'. A no less robust defence was put up for the *Dreadnought*; Cawdor praised it as 'the best fighting battleship in the world'.[8]

As a result of the Unionists' attitude, by the summer of 1906 a pattern of cross-bench agreement in naval affairs had emerged. For the Liberals, Haldane spoke of a 'harmonious' understanding: for the Unionists, Lee could claim in July to have given the government full support thus far. Over a broad range of policy both front benches regarded the Navy as a 'non-contentious and non-Party' subject.[9] The basis of the Unionist position was faith in Fisher and relief that his influence was prevailing upon Tweedmouth and his colleagues; in the Commons on 24 May 1906, Arthur Lee paid open tribute to the First Sea Lord's 'energy and genius'.[10] Fisher had kept in touch with his former collaborators since the change of ministry; on 23 January he wrote to Cawdor to assure him that 'Lord

Tweedmouth is exceedingly loyal to all your decisions and shows such nice spirit as to make me very happy'.[11] Subsequently the First Sea Lord kept Cawdor briefed on the agitation against the Selborne scheme.[12] From the summer of 1906, however, the support of the Unionist leadership for Fisher came under growing pressure within their own party and press. This was due less to his reforms than to the revelation on 27 July that he and the other Sea Lords had approved a cut-back in the Dreadnought construction programme.[13] Until the fall of Balfour's government in December 1905, the attack on the Admiralty had not run on party lines. However, once the First Sea Lord began to cooperate with the Liberal ministry to reduce the shipbuilding programme, Unionist opposition to him was given a party political twist. Fisher was denounced for abetting the 'Potsdam section of the Cabinet' in their pursuit of 'the dangerous phantom of disarmament'.[14] Further grist was provided for this mill in October 1906, when it was announced by the Admiralty that the existing naval Reserve was to be reorganized into a new, independent home-water fleet, to be known as the Home Fleet.[15] The fact that the Home Fleet was to be created from six battleships withdrawn from the three outlying, front-line fleets (the Channel, Atlantic and Mediterranean) and converted from a fully commissioned to a reserve basis gave rise to the charge that it was a barely disguised economy measure: there was general disbelief of Admiralty claims that the new arrangement was designed to improve war readiness.[16] 'We are demobilising our sea-going squadrons for the sake of Free Imports', railed Leo Maxse.[17] Arguing on these lines, London Unionists exploited the Home Fleet issue in the borough elections of October 1906.[18] It was also widely asserted that the pursuit of economy was being allowed by Fisher to damage the Navy in more insidious ways, in that repairs were being neglected, stores becoming depleted, and manpower shortages going unremedied.[19] Bitterness over Fisher's collusion with the Liberals led many Unionists to join the longer-running attack on his administrative reforms. The naval correspondent of *The Times*, James R. Thursfield, a staunch Fisherite, noted early in 1907 how the First Sea Lord's 'irreconcilable critics' had exploited the new situation after July 1906 'for the purpose of getting a new hearing for their old complaints'.[20] As a result, the idea of an inquiry into recent Admiralty administration, spearheaded by the *Spectator*, won many converts among Unionists seeking to punish Fisher. At the same time, the naval reform agitation itself became, as one observer later put it, 'a political campaign and attack on the Government, hitting through and at Sir John Fisher'.[21]

In January 1907 an embattled Fisher described himself to Esher as 'standing on the edge of a precipice to which all great reformers are led, and over which they ultimately fall'.[22] What made the situation critical for the First Sea Lord was the doubtful loyalty of his civil colleagues on the Board. Despite an assurance from Esher that Campbell-Bannerman, Grey, Haldane, Morley and John Burns were fully behind him, he detected 'an official wavering and faltering and lukewarmness' at the Admiralty itself.[23] George Lambert, the Civil Lord, was firmly against any inquiry, but Fisher was suspicious of both Tweedmouth and Robertson.[24] The First Sea Lord had only recently revealed that he was still unhappy about certain features of the Selborne scheme, which was, perhaps, Fisher's most controversial reform; this was worrying for Fisher, because a new parliamentary petition against the scheme was then being organised.[25] How would Tweedmouth respond to it? Robertson's unease about the state of naval opinion and his unhappiness at the extent of criticism of the Admiralty was by this time common talk at Westminster.[26] Fisher was afraid that he was 'coquetting with the "Enquiry" agitators' or at least encouraging them.[27] In fact the First Sea Lord was so alarmed by the situation that he instigated an 'ultimatum' from the Sea Lords to the politicians. At a Board meeting in late January Tweedmouth was left in no doubt that Fisher and his three naval colleagues would not tolerate concessions to the hostile agitation. 'I hope the Prime Minister understands', wrote Fisher to Tweedmouth on 22 February, 'that *any sort* of enquiry however *limited* into any phase of Admiralty policy means loss of confidence and involves our leaving'.[28] Although Fisher continued to believe that Robertson was 'not adverse' to an inquiry, this ultimatum effectively dissuaded the civil members of the Board from seriously entertaining the inquiry proposal.[29] Their nerve was further stiffened by the Cabinet. Ministers had been subjected to insistent lobbying by Fisher; 'there is not one single item of Admiralty policy that has failed,' he maintained, 'beginning with Osborne in December 1902 and ending with the Dreadnought in December 1906'.[30] Though well aware of the controversy surrounding Admiralty policy, Tweedmouth's colleagues were either too busy or disinclined to interfere; 'Of course, I know of the difference of opinion which exists', wrote Grey to a correspondent hostile to Fisher, 'but I cannot pronounce opinions myself upon what concerns another Department'.[31] Once the Sea Lord's ultimatum was made known to them however, ministers took a more positive line – *against* granting any inquiry; they could not contemplate the political uproar which would inevitably follow the resignation of the Board. After attending a Cabinet meeting early in March, Fisher was able to report to Julian Corbett that 'the even tenor of Admiralty policy is not to be interfered with'.[32] During the Commons debate on the 1907–8 Navy Estimates later that month government spokesmen ignored the inquiry issue, and on 17 April Robertson himself announced that:

after the very serious and important changes which had taken place, what the Navy wanted now was a period of rest and reflection during which the experiments [of 1904–5] might be left to work out their own development.[33]

Lambert, speaking eight days later, was even more robust; the policy of the Board, he said, remained 'continuity'.[34] For the moment at least, the door was closed to an inquiry and Fisher had survived an ominous crisis.

It is significant that at the height of his troubles, in late January, Fisher was very concerned to test Balfour's reaction to the inquiry row. He did not disguise Balfour's potential influence on the situation; 'with your kind favour', he wrote to the Unionist leader on 2 February, 'my motto is "J'y suis, J'y reste"'.[35] Balfour gave his favour, both privately and publicly. At lunch on 30 January he told the First Sea Lord that he would 'fight might and main against any sort of inquiry' and that he was resolved to prevent any interference with the 1904–5 reforms.[36] Balfour's attitude reflected his continuing belief in the value of what had been achieved at the Admiralty before the Unionist government fell. Cawdor shared this view, likening an inquiry to digging up plants to see how they were growing.[37] Arthur Lee expressed objection to the principle of outside interference in the work of the Board of Admiralty; 'who is there competent to enquire into them?', he asked.[38] Neither Lee, the main parliamentary spokesman, nor Balfour and Cawdor who between them decided the line of Unionist policy on the Navy, had been swayed by the wave of press criticism during 1906. Fisher was quick to convey their fidelity to the Cabinet, but five weeks later, in the House of Commons, Balfour went out of his way to proclaim his confidence in the First Sea Lord openly, describing Fisher as 'an Admiral of great genius and original powers, whose services to this country . . . had been very great indeed'.[39] This remark is interesting because it shows how clearly Balfour realized that the naval reform issue had to be argued in personal terms. The political significance of his words was not lost upon Fisher, who wrote appreciatively the following day.[40] Balfour's attitude strengthened the First Sea Lord's hand in pressing on the Liberals the case for continuity of policy. The stand taken by the Opposition leader against the anti-Fisher agitation within his own party helped the First Sea Lord to maintain that frontbench consensus in favour of the 1904–5 reforms which had been evident throughout 1906. On 17 April 1907 the survival of that consensus was manifested when Robertson and Lee combined to defeat a backbench motion condemning Admiralty policy.[41] To the dismay of Fisher's enemies, it was clear that the reforms of 1904–5 were not to be a subject of controversy between government and Opposition.[42]

The onset of party political tension over the shipbuilding issue had thus failed to drive a wedge between the Unionist leadership and the Admiralty. Balfour insisted on distinguishing between the two aspects of the Navy debate. He resisted the efforts of Fisher's Unionist critics to conflate the reform and shipbuilding issues. At no point did he allow his unease over the construction issue, or his suspicion of the economy aspects of the fleet redistribution, to obscure the extent of his common ground with the Admiralty on other matters of policy.[43] Contrary to the hopes of some Unionist militants, he was not drawn into seeing the inquiry proposal as a stick with which to beat the Admiralty for either its Dreadnought policy or the Home Fleet. As Sir Charles Dilke observed, to have flirted with the inquiry idea in such a way would have been to risk undermining the achievement of Selborne and Cawdor.[44] Yet Balfour's loyalty to the Fisher reforms entailed defiance of opinion in the Unionist press and on the back benches, opinion which was having its effect on those of Balfour's colleagues who were less directly involved in naval affairs. During the winter of 1906–7 senior Opposition figures were put under pressure by disgruntled officers and anti-Fisher journalists, as well as by MPs. Austen Chamberlain was warned by Leo Maxse that the Sea Lords were acquiescing in dangerous economies.[45] Such lobbying made Arnold-Forster uneasy about the political implications of the Opposition's 'alliance' with the Admiralty; he pointed out to Balfour the danger that the party leadership risked seeming indifferent to the prevailing atmosphere of public uncertainty about current Admiralty policy.[46] At the same time, the Admiralty was itself making it increasingly tricky for the Opposition's naval spokesmen to keep their distance from the militants. Although Fisher privately plied both Balfour and Cawdor with explanatory letters, prints and memoranda, all written in his inimitable style, the Admiralty took no *public* steps to refute the criticisms and allegations accumulating against it. Instead the Board reacted with a stubborn defensive silence. Balfour's first response to the agitation over the Home Fleet was to think of arranging for a debate on the subject in the House of Lords; 'I think Tweedmouth ought to be glad of some opportunity for expanding the Admiralty case', he observed.[47] Tweedmouth declined this offer. In the event no parliamentary debate on naval affairs took place between July 1906 and March 1907, during which time the 'Syndicate of Discontent' was able to damage confidence in the Admiralty both in the country and at Westminster.

Balfour thus found himself in a cleft stick of which the Admiralty was one stem and his own party the other. His reaction to this awkward predicament emerged during the Navy Estimates debate of March 1907 and had two distinguishable themes. First, he and Lee deliberately dissociated the front bench from the extra-parliamentary campaign against Fisher and the Admiralty, and adhered to the bipartisan line developed in 1906. Balfour pointed out that the official Opposition 'had done nothing to embarrass the Government or pour upon them undeserved or unnecessary criticism'.[48] His questioning of the Board's spokesmen, Robertson and Lambert, was studiously moderate and constructive in tone, as was Lee's, with frequent expressions of mutual interest.[49] The *Daily Telegraph* praised 'the patriotic action by the Opposition . . . in refusing to drag the matter into the party arena'[50] It was obvious throughout that Balfour had taken steps to ensure that the performance of the Opposition would be consistent with the cooperative spirit of the previous fifteen months. *The Times* noted that the debate was marked by 'little of the heated controversy which has lately agitated public opinion concerning "The State of the Navy"'.[51] However, the second theme of Balfour's speeches in March was an unambiguous display of anger at the Admiralty's stonewalling attitude to public criticism. He blamed official silence for what he described as 'the whole disquiet in the public mind'. Lee argued that the failure of the Admiralty to make out a reasoned defence had been an open invitation to extremists to attack it, and he reacted sharply when Robertson was evasive under questioning during a debate on 14 March.[52] These Unionist speeches constituted a stern warning to the Admiralty – and to Fisher – that such behaviour was jeopardizing the prospects for cooperation by creating common ground between the official Opposition and Unionist militants. As Balfour put it privately, if the government expected to be treated with confidence by the Opposition then that confidence must be reciprocated.[53]

Enter 'Charlie B.'

Having failed to win the support of either front bench, the agitation against the Fisher reforms had apparently reached an impasse in the spring of 1907: the First Sea Lord's position seemed as secure as ever. During the rest of the year however, the agitation regained momentum, so that the early weeks of 1908 confronted Fisher with a second crisis, his gravest challenge yet. This reversal of fortunes was brought about by the convergence of the long-standing inquiry demand with Admiral Lord Charles Beresford's campaign against the distribution of the fleets in home waters.[54]

'Charlie' Beresford was a brilliant officer, an erstwhile Member of Parliament, a society figure, and a favourite of the public.[55] In social background and bearing he typified the swaggering, aristocratic face of the later Victorian Navy and as such was the polar opposite of Fisher, the self-made bourgeois enemy of tradition. Yet, for all their differences of culture and personality, the two men had long been on amicable terms and Beresford sympathized with Fisher's reforming approach on a number of issues. What soured their relationship was Fisher's promotion to Admiral of the Fleet in 1905. Jacky's new lease of power at the Admiralty dashed Beresford's hopes of succeeding him as First Sea Lord. Frustrated ambition on Beresford's part, and resentful jealousy on Fisher's, proved combustible fuel. 'When two old gentlemen of their age and characters get to loggerheads', wrote Edmond Slade in July 1907, 'there is not much chance of keeping the peace'.[56] Although it is the clash of personalities which has often captured the attention of historians, the quarrel ought not to be dismissed as merely a colourful footnote to Edwardian naval history. Its true significance lies in the fact that it was a catalyst of that crisis of modernization into which Fisher had plunged the Navy in 1904–5. The *opèra bouffe* nature of Beresford's intrigues to topple Fisher after 1906 can too easily obscure the fact that upon their outcome came to depend the fate of an historic set of naval reforms.[57]

It was in the spring of 1907 that Beresford was first drawn into the struggle to topple Fisher. His motive differed from that of the First Sea Lord's veteran critics in that his grievance was not, at first anyway, the Fisher 'revolution' of 1904–5, but the creation of the Home Fleet in 1906. In August 1906 Beresford, then Commander-in-Chief of the Mediterranean Fleet, was designated to succeed Sir Arthur Wilson as Commander-in-Chief of the Channel Fleet, the Navy's premier command afloat. Beresford accepted his appointment on the understanding

Postcard photograph of Admiral Lord Charles Beresford, *c.* 1903.

that his would be the supreme command in home waters and his the responsibility for 'organising the Fleet for war and immediate action'.[58] However, between accepting the appointment and hoisting his flag aboard the *King Edward VII* in April 1907, Beresford was confronted with Fisher's creation of the Home Fleet, a new naval force in home waters.[59] Although he was designated to command both fleets in war and periodically to exercise them together in peace, Beresford objected to what was a significant diminution of his command. He was further angered by Fisher's simultaneous withdrawal of two battleships from the Channel Fleet. From the spring of 1907 until he retired from active service in 1909, Beresford fought to have his command restored to its original scope and importance. He argued that the division of the fleets in peacetime made it impossible for him to fulfil his task of protecting the British Isles from surprise attack. He also argued that the diminished Channel Fleet was badly lacking in the smaller craft, destroyers and torpedo boats especially, which were an essential element in North Sea operations.[60] Beresford bombarded the Admiralty with his complaints and Tweedmouth was forced into a fraught attempt at mediation between the aggrieved Admiral and an obdurate Fisher. As a serving officer Beresford was barred by King's Regulations from seeking public support for his case, so he resorted to proxies. Having sat as a Unionist MP on several occasions since the 1870s, and being a prominent figure in Tory 'society', he had many contacts among Unionist parliamentarians and journalists, to whom he fed damaging information about the condition and organization of the Channel and Home Fleets.[61]

Beresford's entry into the lists against Fisher was a godsend to the flagging agitation against the First Sea Lord's administration, and he won instant sympathy from those delighted by fresh proof of Fisher's 'crimes' against the Navy. It was H.A. Gwynne, editor of *The Standard*, who became Beresford's most important ally. Gwynne, who had turned against Fisher in the wake of the shipbuilding cut-back of 1906, realized that Beresford's call for an inquiry into the situation in home waters might be exploited to undermine that confidence in the First Sea Lord which was still so evident among senior politicians on both sides of the House of Commons.[62] Moreover, because Beresford's inquiry would be more limited in its objective than the inquiry demanded by the bulk of the opposition to Fisher – being focused on the condition of the home-water fleets rather than on the reforms of 1904–5 – and because, as a result, the consequences of granting such an inquiry need not be so drastic, it was possible that politicians impressed by the Admiral's authoritative revelations might at last agree to some outside scrutiny of Admiralty policy. Yet, as Gwynne well knew, the granting of even an apparently narrow inquiry would be a decisive blow against Fisher. What is more, any limitation of its brief would be illusory due to the interrelationship of all aspects of naval policy; an examination of the shortage of destroyers, for example, would immediately raise the question of whether Fisher had been justified in committing so large a proportion of Britain's shipbuilding resources to the construction of a Dreadnought fleet. For his part, Beresford readily lent his prestige to the wider attack on the 1904–5 reforms, asserting that 'nearly all Fisher's '04 schemes are absolutely altered now or are proved to be false'.[63]

It is interesting that it should have been Balfour to whom Gwynne first conveyed Beresford's allegations. Like Fisher, the editor regarded Balfour's attitude to the naval controversy as a buttress of the First Sea Lord's position: 'as long as A.B[alfour]. and his immediate lieutenants are still under the glamour of J.F[isher].', he wrote, 'it is hopeless to expect the initiation of a non-party agitation in the House'.[64] In advance of his meeting with the Unionist leader and Cawdor on 6 July Gwynne was not optimistic about its outcome, and his doubts proved well founded.[65] While expressing concern at the evidence of deficiencies in the Home and Channel Fleets which was put before them, the two men declined to be drawn into a wider discussion of the 1904–5 reforms. Their reaction to Gwynne's evidence was entirely consistent with their supportive attitude towards the Board of Admiralty. Cawdor chose to write to Tweedmouth, giving him notice of a series of parliamentary questions on points raised by Gwynne. 'There are so many rumours and statements about as to the fleet not being up to its prescribed strength', he explained, 'that I think it would do much good in the way of dispelling public anxiety if you could give the information for which I ask'.[66] Putting his questions in the House of Lords on 3 July, Cawdor stressed that his enquiries were not to be construed as hostile to the Admiralty or critical of the Board.[67] He limited his remarks to the specific administrative matters about which there was public doubt – the strength of the two fleets, their readiness for action, and their state of repair. There was no reference to larger aspects of naval policy, no hint of sympathy for an inquiry into the Fisher reforms. In reply Tweedmouth was both friendly and frank, giving a full and detailed account of the state of the fleets.[68]

Cawdor was significantly quick to welcome Tweedmouth's statement; it would 'create confidence', he suggested. What pleased him was that the First Lord's assurances would relieve the Unionist front bench of any need to patronize Gwynne and Beresford. Cawdor had been very wary of having dealings with Gwynne, a man known to be a prime agent in the campaign to overthrow Fisher and his policies. 'We cannot afford to be run by the Standard', he had warned Balfour.[69] Fisher, who seems to have got wind of Gwynne's mission to his Unionist patrons, did his best to alert them to its ulterior aim. 'What is called into question', the First Sea Lord told Balfour, 'is a steady pursuance of the great policy inaugurated under your rule . . . '[70] Beresford's various 'mischievous statements' about the fleets were merely a cover for an attempt to interrupt the continuity of Unionist naval policy.[71] Dismissive of Beresford though he was, Fisher nevertheless took the trouble to send Balfour a forceful Admiralty memorandum entitled 'War Arrangements', which explained the rationale behind the 1906 redistribution and disposed of the charge that the fleets were not organized for war.[72] Fisher's lobbying, Tweedmouth's parliamentary statement, and an Admiralty decision of 5 July to increase the number of smaller vessels attached to Beresford's fleet all relieved Unionist unease about the situation in home waters. They thus gave Balfour and Cawdor additional reason to maintain their distance from Gwynne and Beresford's other Unionist allies.[73] Gwynne did obtain a second interview with Balfour at the end of July, and the naval correspondent of *The Standard*, Leslie Cope-Cornford, kept in touch with Jack Sandars, but their further efforts brought the malcontents no more than a polite hearing at 4 Carlton Gardens.[74] Impressed by Fisher's memorandum, Cawdor declined to go on framing parliamentary questions.[75] Their rebuff was a bad blow to the anti-Fisher camp. Cope-Cornford's verdict was cynical; 'Balfour's administration was so deeply committed with J.F[isher]., that it is almost impossible for Balfour to escape *party* accusations if he moves'.[76] Beresford concurred; the Unionist leader was 'afraid of his skin', he alleged.[77] However, it was not partisan considerations which dictated Balfour's aloofness, but his belief that the 1904–5 reforms had proved their worth. He had no intention of affording patronage, wittingly or unwittingly, to those who wished to turn back the clock of naval reform.

During the summer of 1907 Beresford's friends in Parliament continued to harass Admiralty spokesmen on his behalf; Commons questions on the state of the fleets were an almost daily occurrence in July.[78] But these efforts proved fruitless. Not only did the government shrug off their allegations, but the Opposition front bench also remained unmoved. Because the Beresford lobby on the Unionist back benches was too small to extort Balfour's favour, a new deadlock appeared to have been reached. But it was short lived. In the autumn Beresford's fortunes improved sharply as a result of his adroit association with Lord Roberts' campaign to induce the government to order a reinvestigation by the Committee of Imperial Defence of that hardy perennial, the invasion issue.[79] The Admiral's claim that the fleets in home waters were weak and disorganized acquired new impact when juxtaposed with Roberts' detailed assertion that Germany was capable of mounting a successful surprise attack across the North Sea. By December he was obtaining a wider hearing than before with his contention that, given present naval dispositions, the Germans could land troops in the British Isles within 74 hours of a surprise declaration of war.[80] At this time Beresford began to lobby openly on his own behalf, careless of flouting King's Regulations.[81] Besides holding forth against Fisher and the Admiralty at dinner parties and soirées, he succeeded in obtaining interviews with several Cabinet ministers, including Sir Edward Grey.[82] To Grey, as to others, Beresford urged his case for an inquiry into the state of the Home and Channel Fleets. He was not struggling singlehandedly. Spenser Wilkinson told Grey on 14 January 1908 that 'the separation of the "Home Fleet" was a strategical blunder of the greatest moment' and had 'lost the present admiralty the confidence of strategists'.[83]

This new twist in Beresford's 'Absalomic campaign' brought obvious danger to Fisher.[84] Would the prevailing uncertainty about Britain's insular security, which had led the government to agree in November 1907 to a new investigation by the CID, also win Beresford his inquiry into naval distribution? The First Sea Lord remained adamant that any such inquiry would be 'captured' and exploited by those opposed to the reforms of 1904–5. What Beresford's backers wanted, Fisher knew, was a '"fishing inquiry", that is one in which facts discreditable to the Admiralty, or rather facts which could be represented as such, would emerge from obscurity'.[85] He was able to point to the fact that the strongly pro-Beresford Imperial Maritime League, a body formed by militants within the old Navy League, had as its avowed object 'to upset Sir John Fisher and the Naval Policy for which . . . he must bear the chief responsibility, both under Lord Selborne . . . and under Lord Tweedmouth'.[86] As Fisher saw it therefore, the survival of his finest achievements was at stake in the fight to steel the Cabinet against Beresford. His apprehensions were increased by the knowledge that his rival had also become a pawn in the struggle between the Admiralty and the Cabinet over the 1908–9 Navy Estimates. It was widely rumoured that Beresford was advertising himself as the champion-in-waiting of economy; from the first he had denounced Fisher for wasteful and extravagant administration.[87] This stance won Beresford the support of Haldane, who was quarrelling with Fisher over the conflicting financial demands of the War Office and Admiralty.[88] It also attracted the attention of the Radicals; in February Lloyd George tried to blackmail Fisher into submission over the Estimates by warning him that Beresford was willing to come in as First Sea Lord and to cooperate with the government in a policy of retrenchment.[89]

In self-defence Fisher pounded Lloyd George and other ministers with numerous papers, prints and memoranda.[90] His main advantage was the insubordinate nature of Beresford's activity. In a printed paper entitled 'The Proposed Inquiry into Admiralty policy', which he circulated widely in January and February 1908, Fisher hammered home the argument that for the Cabinet to recognize complaints levelled against the Board of Admiralty by a serving officer would be to raise 'grave questions of constitutional practice'.[91] As in his earlier crisis, Fisher issued threats. He left the Cabinet in no doubt that the granting of *any* inquiry – limited to the distribution of the fleets or otherwise – would cost them his resignation, and that of the other three Sea Lords too; Fisher was more confident of the support of his naval colleagues on the inquiry issue than on the shipbuilding issue and used the fact to telling effect. He also sought to defuse the threat of a *rapprochement* between Beresford and the influential Radical group in the Cabinet by pointing out that Beresford's credentials as an 'economist' were counterfeit:

> The naive thing is that the Government if it acceded to this enquiry . . . would be supporting Lord Charles Beresford's chief plank in his agitation which is the immediate additional expenditure of millions in small cruisers and destroyers which the Admiralty cannot admit as being necessary.[92]

For the Radicals to 'run' Beresford would be to vitiate their simultaneous efforts to break down Admiralty resistance to retrenchment. To confound Beresford still further, Fisher, as we have seen, gave his own promise that naval spending would be cut in the year ahead.

The First Sea Lord was most anxious to prevent the defection of his civil colleagues on the Board of Admiralty. Initially he mistrusted them, complaining to Cawdor that Tweedmouth and Robertson were 'in their normal wobbly state'.[93] But he was worrying unnecessarily. While Tweedmouth conceded that there was 'very strong feeling in many quarters against Fisher', he had confidence in the disposition of the fleets and opposed Beresford's call for an inquiry. On the broader question, the First Lord made no secret of his support for the policies inherited from Cawdor, and showed none of that hesitation about the Selborne scheme which had worried Fisher in late 1906.[94] Fisher continued to be alarmed by Robertson's tendency to equivocate under parliamentary criticism, but the Parliamentary Secretary also remained loyal, as did George Lambert.[95] This unity at the Admiralty had its effect on the Prime Minister. Commenting on the Admirals' feud in its early days, Campbell-Bannerman had moaned that 'the whole thing is honey-combed with personal jealousies and it is hard to have to build a policy on one or other of them'; but in Fisher's earlier crisis the Prime Minister had stood by him and he did so again now, deciding firmly against an inquiry.[96] Fisher's enemies were thus denied the prospect of getting a destructive grip on the reforms of 1904–5.

As he had in the previous spring, Fisher put as much effort into ensuring the loyalty of Balfour and Cawdor as he did into ensuring that of the Cabinet. It is clear that he regarded the two as directly connected and still believed that Balfour's attitude could materially influence events. The source of Balfour's influence on the Liberals lay in the uncontentious manner in which the question of naval reform had been handled by both front benches since 1906. The support of the Unionist leader for the Admiralty, given despite the resentment of many of his own followers, had greatly reinforced Fisher's case for continuity of policy, as well as bolstering confidence in Fisher personally. A declaration now by Balfour in favour of an inquiry might shake ministerial nerves. This danger was far from academic since Fisher knew that Balfour had been impressed by Lord Roberts' evidence on the invasion question.[97] It was possible that Balfour's assessment of Beresford's claims had been altered by the invasion debate in late 1907, and that he might now consider a limited naval inquiry to be justified.

In the event, Balfour's views had not changed. He believed that the Home and Channel Fleets were both strong enough and suitably deployed to prevent a German invasion fleet effecting a successful passage of the North Sea.[98] Yet Balfour's opposition to the inquiry did not rest solely on the lack of credibility of Beresford's claims. He and Cawdor agreed with Fisher that the concession of an inquiry into Admiralty policy at the instigation of a serving officer would be tantamount to 'parleying with mutiny'.[99] Moreover, they disapproved strongly of Beresford's conduct in agitating openly against the Board. Cawdor was most vehement on this point; 'Fisher is unwise in the way he sends about confidential documents', he wrote to Balfour on 5 January 1908, 'but nothing can justify C.B.'s disloyalty'.[100] When Beresford approached Cawdor for an interview, the former First Lord refused to see him. But the most significant aspect of the Unionists' reaction to the prospect of a naval inquiry was their awareness, shared with and sustained by Fisher, that the situation created by Beresford could have damaging implications for the policies that Fisher and the Unionist Board had implemented in 1904–5. 'We are living over an explosive mine', Balfour wrote to a colleague, 'and either Charlie Beresford or some other less important person may at any moment light the fuse'.[101] His fear was that Beresford would respond to the refusal of an inquiry by resigning. Given his considerable public and press following, such a step would be taken amidst a blaze of publicity.[102] The result would be 'a quite unnecessary scandal' which might bring Fisher down and would certainly damage the service because it would make an inquiry inevitable.[103] And an inquiry granted under such circumstances would allow expression to all the destructive forces built up in the Navy since 1904–5.

Fearing this development, Balfour was persuaded that Beresford must be handled with care. He agreed to see the Admiral in person, in order to attempt peaceful persuasion. He also tried to convince an unwilling Fisher that it was in his interest that his rival should be summoned to give evidence before the CID invasion subcommittee; not only might this draw Beresford's teeth, but it would also prevent him subsequently undermining the Committee's findings by claiming to have been 'gagged'.[104] Lastly, Balfour sought to prevent those of his colleagues with whom Beresford was in contact – particularly Sir Edward Carson, the former Attorney-General and now the Admiral's legal counsel – from doing anything that might encourage him to adopt an extreme course.[105] He was particularly anxious that nothing should be done to allow the Beresford issue to upset the consensus between the two front benches on the subject of Fisher's reforms; 'I think among us, by absolutely refusing to treat the matter on party lines, we ought to be able to prevent much damage being done', he wrote.[106] Accordingly, Balfour moved quickly to scotch an attempt by Ernest Pretyman, the former Unionist Civil Lord, to offer himself as mediator between Beresford and the Admiralty.[107] The Opposition leader's containment of Beresford made a vital contribution to Fisher's security because it deterred the renegade Admiral from resigning in protest at the Cabinet's refusal to act. Beresford now found his Unionist friends advising him to stay on at his command.[108] He was forced to conclude that resignation would 'unite both front benches' against him.

It was because Balfour and Cawdor wanted to avert an inquiry that they were irritated by Fisher's aggressive lobbying and 'newspaper "log-rolling"'.[109] His bellicose attitude towards any criticism was encouraging controversy and making matters worse for his friends and defenders. Even a sympathizer such as Austen Chamberlain was offended by Fisher's 'methods'.[110] There was a danger that the First Sea Lord's personality would jeopardize his policy. It was becoming ever more difficult to obtain an objective hearing for his reforms and once he left the Admiralty, as he eventually must, there might be a reactionary backlash against all measures associated with his name.[111] Balfour did not accept the view of Admiral Sir Charles Ottley, another Fisherite, that the First Sea Lord must be 'sacrificed' to save his great reforms.[112] On the contrary, he thought it important that Fisher should remain in office for a further two or three years: but he also thought that the First Sea Lord should do his best during that time to reduce the tension surrounding him.[113] Following a conversation with the Unionist leader in February, in the course of which Balfour made his disapproval plain, Fisher resolved to act more discreetly in future.[114]

Though Balfour disagreed with Fisher over the latter's provocative public profile, he was unstinting in his support for the First Sea Lord against his detractors, especially Beresford.[115] On 9 February the First Sea Lord told a correspondent that the Opposition leader was 'a cordial and good friend' who was 'going to fight tooth and nail against any inquiry into Admiralty policy'.[116] Two weeks later Balfour and Fisher met; from what Balfour said to him 'quite spontaneously and unnecessarily', Fisher concluded that 'he will see me through anything'.[117] Balfour intended these professions of faith to be a weapon in the First Sea Lord's political armoury, and the latter interpreted and used them as such. The eagerness with which he advertised the fact of Balfour's continuing support is a sign of the central place which he believed the Unionist leader to occupy in the naval reform controversy.[118] As the Cabinet weighed the cost of intervening in Admiralty affairs, it was important to Fisher that Balfour's influence be thrown into the scales.

There are two important points to be made about Balfour's willingness and ability to go on giving unequivocal signals of support for Fisher. The first is a point already made, that the controversy over the 1908–9 Navy Estimates had not affected relations between the two men.[119] Fisher actively encouraged Balfour and Cawdor to regard the inquiry and Dreadnought issues as linked. An inquiry, he suggested, 'would show the Navy to be so strong as to play into the hands of the very strong party in the House of Commons who want to reduce the Navy'.[120] Balfour's defence of Fisher's administration at the Admiralty thus merged with his containment of the growing Radical threat to the Navy in 1907–8; in both he continued to look upon Fisher as an ally.

The second point is that Balfour's action in what had become a highly controversial area of the Navy debate was not constrained by new pressures within his own party. Although Lansdowne treated Beresford with disdain – 'there never was a more cheaply acquired reputation than his' – during the autumn of 1907 a number of other senior and influential Unionists had been drawn into Beresford's camp, hitherto a largely backbench preserve.[121] These included Walter Long, Andrew Bonar Law and Lord Curzon, the former Viceroy of India who was now a presence on the Unionist benches in the Lords.[122] Personal acquaintance with Beresford and genuine concern about his allegations played a part in this drift of support to the inquiry campaign. As important perhaps, was a desire to keep in step with backbench opinion. Long and Law, with their extensive backbench contacts, were aware of the restiveness of party militants over Balfour's dogged protection of Fisher. Of course, this restiveness had been much increased by the First Sea Lord's apparent complicity in yet another set of low Estimates. With confidence returning to the Opposition benches in early 1908 thanks to a string of by-election successes, and with the government already looking jaded, there was strong feeling on the back benches and in the press in favour of a combative approach to Liberal policy. Balfour's growing commitment to the cause of Tariff Reform during 1907 was a reflex of this pressure.[123] But his insistence on a cooperative relationship with the Admiralty went against it. The resulting tension in the party explains the progress that Beresford's agitation made among Balfour's senior colleagues. Long complained of the Unionist spokesmen, Cawdor and Lee, 'always backing up and defending the Admiralty'.[124] The striking thing is that this dissatisfaction did not lead to a challenge to Balfour's policy. Due to Cawdor's presence in the Upper House, Balfour had dominated Opposition naval affairs in the Commons, deciding tactics and policy alike. Not one of his colleagues was prepared to question openly his conduct of policy or the sense of common interest with Fisher on which it was based. As a result backbench discontent lacked effective leadership.

On 13 January 1908 Balfour was warned by Sandars, who was following the naval controversy, that 'an explosion of some kind is almost certain to occur, but in which *particular* direction it will expend its force is not quite so clear'.[125] Within a fortnight however, Campbell-Bannerman had decided against an inquiry and it was clear that the explosion would not expend itself in the direction of the 1904–5 reforms. But Fisher's troubles were not yet over. Sandars' prediction proved correct because in March the 1908–9 Navy Estimates brought tension between the parties to a new height. Unionists condemned the government's failure to respond adequately to events in Germany, and, as in 1906–7, they trained their guns upon Fisher, the instrument of Liberal policy. 'Fisher is the villain of the piece', thundered Maxse, 'and until we have got rid of him we shall not get national security'.[126] But, if the new salience of the shipbuilding question swelled the ranks of Fisher's Unionist opponents, it also, paradoxically, worked to the advantage of the First Sea Lord by diverting attention from his reforms. As we saw in Chapter 7, from the spring of 1908 the central preoccupation of all those engaged in the party political debate over the Navy was the Anglo-German naval 'race'. The government's 'neglect' of national security distracted Fisher's Unionist critics from their earlier preoccupation with undermining the 1904–5 reforms. The inquiry agitation steadily ran out of steam. An appeal by the IML in October 1909 for 'a vigorous, impartial and independent enquiry into the whole administration of the Navy by Sir John Fisher' was a low rumble of thunder compared with the storms of 1907 and 1908.[127] There were sporadic challenges to the Dreadnought type (in 1909 and 1910) and to the Selborne scheme (in 1911), but these had no material effect.[128]

It is significant in this respect that when, in the wake of the abolition of his Channel command in the spring of 1909, Beresford at last succeeded in obtaining a governmental inquiry into his charges about the Home and Channel Fleets, it did not have the subversive effect which Fisher had always feared.[129] This was because Asquith, who was by then Prime Minister, insisted on defining the scope of the inquiry very narrowly. As *The Times* observed, the chosen procedure differed widely from 'that suggested by advocates of a general inquiry into the whole conduct of naval affairs by the Board of Admiralty'.[130] But what made it possible for Asquith to exclude the 1904–5 reforms from scrutiny was the fact that, by the summer of 1909, the weight of feeling against those reforms, and the degree of public interest in their fate, was much diminished since 1906 and 1907. By riding out opposition until 1909 Fisher was not only able to 'benefit' from the growing shipbuilding controversy, but also to gain a precious breathing space for the reforms themselves. By 1909, what had been revolutionary and experimental in 1904 and 1905 had proven itself and become routine. While Fisher had fought his desperate battles with the 'Syndicate of Discontent', his major policies had become 'too deeply rooted to be plucked up'.[131] When he retired to Kilverstone in Norfolk in January 1910 he left his achievements intact. 'If Beresford himself came into office tomorrow', Fisher was assured by a friend in August 1910, 'he could not undo your work'.[132]

That Fisher's vision of a Navy fit to win a 'Battle of Armageddon' in the North Sea prevailed against great opposition in the years 1904 to 1910 owed as much to the political skills and energy of the man himself as to the intrinsic merits of his policies. In the final analysis, his grip on office during the vital years 1906–8 depended on the Liberal government of the day. But Fisher always thought that the context in which ministers decided his future could be materially influenced by Balfour. In making the Unionist leader the target of their intrigues, Gwynne and Beresford revealed an identical perception. From 1904 onwards Fisher enjoyed Balfour's constant support; after 1906 there was not one parliamentary division on the subject of Admiralty administration.[133] Not even his growing anxiety over the government's shipbuilding policy, to which a future chapter will return, could undermine Balfour's commitment to working with the Liberal Board of Admiralty in defence of what he deemed to be 'a period of great naval reform'.

CHAPTER 10

'The Last Word of Voluntary Service' 1907–10

'Our County Council Territorial Army'

Between 1903 and 1907 the political debate over army reform had revolved around the Militia issue. From 1907 on, the spotlight would shift to what Arnold-Forster contemptuously referred to as 'our County Council Territorial Army'.[1]

As was shown in Chapter 8, the Unionists' attitude to the passage of Haldane's Territorial and Reserve Forces Bill was primarily determined by its Militia clauses. The creation of the Territorial Force caused them significantly less concern because they recognized that, of the attempts made since 1900 to reform the Volunteers and Yeomanry, Haldane's was the most imaginative and constructive. 'The general view is that as an organization the plan of Haldane's Bill is as good as it can be', wrote Sandars to Balfour on 2 April 1907; 'but many soldiers, while admitting this, declare that *he won't get the men*. I gather the best opinion leans this way.'[2] Scepticism about whether Haldane's organizational framework would be filled in by recruiting, rather than criticism of the principle behind it, was the main theme of Unionist frontbench speeches on the Territorial Force. Balfour and his colleagues repeatedly expressed the view that the conditions of service which Haldane was proposing for the Volunteers and Yeomanry – longer annual training for both, indefinite embodiment on mobilization for the Volunteers, and an altered system of allowances for the Yeomanry – were too harsh and would jeopardize the prospect of a sufficient number of men agreeing to re-enlist in the new force. The farmers, tradesmen and craftsmen who filled the ranks of both forces would resist such changes to a form of service whose very attraction was its compatibility with civilian life. 'Patriotism is all very well', observed Walter Long, 'but a man has to think of his wife and children and other dependants before he volunteers'.[3] (Long might have added employer to the list of interested parties.) Haldane was expecting too much and would either not get his men or get men of an inferior class. Similar arguments had also been used against Brodrick and Arnold-Forster when they, too, had sought to get more for the money that governments spent on the Auxiliary forces.

In the aftermath of the passage of the Act Campbell-Bannerman wrote to Haldane: 'It is a great triumph to have carried such a large body of opinion with you, and I hope you will have as much satisfaction while you proceed to carry out & superintend the working of the details of your magnum opus.'[4] The Secretary of State threw himself into an exhausting campaign of speeches and meetings to ensure the successful launch of both the Special Reserve and Territorial Force in the spring of 1908.[5] In May of that year Beatrice Webb reported him to be in very sanguine mood.[6] By June the Territorials were 183,000 strong, reflecting a steady flow of re-enlisting Yeomen and Volunteers. August found Haldane boasting that his 'new machine [was] working wonderfully smoothly'.[7] Because the preponderance of Unionists over Liberals was as marked in the new Territorial units and associations as it had been in the Auxiliary forces, Haldane was dependent for success on the cooperation of his nominal political opponents. He was fortunate in being able to count on the support of the Unionist party leadership. The favourable outcome of their opposition to Haldane's bill had imposed a moral commitment on Balfour and his colleagues. 'After securing a compromise in respect of the Militia', wrote Wyndham, 'we acquiesced as a party in Mr Haldane's scheme for the reorganization of our land forces and are bound to give it a fair trial'.[8] The active involvement of senior Opposition figures in the old Auxiliary forces made their assistance as valuable to Haldane in implementing his plans as it had been in the task of legislation. From August 1907 onwards those of Balfour's colleagues with connections to the Auxiliary forces worked for their smooth transition to the Special Reserve and Territorial Force. Salisbury had been contemplating scaling down his Militia commitment, but now 'consented to go on at any rate until the new régime has had a breathing space'.[9] He remained colonel of his own Bedfordshire regiment of Militia and presided over its transfer to the Special Reserve in 1908. In September 1909 he reported to Balfour that he was busy with manoeuvres and that conversation at Hatfield was 'entirely about flank movements and extended lines'.[10] Salisbury's usefulness to Haldane was due to his position as a major landowner and leader of the county community as well as to his Militia responsibilities. The local influence of senior Unionists was also mobilized on Haldane's behalf in Wiltshire, where Lansdowne and Long were instrumental in establishing the new County Association of the Territorial Force.[11] Another Unionist involved in the early stages of the Territorial Force was George Wyndham. Despite referring dismissively to the Special Reserve as 'a shelter, competing with the Salvation and Church Army for the manufacture of unemployed', he continued to serve with the Yeomanry in Cheshire – where he was known as 'The Colonel' – and in 1909–10 was a moving spirit behind a plan to set up a Territorial Force War

School.[12] Wyndham's involvement with the Yeomanry was one facet of his devotion to 'a contented and ordered ruralism' and reflected a belief in the duty of 'the gentry of England' to sustain the traditional fabric and cohesion of the county community.[13] In this way, Balfour's colleagues played an important and visible part in the consolidation of the Haldane reforms, even if it may be exaggerating to claim (as did one Unionist by-election candidate in 1909) that the early success of the Territorial Force was 'largely due to the co-operation of Unionists both in Parliament and the County Associations'.[14] Haldane certainly spoke with 'great gratitude' of Unionist support for both the Special Reserve and the Territorials; in June 1910 he offered Salisbury (who accepted) a military KCB in recognition of all that he had done for the Special Reserve since 1907.[15]

Unionist cooperation was important to Haldane in another sense too, in that it lent credence to his claims to have established the basis for continuity in military policy. From the beginning of his career as an army reformer, Haldane had openly declared his aim of achieving continuity in military policy as a means, above all, to economy. He told the House of Commons in March 1906 that he wished to 'lay a foundation which all may accept'.[16] After the gyrations in military policy from 1900 to 1905, this stress on the advantages of continuity made military and political, as well as economic, sense. It recurred in Haldane's speeches in 1907; 'the reorganisation of the Forces of the crown must be a matter not only of successive Parliaments, but of continuous policy', he argued on 19 June.[17] The Unionists reciprocated his sentiments, Long for instance referring to his colleagues' desire to see the army problem 'raised above the level of Party politics, and to seek . . . some working foundation on which might be placed eventually a really efficient and complete system of national defence'.[18] But while the two front benches remained at loggerheads over the Militia issue such statements had a decidedly hollow ring. However, it is clear that Balfour had hoped beforehand that Haldane's proposals would be such as to allow the Opposition 'to treat the question as a non-party one', and when the Secretary of State at last gave way over the Militia he expressed 'enormous relief' that the Unionists would not now be obliged to assume responsibility for yet another abortive attempt at army reform.[19] The Militia compromise translated Haldane's hopes of a bipartisan policy from the realms of platitude to those of reality; 'the Bill [might] now be a national & not a party one', he believed.[20] He sustained this theme during 1908 and 1909, the more convincingly because against the background of Unionist cooperation described above. At Lancaster in January 1909, for example, he reiterated his wish 'to see the principle of continuity largely characterizing foreign affairs extended to our military organization'.[21] However, if the attitude of Salisbury, Wyndham and Lansdowne offered

hope that Haldane's wish would be fulfilled, it was the attitude of the
Opposition leader which was all important. The War Minister made
assiduous efforts to identify Balfour with his policy and to build up his
sense of commitment to it. Despite the growing tensions between
government and Opposition in 1908 and 1909, over the Budget and
Constitution as well as the Navy, Haldane worked across party lines to
involve Balfour in War Office matters. He insisted on consulting him on
certain appointments (notably Kitchener's as Commander-in-Chief in
the Mediterranean in July 1909), sent him confidential papers on
military topics and extended frequent invitations to him to meet soldiers
and War Office officials. In the Navy debate, Balfour's chief source of
inside information about the substance and direction of government
defence policy was a permanent official, Fisher; in the army debate, it
was the Minister himself. Balfour proved responsive to this treatment
and was party to frequent discussions at 'Haldane's hospitable board'.[22]
Like that of his colleagues, his attitude towards the Territorial Force had
initially been cautious; he referred to it as a 'curious experiment' but
determined to give it every chance of success.[23] During 1908, as the
framework created in 1907 was filled in by recruiting, his feelings became
very much more positive. ' I am anxious, as you know, for the success of
Haldane's Territorial Army', he wrote in June.[24] This change is easily
explained. As the conversion of the Militia into the Special Reserve
realized his own policy ideas on imperial defence, so the creation of the
Territorial Force had realized his ideas on home defence by providing
that 'small Home Army thoroughly organised and trained' which was a
vital element of the Blue Water strategy but which, like a reformed
Militia, the Unionist government had failed to bring into being.[25]
Balfour thus had a vested interest in the outcome of the recruiting drive
for the Special Reserve and Territorial Force; if successful, it would bring
to fruition that rationalization of British defence policy which he had set
in train in 1902–3. The 'slow but steady progress' which expanded the
number of Territorials to some 268,000 by June 1909 thus served to
strengthen Balfour's commitment to it; he was 'strongly in favour of
backing up the Territorials', he told Esher in September 1909.[26]
Arnold-Forster's continuing protestations about Haldane's policy made
no headway with either Balfour or Lansdowne.[27]

Curiously for one whose career was to be so dominated by questions
of warfare, Balfour was entirely without the martial pretensions and
equestrian instincts of his class; he preferred golf and tennis on the
Riviera to muddy manoeuvres on Salisbury Plain. He recalled a brief
youthful involvement in the Lothian and Berwickshire Yeomanry as
'pure farce'.[28] His pacific inclinations and his lack of military experience
meant that the substantive help which he could provide Haldane differed
in kind from that offered by his martial colleagues. It was political rather

than military, a matter of supporting Haldane's efforts in speeches and correspondence rather than of engaging directly in recruitment or organization. On the other hand, it extended beyond the immediate issues raised by the Territorial Force. In the early summer of 1908 Haldane came under fierce attack in the Cabinet from the new Chancellor, Lloyd George, and Winston Churchill who, frustrated by the Admiralty's resistance to further naval economies, had determined to force cuts in military spending instead. 'Ll.G. has opened fire – wants to cut down the Army', Haldane wrote on 14 May: 'My reply has been a point blank refusal'.[29] The Radicals' challenge to Haldane, whom they dubbed the 'Minister of Slaughter', laid bare the fragile unity of the Liberal ministry in the wake of Campbell-Bannerman's departure. The still insecure Asquith was trapped uncomfortably between his old friend and ally, Haldane, and Lloyd George, whose hold over backbench Radical opinion gave him the strength to break up the government. Asquith's response was first to concede a Cabinet committee to investigate the scope for reductions, and then to defend Haldane against its findings.[30] The fact that Grey also backed the Secretary of State for War gave the struggle a familiar ring; the old feud between Liberal Imperialists and Radicals seemed to be breaking out again. This was certainly how Haldane interpreted the situation. Since the debate over the Navy Estimates in March he had been predicting a split in the party; 'the fissure is deeper than the mere matter of Army estimates', he wrote.[31] Haldane conveyed this view to Balfour, who responded at once to an analysis which matched and strengthened his own conviction that Liberal defence policy was the outcome of the government's internal tensions. The Unionist leader acted to help Haldane by ensuring that the Opposition in Parliament did nothing to embarrass him while he fought his Cabinet battles.[32] In particular, Balfour prevented an adjournment motion from the Unionist benches when in July Repington of *The Times* made public the facts of the Cabinet row, including the revelation that Churchill – 'playing his father's part again' – had been allowed a room at the War Office and access to its officials for the purposes of working up his case against the excessive size of the Expeditionary Force.[33] Balfour's sensitivity to Haldane's difficulties irritated Arnold-Forster, who had enjoyed no such sympathy from his leader, but its logic was understood by other frontbench colleagues.[34] Balfour gave Haldane further tactical support in the spring of 1909 when the 1909–10 Army Estimates came under attack from the Liberal backbenches.[35]

The support he received from Balfour and other Unionists was also of great importance to Haldane in his struggle to overcome the challenge of the National Service League. That struggle dominated the army debate after 1906 as much as German policy dominated the navy debate, and Haldane and the League were not alone in having a major stake in its outcome. In bringing Balfour's concept of imperial defence to fruition, the reforms of 1906–7 had identified the Unionist leadership with Haldane's policy and thus given them a vested interest in seeing the Secretary of State for War prevail over his opponents. The remainder of this chapter will examine the consequences of this situation for the Unionist party in the years 1908 to 1910.

Bolts From The Blue

During 1906, under Roberts' leadership, the League not only expanded its membership, but also refined its goals.[36] Whereas the Norfolk Commission of 1904 had advocated compulsion to meet the need for expansion, the NSL chose instead to base its case on the necessities of home defence.[37] Its stress on raising 'a National Militia for the defence of these islands' made excellent political sense.[38] As Arnold-Forster observed, the League's leaders knew that 'if they were to propose conscription for foreign service . . . they would utterly fail to move public opinion'.[39] The susceptibility of the British public to periodic invasion scares in the years after 1900, and the enormous popularity of alarmist novels such as William Le Queux's *The Invasion of 1910* (published in 1906), encouraged the NSL to regard the issue of home defence as the most promising terrain for a battle with the voluntary principle.[40] But it was not only such political or tactical considerations which influenced the League's choice of platform. Roberts was deeply antagonistic to the Blue Water doctrine and Balfour's celebrated statement of 11 May 1905 had been a significant factor in his estrangement from the Unionist government.[41] In Roberts' view, Blue Water thinking lulled the public into an entirely misplaced confidence in Britain's insular security. To rely on the Navy alone to safeguard the British Isles against invasion in the absence of the Regular Army was to court disaster. What guarantee was there that the fleet might not be drawn away in war, perhaps to cope with a threat to Egypt, leaving Britain in the feeble custody of the Auxiliary forces? The scenario darkened further if the possibility of the fleet falling victim to a 'Bolt from the Blue' was admitted. And if, to avert these dangers, the fleet were to remain in home waters, what protection could be offered Britain's imperial possessions, whose security rested on the flexibility of British sea power and the ability to reinforce rapidly and safely by sea? It is mildly ironic that Roberts, hero of 'Queen Victoria's Little Wars', should so challenge the Balfour government's preoccupation with the military defence of Empire and try to focus attention on the military defence of Britain. He rejected the Unionist thesis that compulsion was inappropriate to Britain's needs because those needs were, above all, imperial. 'Our scattered possessions', he argued, 'have necessitated our keeping an Army raised on Voluntary principles for service overseas, & this Army has been the cause of confounding in people's minds the *policing* of the Empire, which must of necessity be always undertaken by volunteers, & *national defence*, which is, or ought to be, the direct concern of every citizen'.[42]

Haldane's attempt to create a viable volunteer home army in accordance with the Blue Water theory was thus a direct challenge to the NSL. But from a different angle, the creation of the Territorial Force from the patchwork of the Auxiliary forces can be seen to have marked a great advance in their campaign. It certainly did not constitute 'a mortal blow' to it.[43] Writing to Kitchener on 4 October 1906, Esher predicted that Haldane's scheme would be 'the last chance which . . . will ever be given to the voluntary system'.[44] Haldane's vaunted methodical and clear-thinking approach, his insistence on avoiding hasty action and on broad consultation, all these aspects of his approach to the problem of army reform have impressed historians more than they did some contemporaries, including Balfour.[45] But their main effect was to give currency to the idea that his failure would be conclusive proof of the bankruptcy of the voluntary principle. This is why Milner, a Vice-President of the NSL and after Roberts its leading figure, could write that 'Haldane is ultimately going to prove our case.'[46] Haldane himself admitted to Repington in 1906 that, following the failures of Brodrick and Arnold-Forster, his attempt at reform must be regarded as 'the last word of voluntary service'; if he, too, failed, then the country must look elsewhere for a solution.[47] And it would seem that Campbell-Bannerman had a similar sense of the high stakes for which his Secretary of State for War was playing.[48] Whether or not such statements should be taken as a deliberate ploy to frighten fellow Liberals into backing Haldane, they played into the hands of the League by lending its arguments a greater relevance and political legitimacy.

Haldane's success in creating a new home army organization did not disappoint the NSL. Roberts described the Territorial Force as 'the greatest step forward in the direction of a national army which has ever been made officially'.[49] A new framework of military organization had come into being, enjoying a broad measure of political support. If Haldane could not fill that framework by voluntary recruitment, there could be no alternative to compulsion. In short, Haldane's very success had lit a fuse under the voluntary system. This explains the almost desperate way in which he flung himself into evangelizing the Territorial Force between 1907 and 1909. Opinions differed within the League as to the stance it should adopt while voluntarism was put to its 'final' test. On the one hand, Milner and Repington argued for standing back and giving Haldane a 'fair field'.[50] 'I do not want the League to be accused . . . of having contributed to the failure [of the T.F.] by damning the thing in advance', Milner told Roberts.[51] However, Roberts, encouraged by

Garvin of the *Observer*, believed in a more active policy; 'the right way with the public', Garvin advised, 'is to expose the futility of Haldane's scheme as it stands'.[52] This counsel resulted in a vigorous public and parliamentary campaign in the spring of 1908 against Haldane's plan to raise a volunteer Territorial artillery. But for much of 1907 and 1908 however, Roberts' energies were expended in a different direction – in challenging the validity of the Blue Water doctrine endorsed by the CID in 1905.

'The man who believes in invasion believes in conscription', wrote Arnold-Forster in 1909, exactly describing Roberts' position.[53] If it could be shown that large-scale invasion was a possibility, then the case for the Territorial Force would crumble. As even Haldane conceded, such a force was sufficient only for dealing with raids on the pattern envisaged by the CID in 1903.[54] Roberts' case was that the changed diplomatic configuration resulting from the *entente* of 1904, together with the growth of the German Navy, had raised the possibility of an attack on the British Isles across the North Sea rather than the Channel, an eventuality not considered by the CID. Working with Repington, Sir Samuel Scott and Lord Lovat, he assembled a large quantity of information on subjects such as German shipping capacity, dockyard facilities and railway tonnage, all of which was intended to prove the vulnerability of Britain's east coast to a surprise descent by a German invasion force.[55] Additional material on the naval situation was supplied by Beresford, who was in contact with Roberts through Repington; as suggested in the last chapter, the maverick Admiral saw Roberts as a useful ally in his campaign against the Home Fleet.[56] Although any decision in their favour would obviously be taken by the government, it is significant that Roberts and his associates first approached the Leader of the Opposition.[57] They recognized the oracular role that Balfour had won himself in the field of defence policy. If he could be persuaded to repudiate his 'heresies about invasion', public opinion would surely be impressed and the government left with no option but to re-examine the strategic first principles upon which the Haldane reforms were based.[58] To Repington's delight, Balfour not only agreed that events since 1905 justified a reconsideration of the CID's findings on the invasion issue, but also agreed to forward the views of the lobbyists to Clarke.[59] This intervention resulted in a fresh subcommittee of the CID being appointed in November 1907 to review the whole invasion question.

In the event, the 1907–8 invasion inquiry reaffirmed the conclusion arrived at by its predecessor in 1903, although Roberts did obtain an official acknowledgement that 'the new organisation of the army at home' must be sufficient to secure Britain against an invading force of up to 70,000 men, it being agreed that any larger force would be intercepted and destroyed by the Navy.[60] Having helped initiate the inquiry, Balfour also contributed to its findings. He was invited by Asquith to give evidence to the subcommittee, an instance of non-partisan cooperation which Esher described as 'quite unique in the history of political administration'.[61] On 29 May, in a presentation which (Esher reported) held an admiring audience enthralled, Balfour came down squarely against the contention that the Blue Water doctrine no longer held good. While acknowledging that Germany did have the capacity to mount an invasion, he dismissed the idea – central to Roberts' case – that surprise was possible, and contended that any attack would fail if Britain retained naval superiority in home waters and a home army sizeable enough to force an invader to send 100,000 or 150,00 troops. Balfour also stressed his belief, shared with Fisher, that the development of submarines and wireless telegraphy had greatly added to the advantages of maritime defence.[62] There is absolutely no evidence to indicate that Balfour's views, with which the subcommittee's verdict agreed, were based on anything but the merits of the case put before him; his masterly exposition before the committee revealed his fascination with the technological and strategic complexities of the subject. By no stretch of the imagination should the episode be interpreted as Balfour choosing 'to take advantage of the opportunity to provide opposition to the Government'; such an interpretation is based on a profound ignorance of both Balfour's approach to defence issues and the working of the CID.[63] It is nevertheless true that the committee's findings were politically advantageous to the Unionist leader. The relationship between the four elements of Unionist policy as it had developed between 1903 and 1907 – naval primacy, an 'imperial' Regular Army, a reformed Militia, and an organized Home Army – followed logically from the Blue Water doctrine. So, by restoring the credibility of the strategy that underpinned Unionist policy, the CID subcommittee of 1907–8 had, in effect, endorsed the policy itself. It is certainly the case that the outcome of the invasion inquiry influenced Balfour's conduct of the defence debate during 1908; it not only reinforced his concern for Britain's naval situation, but also encouraged him to support the Territorials.

It is interesting that those of Balfour's colleagues most closely identified with the Blue Water policy reacted similarly to the invasion inquiry. Salisbury, Selborne and Arnold-Forster all took the view that invasion was no more possible than in 1905; even if it was, insisted Arnold-Forster, the correct response would be to increase the Navy, not the Army.[64] On the other hand, Midleton, detached from the policy consensus which had emerged from the ashes of his administration, took a different view. It will be recalled that the invasion issue had bulked large in his thinking as War Minister.[65] He now warned Balfour that the party might suffer political damage if his Blue Water statement of May 1905 was discredited, and that Balfour himself would be open to accusations that he had misled the country.[66] But this argument – easily met by the point that it had always been intended that the conclusions of the CID should be subject to constant review and periodic revision – may have masked Midleton's true interest in the invasion inquiry.[67] If the Blue Water consensus was to be undermined as a result of Roberts' initiative, Unionist policy would have to be reshaped and the way would then be clear for Midleton to recover the influence he had lost in defence matters in office. At this stage, however, handicapped by his lack of a political following, and having only recently returned to Parliament, Midleton did not have the political authority to impress his views on either Balfour or other colleagues.[68]

If their invasion agitation proved a blind alley for the NSL, there was precious little joy to be had elsewhere. Continued efforts to familiarize leading Unionists with the case against the Territorial Force evoked a range of responses. At one end of the range were Balfour and Salisbury, who showed no sign of wavering from the policy settled in 1907. Salisbury not only maintained that 'a large conscript Army is not required for home defence and cannot be used for foreign service', but also rejected compulsion on more general grounds.[69] He associated it (like Tariff Reform) with 'Milnerism . . . a complete change in our method of Government from the English system to the German system: from freedom to compulsion'.[70] Britain would not tolerate the 'drill sergeants' methods' acceptable in Germany, a country unused to 'real' freedom whose citizens had 'grown up in the barrack square'. Salisbury's criticism reflects his insulation from the currents of Social Darwinism and ideas of national efficiency which swept along many on the Right before 1914. They also recall Balfour's remark to Roberts in 1905 that compulsion could not be introduced into Britain without a social 'revolution'. For both men, their support of Haldane's army reforms had a significance broader than the purely military issues involved.

At the other end of the range of Unionist responses to the NSL were Midleton, Curzon and Wyndham, all markedly sympathetic. Midleton was convinced that the Territorial Force had 'utterly failed' as early as July 1908 when he sent Selborne a scathing account of some Territorial units he had seen on a recent visit to Leeds. They were, he wrote, 'the smallest, squinniest, whitest and most decrepit looking fellows': 'where there was a policeman beside them, he looked as if he could have tackled three of them easily'.[71] Midleton's deliberate distancing of himself from official Opposition policy supports the theory that he anticipated that the centre of gravity in the defence debate would soon shift towards compulsion. Having stated publicly, when Secretary of State for War, that his loyalty to the voluntary system was contingent upon its ability to provide for Britain's military needs, he was well placed to exploit evidence to the contrary.[72] On the other hand, Midleton was constrained by frontbench responsibilities from speaking out freely in Parliament.[73] Curzon, a Vice-President of the League since 1906, was equally convinced that Haldane was 'trembling on the brink of a tremendous failure' and that compulsion would follow.[74] Unfortunately for the League, at this time the former Viceroy was no more influential within the Unionist party than Midleton and thus no more able to challenge Balfour's policy. Worse, their bitter public quarrel over Indian army reform in 1905, which had resulted in Curzon's resignation as Viceroy, had badly soured relations between Curzon and Midleton, and now stood in the way of their combining forces on the League's behalf.[75] 'They still do not speak to each other', wrote the Unionist peer Lord Newton, one of the League's founders, 'and I am occasionally called in as a kind of interpreter or shock absorber'.[76] Nor was there any bond between either of the warring peers and Wyndham who, despite his active engagement in the Yeomanry, consistently offered a sympathetic hearing to Roberts and other League members. He also attended League meetings, including its Annual General Meeting in June 1909.[77] Wyndham's sympathy for the cause stemmed less from the detailed military considerations put forward (which he rarely addressed), than from the Social Darwinist outlook which he shared with others on the Right and which led him to see the value of compulsory training in national efficiency terms.[78] Although Newton described him as 'a very valuable convert', Wyndham's value to the League was always limited; not only by his rather isolated position within the party – his reputation had not recovered from the Macdonnell débacle of 1905 – but also by his shadow Cabinet involvement, his parliamentary responsibilities as a party spokesman on army affairs (increasingly important after Arnold-Forster's death in March 1909) and his loyalty to Balfour's decisions as leader.[79] In fact, the relationship between Wyndham and the NSL is an excellent lesson in why historians of Edwardian Unionism should be very wary of equating the involvement of frontbench figures in pressure groups, or their expressions of support for radical causes, with the existence of acute vertical tensions within the party. It is easy to present Wyndham as an exemplar of the Radical Right; one needs only to emphasize his affinities with militant or 'forward' elements in the party and press. In fact, however, Wyndham is more usefully seen as a 'Mandarin', subject to a range of political disciplines that separated him from backbench activists with whom he shared views. Thus his interest in compulsory military service did not interfere with Wyndham's loyal support of Balfour's policy.

Between the opponents and supporters of compulsory service, an assortment of views can be identified at the upper levels of the Unionist party during 1908 and 1909. Arthur Lee found common ground with the League on the question of Haldane's Territorial artillery, which he

'Dover and War', cartoon of George
Wyndham MP by 'Spy', *Vanity Fair*, 20
September 1900.

regarded as 'tom foolery in peacetime and sheer murder in war', but was
too junior and too ambitious to risk stepping out of line with Balfour's
policy.[80] Arnold-Forster continued to breathe fire and brimstone towards
the Special Reserve, but was as violently opposed to compulsion.[81]
Austen Chamberlain, a considerably more powerful political figure than
either Curzon or Midleton, made sympathetic noises to League lobbyists
such as Leo Maxse who canvassed him for support, but he did nothing
concrete for them.[82] Though unhappy about aspects of the Haldane
scheme, privately he remained unconvinced that compulsory service was
either 'financially practicable' or, given the limited resources available
for defence, 'the best way of spending our money'; as a former Civil Lord
of the Admiralty, whose correspondence reveals him to have shown a
greater interest in naval than military questions, Chamberlain was
naturally reluctant to see further pressure on the Navy's budget. He
therefore commiserated with Maxse about the party's lack of any 'very
definite counter policy' to that of the government, but explained that
personally he had 'too much on hand with Tariff Reform' to take up what
was another 'big question'.[83] A similar excuse was offered by Andrew
Bonar Law, a prominent Tariff Reformer and a rising star within the
Unionist party. 'I am certainly not opposed to [compulsory service]', he
wrote to Fabian Ware, the editor of the *Morning Post*, in September

1908, 'but it is a very big thing in itself, and we have enough to do, in my opinion, with the change in our Fiscal System without attempting to identify the party with this proposal also'.[84] Like Chamberlain, Law thus kept his distance from backbench activists on the army issue by emphasizing his common cause with them on the fiscal question.

Among those frontbench Unionists who, unlike those mentioned, had neither relevant ministerial experience or associates in the National Service League, the prevalent attitude towards the army controversy seems to have been one of detachment, even indifference. The most powerful disincentive to action in what was notoriously an uncongenial area of policy – even for those with some knowledge of its intricacies – was the close grip that Balfour maintained on the subject. Like naval policy, army policy was one of the few subjects which came firmly within the direct and self-determined jurisdiction of the party leader. That jurisdiction was actually greater in army affairs because of Arnold-Forster's eclipse since 1905; the party's policy in Opposition was identified with Balfour, and not with the former minister. A contrast with naval affairs is tempting, where Cawdor retained influence and responsibility greater than that of Arnold-Forster; but the contrast is more apparent than real, since, as we have seen, Balfour's effective control of naval policy was not thereby weakened.

For a variety of reasons, therefore, the NSL received insignificant support from the Unionist front bench in either house of Parliament before the spring of 1909. Repington hazarded his own cynical explanation: 'the Tory leaders fear compulsion', he observed to Maxse in May 1909, 'because they fear to arm the people & prefer the better class T.F. . . . a conservative force [which] will not paint the towns red if there are riots or troubles'.[85] Dark fears or not – and there is not a scrap of evidence to bear out Repington's allegation – what dissatisfaction there was with Haldane's policy did not translate itself into enthusiasm for what the League and the Secretary of State regarded as the only alternative. To the League's annoyance, Balfour declined 'to touch compulsory service in any shape or form with a bargepole' and not one of his colleagues chose to dissent from this.[86] Nor was there any detectable opposition to his cooperative attitude towards Haldane's administration. A vital factor here was undoubtedly the continued growth and consolidation of the Territorial Force which continued to engage the interest and efforts of 'Tory peers and squires . . . working on the associations'.[87] Speaking on the Army Estimates in March 1909, Haldane described it as the strongest bulwark ever forged between the country and compulsion.[88] By July the force totalled 268,000 men, just 47,000 below establishment. Recruitment was much helped by the naval crisis and the renewed invasion 'bogey'.[89] Performances of Du Maurier's invasion melodrama *An Englishman's Home* prompted a stream of recruits to the London Territorials, welcomed to arms by a recruiting sergeant posted in the theatre foyer.[90] The healthy existence and 'immense potentialities' of the force were the most effective advertisement for Balfour's policy and a formidable obstacle to the NSL's efforts to sow doubts in Unionist minds about the security of the nation's defences.[91] 'It is most unfortunate', wrote Roberts grumpily, 'that not a single man on the Front Opposition Bench seems to care one straw about Home Defence.'[92]

Lord Lansdowne's Graceful Trimming

Attributing his lack of progress to Unionist indifference spared Roberts the pain of recognizing the strength of the interlocking strategic, military, financial and political arguments which bound the Opposition to the military status quo. The only consolation available to the League was its growing and increasingly vocal band of supporters on the Unionist back benches in the House of Lords. This marked a real advance on the position in 1907, when, during the debate on Haldane's reforms, the commitment of most Unionist peers to the voluntary system had been manifested in their defence of the Auxiliary forces. Since 1907, partly as a result of Roberts' tireless propaganda effort, partly (perhaps) because the advent of the Territorial Force had diluted old loyalties to the Auxiliary forces, the League had won over a significant number of Opposition peers. Being unelected, peers were undoubtedly less sensitive to the electoral implications of compulsory service than both their Commons counterparts and frontbenchers in either house. The presence in the Upper House of both Roberts and Milner ensured active leadership, and in debates and resolutions through 1908 the compulsionist lobby scored a series of propaganda blows against Haldane. But each of these blows was also a challenge to the Opposition leadership, and to Lansdowne in particular, who was compelled to preserve his detachment from dissident backbench opinion by means of what Milner called 'graceful trimming'.[93] As the League's grip on the Unionist peers became stronger, Roberts tended increasingly to focus his strategy on the possibility of gaining support from Balfour and the party leadership. Growing Unionist support undermined the League's declared policy of non-partisanship, a policy which had been adhered to throughout 1906 and 1907.[94] Though Lord Newton argued that the organization's strength lay in its avoidance of a direct appeal to either party, and that to enter into party allegiance would kill all hopes of legislative success, such arguments could not counterweigh the strong gravitational pull towards the Unionist party which marked the League's development in 1908. The growing number of Unionist adherents to the League in the constituencies, coupled with the solidity of Liberal support for the

Territorial Force and the continued scarcity of Liberals in the ranks of the League, served to create an obvious association in the public mind between the League and the party. This trend was reinforced by both the general heightening of party tensions after Asquith's accession to the premiership, and a deepening dismay at the drift of government naval policy. By early 1909, such factors seem to have convinced Roberts that the Liberal party could be written off and the polarization of party attitudes over the naval question in March was the final straw. To believe, in these circumstances, that compulsory service could come by bipartisan agreement was fanciful. The League's tradition of bipartisanship had become obsolete and a handicap. 'I hoped . . . to have got [compulsory service] accepted by the nation as a non-political and non-party measure', Roberts confided to Strachey in May 1909, 'but the recent disclosures about the Navy satisfied me that this was no longer possible'.[95] Strachey concurred: 'if we do not do something before the next general election to commit the Unionist party to national service, we might as well just throw up the sponge in regard to that policy'.[96]

During 1909 the growing likelihood of an election and the possibility of a change of government brought with them the prospect of Haldane's much-vaunted 'continuity' being put to the test. Although he had written confidently to Kitchener on 8 July that the Opposition leader was 'anxious to lay the foundations of continuity in military policy', the Secretary of State was clearly relieved by Balfour's comments at a dinner party the following week: 'Last night was very useful and the young Generals were made very happy by what you said', he wrote appreciatively.[97] Esher's forecast that Balfour would appoint Salisbury to the War Office in the next Unionist government offered further cause for confidence.[98] Yet at the beginning of November Haldane seems to have suffered a further bout of nerves and took the opportunity of a walk along the Embankment with Balfour to obtain 'a very satisfactory assurance of carrying on my Army policy in case he came in'.[99] Balfour's readiness to give such forthright assurances confirms the impact of the naval crisis on his thinking. More fundamentally, it confirms the point that current Liberal policy had been prefigured in his own scheme of army reform of 1905. His 'public & generous endorsement' of Haldane's reforms in the Commons in March, and his various private statements, were a matter of policy rather than altruism.[100] It is this which explains the ease with which his colleagues suppressed their misgivings. The tone of Balfour's comments on the Army was used by the press to confirm his image, cultivated in the naval debate, for resisting partisanship on defence issues. In a leader on the Navy on April 1909, *The Times* noted that Balfour had 'steadily refrained from attempts to make party capital out of the Army scheme'.[101] Indeed, the moderation of the Unionist leader's stance in the army debate would become more conspicuous from this point on as relations between government and Opposition on the naval issue rapidly deteriorated.

The obverse of this coin was growing tension between the Opposition and the National Service League. In April, when the Liberal MP for South Warwickshire, Captain Kincaid-Smith, resigned his seat to contest the ensuing by-election on the platform of compulsory training for the Territorials, Balfour declined to respond to Milner's request that he dissuade the local Unionist party from offering opposition.[102] He refused to 'call upon the party in Warwickshire to vote for a man who is against us on all the *main* principles of our case because he is standing in favour of Universal Training – a question which is not included in our official programme'.[103] When local Unionists chose P.S. Foster to contest the seat, Balfour wrote him a letter of support.[104] The League's executive now shrank from calling on their Unionist supporters to vote for Kincaid-Smith; to avoid a damaging split they opted instead for the humiliating position of neutrality.[105] Foster's decisive victory in a high poll was a major setback for the League and a vivid reminder to Balfour and his colleagues of the electoral cost of infidelity to the voluntary principle. 'To suppose that the Unionist party will take up an unpopular proposal which will lose votes is an extraordinary hallucination', wrote a dejected Newton. The episode as a whole contained three lessons, other than that Roberts knew as much about English party politics as 'a Patagonian'.[106] First, it had shown how fragile was the League's cross-party support at a time of growing party political polarization. Second, it had shown that party commitments had priority over compulsionist sympathies at the Unionist grass-roots and that 'dislike of the present Government, of the Budget and the dread of Socialism' would impose severe limits on the League's ability to encourage internal Unionist dissent on the army issue.[107] Finally, it had shown that, for all its lengthening roll of Unionist members in the country, the League continued to lack influence at the higher levels of the Unionist party.

Tension between the League and the party came to a head in the House of Lords in July 1909 when Roberts and Milner introduced a bill designed to convert the Territorial Force to a compulsory basis. The bill proposed that men between the ages of 18 and 30 should be liable for Territorial service; that the period of compulsory initial training should be 4 months for infantry, 4–6 months for other arms; and that there should be a 15-day period of compulsory training in each of the first three years.[108] The political purpose of the exercise was, Milner explained, to 'take a sufficient number of leading Unionist peers (Curzon certainly & I hope Cromer) with us to make the Party leaders realise that this is no longer an academic question & that there is a body of conviction who has got to be reckoned with'.[109] A week before the debate on 12 July, an amendment to the Roberts bill was laid down by the Duke of

Northumberland. This acknowledged the need for a home army adequate in size and training, but it also expressed unwillingness to accept a measure whose cost was unknown and which did not have the backing of the government's expert advisers.[110] Milner detected subterfuge, believing that the amendment had been inspired by Lansdowne. The deft reference to the military advisers would 'leave the door wide open for [the Opposition] to adopt the opposite line in future, when the 'military advisers', no longer primed by Haldane, will of course be much more ready to declare the T.A. insufficient . . .'.[111] In fact the conspiracy went deeper. Northumberland's amendment was the fruit of consultation between Lansdowne, Balfour and Haldane. 'Two can play the game of strategy!' observed Haldane slyly.[112] Cushioned by the government's large majority in the Commons, the Secretary of State for War could not feel seriously threatened by Roberts' action in the Upper House, but he had no desire to see Balfour's freedom to support him circumscribed. Thus, in a curious reversal of roles, Haldane considered what action he might take to assist the Unionist front bench in resisting backbench pressure. 'The stress and burden of the day will fall on the official opposition', wrote the Under-Secretary for War, Lord Lucas, 'but I think that . . . we ought to help them as much as we can by damning the bill in unmeasured terms'.[113] With ministerial support the Northumberland amendment was carried by 123 to 103, a result which Haldane deemed 'very satisfactory'.[114] Roberts could take comfort from the fact that 98 Unionist peers had voted for his bill and from the seriousness with which the party leadership had taken the revolt, but the outcome was still disillusioning. In a letter to *The Times* on 12 July Newton vented the League's frustration; 'if the official Unionist leaders . . . prefer to support Mr Haldane's policy rather than the only practical alternative, what serious value can be attached in future to their criticisms of the military policy of the present Government?'[115] Despite his excuses to Roberts, Midleton's action in seconding Northumberland's amendment was a strong reminder to the League that the support of those whom Maxse dubbed pejoratively as 'practical politicians' was not to be relied upon when party pressures were brought to bear.[116]

The cross-bench collaboration of July 1909 is particularly striking in that it occurred in a context of rapidly deteriorating relations between government and Opposition over the so-called 'People's Budget' and the Navy.[117] What Newton saw as the Opposition's failure to oppose should in fact be seen as the high water mark of that era of bipartisanship in military affairs inaugurated in June 1907 with the Militia agreement. This bipartisanship has been described by Scally as 'a triumph of the national, "non-party" principle and a manifest example of the possibilities of joint effort among imperialists in the government and the opposition', but that is misleading in two ways.[118] Not only because those most closely identified with social imperialism and national efficiency – Milner and Co. – were opponents, not supporters, of the policy settled in 1907, but also because, for those in Opposition who actually made the 'joint effort', ideology, of Empire or otherwise, did not enter into it. What motivated Balfour and Salisbury were the more prosaic forces of policy and politics. 'If Balfour returns to office', Repington had predicted in May 1909, 'he will continue on Haldane's lines because every other possible alternative has been tried & has failed, or else has been examined & rejected'.[119] Much as the League deplored it, the Northumberland amendment was 'nothing more or less than a vote of confidence in Mr. Haldane and his military advisers'.[120] The commitment of the Unionist party to Haldane's policy, and to the voluntary principle, was confirmed three days later when Balfour dined with Haldane to meet the General Staff and told them that 'they might "count on" his adopting & carrying on the policy when he came in'.[121]

CHAPTER 11

Dreadnoughts and Politics 1909–11

Asquith's 'Curious and Characteristic Solution'

By the autumn of 1908 it was clear that the forecast of German shipbuilding which the Liberal government had offered Parliament in March had been wildly optimistic. During the year the Germans had not only laid down the four Dreadnoughts of their 1908–9 programme, but also begun work on the four of 1909–10 for which the Reichstag had yet to vote credits, a development which suggested that the rate of German construction was no longer bound by the constraints of parliamentary finance.[1] This 'acceleration' had only been made possible by recent expansion in the German dockyards and at Krupps of Essen, the major supplier of guns, gun-mountings and armour to the Imperial Navy.[2] The growth of Krupps' productive capacity also removed any doubt that the Germans *could* now match the average British construction period of two years. It was realized at the Admiralty in London that if the Germans were to repeat in 1909 and 1910 the action taken in 1908 – building eight vessels in each year rather than four – and if those vessels were completed in two years, they *could* have 21 Dreadnoughts complete by the spring of 1912 and 25 by the autumn. Since, at the end of 1908, Britain had 12 Dreadnoughts built or building, to match these possible German totals she would have to complete 9 new Dreadnoughts by the spring of 1912 and a further 4 by the autumn. Even this massive effort would achieve a mere parity; only if the two most modern pre-Dreadnoughts, *Lord Nelson* and *Agamemnon*, were taken into account would Britain enjoy a margin of superiority. For the Board, Fisher insisted that 'the *safe* and *right* thing to do' was to build 6 new British Dreadnoughts in 1909–10, while making preparations to build more in 1910–11; of course, if German construction slackened off during the year, Britain could follow suit.[3]

The Board's demand confronted the Liberal ministry with a stark choice between priorities. To agree to six new Dreadnoughts would be to defeat the government's domestic political objectives.[4] But to reject the Board's demand was to risk a serious deterioration in Britain's naval position. The attempt to frame Estimates which would reconcile these conflicting priorities reopened the Liberal Imperialist–Radical schism which had characterized Liberal politics in the decade bisected by the South African War. Contrary to the assumption of Conservatives, since 1906 the Navy issue had caused strikingly little factional tension within the Liberal Cabinet; its main effect had been to strain relations between the government and its backbench supporters. Persuaded that objective naval circumstances justified a relaxation of Britain's construction effort, the former supporters of Lord Rosebery had approved the policy of retrenchment pursued since 1906. In February 1909, however, what one minister referred to as 'the seam in the Cabinet' was exposed.[5]

The Radical ministers – Lloyd George, Churchill, Morley, Burns and Harcourt – would agree to no more than four new Dreadnoughts in the coming year. They scoffed at McKenna's 'fatuous' Estimates and dismissed his projections of German strength; 'I believe the Admiralty are procuring false information to frighten us', Lloyd George warned Churchill, who refused to credit that the German naval programme was suddenly to be freed from all political and financial restraint.[6] Pressure from their supporters at Westminster and in the country only stiffened the Radicals' determination to stand firm; Morley and Churchill talked of resignation and of the breakup of the government.[7] Charles Masterman was convinced that a six-ship programme would be 'the beginning of the end' for the Liberal party.[8] Other ministers, however, ranged themselves behind the Board of Admiralty. For the first time since 1906, a distinctive Liberal Imperialist position developed in the Cabinet. Grey warned Morley that he could not stay in the government unless the Estimates provided 'a sufficient margin of safety against possible naval strength in 1912–1913'.[9] 'I like others advocated retrenchment at the last election', the Foreign Secretary wrote to Asquith, 'but I always excepted the Navy from my promises, and in any case promises must be subordinate to national safety'.[10] Haldane and Crewe also backed McKenna, Crewe maintaining that it would not be possible to propose fewer than six new ships 'without the suppression of material facts and the refusal to admit reasonable inferences from those facts'.[11]

Throughout February 1909 an acute sense of crisis enveloped the Cabinet, with ministers and observers alike predicting its imminent demise. There were those on the fringe of events who wished the government to fall on the Navy issue. H.W. Massingham, editor of the *Nation*, hoped that the crisis might result in a new Radical ministry under Morley, one purged of Liberal Imperialist influences.[12] The government only survived because of Asquith's skill in fashioning what Churchill called 'a curious and characteristic solution'. 'The Admiralty had demanded six ships: the economists offered four: and we finally compromised on eight'.[13] After prolonged argument and negotiation, at a Cabinet meeting on 24 February the Prime Minister proposed that the

Estimates should provide for the construction of only four Dreadnoughts immediately, rather than the six demanded by the Board.[14] However, he also proposed that a footnote to the Estimates should give the government powers to build four more Dreadnoughts later in the year if events corroborated the Admiralty's predictions about German policy.[15] The inwardness of the compromise lay in the contingent status of the second four Dreadnoughts. It was because this was interpreted in diametrically opposed ways by the parties to the dispute that the compromise worked. Believing that events in Germany during the months ahead would discredit the Admiralty's analysis of German shipbuilding policy, the priority for the Radicals was to prevent a premature commitment to ships which would not be necessary; this they had done. For them, the contingent status of the second four Dreadnoughts was a matter of substance. For the Board of Admiralty, on the other hand, the construction of the ships was a foregone conclusion and their contingent status a matter of form.[16]

The Prime Minister was playing a crafty game. His instincts on the issue aligned him with the Radicals.[17] Consistent with his conduct since 1906, Asquith was determined to avoid unnecessary naval expenditure; 'no surplus, however large, would justify the laying down of a ship that was not needed for security', he wrote.[18] He did not believe that the German government intended to utilize Krupps' increased capacity, nor that its finances would permit a vastly increased naval effort. He did not, therefore, expect the need for the contingent vessels to arise. He was confirmed in this view by statements made to Grey by the German ambassador, Count Metternich; Metternich denied any intent in Berlin to exceed the statutory programme and explained the apparent acceleration of work on the 1909–10 programme as an initiative by contractors hard pressed by a slump in trade.[19] But in order to persuade McKenna and Fisher to abandon their initial demand for six Dreadnoughts and agree to the package Asquith had to disguise his views. While rejecting Fisher's efforts to get him to sanction the placing of orders for all eight ships at once, he gave the Board a verbal assurance that the contingent ships would definitely be ordered in the coming year.[20] Doing so in no way tied his hands. If, as he and the Radicals anticipated, the Admiralty were proved wrong about German policy, then the case for further construction would dissolve and with it his assurances. If the Admiralty were proved right, then, assurances or no, the contingent Dreadnoughts would have to be built. This skilled avoidance of commitment in the hope of a favourable turn of events is a classic instance of Asquith's political technique, the strategy which opponents dubbed 'wait and see'. The compromise can thus be compared with Asquith's parliamentary 'pledge' of March 1908. In both cases the Prime Minister had bought time.

'We have had a very serious Cabinet today', Haldane reported to his mother on 24 February, 'but I think we have got around the corner and over a crisis which might have split us'.[21] Asquith had indeed saved his ministry. In doing so, however, he had brought the wrath of the Opposition down upon his head. Their reaction to the 1909–10 Estimates is the subject of the next section of this chapter. Before returning to the Conservatives, it will be convenient to outline Liberal policy from the spring of 1909 to the end of 1911 since this is essential background for the third section of the chapter, which describes Opposition policy during Balfour's last two years as party leader.

The four contingent Dreadnoughts of the 1909–10 programme were eventually built: but not for the expected reason. Asquith's scepticism about German shipbuilding proved to be well founded. Far from acceleration, in May 1909 the British naval attaché in Berlin reported a general slowing down.[22] On the other hand, Grey's attempts in 1909–10 to reach an agreement on naval arms limitation with Berlin proved unsuccessful. As one scholar puts it: 'The curious diplomatic minuet of these years was not simply a question of chronology – with Berlin wanting a pledge of British neutrality as a precondition for naval limitation, and London wanting a halt to German fleet expansion before it would consider a political settlement – but an indication that in neither field was compromise possible.'[23] In the Mediterranean, a fresh and unexpected naval challenge to Britain was emerging. The adoption of new Dreadnought programmes by Germany's Triple Alliance partners, Austria and Italy, early in 1909 left the British government no choice but to go ahead with the contingent ships, despite the good news from Germany.[24]

Coupled with the unexpectedly high cost of the old-age pensions scheme introduced in 1908, and a shortfall in tax yields as a result of an economic downturn in 1907–8, the adoption of a construction programme 400 per cent greater than that of the previous year made an already parlous financial situation considerably worse.[25] The government's solution to the crisis of public finance was Lloyd George's celebrated 'People's Budget' of April 1909. The Budget, which contained steep rises in income tax, death duties and stamp duties, as well as a tax on incremental land values, was a masterly political initiative designed both to reinvigorate the fortunes of the Liberal party and to prove that the needs of the modern British state could be met without resort to tariff reform.[26] Its rejection by the Unionist-controlled House of Lords in November 1909 not only precipitated the fiercest phase yet in the fiscal controversy, but also opened a new and ultimately decisive chapter in British constitutional history, one which would encompass two general elections in 1910 and would only close with the stormy debates over the Parliament bill in the baking summer of 1911.

The new taxes introduced in 1909 greatly improved the government's financial position. Revenue in 1909–10 and 1910–11 was some 10 per cent above the level of 1908–9. An economic upswing helped matters by improving tax yields.[27] The Navy benefited from the government's rising income; naval expenditure, which had totalled £32.2 million in 1908–9, amounted to £42.2 million in 1911–12. As in the phase of retrenchment between 1906 and 1909, the key financial determinant after 1909 was construction. Following the eight-ship programme of 1909–10, five Dreadnoughts were built in 1910–11 and five more in 1911–12. (An additional two Dreadnoughts were built for Britain at the expense of the Australian and New Zealand governments.) Britain's naval position was thus secured in the face of continued building by the powers of the Triple Alliance. In the three years 1906–8, the Liberal government agreed to the construction of eight Dreadnoughts; in the three years 1909–11 they agreed to eighteen. The events of 1909 thus mark a distinct watershed in Liberal policy. As will be noted in a later chapter, the trend to large programmes and high Estimates would continue until 1914.

By then the two-power standard was no longer official British policy. In the spring of 1909 the two next strongest naval powers were Germany and the USA. In May 1909 Asquith made it clear to the House of Commons that the government did not regard a German–American combination against Britain as 'reasonably probable' and that the friendly USA was excluded *de facto* from the Admiralty's calculations of the two-power standard.[28] This was a decision which the Unionist government had taken in principle in 1900–2 but which they had chosen to conceal, thus preserving the credibility of the two-power standard. Now Asquith's declaration of what had in fact been British government policy since 1900 destroyed it. It was not only the quickening growth of American naval power which made the demise of the two-power standard inevitable; the fact was that Germany's strength threatened to so exceed that of the USA that even a margin of 10 per cent over their combined strength would not assure Britain superiority over Germany alone.[29] From 1909 the Admiralty unofficially based its policy on the more exacting standard of equality with Germany plus 60 per cent. It was a bitter turn of events for Liberals who had seen the dropping of the two-power standard as the key to retrenchment.

'Asquith Deserves To Be Hung . . . '

'The increasing tension between the two countries gives me profound anxiety', wrote Balfour of Anglo-German relations in the early summer of 1908.[30] He regarded naval rivalry as the major cause of tension and told the German ambassador in July that the steady expansion of the German fleet was at the root of ill-feeling in Britain.[31] Unguarded comments on Anglo-German relations by the Kaiser in an interview with the *Daily Telegraph* in October 1908 not only confirmed Bismarck's comparison of the Kaiser with a balloon – 'if you do not hold fast to the string, you never know where he will be off to' – but also brought that ill-feeling to a new pitch.[32] Balfour's personal anxiety about the German naval 'threat' was greatly intensified by the aggressive tenor of German foreign policy during 1908. In the autumn, a sharp Franco-German clash over Morocco (the 'Casablanca affair') was quickly followed by a more threatening Balkan crisis (precipitated by Austria-Hungary's annexation of Bosnia-Herzegovina) during which the government in Vienna was offered German support for a war with Russia.[33] From late 1908, German policy and arms were increasingly seen as a direct menace to the peace of Europe. Wyndham expressed the attitude of many leading Unionists when he asserted that the Germans were bent on war, 'not, necessarily in the immediate future, but some day, and pretty soon'.[34] Visiting Balfour at Whittingehame, his Scottish estate, in mid-September, Lady Selborne found him 'much preoccupied with the German scare' and 'quite convinced that the Germans are determined to sweep us out of the way'.[35] In fact, Balfour's assessment of the situation was much influenced by contact with members of the government. By the first week of November the Cabinet considered the European situation critical and Asquith was forced to contemplate British intervention in a continental war.[36] So grave was the outlook that the Prime Minister took the precaution of briefing the Opposition leader. 'Asquith asked me to speak to him last night after the House rose', Balfour wrote to Lansdowne on 6 November. The Prime Minister had appeared 'extremely perturbed' about the European situation and had said that 'incredible as it might seem, the Government could form no theory of the German policy which fitted all the known facts except that they wanted war'.[37] It was because Asquith so impressed Balfour with the fragile state of Anglo-German relations that the Opposition leader tried to dissuade Lord Roberts from staging a Lords debate on the invasion issue later in November.[38] And Balfour's sense of concern can only have been heightened when in December the Prime Minister took the novel step of formally requesting Esher to brief the Unionist leader on various strategic plans then being considered by the CID.[39]

Apprehension about the international situation inevitably reinforced the Unionists' determination to see a resumption of large-scale shipbuilding in 1909. 'I am not satisfied that war with Germany is inevitable a few years hence . . . ', observed Selborne, 'but it can only be avoided if, in the interval, we make ourselves so strong at sea as to make any attempt to attack us obviously absurd'.[40] Unionists were strengthened in their view that a new programme of at least six ships was necessary by reports of the expansion at Krupps and in the German dockyards. *The Times* had also revealed the start of work ahead of time on the German Dreadnoughts of 1908–9 and 1909–10.[41] On 24 November 1908 Cawdor questioned the government in the Lords about Britain's capacity for producing the vital warship components, guns, gun-mountings and turrets.[42]

The Opposition greeted the new Estimates with a mixture of incredulity and anger. Their autumn campaign had apparently been futile. 'Asquith deserves to be hung', snapped Austen Chamberlain; 'It is inconceivable how any body of responsible men with the knowledge which the Government have before them can so play with the gravest issue which we have had to face for years.'[43] There was also criticism of the Sea Lords; 'all the bluster about the Bd. of Admiralty being determined to resign if they did not get 6 Battleships seems to have ended in smoke!', wrote Cawdor.[44] The Unionists' anger intensified during the Estimates debate on 16, 17 and 18 March. Anxious to divert a planned attack by Radicals of the backbench Reduction of Armaments Committee, McKenna and Asquith deliberately dramatized the seriousness of the situation produced by developments in Germany.[45] They not only conceded that the government had miscalculated the pace of German shipbuilding in 1908, but also acknowledged that its information remained imperfect; 'we do not know, as we thought we did, the rate at which German construction is taking place', said the First Lord.[46] As far as the future went, McKenna spelled out three important assumptions on which government policy was based; first, that because they were to be built in batches, new German Dreadnoughts could not be completed in less than three years; second, that any work done thus far on the four ships of 1909–10 was merely preliminary; and third, that work on the four German Dreadnoughts of 1910–11 would not be brought forward into 1909–10. The second and third assumptions reflected Count Metternich's assurances, of which Parliament was now told. These assumptions led the government to forecast that the maximum number of Dreadnoughts Germany could have by 1912 was seventeen, and it was as 'a most reasonable and business-like response' to this possibility that the provision of four contingent Dreadnoughts was justified.

McKenna's revelations electrified the House of Commons; 'The tea hour came and went and not a man stirred.'[47] He certainly succeeded in disarming the Radicals.[48] The candour and stern tone of McKenna and Asquith alike weakened resistance to both the increased Estimates and the shipbuilding programme. Frustration rather than anger or vituperation characterized the reaction of the 'economists' to the death-knell of economy. Regretfully, they faced facts. 'So far as I am concerned', said John Ward, 'I am going to give no Vote . . . which at some future time when the defences of the country are put to the test I may be sorry for'.[49] However, the government's tactics unexpectedly backfired, as Austen Chamberlain observed:

The fact is that the Government altogether miscalculated the forces at work. They thought they had got to justify their estimates against a Radical attack on the size of the programme and they prepared their speeches from this point of view. But they were quite wrong. All they said in their defence against the Little Navy men served only to strengthen the real attack – the charge that they are not doing enough.[50]

It was Balfour who turned the debate on to this new axis. He spoke immediately after McKenna, seizing the attention of the House with his 'evident earnestness'. Garvin described his speech as one of 'measured but extraordinary power, which showed once more that in a crisis he can be as firm as steel'.[51] The case argued by Balfour on the 16th, and developed by Opposition spokesmen over the next three days of debate, was clear-cut. How could the government justify taking an optimistic view of the future when, by its own admission, it had completely mis-judged the rate of German construction in March 1908 and when (as McKenna's speech had revealed) it lacked hard evidence of current activity in the German dockyards? Ministers were 'living in a fools' paradise', believing what it suited them to believe. The Unionists argued that given the uncertainty over both Germany's intentions and her recent progress, British policy must be determined by the only certain element in the situation – Germany's constructive potential. If the enormous resources of Krupps and the German dockyards were utilized to the full, the scales of naval advantage would tilt dramatically in Germany's favour.

The government should not rely on the protestations of the German ambassador to insure Britain against this contingency, but on iron and steel. The only safe course of action was to expect that Germany *would* start eight new Dreadnoughts in 1909 and complete them in two years. This would give her 21 Dreadnoughts in the spring of 1912, not 17 as McKenna forecast.[52] Accordingly, the contingent British Dreadnoughts should be ordered at once. Only thus could Britain depend on having 20 Dreadnoughts complete by the spring of 1912 and so minimize her inferiority.

This was the case hammered home by Lee, Pretyman, Law and Chamberlain, as well as by Balfour himself, over the next three days.[53] Other lines of attack included criticism of the government for not having informed Parliament sooner of the acceleration of German shipbuilding, and a more general charge that the present crisis might have been averted had the government behaved more cautiously between 1906 and 1908; 'All the efforts which have been devoted to building up our great Navy, to put it beyond rivalry are, by a year or two's neglect, rendered futile and useless', complained Chamberlain. The government responded to all this with a dogged defence of its policy.[54] Asquith dismissed as 'a physical impossibility' Balfour's suggestion that Germany could have 17 Dreadnoughts as early as November 1911 and evaded the Opposition's central point about the proven fallibility of the government's powers of prediction. By the end of the debate on 18 March it was plain that the Unionists had made no progress whatsoever. Their frustration was the more intense because this was not the turn of events they had expected; they entered the debate firmly believing that the government would yield to pressure.

This belief originated with Fisher. At 10 p.m. on 15 March, the eve of the Estimates debate, Lord Esher had called on Balfour at 4 Carlton Gardens. He arrived hotfoot from the Admiralty where he had been closeted with the First Sea Lord. Esher was playing one of those conspiratorial behind-the-scenes roles which he so relished. We saw him in action in 1907, shuttling between Haldane and the Opposition over the Militia issue.[55] On this occasion his mission was to enlist the Unionist leader's help for Fisher in securing immediate orders for the contingent Dreadnoughts. Finding Balfour out, Esher explained Fisher's view of the situation to Jack Sandars, who sat down at midnight to draft a memorandum for his chief.[56] Fisher's analysis can be briefly summarized. The Board of Admiralty were set on ordering the contingent ships without delay; this offered the only hope of insuring Britain against the possible 'catastrophe' of 25 German Dreadnoughts at sea in 1912. The government recognized the necessity for the ships and was committed to them, but had chosen to delay the second four for fear of alienating the Liberal rank and file. In other words, the footnote was a device to mask the government's true position. The key point, however, was that, according to Fisher, the government wanted to be *forced* 'to surrender their virtue & be committed to the 8 ships at once'. Parliamentary pressure from the Opposition, combined with the press agitation being mounted by Fisher's journalistic friends such as Garvin of the *Observer*, could neutralize the government's fear of the 'economists'.[57]

In previous years, Fisher had always urged restraint on Balfour. On this occasion, having failed to persuade Asquith to allow orders for the contingent Dreadnoughts to be placed at once, the First Sea Lord wanted the Opposition leader to take the offensive and make the ships 'parliamentary sure'.[58] The only explanation Fisher could come up with for Asquith's compromise formula was fear of his party's Radical 'tail'. While untrue, this analysis naturally impressed Balfour who, as we have seen, habitually interpreted Asquith's conduct in just such terms. Fisher's story was entirely consistent with what Balfour – encouraged by Esher – saw as the Liberals' 'way of doing business' in naval affairs.[59] The other significant point about Fisher's appeal to arms is that it offered the Opposition a chance to influence what otherwise appeared to be a hopeless situation.[60] Esher's dramatic visit led the Unionists to believe that, in pressing for action on the contingent Dreadnoughts, they would be pushing against an open door.

By the end of the third day of debate this expectation had dissolved. 'Asquith jumps about like a parched pea in a frying-pan and doesn't know which way to face', observed Austen Chamberlain of the Prime Minister's efforts to defend the new programme against complaints from both Radicals and Unionists.[61] But, however uncomfortable his position, the Prime Minister gave no sign that he was preparing to challenge the 'economists'. Astonishingly, this unexpected turn of events did not lead Balfour and his colleagues to question Fisher's analysis. They simply concluded that Asquith was more politically craven than they had assumed. This was perhaps less offensive than the truth would have been, but it was no less infuriating. Senior Unionists were appalled at the lengths to which Asquith seemed prepared to go in subordinating naval policy to the pressures of internal Liberal politics. With only one day of debate remaining, Balfour had urgently to review his options. Already there was talk in the Unionist press of accepting the inevitable and renewing the fight for the contingent Dreadnoughts later in the year.[62] Balfour, however, was determined not to let the debate end without some formal expression of the Opposition's dissent from government policy. The obvious course would have been to move an amendment to the Estimates in favour of increased expenditure on construction. Yet according to parliamentary procedure, only amendments in favour of reduction were permissible and, as Balfour put it drily, 'to move a reduction when you want an increase is not an effective way of expressing your opinions'.[63] Abstention was ruled out for the same reason. In these circumstances there remained only a vote of censure, the ultimate means by which an Opposition could register its profound disagreement with the policy of the government of the day. This course of action was not without disadvantage since it would undoubtedly rally to the government those Liberals whose sympathies in the debate had hitherto been with the Opposition; Balfour would be 'giving the Imperialist Liberals and the Economist Radicals an excuse for voting together'.[64] Moreover, a censure motion would inevitably give rise to accusations of partisanship which could damage the credibility of the Opposition's case against the government. The Liberals would be quick to denounce their opponents for seeking to make political capital out of the situation.

Despite these risks, Balfour was convinced that no other 'politically practicable' course was open to him.[65] Besides, a censure motion was an appropriate index of both his anxiety about the naval situation – Esher claimed never to have seen Balfour so upset – and his disgust at the government's response to that situation.[66] Other senior Unionists concurred in his decision.[67] There was some hope on the front bench that the censure motion might retrieve the situation altogether. It was possible that the Prime Minister would consider braving the Radical storm over the contingent ships preferable to the loss of prestige at home and abroad which a censure of the government's naval policy would entail. Even at this stage, after three days of acrimonious debate, the Unionists had not lost hope that the Liberal Imperialists would stop 'thinking only of how to placate their little-Englanders'.[68] Hence Alfred Lyttelton's belief that the very prospect of a censure motion would 'strengthen the hands' of Asquith and Grey and 'stiffen their resolution'.[69] Chamberlain was heartened by signs of a 'pro-Navy' reaction on the Liberal benches.[70] Considerations of this kind explain why Balfour chose to delay moving the vote of censure until the close of the concluding session of the Estimates debate on 22 March. He was giving Asquith yet another chance to make his long-awaited stand against the Radicals.[71] 'Though the sands are running out', warned *The Times*, 'there is yet time for the Government to repair one of the greatest political blunders of modern times . . .'.[72]

On the morning of 19 March the Cabinet decided that 'in view of the attempts . . . being made in some quarters to manufacture something like a Navy scare', the Prime Minister should make a further statement in Parliament on the 22nd.[73] Rumours to this effect circulated almost immediately. On his arrival at the Commons that afternoon Balfour heard that Asquith intended to pledge the government to unspecified action on the contingent ships later in the year – far less than the Opposition demanded – and, exploiting 'a not very clearly worded phrase' in Balfour's speech of 18 March, to claim the Unionist leader's support.[74] Unwilling to be outmanoeuvred, Balfour stole Asquith's thunder by promptly tabling his censure motion; Margot Asquith's boast that her husband's speech would 'put everything right and be a great triumph for him' proved premature. Austen Chamberlain thought it a pity 'that the situation could not have been allowed to develop for another two or three days on entirely non-party lines', but accepted Balfour's reasoning.[75]

The text of the censure motion was published on the morning of 20 March: 'That in the view of this House the declared policy of His Majesty's Government respecting the immediate provision of battleships of the newest type does not sufficiently secure the safety of the Empire.'[76] *The Times* approved Balfour's action on the grounds that he had 'exhausted the resources of an Opposition in the way of friendly appeals'; the government's intransigence had made 'other methods' unavoidable.[77] Predictably enough, the Liberals saw matters differently. Balfour was accused by Walter Runciman of having 'dragged [the Navy] into the party arena' and of indulging in 'an amount of alarmist talk on the Navy . . . almost unequalled in Parliamentary history'.[78] In the Commons on 22 March Asquith denounced the Opposition's 'unscrupulous' and 'unpatriotic' agitation and dismissed what he called 'the absurd and mischievous legends' about Britain's naval weakness.[79] Balfour reacted furiously to the Prime Minister's strictures, repudiating the charge that he and his colleagues were politicizing the Navy issue.[80] The censure, he retorted, was the Opposition's only possible response to the government's failure to recognize the gravity of the situation. By this stage there was a marked animus in exchanges between the two party leaders. It seemed to the veteran lobby correspondent, Henry Lucy, that Asquith was incensed by the Opposition leader's refusal to accept his assurances.[81] In view of his bipartisan support of Fisher and his previous restraint on the shipbuilding issue, Balfour bitterly resented the imputation of partisan irresponsibility. His anger was shared by his colleagues. 'He [Asquith] knows as well as your own followers do', wrote Walter Long, 'how careful you have been to abstain from anything of the kind'.[82] To Unionists like Long, it was the government itself which had politicized the Navy issue by letting the Navy Estimates become the shuttlecock of various Liberal factions.

The debate on the 22nd disabused Unionists of the notion that the mere prospect of a censure motion – the first of his premiership – might spur Asquith into action in defiance of the Radicals. If anything, the Prime Minister seemed more obdurate. This was certainly Fisher's view, conveyed to Balfour and Cawdor at a meeting on 24 March, their only encounter during the crisis. The First Sea Lord believed that the censure motion had made 'some more definite promise from the Prime Minister' less, rather than more, likely to be forthcoming.[83] He remained anxious to draw Asquith into some public commitment but now felt that confrontation was not going to secure results; a softer line might be more productive. Balfour and Cawdor apparently recognized Fisher's logic. In the days preceding the censure debate they tried to build what *The Times* called 'a golden bridge between the parties'.[84] Speaking at Newton Abbot on 25 March Cawdor made it clear that the Opposition would welcome a pretext for dropping the censure motion; 'those with whom I act would give much if we found tomorrow morning that the Government were going to do what the people of this country want'.[85] On 26 March, the 'Political Notes' column of *The Times*, a recognized channel for unofficial frontbench statements, announced that Lee would move the censure motion at the outset of the debate on the 29th, so allowing Balfour to wind up. 'Such an arrangement does not, of course, indicate any change in the attitude of the Opposition, but if the Ministerial pronouncements on Monday are considered more satisfactory, it would enable the leader of the Opposition to review the situation.'[86] There was no doubt, however, that to induce Balfour to withdraw his motion the government would have to order all eight Dreadnoughts at once. On 28 and 29 March Sandars had heard from another informant in the Admiralty, the Fourth Sea Lord Francis Bridgeman, that any delay in ordering the contingent ships would make effective progress on them impossible during the coming year.[87]

Of course, there was no chance of the government conceding this point. The Unionists' delusions were punished in the censure debate on 29 March. As previously announced, the Opposition's case was prosecuted by Arthur Lee, who gave 'one of the best performances of his parliamentary career'.[88] In a packed and excited House of Commons, Lee argued incisively that the government were underestimating the threat posed by Germany's gigantic shipbuilding resources and taking risks with Britain's security.[89] Even on the government's own figures, Britain would have only a bare margin over Germany in 1911. 'We ought never to have been reduced', he suggested, 'to the position of estimating whether these small differences in calculation in numbers are vital to our naval supremacy or not'. Having set out the indictment, Lee offered a reprieve. Insisting that he and his colleagues had no wish to see the Navy immersed in 'the whirlpool of party politics', he declared that the Opposition would be 'only too glad to have an opportunity of withdrawing this Motion now if the Government would endeavour to recognize the force of the arguments which we have laid before them'.

The government made no such endeavour. They declined to walk the 'golden bridge' extended towards them. It was Sir Edward Grey who rose to kill Unionist hopes of a breakthrough. The Foreign Secretary defended the government's judgement on the subject of Germany's potential naval strength, laying stress on Metternich's declaration that Germany would not have thirteen Dreadnoughts at sea before the end of 1912.[90] The government now believed it had over- rather than under-estimated the 'acceleration' of the German shipbuilding programme. Grey rejected the demand that all eight Dreadnoughts be ordered at once, reserving a decision on the contingent ships until July, and roundly condemned Balfour's decision to move a vote of censure: 'To make the Navy a party question by any unnecessary, premature or exaggerated anticipation of alarm is the greatest political crime that can be committed', he declared. Though most of his speech was devoted to beating off the Opposition's attack, Grey was also attentive to the 'economists'. He deplored the naval arms race as a 'satire . . . on civilisation', while arguing that Britain had no choice but to arm at a time when other powers were doing so relentlessly. Liberals should trust their government to do only what was essential in the national interest and, meanwhile, support it against an unprincipled, alarmist and exaggerated Unionist attack. Grey's speech delighted his colleagues. Haldane thought it 'admirable . . . perfect in tone and good in its points'.[91] Asquith said that Grey had put the government's case 'unanswerably'. The Prime Minister's own speech was correspondingly

'Our Army Critic', cartoon of Arthur
Lee MP by 'Spy', *Vanity Fair*, 23
January 1907.

brief, though long enough for him to pour a generous measure of scorn on
the Opposition's arguments and motives; the *Standard* called it 'one of
the most violent party speeches on record'.[92]

Grey's and Asquith's speeches on 29 March were a bitter return on the
hope invested in them by the Unionists since December 1905. The
disillusioning effect of Grey's performance was the greater because most
Unionists looked upon him as an 'irreproachable patriot' and an ally
across the party divide in matters of national defence.[93] Grey's apologetic
tone in justifying the Estimates to the Radicals seemed to confirm the
picture of a Liberal Imperialist group running scared of their party's
'Brunnerite' tail. Suddenly, brusquely, it seemed all too obvious that the
Unionists had been deluding themselves to think that the Liberal
Imperialists would ever draw the line and say to the Radicals, 'no
further'. Balfour had been too trusting.

When the Unionist leader rose to speak he knew that a division on the
censure motion was now inevitable and that his words would mark the
start of a new partisan phase of the Edwardian Navy debate. He began
with a robust defence of his own conduct, which is worth quoting at
length for the light it sheds on his view of events since leaving office:

> On this question I have pleaded with the Government for the three
> years that they have been in power . . . . When the Government

announced their intention to drop one of the Dreadnoughts in 1906 . . . and in 1907 and 1908 . . . I anticipated all the great points which we now have before us – . . . the absolute necessity of counting your fleet of the future in Dreadnoughts, and not in other ships, the rapidity of the Germans in building Dreadnoughts, the growth and increase in the German power of output – all these . . . crucial and critical issues of the controversy, I brought before the House to the best of my ability, and in no party spirit, followed by no party division, year after year. And in this year, 1909, when the question had reached what I conceive to be not merely a critical, but a dangerous phase, I waited during three nights' debate for some hope from the Gentlemen who now carry the destinies of the country in their power before I ventured on the step of asking this House to . . . take a formal decision upon a matter in which, I believe, the interests of this country are vitally concerned. Will anyone say that that procedure is one which is of a party type?[94]

As he had since the first day of debate, Balfour narrowed the issue to one of confidence. Grey and Asquith had appealed for the confidence of the House and country. Sandars, scribbling notes in the Visitors' Gallery, had written at this point: 'Why should we trust them? They knew everything: they quarrelled for three months – then compromised: They gave us less than they wished.'[95] Balfour rested his case on the naval rather than political aspects of the situation. The fact that McKenna had several times during the debate revised his account of recent progress in the German dockyards showed, Balfour contended, that it was beyond the government's power 'to know with certainty and security' what was going on in Germany. In the light of this, and given that Germany's capacity for construction was at least equal to Britain's, it was 'perfect madness' to depend upon margins as small as those the government were ready to contemplate. 'Is that the way national interests should be treated?' Balfour asked, in concluding a hard-hitting and sombre speech.

The Opposition's censure motion was rejected by 353 votes to 135 shortly before 11 p.m. The debate had been intense and passionate. It left the gap between the two parties wider than ever. Battle had been joined on the naval issue for the first time since 1906. But where and how would it be fought? Before the debate a pessimistic Cawdor had predicted that the Opposition might find themselves with no option but to 'rouse the country' against the government's naval policy.[96] These words now proved prophetic. If it was to be won, the struggle for the eight Dreadnoughts could no longer be confined to Parliament. If the terms of the Navy debate were new after the events of March 1909, so must be the arena.

'We Want Eight And We Won't Wait!'

The parliamentary exchanges of March 1909 precipitated the greatest Navy 'scare' of the Edwardian period. For more than a fortnight the Navy was the dominating issue in British politics.[97] The war of claim and counter-claim being waged across the floor of the House of Commons evoked an 'excited and anxious' reaction on the part of press and public. On 22 March the Liberal *Daily News* reported that, far from subsiding, the 'panic' over the naval position was 'rising more and more loud'.[98] 'It is impossible to open a newspaper', said one observer, 'without seeing nearly a page devoted to the alarm felt throughout the country'.[99]

In fact, as one historian has pointed out, 'the 1909 naval panic was largely an issue in London and southern England as opposed to most other regions'.[100] But it was intense nevertheless. The First Lord's revelations, which had so stunned the House of Commons on 16 March, persuaded a substantial section of British public opinion that the trident was slipping from Britannia's grasp and that Germany was within an ace of snatching it. There was even grudging admiration for the way in which Tirpitz and Krupps had demolished British naval supremacy in just a few years; 'Since Rome became web-footed to cope with Carthage, there has been no more brilliant and formidable achievement of its kind in the whole of history.'[101] The dangers of the situation were trumpeted by both the Navy League and Imperial Maritime League.[102] Also active were those non-naval pressure groups which hoped that their own causes would benefit from public anxiety; the National Service League, which saw a loss of public faith in Britain's naval defences as grist to the mill of compulsion, and the Tariff Reform League, which argued that the needs of the Navy could only be borne by a broadening of the basis of taxation.[103] These activities overlapped with those of Unionist constituency organizations, which held meetings to protest against government policy. Spoiling for a fight after three years in Opposition, Unionist activists seized on the naval question as a vote-winning stick with which to beat their Liberal opponents. At Croydon, where a by-election was due following the death of Arnold-Forster in February, the Unionist candidate, Sir Robert Hermon-Hodge, made the Navy the main theme of his winning campaign.[104] News of his victory reached the House of Commons during the censure debate on 29 March; when Asquith rose to speak he was taunted with Opposition cries of 'Croydon! Croydon!' In many instances meetings across the country were addressed by leading party figures. Austen Chamberlain spoke on the Navy at Limehouse on 19 March, and it was at Wigan on 27 March that George Wyndham coined the famous jingle by which the crisis (and indeed the whole Dreadnought era) has come to be identified – 'we want eight and we won't wait'.[105]

The campaign was not orchestrated from Westminster; it developed spontaneously and gathered momentum as the parliamentary struggle intensified. Gwynne of the *Standard* claimed that:

> Never within the last quarter of a century, not even on the Home Rule Bill of 1886, not in the dark days of 1896, not in the most anxious crisis of the South African War, has the dominant feeling of the country been more strikingly displayed.[106]

But, as their speeches 'on the stump' indicate, senior Unionists were swift to encourage the agitation once under way; it would be naive to think that they were not alert to the chance of electoral advantage. The significance of the out of doors agitation changed after the vote of censure. Until then, their campaign in the country had been ancillary to the Unionists' parliamentary fight. After the censure debate, with the parliamentary battle lost, the campaign in the country acquired decisive importance. For the first time since 1906 the mobilization of public opinion displaced parliamentary manoeuvre as the centrepiece of Opposition strategy on the Navy issue.[107] At the same time, the Navy debate acquired a strongly partisan tone for the first time since 1906; events in Parliament had created a deep gulf between the parties and provoked bitter recriminations on both sides. It was Balfour himself who signalled these transitions. Within twenty-four hours of the censure debate he delivered his first fighting platform speeches on the Navy as Opposition leader. On 30 March he spoke at a meeting of the Metropolitan Division of the National Union at the Agricultural Hall and received a standing ovation from an audience of 10,000; the following afternoon he addressed a packed meeting at the Guildhall.[108] From platforms bedecked with the Union Jack, and to audiences warmed up by a round of patriotic songs and anthems, Balfour hammered home the case that he and his colleagues had been making in Parliament; the government had 'neglected the interests of the Empire in its most important and vulnerable point'.

Anxious to keep public attention focused on the naval issue, Balfour authorized a nationwide series of meetings to be addressed by leading party figures.[109] The campaign was formally begun by Pretyman, who spoke at Ipswich on 6 May; later that month Lee spoke at Nottingham, Glasgow, Liverpool, Leicester and Swansea. On 7 May Balfour made the Navy the main subject of his speech to the annual assembly of the Primrose League at the Royal Albert Hall.[110] He condemned the government's willingness to rest national security 'upon the turn of a die, the accident of a torpedo, the possibility of a submarine mine'. Marder argues that the force of the agitation for the eight Dreadnoughts was 'largely spent' by May.[111] While true of the national press, this is far from true of the Unionist Opposition. Their agitation was gaining fresh impetus. Whereas a year earlier Balfour had been the subject of criticism in Unionist backbench and press circles for his alleged 'passivity' in naval affairs, now he was lionized.[112] Gwynne praised his 'courage and pluck in the face of an overwhelming numerical superiority in the House'.[113] Garvin claimed that the Opposition leader had 'shown nothing less than greatness' in the crisis.[114] Both men believed that Balfour's action on the Dreadnought issue had won him the admiration of the country and would benefit the party. Their view was shared by *The Times*, whose editor, G.E. Buckle, had given Balfour energetic support during the parliamentary crisis: 'Never before in his career – not even when he was fighting the League in Ireland – has Mr Balfour won the enthusiasm and confidence of his fellow countrymen so completely', ran a leader on 5 April.[115] Thanks to the naval issue, Balfour's authority as leader of the Unionist party was stronger in the first half of 1909 than at any time since 1906.

Balfour's object was to bring public opinion to bear on the government when, in July, it took a decision on the contingent ships. A counterweight was required to the influence of the Radicals, whose determination to avoid further construction was signalled by Churchill in an open letter to his Dundee constituency chairman on 14 April, and by Lloyd George when introducing what would come to be known as 'The People's Budget' on 29 April; in discussing the rising costs of naval defence, the Chancellor argued that it would be 'an act of criminal insanity to throw away £8,000,000 of money which is so much needed for other purposes on building gigantic flotillas to encounter mythical armadas'.[116] In the event, the government decided to proceed with the contingent ships. Its decision was due entirely to the Mediterranean naval outlook; in announcing the news to Parliament on 26 July, McKenna barely alluded to German shipbuilding.[117] The Opposition's noisy agitation had no discernible influence on the outcome. The Radicals, however, thought otherwise. Alleging that the disappearance of the spectre of German 'acceleration' had forced the government to use Mediterranean developments as a pretext for action, they claimed that ministers had been intimidated by 'the coercive policy of the Opposition'. Paying a back-handed compliment to the efficacy of the Unionists' extra-parliamentary campaign, John Dillon warned the government against trying to 'buy off a man-eating tiger with a small dose of blood'.[118]

Unionist satisfaction at the turn of events was marred by the fact that the government not only postponed laying down the keels of the contingent Dreadnoughts until April 1910, but also made no financial provision for work in the interim. Even so, they supported the government in the division lobby against hostile Radical votes; Balfour commented acidly on the 'pitiable spectacle' presented by a ministry dependent on Opposition votes to defend its naval policy against its own supporters.[119] The Unionists exaggerated their own influence on events, seeing the government's action as a vindication of their tactics since March. It confirmed them in the view that, as Lee put it, 'the present Government is one which yields only to pressure and agitation'.[120] Austen Chamberlain believed that the government would be 'sleeping still' had it not been for the outcry raised by Balfour's 'revelations' confirmed by their own admissions.[121] By bringing public opinion to bear in the Navy debate, the Opposition had (it seemed) overcome that parliamentary weakness which had condemned them to passive resistance to Liberal policy between 1906 and 1908. The task facing Balfour was to keep public opinion mobilized. In part it was a matter of educating the public. The *Daily Telegraph* claimed that events in March had 'revolutionised the average man's conception of the naval situation', but Balfour was less confident.[122] He believed that Britain would only retrieve her naval superiority over Germany if the public realized just how close to losing that superiority it had come since 1906.[123] Without a true appreciation of the dangers confronting it, the country would be less ready to shoulder what must be a heavy financial burden. Balfour's aim during the rest of 1909 and during the election campaign of January 1910 was to shake the British public from that complacency about the Navy which was perhaps the most dangerous legacy of the Victorian 'Pax Britannica'. A second motive for carrying on the naval agitation was to keep up pressure on the Liberal Imperialists. Dented and tarnished though it might be, Unionist faith in the Cabinet's 'sound men' persisted. It was hoped that, if sustained, the new mood of public resolution would embolden the Liberal Imperialists against a further capitulation to Radical brow-beating in 1910. 'Those who have held out . . . against the forces of sentimentalism and surrender need the continuous support of public opinion to prevent a relapse in to the disastrous policy . . . identified with the Campbell-Bannerman Administration', argued Lee.[124] If the government did its duty in future, said Balfour, it would be 'because those members of the Cabinet who see the . . . great national dangers which are before us know they have behind them the backing of the country'.[125] The shift from a parliamentary to an extra-parliamentary emphasis in Unionist strategy thus left undisturbed the tissue of misconceptions underlying Opposition policy.

Mobilizing public opinion on the Navy issue was not as easy in the autumn of 1909 as it had been in the spring. 'Questions of naval and military policy have been somewhat overshadowed of late', observed *The Times* on 27 August, 'by the acute domestic controversy which at present absorbs the energies, and embitters the life, of members of Parliament . . . '.[126] The source of that controversy was Lloyd George's budget and the constitutional crisis to which it gave rise. From its outset, Balfour was anxious that the 'overmastering excitement' of the political crisis should not submerge the naval issue.[127] When the prolonged autumn election campaign got under way, the Unionists' nationwide naval agitation was already several months old. Having already invested much energy and political capital in keeping the naval outlook clearly in the public eye, it is not surprising that Balfour determined to make the profound differences between government and Opposition on the naval issue a central part of the Unionists' appeal to the country in January 1910. Those historians who interpret the Unionists' attention to the Navy in December 1909 and January 1910 as a strategy cynically adopted for the election ignore their intense activity on the subject in the previous eight months. Balfour regarded the Navy, the Budget and the Constitution as the three dominant issues before the electorate. The Navy featured prominently in his election address, published on 11 December, and in speeches across the country he routinely condemned the government's conduct of naval policy since 1906; 'What more can be said against any Government', he asked an audience at York on 12 January, 'than that they have not proved themselves efficient to carry out adequately the great trust of national defence?'[128] These were not merely sentiments for public consumption; 'I have the profoundest distrust of the policy of the present Government in respect of this all important part of their administrative duties', he wrote privately in December 1909.[129] Austen Chamberlain took the view that, regardless of any of the other issues before the electors, the Liberals' naval policy was in itself sufficient to condemn them as 'unfitted to exercise the powers which they now hold'.[130] Senior Unionists, including Balfour, did not pledge the party to specific policies if returned to office. They confined themselves to general declarations of intent to put Britain's naval security beyond doubt.[131] Balfour resisted demands from within the Unionist party and press for the adoption of the 'two-keels-to-one' standard as official party policy. First canvassed in 1907–8 when the German 'menace' first loomed large, the case for the 'two-keels-to-one' standard had strengthened during 1909 as the insufficiency of the two-power standard became evident. As a concept it appealed to Germanophobes in the Tory ranks and to those convinced that the Unionist party's best hope of electoral success lay in articulating a clearly defined 'patriotic' policy. Prominent among the latter was J.L. Garvin, who saw the 'two-keels-to-one' policy as 'something big and bold and broad and vivid to strike [the] national imagination', and urged its political merits on Balfour throughout the autumn of 1909.[132] Balfour, however, while not opposed to the idea, stuck to his 'general rule' of Opposition, namely to avoid committing the party to a specific policy while out of office and lacking full information. To do so he regarded as a recipe for both bad policy and possible political embarrassment.[133] Similar thinking explains his aloofness from the associated proposal for a Naval Loan of £50–100 million to finance a huge construction programme.[134] There was also the additional problem, recognized by Lansdowne, that without official information the Unionists could not know whether even this sum would be sufficient.[135]

As was acknowledged by the chief whip, Sir Alexander Acland Hood, the Unionists' highlighting of the Navy issue brought them electoral benefit.[136] Neal Blewett's study of the January 1910 election provides evidence of the positive impact of the naval campaign on the Unionist poll, particularly in southern England and conspicuously in the dockyard towns; the Liberals lost seats at Devonport and Portsmouth.[137] This explains the violence with which Liberals condemned their opponents' campaign, The air was acrid with accusations that the Unionists were deliberately manufacturing a naval scare; McKenna denounced 'ridiculous fictions' and 'wild exaggerations' spread 'solely for electioneering purposes'.[138] The opprobrium reached a crescendo after a speech by Balfour at Hanley on 4 January, in which he acknowledged that many people thought an Anglo-German conflict inevitable.[139] Churchill described the speech as the lowest point of 'the most contemptible policy ever pursued by a great party'.[140]

In the event, whatever its local effect, the naval issue won the Unionists insufficient votes to dislodge their opponents from power. Once the Liberal victory was known, Esher noted ruefully that it could not be construed as a 'clear pronouncement in favour of an overwhelmingly strong Navy'.[141] The election nevertheless transformed the complexion of the Edwardian Navy debate by strengthening the parliamentary position of the Unionists and weakening that of the Radicals. While 273 Unionist MPs now crowded on to the Opposition benches (as against 168 in the previous Parliament), the number of recognized 'economists' fell from above 100 to below 40.[142] The Reduction of Armaments Committee, prime mover in the Radical agitation between 1906 and 1909, was not formally reconstituted in the new Parliament.[143] The eclipse of the 'Little Navy' element had begun on the hustings; 'if any member of the new Liberal majority has preached a reduction of our armaments', observed *The Times*, 'he has preached it in a very modest and unobtrusive way'.[144] The Radicals were to be further hamstrung by the general political context in the wake of the election. 'Resistance to expenditure of all kinds was never at a more feeble ebb', bemoaned Churchill.[145] The vulnerability of the ministry, which lacked an overall majority and was dependent on Irish and Labour votes for survival, meant that the 'economists' could no longer vote against it with impunity.[146] Nor could their Irish and Labour allies, whose hopes of Home Rule and social reform were pinned on Asquith's premiership.[147] As Arthur Lee put it neatly, the political crisis had 'forced the Peace-at-any-Price party to prefer party to peace'.[148]

These developments provided the political basis for that shift to large construction programmes and rising Navy Estimates which marked Liberal policy in 1910 and 1911. The first evidence of the Liberals' 'new course' was the 1910–11 Navy Estimates which provided for five new Dreadnoughts and a financial increase of more than £5.5 million over 1909–10.[149] The new programme was a response to the continuing progress of Austrian and Italian shipbuilding which, as Marder observes, had had a 'decisive impact' on British naval policy.[150] Though Grey had argued in a memorandum of 31 January that the government should agree to substantial Estimates in order to defeat Balfour's 'endeavour to destroy confidence in us and get it for himself on the question of the Navy', as with the contingent Dreadnoughts in July 1909 it was naval realities rather than political pressures which forced the government's hand.[151] Outsiders thought differently, however. Fisher exulted that the Unionists' campaign had 'effectively crippled Lloyd George & Co. as regards the Navy' and the Unionists themselves agreed.[152] 'They [the government] have found out that their Little Navy line did not pay and have altered their policy accordingly', wrote Austen Chamberlain.[153] The prevalent feeling among Balfour's colleagues was that the new Estimates brilliantly vindicated his decision to take the Navy issue to the country.[154] 'For the first two or three years it was in power the present Government yielded to pressure below the Gangway', said Lee in the Commons on 14 March, 'but . . . during the last twelve months it has yielded to pressure from this side of the House'.[155]

The new direction taken by the policy of the government produced a corresponding change in that of Opposition. Unionist anxiety about the naval outlook diminished steadily through 1910 and 1911. In December 1909 Balfour had thought the naval situation 'full of peril'; by 1911 the tone of his speeches and comments had become much less urgent.[156] The naval question occupied a lower profile in Unionist politics during 1910 and 1911 than at any point since 1907. The Dreadnought issue all but disappears from Balfour's correspondence in his last year as leader. The most striking result of this new sense of security was the abandonment by the Unionist leadership of systematic extra-parliamentary agitation on the Navy issue and a return to parliamentary opposition. In the December election of 1910 the party battle lines were drawn up squarely on the issues of Tariff Reform and the Constitution, not on the Navy. Balfour made only a passing reference to it in his election address, while Chamberlain, Long and Wyndham ignored it altogether.[157] Although Garvin and others continued to believe the Navy a vote-winner, and although 89 per cent of Unionist candidates referred to defence in their election addresses (compared to 37 per cent Liberal and 25 per cent Labour), the party leadership made no effort to exploit the issue.[158] The efforts of constituency activists and journalists received no deliberate official sanction or encouragement. This is a significant fact overlooked by historians who argue that the Navy was central to the Unionist party's electioneering strategy in 1910.[159] Since the electoral incentives for highlighting the Navy remained constant throughout the year, the fact that the Unionists fought the first election of 1910 on the Navy but not the second would tend to confirm the view that political self-interest was not the determining factor in their treatment of the Navy on the hustings. The changing political priority which the party leadership attached to the naval issue reflected a changing level of concern about the naval situation. It is because their concern diminished during 1910 that the two Unionist election campaigns present such a contrast.

In Parliament in 1910 a distinctly calmer atmosphere had prevailed in naval affairs. The session of 1910 was 'marked by no such stormy debates on naval topics as characterized its two immediate predecessors'.[160] Austen Chamberlain described the debate of March 1910 as 'dull' and 'uneventful'.[161] While critical of the details of Liberal policy, and violent whenever ministers adopted an apologetic tone towards the Radicals, the Unionists' opposition was generally subdued. The government's new course had drawn their sting. As Sandars remarked of the 1910–11 Estimates: 'This is a very extended programme, and I do not think we shall have any serious criticism to offer on the score of sufficiency, especially as it is accompanied by a substantial programme for cruisers and smaller craft.'[162] The 1911–12 Estimates prompted a similar response. In Parliament during 1910 and 1911 the Opposition stood by the government in the division lobby whenever the Radicals pressed motions for reduction. The duty of the Opposition, said Lee on one such occasion, was 'to defend the Navy'.[163] Senior Unionists remained convinced that internecine divisions were the key to Liberal policy. News reached Balfour during 1910 that Lloyd George and Churchill were conspiring to prevent further large-scale shipbuilding.[164] At this time Lloyd George was becoming increasingly restless on the subject of armaments and increasingly sensitive to pressure from the 'advanced' wing of the Liberal party.[165] Such news revived Unionist suspicions that, under pressure, the government would 'do the least rather than the most possible' for the Navy.[166] 'I still trust that the government will give us good Naval Estimates', Balfour wrote to Northcliffe on 17 December 1910, '[but] it all turns on whether they are more afraid of the Germans or of their own tail'.[167] To tip the scales, during the autumn of 1910 Balfour publicly offered the government the Opposition's support in carrying out strong naval measures against Radical objections.[168] The appearance of the 1911–12 Estimates, with provision for five new Dreadnoughts, enabled Balfour to redeem his promise to support the government against the 'Little Navyites'. In March 1911 two Radical motions for reduction were comprehensively beaten by cross-bench majorities.[169] A backbench 'economist' complained that 'the Leader of the Opposition is always helping the First Lord of the Admiralty, and we poor economists have to fight them both'.[170] This return to the political pattern of 1906–8 was self-conscious and allowed Unionist spokesmen once more to pride themselves on their non-partisanship in naval affairs.[171]

The nature of Unionist policy in 1911 contributed to the growing restiveness of the party under Balfour's leadership. Balfour's policy in 1910 and 1911 was essentially reactive, as it had been between December 1905 and March 1909. While he no longer believed in the two-power standard, he still refused to commit himself to a policy of 'two-keels-to-one'. The Opposition lacked a definitive naval policy around which the party could rally, an equivalent of the 'We Want Eight' slogan which had galvanized party energies in 1909–10. As in the military debate, where Unionist policy was similarly undefined, the result was frustration and anger among party militants and activists who wanted to differentiate the position of the parties across the whole spectrum of policy issues. Nor was Balfour's resumption of constructive parliamentary opposition in tune with the mood on the back benches and in the constituencies where, after nearly two years of almost continuous campaigning, Unionist activists were in no mood for compromise.

So, while it made sense from the front Opposition bench, Balfour's conduct of the Navy debate in 1911 did his cause as leader no good. Until 1909 a constructive Opposition strategy had been intelligible to the party: after March 1909 it was not. The clock could not be turned back. In part this was due to the very real anxiety over the naval position generated by the Dreadnought crisis. In part it was due to the bitterness and polarization which had entered British politics since the spring of 1909. The Unionists' extra-parliamentary campaign had contributed substantially to both these developments. In a sense, therefore, Balfour was the victim of his own success.

CHAPTER 12

The Crisis of the Voluntary System 1910–11

The Decline of the Territorial Force

On 7 April 1909 Lord Roberts wrote to Balfour to explain why he had concluded that the National Service League's cause could no longer be kept 'free from Party politics' and inviting the Unionist leader to combine his crusade for Dreadnoughts with a campaign for compulsory service.[1] Roberts clearly hoped that the alarm over Britain's naval vulnerability had opened Balfour's mind on the matter of home defence. Bobs was, however, hoping in vain.

Balfour's concern over the naval situation has to be seen in a long perspective. The naval supremacy which the Liberal government seemed to have squandered had been the foundation of British defence policy throughout the late Victorian period. The Defence Committee statement of 1896 had acknowledged the extent to which sea power was the cardinal element in the system of imperial defence.[2] Upon it depended Britain's ability 'to maintain the largest empire the world ha[d] ever seen with the the military capabilities of a third rank Power'.[3] This imbalance between Britain's military and naval efforts, although a product of history, was also dictated by financial considerations and the susceptibilities of the Victorian public mind. It was an underlying assumption of Balfour's attempt to rationalize and formulate a coherent defence policy for Britain in the wake of the South African War. It received precise articulation in the 'Blue Water' doctrine adumbrated by the Prime Minister in the Commons in May 1905 and was embodied in Balfour's own army reform scheme of the same year. The Balfourian 'system' combined three elements, a dominant Navy, a Regular Army devoted to service overseas and a small-scale home defence army.[4] This balanced system recognised the realities of electoral opinion and the imperatives of public finance as well as the requirements of imperial defence. The Unionists carried their commitment to it into Opposition when it guided their response to Liberal policy. Their campaign to protect the two-power standard after 1906, their insistence on Militia reform and their backing for the Territorial Force from 1907, were complementary aspects of a coherent approach to imperial defence with its roots in the late nineteenth century. Balfour infused that approach with both his own deep-seated navalist convictions and his preoccupation with India. Notwithstanding the Anglo-Russian Central Asian agreements of 1907 or the growing tension with Germany in the North Sea, his outlook was little changed in this respect from 1903; in May 1908 he reminded Esher of 'the fundamental obligation of keeping adequate reinforcements for India, which are just as necessary now as they ever were'.[5] The integrity and justification of Unionist military policy as it had evolved since 1903 depended entirely on the guarantee of naval supremacy. The real significance of the events in Parliament in March 1909 is that they seemed to have removed that guarantee, so threatening to overthrow the system of imperial defence of which Balfour was architect and Haldane craftsman. Lord Rosebery identified the crux of the matter in a letter to *The Times*; 'what becomes of the Blue Water school?', he demanded.[6]

The crisis of the Blue Water school came as manna from heaven to the compulsionist lobby. By exposing Britain's slender margin of naval security it seemed to strengthen their case for 'transferring the centre of gravity from that part of the army which can fight abroad to that part which can't'.[7] And, by raising the spectre of invasion on a scale larger than the CID had ever allowed possible, it inevitably suggested that new and more exacting criteria must be applied to the Territorials. Of the result of such a test, Roberts was in no doubt; 'Haldane's Army, as at present constituted . . . would be quite useless against such a force as Germany could land here, if she had command of the sea for only 48 hours', he warned.[8] The solution to the problem created by the shipbuilding cut-backs was to adopt compulsory training for home defence, thereby 'providing Haldane's admirable framework with the required number of adequately trained men'.[9]

Balfour's response to the naval situation differed diametrically from that of the NSL, but was no less predictable. Personal conviction and long-standing strategic views dictated that, rather than accepting the collapse of his policy, he should commit his energies to repairing its shaken foundations. His campaign in 1909–10 to secure the eight Dreadnoughts has to be seen in this light. The naval crisis confirmed, rather than weakened, his commitment to Blue Water principles. It reinforced, rather than undermined, the strategic, financial and political priority which he attached to the pursuit of naval security. Unlike others, Balfour did not see a military alternative to increased naval construction.[10] Indeed, the logic of the situation bound him even closer to existing military arrangements. It was not just that the success of the naval campaign would obviate the need for changes in military policy; but that Britain's naval supremacy could only be lastingly maintained if the Territorial Force flourished. Its failure could only mean political and financial distraction from the paramount task of beating off the German naval challenge.

Unionist defence policy for the remainder of 1909 corroborates this assessment of Balfour's outlook. The nationwide party campaign for the additional Dreadnoughts was accompanied by an even closer identification of official Opposition policy with Haldane. In March 1910, at an acute stage in the political crisis over the Budget, Haldane confided to Sir Almeric Fitzroy that he had no fears for the future of his policy in the event of a change of government.[11] His confidence seemed well founded in that the election campaign of December 1909–January 1910 had confirmed the existence of a party consensus on military policy. 'The disappearance of the Army from the party platform is one of the few gratifying circumstances connected with the political crisis', wrote Repington of *The Times*.[12] The army issue was conspicuously absent from the official Unionist platform, in sharp contrast to the priority given to attacking the Liberals' treatment of the Navy. As explained earlier, the Opposition's naval campaign, launched a full nine months before the election, was the manifestation of a deep rift between the parties. In military affairs there was no such rift and thus no pressure or incentive for the Opposition to differentiate its attitude from that of the government. Indeed, there was an obvious risk of distracting public attention from the naval issue which Balfour had worked so hard to push to the centre of the political stage in 1909 and which he and his colleagues regarded as one of the three dominating issues of the election. The Unionist press followed the lead given on the platform by the parliamentary leadership in concentrating the public mind on Dreadnoughts.[13] So, ironically, did the government; by taking up the Unionist gauntlet of debate on the naval issue, ministers contributed to the marginalization of military questions. It is noteworthy, however, that one of the few Liberal speeches to refer to Haldane's reforms advertised the existence of a policy consensus. At Haddington on 3 January, Asquith confidently predicted that 'if the Tory party were to return to power tomorrow you would find that they had turned their back once and for all upon those clumsy, costly and ill-starred experiments for which they were responsible when they were last in office, and that they would proceed upon the lines which Mr Haldane's foresight and statesmanship had laid down'.[14]

In these circumstances, and given the general preoccupation of public and politicians with the fiscal and constitutional issues, the compulsionists found it harder than ever to obtain a hearing in the Unionist party. 'I always hammer away at defence', complained Milner in November, 'though in this hubbub one gets little attention for anything except Tariff'.[15] No less powerful a competitor for attention was the Navy. This was not only the subject on which leading party figures focused their defence speeches, it was also that which aroused greatest public interest. Whereas enthusiasm for the policy of the NSL seems to have been confined to parts of the south-east, interest in and concern for the Navy was a staple element in Unionist electioneering nationwide.[16] The NSL was thus the victim of the Opposition leadership's successful mobilization of party and public opinion on the naval issue since early 1909. The election also dramatically confirmed the priority of party ties and commitments over those of leagues and pressure groups. In the context of intense party polarization, the overlap between its membership and the Unionist party seriously handicapped the League ; the League's activists were powerfully diverted into the Unionist party's struggle to regain power and its leaders came under pressure not to draw attention from the main question, the replacement of Asquith's government.[17] The electorally charged nature of the army issue was plainly an important consideration. Even those who accepted much of the League's case had to acknowledge the justice of Lansdowne's warning that 'the raising of the question at this moment might do harm to the Unionist cause'.[18] Such realism was evinced by H.A. Gwynne; 'What we have to ask ourselves', he wrote, 'is whether we can do more good for the country by coming to power on other cries than this of compulsory service, or whether it will be better to go gloriously to destruction with this absolutely necessary cry inscribed on our banners?'[19] Such calculations, at all levels of the Unionist party, helped to make the January 1910 election the low point of NSL influence; the League could have nothing to hope for from a Unionist victory. By the same token, the election represents the high point of Balfour's attempt to build a system of defence appropriate to imperial needs. Two years earlier Arnold-Forster had scorned his leader's view of military questions as a 'purely fancy picture . . . evolved out of his own consciousness, and from a variety of tags of conversation, scraps of speeches and misapplied general propositions', but in the spring of 1910 that 'fancy picture' rested on solid political and electoral foundations.[20]

There had never been any question that the failure of the Territorial Force would bring the voluntary principle into final disrepute and open the way to compulsion. But until the spring of 1910 all the evidence pointed the other way. Compulsion seemed to have been banished from the British political agenda and the voluntary system to have had the 'last word' after all. But, during the course of the next eighteen months – Balfour's last as Unionist leader – the picture changed dramatically. What happened is the subject of the rest of this chapter.

The catalyst was a decisive slump in recruitment to the Territorial Force during the course of 1910. The government's decision to resume large-scale battleship construction seems to have calmed public anxiety about invasion, and so dampened enthusiasm for enlistment. Not only

did the inflow of recruits halve in the first six months of the year, but the
rate of men seeking discharges also quickened.[21] The Special Reserve
was in no healthier a condition; during 1910 it was the subject of urgent
investigation by a War Office committee.[22] Had Arnold-Forster been
right after all, in warning against 'a go-as-you-please Army, in which
everything will be arranged to suit the convenience of the individuals,
and nothing to suit the exigencies of war'?[23] The Unionist MP Mark
Sykes attributed the decline in recruitment to 'intense work, greater
luxury, more sport and more amusement' among the rich, and to 'high
wages, trips, football matches and cinematograph shows' among the
working classes.[24] Lord Esher wrote in similar vein in the September
issue of the *National Review*; he suggested grimly that 'the sirocco of
democracy' was 'withering in our people the spirit of sacrifice'.[25] Coming
from a man who was not only chairman of the London County
Territorial Association, but also a recognized ally of Haldane, Esher's
assertion that the Territorial Force would never get the 60,000 recruits
it required annually made a significant contribution to the crisis of
confidence in the voluntary system and deeply distressed the Secretary
of State.[26] In public Haldane refused to admit that his scheme was
foundering, but his private mood was less sanguine.[27] Beatrice Webb
found him 'rapidly ageing . . . worried and depressed about his War
Office administration – in a very different state of mind from the buoyant
self-confidence and delight with which he undertook it'.[28]

Aside from the problem of dwindling recruitment, Haldane had to
contend with the agitation of an invigorated National Service League.
The Territorials' precipitate decline transformed the League's fortunes.
Its membership rose from 35,000 in 1909 to 91,142 in 1910–11 and
98,931 in 1912. Now 'a large, vigorous and flourishing organisation', its
expansion after 1909 mirrored its earlier growth in occurring chiefly in
social groups and geographical areas in which the Unionist party was also
strong.[29] Thus the League's largest branches were to be found in London,
the Home Counties and Lancashire. The Unionist press was also more
productive soil than before. Roberts always recognized that his efforts
in Parliament were 'of no use unless . . . supported by the Press' and
assiduously cultivated pressmen.[30] The League's most faithful champion
was Maxse, whose tirades against 'that oily Jesuit the Secretary of State
for War' were a regular feature of each month's *National Review*.[31]
However, sensitive to public opinion and to what Garvin termed 'the
business point of view', even sympathetic editors were generally wary of
giving column space to the League.[32] The effect of the newspapers'
absorption in naval matters was that, as Garvin pointed out to
Repington, 'we have all been far kinder to the Liberal Minister for War
than we were to his Unionist predecessors'.[33] From 1910 this changed
because the combination of the recruiting crisis and the loss of interest
and excitement in naval affairs in the wake of the government's 1910–11

shipbuilding programme made military policy the focus of attention and controversy in the defence debate for the first time since 1907. Hence the 'full chorus of abuse' in the Unionist press of which Haldane complained in July 1910.[34] In Parliament, too, the League's presence in the Unionist party strengthened at this time. It is ironic, in view of its difficulties during the election campaign, that the outcome of the polls proved highly favourable to the League. The January 1910 issue of its journal claimed a total of 155 friendly MPs, as against 43 before.[35] Of a list of 105 sympathetic MPs published by the League in March, only three were Liberal, the remainder Unionist. The League therefore claimed to enjoy the support of two-fifths of the parliamentary Unionist party. It had achieved a base of support in the Commons to match that which it already enjoyed in the Lords and thus seemed well positioned to intensify the pressure on the Unionist leadership. The circle of League adherents overlapped with a wider circle of Unionist MPs who, while perhaps not committed to compulsion, were nevertheless very critical of Haldane's policy and keen to see it subjected to tough scrutiny. The general acrimony of party politics at this time inevitably affected the army debate. Between 1906 and 1910 Haldane had been shielded by Balfour from partisan attack; 'No War Minister has ever had such powerful assistance as Mr Haldane has received', observed Garvin.[36] But the Unionist 'new boys' of 1910, such as Henry Page Croft, were fired up by the electoral fight, conscious of their party's newfound strength in Parliament, and unwilling to see any aspect of Liberal policy go uncontested.[37] 'The W.O. will not have the comfortable time of the past 4 years', wrote Esher in February. 'The Opposition now is powerful and vicious. Every mistake will be severely handled.'[38] These aggressive instincts were to be embodied in the Reveille Movement of September 1910.[39] As far as military matters went, the question was whether backbench pressure, together with the groundswell of compulsionist sympathy throughout the Unionist party in the country, would be sufficient to shake Balfour's habit of collaboration with Haldane. More fundamentally, would the incipient collapse of the Territorial Force open the Unionist leader's mind to departures in policy? The attitude of the party leader inevitably remained the focus of Roberts' attention. Given the nature of policy-making within the Unionist party, it had to be; unless Balfour chose to do so, the party would never raise the flag of compulsion.[40]

On the other hand, it mattered greatly how Balfour's senior colleagues responded to the crisis facing Haldane. The almost constant electioneering of 1909–10, together with the greatly changed parliamentary landscape, appears to have introduced a new openness into Unionist policy-making. More frequent 'shadow cabinet' consultation took place and leading figures were more forward in presenting their opinions on policy matters to Balfour than hitherto. With the credibility of the

Territorial Force much weakened, the pressures were now for leading men to take a view on the military issue. Lobbying by backbenchers added further incentive; it is interesting, for example, that Walter Long, ever-sensitive to currents of opinion on the back benches, adopted a higher profile in army affairs at this time.[41] If a new frontbench consensus were to emerge in favour of applying compulsion to 'salvage' the Territorial Force, Balfour's grip on party policy might be loosened.

In the event, opinion did shift. 1910 saw increasingly outspoken criticism of Haldane from senior Unionists coupled with growing support for some measure of compulsion.[42] Existing sympathizers of the NSL became more assertive, with Midleton trying to organize meetings between Roberts and Balfour, Curzon continuing 'a tower of strength' to the League, and Lee and Wyndham expressing compulsionist views in Parliament.[43] In the Commons, during the Army Estimates debate in March, Lee dealt harshly with Haldane, claiming that his failure must hasten the advent of compulsion.[44] In June, following poor recruiting figures, Wyndham rubbed in the shortcomings of the Territorial Force, and expressed scepticism as to whether, even if at full strength, it was adequate for its purposes; like Lee on the earlier occasion, his preference for compulsion was patent.[45] Wyndham made no secret of 'agreeing with the principles of the League', although as a potential Unionist War Minister he would not commit himself to policy details.[46] He now began to appear more frequently on NSL platforms and in June 1911 moved a resolution at the League's annual meeting in the Queen's Hall.[47] The compulsionist cause had made two significant converts by that time – Lansdowne and Long. In June 1909 Lansdowne had agreed with Roberts that compulsion for home defence was becoming 'less repugnant' to British opinion.[48] Nevertheless, he still held that public opinion was not ready to accept compulsory service in that or any form. Consequently, he had backed Balfour's policy stance on the matter and been careful to avoid 'tarring [the party] with the brush of conscription'.[49] By 1911, however, Lansdowne appears to have undergone a gradual change of heart on the issue, although his conclusion differed from that advocated by the League. 'The more I consider the question', he wrote to Salisbury in April of that year, 'the more I am disposed to think that what we want is universal military training to be put in between *aet* 14 & 17'.[50] Long, for his part, had explained to Balfour in October 1910 that, while he did not agree with those claiming that the Territorial Force was a 'complete failure', he did believe that 'Haldane's plan has not produced & will not produce enough *men* & that we must find a way to do this.'[51] By the spring of 1911 he was describing himself as 'strongly in favour of doing something in regard to Compulsory Training and Universal Service'.[52]

For various reasons, however, this new receptivity towards compulsion on the part of former ministers interested in the defence debate was not to be reflected in any outward change in party policy.

The first was disagreement, and uncertainty, about what exactly was required or practicable.[53] As the decline of the Territorial Force brought the prospect of compulsion nearer, the programme of the NSL was scrutinized more closely than before. This attention to detail is evidence of the ground gained by the League since the end of 1909. The question most often asked was, would the period of compulsory training proposed for the Territorial Force make as much difference to its efficiency as the League claimed? Under scrutiny the vagueness of the League's policy on a number of points, such as the number and training of officers, became evident. The most glaring imprecision came in the matter of cost. To politicians considering the subject seriously for the first time, these practical difficulties were a compelling reason (and a good excuse) for avoiding hasty commitment. Austen Chamberlain thought it 'very difficult to form a just judgement . . . without special information'.[54] The generalized nature of Walter Long's pronouncements can be explained similarly. To Midleton, anxious to exploit the newly favourable mood among his colleagues, the League's lack of any detailed and authoritative proposals appeared a serious handicap. Without detailed evidence, Chamberlain, for instance, could not be persuaded that compulsion offered a solution to Britain's military problem, 'the most difficult in the world'.[55] So Midleton suggested to Milner in April 1910 that the League should create an investigatory commission (on the lines of the Tariff Reform Commission of 1903) to pronounce on the points at issue. 'What we want to hear is say, Given $\frac{1}{2}$ regular officers, $\frac{1}{2}$ regular N.C.O.s, & a nucleus of privates, with what training could a regiment [of Territorials] be made fit to march in England against Continental troops.'[56] Midleton's idea was that the report of such a commission, whose members would be distinguished soldiers, would not only resolve doubts about the feasibility of applying compulsion to the Territorial Force, but also reassure politicians about the state of military opinion. He maintained that 'the doubt which exists in the minds of politicians as to the effect upon the electorate of proposing national service would be largely dissolved if they could see their way to some scheme which was likely to be permanent and . . . was recommended by anything like a consensus of military authority'.[57] The volatility of military opinion since 1895 had hardened his Unionist colleagues against taking steps in policy which might subsequently be disavowed by experts, argued Midleton, himself the celebrated victim of such a disavowal. He was convinced that his party would not contemplate compulsion unless convinced that it would enjoy the support of successive War Office officials.

Midleton's initiative is interesting because it indicates that leading

Unionists, whatever their private doubts, were positively influenced by
the weight of expert opinion behind Haldane.[58] What made the active
cooperation of the War Office soldiers in Haldane's policy so impressive
was, of course, the contrast it presented with events between 1900 and
1905. Haldane had apparently achieved a degree of expert consensus
which had eluded his hapless Unionist predecessors. The extent of that
consensus was known to the Opposition through Balfour's regular
contact with the General Staff and other officers. In effect, after 1907
there were two rival blocs of military opinion in Britain. One, based on
the War Office, embraced the Army's younger, more progressive and
active soldiers such as Haig, Sir Ian Hamilton and Sir John French; the
other, centred on the NSL, was composed mainly of lesser-known
soldiers or those of a previous generation such as Roberts. The most
influential active officers to support compulsion openly were Sir William
Nicholson and Sir Henry Wilson.[59] The Balfour–Haldane relationship
after 1907 identified Unionist policy squarely with official opinion, as
was explicitly demonstrated by the wording of Northumberland's
amendment in July 1909.[60] Balfour's repeated assurances of continuity of
policy were an expression of confidence in the current army establishment as against its critics; one might see a parallel here with his support
of Fisher against the 'Sanhedrin of Admirals'. Deference to expert
opinion thus reinforced – and might mask – the various military and
political reasons for backing the Territorial experiment. Consequently,
while Haldane's advisers remained committed to the voluntary system,
the League would find it hard to sow doubt in Unionist minds.[61] Hence
the advisers often shared the League's brickbats with their minister;
'Haldane ought to be removed and the four members of the Army
Council placed upon retired pay', wrote Roberts in late 1911.[62] The
object of Midleton's commission proposal of 1910 was to undermine the
credibility of the War Office by presenting to the public and the
Opposition an alternative military consensus. Although the idea did not
materialize, it casts light on an important aspect of the Unionists'
commitment to Haldane.[63]

The second obstacle to the NSL's progress was the continuing impact
of the general political situation. There were two main aspects of this,
other than the absorption of party leaders in other questions, the first
being the need throughout this period for the Opposition to avoid any
policy departures which might lose votes and so block the path back to
power. The electoral parameters of the army debate were more clearly
defined in 1910 than at any point since 1903. Midleton admitted to
Milner that his colleagues continued to regard compulsion as 'an
enormous burden on the country' which would exact 'a great political
sacrifice' from the party that proposed it.[64] There was a general belief

that the adoption of compulsion would reduce the party's chances of regaining office by 50 per cent.[65] Such considerations weighed even with the compulsionist sympathizers on the Unionist Army Committee in the House of Commons among whom Long found apprehension 'that if these questions were to be included in the Party Programme they might bring us some trouble and difficulty'.[66] Once again League supporters showed a good grasp of political realities or, put less charitably, lacked the political courage of their convictions. Now back from South Africa and re-engaged in the political fray, Selborne, though still personally opposed to compulsion, argued that it was the kind of deeply controversial subject for which his political hobby-horse, the referendum, was suited; it entailed, he wrote to F.S. Oliver, a burden which must be 'taken upon their shoulders by the people themselves, and not only by their representatives'.[67] The second political aspect of the issue was its potential impact within the party itself; since many 'Tory peers and squires' continued to work on the Territorial county associations, and many more objected to compulsion, for the party to abandon voluntarism could produce internecine rifts at a time when cohesion, in the interests of victory, was of the essence.[68] With the Tariff Reform debate having erupted again in November 1910 as a result of Balfour's pledge to submit food taxes to a referendum, the time was hardly right for a further test of party unity.[69]

Such factors help explain why frontbench sympathy for compulsion was not translated into action. Much of what new sympathy there was remained a matter of private comment; reference to the issue was cursory and infrequent rather than sustained, reluctant rather than interested. No attempt was made to raise the priority given to army issues in parliamentary or party debate. Roberts protested that the Unionist front bench knew little and cared less about army matters, and that they missed frequent opportunities to score points off Haldane.[70] His complaint echoed that heard from the Beresford faction between 1907 and 1908; in both cases activists grew frustrated at what seemed to them to be frontbench apathy. In both cases, however, apathy was the least appropriate explanation; cool calculation was involved. An examination of the election addresses and speeches of leading party figures at the time of the second general election of 1910 reveals a striking failure to mention, let alone discuss, the military question in public. The consistency in this respect confirms the suggestion of this account that there was a basic uniformity in the approach of senior Unionists to the army debate. Whatever the variation between their individual views on the military problem, those views were consistently subordinated to party political interest. That interest just as consistently dictated caution, both in Parliament and on the platform.

Balfour deliberately excluded the army from his agenda for the election campaign.[71] He studiously avoided public comment on military affairs throughout 1910 and 1911, making no effort to resolve the confused and uneasy state of opinion among his colleagues.[72] Yet like them, Balfour had been influenced by the declining fortunes of the Territorial Force. In contrast to the period 1907–9, there is a marked absence of positive comment about the Force in his speeches and correspondence during 1910 and 1911. Privately, he acknowledged the strength of the case against the Territorials and found the logic of Wyndham's argument that the force had exposed the limits of the voluntary system 'convincing and most disturbing'.[73] Why he should be so disturbed is easy to understand. Having defused the threat posed to the 'Blue Water policy' by the naval reductions of 1906–9, Balfour was now confronted with a new challenge to it. Another piece, it seemed, was being removed from the defence policy jigsaw so laboriously assembled since 1903. Given this concern, why was the Unionist leader not moved to action?

The first point to make is that Balfour's concern had limits. The shortfall in Territorial recruitment was a problem of lesser magnitude than the recent growth of German naval power. By securing the country against invasion, the 'recovery' of British naval supremacy in 1910–11 had removed the possibility that the Territorial Force might be called upon to repel anything more serious than a raid. 'If the Army remains as it is, I do not think our national existence is imperilled', wrote Balfour to Midleton in March 1911.[74] 'If the Navy is not strong enough, we perish.' Such a remark was entirely consistent with Balfour's outlook on national defence since the 1880s. In the circumstances of 1910–11, however, it acquired a fresh significance. Hitherto, naval supremacy and adequate land forces at home had been complementary parts of an overall system of defence; Balfour had always criticized the NSL for tending to present them as alternatives, a tendency the League always tried to avoid.[75] Now Balfour was himself falling into the same trap. He was arguing, in effect, that provided the Navy remained dominant, deficiencies in Britain's land defences could be tolerated. He refused to contemplate the obvious military solution to the problem, reiterating his 'great many reasons, military and political' for objecting to the adoption of compulsion.[76] He continued, above all, to regard it as a dangerous diversion from the task of naval mastery; the £8 million which was estimated by the League to be the cost of its programme would, if available, be better spent on Dreadnoughts.[77] If the Navy was supreme, Britain had no need of a compulsorily raised home army. On the other hand, if such an army were to be adopted, Britain might not be able to afford the supreme Navy without which no military force would suffice. Nor can Balfour have needed reminding that, as Esher put it, 'an armed force at home, able, beyond doubt, to hold its own against any probable invading enemy, would gradually but surely lead to the weakening of the Fleet'; compulsory training would present the Radicals with a crushing argument for cuts in the Navy.[78]

In the light of this reasoning, the relationship between Balfour's high profile on naval questions and his low profile on army questions becomes intelligible. Shaped by his navalist instincts, and his opposition to compulsion, his response to the *military* crisis of the voluntary system took a *naval* form. But Balfour was not only prepared to discount the evident weaknesses of the Territorials; he was also determined to prevent them becoming a political issue at all. To some extent this was a matter of political self-interest. Since 1907 the root issue in the army debate had been the 'last word of the voluntary system'. The debate had become structured as a stark choice between conflicting alternatives; voluntarism versus compulsion, Haldane versus the NSL. This polarization, for which Haldane bore major responsibility, admitted of no compromise positions. To repudiate or question the Secretary of State's efforts was to lend strength to the League, as the Esher episode had shown. Because Haldane had cast his scheme as 'a last alternative to some form of compulsion', any change in the Unionist position was fraught with electoral risk; in the circumstances of 1911 it would inevitably have been trumpeted by the League, and interpreted by the government and public opinion, as a move towards the compulsionist camp.[79] By creating a party consensus in the army debate, the early success of the Territorials had obscured the fact that the Secretary of State for War occupied the only politically safe ground. It was only the decline of the Force which made it obvious and an awareness of this must have coloured Balfour's attitude. But, like his position on successive defence issues, the Unionist leader's refusal to allow the Territorial Force to become an issue between the parties was more than tactical. It seems clear that he remained committed to the framework of military organization created since 1907, regarding it as the best job yet done with Britain's given military resources. Balfour reminded Esher in August 1910 that, for all its shortage of men, the Territorial Force was 'much better than the old Volunteers'.[80] He also assured Esher that, if re-elected, he intended to maintain continuity at the War Office; 'I am not aware', he wrote, 'of any practical substitute for a voluntary second line – or first line either'. The corollary of this was continued support for Haldane's present efforts to revitalize the flagging Territorial Force and defend it against its detractors in the NSL and elsewhere.[81] Haldane commented on their bond in February 1911; 'I can generally manage Arthur Balfour', he wrote, 'for he & I see a good many things from the same point of view'.[82] The Secretary of State had continued to involve Balfour in his activities

throughout 1910, notwithstanding the fast and furious party struggle
raging around them. At the height of the row over Asquith's negotiations with the Irish Nationalists in March, he sought the 'assent' of the
Opposition leader to the appointment of General Ewart to be Director-
General of the Territorial Force. 'I do not like to take steps in Army
matters much in advance without consulting you', Haldane wrote.[83]

Balfour's passive approach to the military situation did not enjoy the
support of his frontbench colleagues. For the first time since 1902 – a
significant statistic – there arose serious dissatisfaction with his conduct
of defence policy. That dissatisfaction did not, however, manifest itself
in pressure on Balfour to espouse a compulsory solution to the plight of
the Territorial Force. As will be clear by now, the political dangers
inherent in any such action were universally recognized and lost none of
their force during this period. For all their private mutterings about compulsion, leading Unionists saw the virtue of public discretion. Where
Balfour encountered dissent was in his continued willingness to shield
Haldane from partisan criticism and in his disinclination to find some
other way of distinguishing Opposition policy from that of the government. Here one must again bear in mind the general political context of
1910–11; as a period of intense bitterness and fundamental conflict
between the parties moved towards its crisis over the Parliament bill in
July 1911, the Unionist party experienced a series of sharp internal disputes over a range of issues, the common theme of which was growing
backbench militancy and an increasing strain on the authority of the
leadership at Westminster.[84] Pressure on the front bench to take the
fight to the government mounted in the wake of the abortive Constitutional Conference, which many activists on the back benches and in
the press had regarded as a futile and unjustified interruption to the party
struggle. Against this background – which historians see as the climax of
the 'crisis of Conservatism' – criticism of Balfour's leadership became more
strident, the major themes being his alleged failure to articulate clear
policy positions and his supposed willingness to subordinate principles to
tactics.[85] The chief mouthpiece of such sentiment was Maxse, who
lambasted 'Mr Balfour's too friendly relations with the other side with
whom he is frequently prepared to do a deal at the expense of
Unionism'.[86] Defence was central to Maxse's indictment and to his
vigorous 'Balfour Must Go' campaign of September to November 1911.
'Of late years', he asserted in November 1911, 'the Opposition has had
no policy whatsoever as regards National Defence . . . . We seem to have
tacitly abandoned the two-power standard without having replaced it by
the two keels to one standard, and we have quietly looked on while
Haldane has reduced the regular army and has wasted six years over this
territorial fiasco.'[87] In Maxse's view, Balfour had let Haldane off 'much
too cheaply'; it was deplorable that the Opposition should have

'bolstered up' a man 'who at a most critical moment in the history of this country has made us relatively weaker as a military power simply because he feared to look facts in the face and preferred to pretend that paper forces could cope with armies made of flesh and blood'.[88] Maxse's comments show how the the combination of acute party political tensions and the decline of the Territorial Force had brought Balfour's support of Haldane into a harsh new political light.

Growing backbench irritation was bound to affect Balfour's colleagues, keen to maintain their influence within the party at a time of political turbulence. In 1910–11 one finds signs that they felt uncomfortable pulling their punches in the army debate and chafed at Balfour's insistence on restraint. Haldane observed how, in Balfour's absence from the House of Commons during debates on army affairs, the tone and substance of Opposition speeches acquired a new belligerence; 'Mr Balfour was away & they did not behave well', he wrote of Opposition obstruction of the army vote in July 1910.[89] From outside, Roberts moaned that 'Balfour believes in Haldane, and all on his side of the House follow his lead.'[90] But this was to underestimate the strain that Balfour's fidelity was producing. Their angry parliamentary outbursts in his absence, a kind of schoolboyish defiance, were one symptom of unease. Private comments were another, like Lee's cryptic accusation that Haldane had 'bamboozled' the Opposition leader.[91] Cross-bench collaboration went against the grain in circumstances when, as the chief whip advised in September 1911, the key to maintaining party morale and unity was 'aggressive and sustained criticism of everything the Govt proposes'.[92]

However, as important a cause of dissatisfaction was the feeling among Balfour's colleagues that the party had come to lack a coherent and publicly identifiable military policy, a sentiment much to the fore in the early activities of the Halsbury Club. The Club's founders and members were brought together in the wake of the passage of the Parliament Act by a desire to rebuild party morale and regain fighting momentum ahead of the anticipated clash over Home Rule.[93] They had also been joined in opposition to Balfour's decision to allow the Parliament bill to pass rather than risk a massive Liberal peer creation. The Club's leading figures included a range of militants such as Milner, F.E. Smith, L.S. Amery and George Lloyd, alongside frontbenchers such as Chamberlain, Selborne, Wyndham and the Cecil brothers, Lords Hugh and Robert; it was only because of the influence of this last group in restraining their militant associates that the Club professed loyalty to Balfour. Neverthe-less, the Halsbury Club's stated object of 'work[ing] out the problems connected with the great questions for which a solution had to be found' implicitly condemned the party leader for having failed to formulate a distinctive party policy on a range of issues from the Constitution to

unemployment.[94] This was a charge levelled repeatedly in the press and
constituencies since 1906 and a deliberate challenge to Balfour's 'general
rule' – imposed by him in the Navy debate since 1909 – that a party
should refuse to formulate detailed policy until in power and in a position
to put plans into effect. Prominent among those issues to which the Club
proposed to devote constructive attention was national defence.
Wyndham, who became chairman of a subcommittee on defence
matters, urged the need to 'speak more plainly about national dangers
and National Defence'.[95] Austen Chamberlain confessed himself 'glad to
see National Defence more frankly discussed and more closely studied'.[96]
In part this was a reaction to the ambiguity in Unionist naval policy since
the eclipse of the two-power standard. Above all, however, it was a
reaction to the ambiguity of the party's position on the military issue. 'So
far as I know' wrote Selborne, 'the party has no policy on these
subjects'.[97] The interest of the Club in defence was symptomatic of twin
concerns among ministerial Unionists: first, that Haldane's policy had
failed and that the country required an alternative, albeit yet unspecified;
second, that the Unionist party should reassert its independence of
Haldane, extending to the military sphere the kind of partisan choice
available to the electorate in every other area of policy.

In retrospect, the first nine months of 1911 can be seen as a period in
which Balfour's authority as party leader steadily diminished. By the
autumn he was weary and dispirited; in November he lost the will to
struggle on and resigned, throwing the party into temporary turmoil.[98]
Balfour's handling of army affairs, and particularly his kid-gloves
approach to Haldane, had contributed to the crisis of his leadership by
antagonizing militants such as Maxse. It had also contributed to the
general sense of drift and lack of purpose within the party of which the
Halsbury Club was a product, and thus to the erosion of Balfour's
authority over his colleagues which was a conspicuous feature of the
period from June to November 1911. By the autumn of 1911 the
consensus within Balfour's shadow Cabinet was more closely aligned
than before with those on the Unionist back benches and in the press
who wanted the party to abandon Haldane and declare for compulsory
training. The outward continuity of Unionist policy during Balfour's last
year or so as leader masked the final fragmentation of that frontbench
consensus in favour of Haldane's policy which had characterized the
period 1907–1910.

However, as in previous phases of the army debate their position
on the front bench imposed restraints on Balfour's colleagues. The
frontbench perspective amounted, as we have repeatedly seen, to a
narrower vision of the politically possible than was enjoyed from the back
benches or editorial offices. It also embraced a range of less cynical
disciplines, Wyndham's 'political predilections' and 'personal ties'.[99] By

the autumn of 1911, the most obvious of the latter was deference to Balfour. After six years during which he had dominated the defence policy of the party, his presence was a formidable obstacle to action by his colleagues, particularly since they shared no more than a general desire for change and had no specific policy to oppose to his. It is worth suggesting that their position was further weakened by the 'Balfour Must Go' campaign; loyal colleagues had no wish to see their policy differences with Balfour unwittingly fuel Maxse's *putsch* against his leadership. A clue to Wyndham's attitude is to be found in a letter he wrote to Balfour in 1903, when his support for the policy of Tariff Reform threatened to distance him from Balfour. 'In a difficult "cas de conscience" I hold that primary loyalties override all else. I shall therefore stick to you, through thick and thin', Wyndham assured the then Prime Minister.[100] One may only speculate on what might have happened had Balfour not resigned the leadership of the party. By November 1911 tensions seemed to be coming to a head. Would he have acknowledged the views of his colleagues and agreed to rethink military policy? Or would he have driven them into open dispute by refusing to shift from the policy ground on which he had stood since 1903? Since his objections to compulsion did not diminish after 1911 one can hazard that, had he not resigned, the likeliest outcome would have been a row.[101] In the event, his departure left the problem of resolving the dilemmas of Unionist policy to his successor Andrew Bonar Law. Law's was to be a thankless inheritance in many ways, but in none more so than in the sphere of military policy. His difficulties are the subject of the following chapter.

The Continental Commitment 1911

In the summer of 1911, in response to a French expedition to Fez, the German government dispatched a warship, the *Panther*, to the Moroccan port of Agadir.[102] This *démarche*, which triggered a European war scare which would last several months, had two main purposes; to challenge France's preponderant influence in Morocco and to achieve a diplomatic success which would ease the domestic political difficulties of the government in Berlin. It was also intended to test the cohesion of the Anglo-French *entente*; the expectation in the Wilhelmstrasse was that Britain would not risk war with Germany to safeguard France's creeping protectorate in Morocco and that France, humiliated, would repay *la perfide Albion* by seeking a German *rapprochement*. In the event *der Panthersprung* backfired. A trenchant speech by Lloyd George at the Mansion House on 21 July left Berlin in no doubt that Britain would not stand aloof.[103] At the height of the crisis, on 23 August, the CID met to consider Britain's strategic options in the event of the government deciding to intervene militarily to help France resist German aggression.[104] At the War Office an atmosphere of 'semi-scare and scramble' prevailed as officials rushed to ready the British Expeditionary Force for mobilization.[105] The government opened discussions with the railway companies and trade unions to ensure the smooth passage of troops to the ports. The crisis blew over in the autumn, when a Franco-German colonial agreement was signed, but it had exposed the underlying strength of Britain's alignment with France. It was not any sense of formal obligation which motivated the Asquith government to prepare itself for war, but rather a sense of Britain's own self-interest. A crushing German military victory over France would not only give Germany continental hegemony, but could also give her access to the Channel ports and thus the means to threaten both Britain's island security and her maritime empire.[106] A crushing German diplomatic victory would destroy the *entente* which had been the basis of British policy since 1904, reopening old Anglo-French frictions in the Mediterranean and Africa, jeopardizing Britain's *entente* with Russia, and crippling her diplomatic freedom of manoeuvre towards Germany. It was these hard-headed political and strategic interests which dictated the response of Sir Edward Grey and his colleagues to the *Panther's* provocative leap.

The significance of the Agadir crisis for a study of Unionist defence policy is twofold. First, as will be explained in the next chapter, it had a decisive influence on the attitude of the Opposition to the problem of the Territorial Force in the years 1912–14. Second, and to be discussed here, it forced the Unionist leadership to confront the prospect of Britain's involvement in a Franco-German war. The Unionist government had secured the *entente* and bequeathed it to their successors. In Opposition they supported its continuation and its *de facto* extension to Russia in 1907. But the significant point is that they regarded it simply as a *diplomatic* arrangement. The evidence suggests that Balfour and his colleagues were not aware before September 1911 of the military dimension which had been added to the *entente* by Grey and Haldane in January 1906. Nor, despite Balfour's close contacts with Esher who was a permanent member of the CID, did they know of the plans for British military cooperation with France which were devised at the War Office after 1906 and which were discussed at the CID in 1908–9. Although it dimmed from 1908–9, the vision of future war which informed Unionist comments on military policy had Central Asia as the theatre and Russia as the enemy. When Unionists talked about or wrote about war with Germany between 1906 and 1911 it was wholly in naval terms. They also envisaged an Anglo-German war rather than one between Germany and the *entente* powers together. The Agadir crisis transformed their outlook. At Balmoral in early September Balfour first learned from Sir Edward Grey of the Anglo-French military conversations and realized that the loose *entente* of 1904 had changed character to the point where there was now prospect of Britain joining France to fight Germany on land in Europe.[107] 'It came upon me as a shock of surprise', wrote Balfour in 1912, '. . . when I found how rapidly after I left office the Entente had, under the German menace, developed into something resembling a defensive Alliance'.[108]

Yet there was universal support on the front Opposition bench for Asquith's readiness to render military assistance to France.[109] At Balmoral in September Balfour promised the government full Opposition support if war came.[110] Austen Chamberlain typified his colleagues' view in arguing that 'nothing but the clear indication that we should take a hand in the fighting had restrained Germany from attacking France'.[111] The Unionists' attitude in the summer of 1911 cannot be attributed to a previous preoccupation with the military balance of power on the Continent. For this one searches the archives and Hansard in vain. It was rather the result of almost a decade of concern over German *naval* expansion, heightened since 1909 and coupled with a general sense, which the Agadir episode confirmed, that Germany's ambitions were a threat to peace. 'A war entered upon for no other object than to restore the Germanic Empire of Charlemagne in a modern form appears to me at once so wicked and so stupid as to be almost incredible', observed Balfour in March 1912: 'And yet it is almost impossible to make sense of modern German policy without crediting them with this intention.'[112] As Keith Wilson has argued of Grey, Unionists did not regard maintaining the integrity of France against Germany as an alternative to defending the Empire.[113] Because the domination of Europe by a great military power which was also Britain's greatest rival at sea would ultimately make the retention of British naval supremacy impossible, maintaining the integrity of France was also a vital British interest.[114] The key to imperial security lay in what Garvin called 'the old historic situation in Flanders'.[115] Detachment from European war could also jeopardize the 'very existence of the Empire' in another sense since failure to support France would expose Britain to the charge of *perfide Albion*, destroy the *entente* and reopen the old imperial struggle with France and Russia in the Mediterranean, Near East and Asia. A vengeful France, a humiliated Russia and an ascendant Germany would be a nightmare combination against which Britain could not hope to contend successfully.[116]

The Radical Lord Loreburn, a critic of Grey, believed in December 1911 that a Unionist government would 'not be deeply committed, like Grey, to an extravagant championship of France', but this was misguided.[117] In June 1912 Balfour even wrote a memorandum for Grey favouring the conversion of the informal *entente* into a formal alliance.[118] In the Commons in July 1912 Bonar Law described the preservation of close relations with France as the keynote of British foreign policy and

endorsed the broad lines of Grey's diplomacy.[119] The Unionists' support
for the dispatch of the British Expeditionary Force to France in a future
Franco-German war was unswerving from 1911 to 1914 and, as will be
seen in the next chapter, dictated their approach to questions of military
policy. It might be supposed therefore that 1911 marks a final shift away
from the imperial orientation which had characterized Unionist defence
policy since the South African War. But this was not to be the case.
While their attention focused increasingly on the contingency of a
European war, the Opposition continued to regard problems of defence
policy from an 'imperial' perspective. A concern for the vulnerability of
Britain's interests in 'the whole of the Eastern world from Tripoli to the
China Sea' runs through official Opposition speeches in the years 1912 to
1914. It is evident in discussions of the future role of the Expeditionary
Force, when Unionists emphasized what Curzon called 'the Imperial
call'. He reminded the House of Lords in April 1913 that the British
Empire had a land frontier of some 20,000 miles and that the Expedi-
tionary Force was as likely to have to defend that frontier in Egypt or
India as to fight in Belgium.[120] It was in the debate on naval policy that
imperial considerations most conspicuously coloured Unionist policy.
The Opposition consistently expressed unease about the extent to which
Britain's naval resources were being absorbed by the task of matching
Germany in the North Sea. They argued that superiority in home waters
was being maintained at the expense of the Navy's wider imperial role.
As Leo Amery put it in July 1912:

> To meet the menace arising in the narrow seas, we have abdicated the
> primary function of the Navy in the defence of the British
> Empire . . . to command the seas which unite our scattered Empire, to
> keep open the ocean highway for our supplies of food . . . and for the
> passage of those troops which may be required to safeguard and protect
> any part of the Empire.[121]

Wyndham and others argued that the corollary of increased naval
concentration in home waters was a strengthening of Britain's imperial
garrisons. No longer protected by local sea command, they must be made
self-reliant.[122]

The Unionists reacted strongly when in 1912 the Admiralty proposed
to meet the German Navy Law of 1912 by reducing Britain's naval
presence in the Mediterranean to a squadron of armoured cruisers.[123]
They argued that it was essential for Britain to retain a battleship fleet in
the Mediterranean for the purpose of defending the routes to Egypt, India
and Australia. 'A naval force in the Mediterranean strong enough to
overcome any probable combination against us is essential for the continued existence of the British Empire', Law told the Commons in July
1912.[124] Lee countered the government's claim that the Mediterranean

could be reinforced in war by contending that sea power had a vital peacetime role to play; it guaranteed 'that vast, intangible, but at the same time vital asset of our prestige amongst the Mahommedan peoples and other dwellers on the shores of the Mediterranean'.[125] Selborne, who led the Opposition's campaign against the withdrawal from the Mediterranean, asserted that 'the prestige of this Empire in the Mediterranean is just as solid a material asset to this Empire as . . . coal-mines . . . or the gold in the Bank of England'.[126] Despite their commitment to the *entente*, Unionists were hostile to the suggestion that Britain should look to an agreement with France as a substitute for independent sea power in the Mediterranean. 'This country', declared Selborne, 'ought never to be in the position of having to depend . . . on the loyalty, efficiency and courage of some ally for the protection of all our interests in the Mediterranean'.

In the event, resistance to its plans from the War Office and Cabinet forced the Admiralty to agree to keep in the Mediterranean a battle fleet equal to a one-power standard. Although the objections of Unionists were not of primary importance to the outcome of what became a vigorous ministerial dispute, they do illustrate the point that the Opposition's strategic horizons did not change overnight in 1911. Their new preoccupation with the Franco-German frontier, where 'every night in the year . . . sentries stood facing each other with loaded and . . . cocked rifles', did not efface a traditional Unionist concern for what Lansdowne called 'our old position in the Mediterranean'.[127]

CHAPTER 13

New Leader, Old Realities 1911–14

From Balfour to Bonar Law

'Arthur . . . takes too scientific a view of politics', remarked George Wyndham of Balfour in February 1911; 'He knows that there was once an ice age, and that there will someday be an ice age again. This makes him indifferent.'[1] Balfour is frequently depicted in such terms as a man whose intellect ruined him for politics; he is seen as incapable of the passion and conviction required for effective leadership. It will be clear from the account presented of him here that such a view must be qualified. The anger and energy of his campaign in 1909–10 to restore Britain's naval security reflected a profound conviction that Britain's 'national and Imperial structure' was founded on naval supremacy and that to maintain that supremacy was the paramount responsibility of any British government. His role in the Navy debate shows that he was neither temperamentally nor intellectually incapable of supplying the positive and pugnacious leadership called for by his Radical Right critics.

Indeed, the insecure nature of Balfour's authority over the party after the tariff split in 1903 – on which historians place much stress – is not visible in the defence debate until the last eighteen months of his leadership. Defence policy was comparatively uncontentious throughout the period 1906 to 1910. Such criticism as there was emanated from a random collection of journalists and backbenchers – haters of Fisher or advocates of compulsion – who failed to weaken the loyalty of Balfour's frontbench colleagues to his policy. Only in 1910 did the frontbench consensus crumble on the military question and even then dissent was constrained by a common political prudence. Because they invariably emphasize the importance of extra-parliamentary politics, in which his leadership has serious weaknesses, and focus on socioeconomic issues on which he spoke in dated tones, most accounts of Balfour's leadership leave one wondering why it was that he was not driven out sooner. A study of the defence debate provides an answer by directing attention to Balfour's mastery in the parliamentary sphere – Garvin attributed to him an 'unrivalled ascendancy over the House of Commons' – and to issues

'Dialectics', cartoon of A.J. Balfour by 'XIT', *Vanity Fair*, 27 January 1910.

on which he spoke with almost oracular authority.[2] There was no other statesman of the period, not even Churchill, whose political reputation derived so largely from an identification with defence policy. Garvin wrote to him in June 1912: 'There is not another man but yourself who really moves the national mind on these questions.'[3] In his memoirs Repington recalls NSL speakers being met with 'Why should we serve? Mr Balfour says invasion is impossible.'[4] The attention he received from pressure groups is as clear an index of his authority as the support he received from colleagues.

Balfour's knowledge of military and naval issues was amateur but extensive. One need only refer back to his army reform scheme or to a speech in Glasgow in October 1910 when he delivered a brilliant *tour d'horizon* of naval policy.[5] What fascinated Balfour most was the impact of technological change on warfare. Fisher acknowledged their 'common bond in the submarine and the big gun'.[6] At Weymouth in May 1912 Balfour actually travelled in a submerged submarine.[7] Three years earlier he had been present at a flying demonstration by Wilbur Wright at Pau.[8] It would be wrong, however, to overemphasize the technical nature of his interest in defence issues. J.A.Spender described Balfour as possessing 'a very cool executive sort of brain which made his counsel of high value in the wide range of imperial and strategic problems into which party politics do not enter'.[9] This is supported by Professor Mackay's picture of Balfour as an 'intellectual statesman' but called into question by the evidence presented here. Balfour took an intensely *political* interest in defence questions. On the one hand, he was moved by considerations of political feasibility; what defences could Britain afford and what means of defence would her political culture permit? On the other hand, he consistently saw defence policy in party political terms. Between 1902 and 1905 this entailed framing policy to fit parliamentary imperatives and between 1906 and 1911 electoral ones. The saga of compulsion illustrates this perfectly.

From a different perspective Balfour can indeed be seen to have approached defence issues in a non-partisan manner. We have seen this in both naval and military policy after December 1905. His support for Haldane – 'the spoiled darling of party politics' as Arthur Lee dubbed him – and Fisher had the effect of insulating important matters of policy from the icy blasts of adversarial politics. If, as the historian Julian Corbett believed, Fisher's five years as First Sea Lord marked an epoch 'as clearly and indisputably as Nelson did his', then some measure of the credit for the reform of the Edwardian Navy belongs to Balfour, on whose political patronage Fisher leaned so heavily.[10] Party advantage was also sacrificed in Balfour's willingness to align the Opposition with the Liberal Imperialists to defeat Radical agitations for economy. Balfour was not slow to take credit for his action, declaring grandiloquently:

> Never in the history of Opposition has so much trouble been taken to keep . . . the defence of Empire as far as may be outside the area of party controversy.[11]

The validity of the claim was recognized not only by friends such as Esher, but also by opponents.[12] 'It would be unfair not to do justice to Mr Balfour's patriotism with regard to the Navy', conceded McKenna in 1910; 'there is no one who has done more than he to help the Navy out of party discussions'.[13] Of course, Balfour's restraint was not a matter of sentiment or disinterest but the instrument of policy. He cooperated as long as doing so produced results. When it did not, as in 1909–10, the gloves came off.

Balfour's cross-bench instincts were given freer rein after his resignation. Between 1912 and 1914 he enjoyed friendly links with the new First Lord, Winston Churchill, and with Haldane's successor, Jack Seely, who briefed him on policy and sent him confidential papers and documents.[14] Churchill regularly invited him to join parties on the Admiralty yacht *Enchantress* for naval manoeuvres; 'I am arranging this plan almost entirely for you and the Prime Minister', Churchill wrote on one occasion in June 1913, '& I do hope you will be able to come. There will be no ceremonies of any kind, & nothing but naval officers, naval exercises, & naval arguments'.[15] Balfour's new role as 'confidant & adviser' to the government on defence matters was a source of amusement rather than embarrassment to his colleagues since, treating his resignation as retirement, the former leader chose not to take an active part in parliamentary defence debates in the immediate pre-war years.[16] In 1913 Balfour's status as a cross-bench guru on defence issues was formalized when Asquith invited him – as an expert – to sit on a subcommittee of the CID set up to reinvestigate the invasion issue. The peculiarity of Balfour's role is well illustrated by his arriving at the committee's final meeting on 26 March 1914 fresh from addressing a major anti-Home Rule rally: 'I spent the first part of the afternoon abusing the Government in the City', Balfour remarked to Hankey, 'and the second part in solving their difficulties in the House of Commons'.[17]

Balfour was succeeded as leader by Andrew Bonar Law, a dour Scottish ironmaster elected to Parliament in 1900.[18] Law had been Parliamentary Secretary to the Board of Trade in the government of 1902–5 but lacked experience of defence matters. Through the Tariff Reform movement, however, in which he was an influential figure, he had been brought into contact with people interested in defence issues and had become well informed. He had spoken from the Opposition front bench during the dramatic Navy debate of March 1909. As a rising star in the party, Law was wooed by both the NSL and Beresford but, significantly, had been careful to avoid commitment to either.[19] There is no evidence to suggest that he disagreed with party defence policy under Balfour or that he came to the leadership with strong independent views.

Law had emerged as a candidate for the leadership when it became clear that neither of the principal contenders, Austen Chamberlain and Walter Long, could command a majority of support among Unionist MPs.[20] As a compromise selection, Law's authority was insecure, and as a result he was more open to pressure from influential colleagues than Balfour had been. With the experienced Lansdowne remaining leader of the Unionist party in the House of Lords, Law would be denied the autonomy in policy that Balfour had enjoyed. This was nowhere more true than in the sphere of defence where his inexperience further weakened his hand. The new leader was surrounded by colleagues with ministerial experience and firm views on defence matters who were looking for a greater influence over party policy than had been possible in the Balfour 'era'. Had Balfour not deliberately withdrawn from active engagement in the defence debate, Law's position would have been further embarrassed.

Although one of the most frequent complaints about Balfour as leader had been his failure to convene regular 'shadow Cabinets', by early 1913 Law too had begun to avoid summoning that body on the grounds of its

excessive size and unwieldiness.[21] The formulation of party defence
policy devolved on to a smaller group of interested ex-ministers who also
filled the parliamentary gap left by Balfour's withdrawal from an active
frontbench role. Following Cawdor's death in 1911, Selborne assumed
responsibility for naval policy, with Arthur Lee (supported by Ernest
Pretyman) continuing to speak for the Opposition in the House of
Commons. The responsibility for Unionist military policy was less clearly
defined though the most conspicuous feature of the pre-war years is the
recovery of influence by Midleton and the emergence of Curzon into
the front rank. Midleton's attempt to secure overall responsibility for
Opposition policy led to friction with George Wyndham, who was now
chief spokesman in the Commons and had expectations of being War
Minister in the next Unionist government.[22] This confusion, which Law
did nothing to resolve, persisted until Wyndham's sudden death at
Fontainebleau in June 1913. With Arthur Lee succeeding Wyndham as
Commons spokesman on army affairs, Midleton's primacy was now
assured. There was now no one on the Commons front bench with War
Office experience. By 1913, therefore, the naval and military policy of
the Opposition lay in the hands of peers. (It is paradoxical that whereas
under the patrician Balfour Unionist policy had chiefly been decided and
articulated in the House of Commons, under the *bourgeois* Bonar Law it
emanated from the House of Lords.)

The trend towards a collective defence policy in the pre-war years was
accentuated by Law's growing preoccupation with the Irish crisis. 'The
son of a Presbyterian minister who had been born in Ulster and had died
in Ulster', Law had a deep personal stake in the fight against Irish Home
Rule.[23] This was to be the dominating issue of his leadership and to
absorb the greater part of his energies. All other political questions were
cast in its shadow. Law was not, as Arthur Lee later alleged, 'entirely
sceptical and apparently uninterested' in defence matters, but his interest
was not deep enough to resist the pull of the unfolding Ulster crisis.[24]
Defence issues were a distraction from the overriding goal of saving the
Union and, worse, a potential source of internal disunity at a time when
the Unionist party most needed cohesion. If Law never gave defence
matters the attention that Balfour had, this was due as much to fear of
the consequences as to preoccupation elsewhere.

'You've Made Me Love You'

In October 1911, much to the chagrin of Haldane who had wanted the
post himself, Winston Churchill, then Home Secretary, was appointed
First Lord of the Admiralty with a brief to overhaul the war organization
of the Admiralty and to improve coordination between Admiralty and
War Office.[25] It was the Agadir crisis which had placed Admiralty reform

on the political agenda. When the CID convened at the height of the crisis on 23 August, Asquith and other ministers present were appalled to discover the 'puerile' state of naval war planning and the extent to which the Admiralty had reneged on an undertaking given at the CID in 1909 to cooperate with the General Staff in preparing contingency plans for despatching the British Expeditionary Force to the European mainland.[26] Asquith's decision to replace McKenna with the Radical Churchill was less eccentric than it would have been two years earlier when Churchill was raging against the Admiralty's demand for eight Dreadnoughts.[27] The events of the summer of 1911 had propelled Churchill from militant Little Navyism to a hard-headed conviction of the German 'threat' and a determination to ensure that Britain would have the military and naval means to assist France resist German aggression. 'Liberal politics, the People's Budget, Free Trade, Peace, Retrenchment and Reform – all the war cries of our election struggles began to seem unreal in the presence of this new preoccupation', he subsequently wrote.[28]

There are several accounts available of Churchill's administration of the Navy between October 1911 and August 1914, in addition to his own vivid record in *The World Crisis*.[29] Here it is only necessary to sketch

'Tenants' Fixtures', cartoon from *Punch*, 1 November 1911.

the main outlines. By establishing an Admiralty War Staff in 1912, Churchill succeeded in his primary purpose of bringing greater direction and clarity to naval war planning. Inter-service coordination was improved by means of the so-called 'High Level Bridge', a liaison committee also set up in 1912. In the technological sphere, Churchill's pre-war period as First Lord saw the Navy's adoption of oil fuel – an innovation more far-reaching even than the *Dreadnought* – and the intensive development of aeroplanes, airships and submarines. In 1913–14 a new qualitative peak was reached in warship construction with the laying down of the *Queen Elizabeth* class, battleships with 15-inch guns, heavy armour and a speed of 25 knots.[30] Qualitative advance was accompanied by a quantitative increase in construction made inevitable by the failure of persistent British attempts to secure a naval arms limitation agreement with Germany – in 1912 via Haldane's mission to Berlin and in 1913 via Churchill's proposal for an Anglo-German 'naval holiday'.[31] Agreement proved impossible for the same reasons as it had in 1909–11; Britain refused to pay the Kaiser's price for staying Tirpitz's hand – a pledge of her neutrality in a continental war.[32] The result was the German Navy Laws of 1912 and 1913, which not only substantially increased the size of the German fleet but also greatly enhanced its immediate war readiness. Churchill's response to this development was to make public the government's commitment to maintaining a 60 per cent margin of superiority over Germany's existing Dreadnought programme and to further pledge that Britain would lay down 'two keels to one' for every additional German Dreadnought built.[33] The two-power standard was thus laid officially to rest. Yet, as Sumida notes, 'the replacement of the two-power standard by the one-power standard did not result in a significant change in the accepted measure of British naval security'; the new standard entailed building just two ships fewer than the old.[34] Through to 1914 Britain retained a commanding lead over Germany in Dreadnoughts and, during 1913–14, actually enjoyed superiority over Germany and the United States combined.[35] Coupled with qualitative changes, particularly the 15-inch gun, this policy pushed the Navy Estimates from £41,471,037 in 1911–12 to £51,609, 402 in 1913–14.[36] A sharp increase in tax yields over the same period enabled these costs to be borne without detriment to the government's social reform programme and thus without provoking political tensions such as those which had racked the Liberal party during its first five years in power. It was only the 1914–15 Estimates, providing for an increase of some £3 million, which came close to shaking the government. Seeking to rally Radical opinion, Lloyd George made a tough stand against Churchill's demands; the allies of 1909 were now antagonists. After a protracted Cabinet crisis, a saving compromise emerged by which Lloyd George swallowed his objections to the 1914–15 Estimates in return for Churchill's formal pledge of major cuts in 1915–16.[37] The outbreak of war six months later cheated the Chancellor of his stake in the bargain.

Churchill had been a distrusted and unloved figure in the Unionist party even before he crossed the floor to the Liberals over the tariff issue in 1904. This 'treachery', and his subsequent ministerial career as a voluble tribune of retrenchment and 'socialistic' reform, won him a prominent place in the demonology of many Unionists. Accused of recklessness and lack of principle, he aroused bitter hostility, resentment and envy but never indifference. Against this background, it is remarkable how calmly his Unionist opponents reacted to Churchill's appointment to the Admiralty. There was a general acknowledgement of what one observer called his 'volte-face from little-Englandism to jingoism' and a general disposition to give him a fair chance to prove himself a champion of the Navy.[38] This was most marked among Unionist editors. Garvin, now editing the *Pall Mall Gazette*, determined to give 'Winston fair play and to defend him against prejudice on our side if he means to be at least as strong as McKenna who has played under great difficulties a patriotic part'.[39] Gwynne of the *Morning Post* took an identical line.[40] More remarkable (and ironic) was the attitude of Maxse, who had hounded Balfour for his 'leniency' to McKenna and Haldane; he now urged Law to back Churchill and Lloyd George, his fellow-traveller. The Opposition, he wrote in mid-November, could do 'far more than has yet been done to strengthen the hands of the few men in the Cabinet who are abandoning their ostrich-like attitude'.[41] There is some evidence of similar thinking among Unionists at Westminster. When consulted by the Whips' office about their approach to the new Board of Admiralty in November 1911, Sandars, whose days of influence were now numbered following Balfour's recent resignation, 'begged *them* to go slow & to avoid any appearance of hostility to it, simply because it was the work of W.Churchill'.[42]

This would appear to have been the official frontbench position in advance of the Navy Estimates debate of March 1912. Hopes that Churchill would prove 'sound' as First Lord were then vindicated when he declared his policy of a 60 per cent Dreadnought superiority over Germany; this meant building 25 vessels between 1912 and 1916 as against Germany's published programme of 14. Churchill pledged that the three Dominion Dreadnoughts constructed since 1909 – *Australia, New Zealand and Malaya* – would be treated as additional to the requirements of the 60 per cent standard.[43] Lee welcomed the Estimates as evidence that the Admiralty were determined on 'a clear, steady and resolute policy with regard to our naval affairs' and promised Opposition support.[44] Not since 1906 had such harmony prevailed; Churchill thanked his opponents for their 'kindness'. As Sandars had predicted, the First Lord had 'put himself straight at once by some striking declaration or act of policy'.[45] Weeks later, the new Budget's provisional allocation of a £6.5 million surplus for naval purposes was greeted as 'a great triumph for the supreme Navy Party' and a coup for Churchill personally.[46] The First Lord's unequivocal assertion of Britain's determination to guard her naval supremacy in speeches during 1912 and 1913, together with his plain speaking on the German naval challenge, gratified Unionists used to a less robust tone from Liberal First Lords.[47] Yet as early as the summer of 1912 the Opposition were alleging that the Admiralty shipbuilding programme fell short of what was needed to give effect to Churchill's pledges. In the Navy debates of 1913 and 1914 Lee maintained that Britain had built, was building or had projected 3 or 4 fewer ships than were needed to realize the 60 per cent standard and that, despite his protestations to the contrary, Churchill was including the Dominion Dreadnoughts in his calculations.[48] When a Canadian offer to build three Dreadnoughts for imperial purposes was withdrawn following the refusal of the Senate to ratify the relevant bill, the Opposition insisted that the Admiralty should build them anyway, in addition to the vessels which, they argued, were needed to make good the 60 per cent standard.[49] Lee rejected Churchill's response to the Canadian disappointment – an acceleration of existing British construction – along with his claim that the superior technology of the *Queen Elizabeth* class compensated for any temporary numerical shortfall. These various points were the subject of a spirited argument between Churchill and Lee which ran from debate to debate in the pre-war years. It is a reflection on their basic confidence in him that the Opposition never actually accused Churchill of abandoning the 60 per cent standard; there was to be no reversion to the tedious shadow-boxing which had characterized the two-power standard debate in 1906–8.

However, in 1913 and 1914 the continued expansion of the Austrian and Italian fleets led the Opposition to challenge the sufficiency of the 60 per cent standard itself. They argued that maintaining a 60 per cent margin over Germany in the North Sea left the Navy unable to fulfil its role as protector of imperial interests worldwide. Reversing Churchill's axiom that 'it wd. be vy foolish to lose England in safeguarding Egypt', Arthur Lee contended that 'safety in the North Sea [would] not prevent disaster if we are found wanting in the Mediterranean and the Pacific and in other seas'.[50] The safety of its 'outer margins' was no less vital to the existence of the Empire. When pressed by Churchill to explain what wider standard the Opposition would substitute for 60 per cent, Lee (while not concealing his own enthusiasm for 'two keels to one') evaded the issue by arguing that the responsibility of an Opposition was not to lay down alternative policies but to ensure that the government of the day fulfilled its pledges.[51]

The Unionists' refusal to advance an alternative policy reflected a conventional view of the constitutional role of an Opposition in the British political system. It was, however, also a convenient mask for the fact that the Opposition had political reasons for not pronouncing positively on policy. In November 1911 it had seemed inevitable that the Opposition would take deliberate steps to differentiate its policy from that of the government; Balfour's unwillingness to make the 'two-keels-to-one' standard official Opposition policy had antagonized the many in his party who saw it not only as the obvious replacement for the defunct two-power standard, but also as a rallying cry and an electoral ace. A growing (and justified) sense that the party lacked a definite policy on the Navy undoubtedly contributed to the crisis of Balfour's authority in the autumn of 1911. Giving the party such a policy had appeared to be a priority for the new leader and Law immediately came under pressure from advocates of the 'two-keels-to-one' standard. Within weeks of his election, he was being assured that an endorsement of the formula would be received 'with enthusiasm' by his supporters and would be 'extremely popular' in the country.[52] In the event, Law did not respond to these inducements. Despite a strong appeal from Arthur Lee, he made no reference to the standard in his first major speech as leader at a rally in the Albert Hall on 26 January 1912.[53] In fact, no action was taken in the matter until the summer of 1912 when Selborne, rather than Law, began to canvas the opinion of his senior colleagues on the issue.[54]

Selborne argued for a standard in battleships and battle cruisers of 'two-keels-to-one' against the next largest European navy; in other words, an increase on the 60 per cent standard proclaimed by Churchill in March. 'I think that . . . it would be safe and not excessive and that as a formula it would be understood by the public', Selborne wrote to Law, Lansdowne and Austen Chamberlain on 29 August.[55] In support of his claim that such a standard would not impose an intolerable financial burden on Britain, Selborne pointed out that it would only require the construction of three more ships than the government's own standard committed it to build by 1917. This information impressed Austen Chamberlain, who readily accepted the need for 'a simple and easily comprehensible formula' in place of the two-power standard and doubted the adequacy of the 60 per cent standard, but, as Chancellor-in-Waiting, had hitherto declined to endorse 'two-keels-to-one' because he believed it to be prohibitively expensive.[56] Law and Lansdowne expressed a different reservation about Selborne's proposal. Would the adoption of a 'two-keels-to-one' standard not handicap Britain in responding to further increases in Italian or Austrian shipbuilding?, they asked. While not disagreeing with a change in principle, both preferred, as Lansdowne put it, 'to avoid tying ourselves to a programme of construction the extent of which will be determined by the rate at which other Powers may think proper to build'.[57] This concern Selborne met with an assurance that the 'two-keels-to-one' standard must be regarded as 'a building formula which would not exclude any additional programme that might be necessary' in response to events abroad.[58]

Thus Selborne's initiative in August 1912 established a consensus among the key policy-makers on the merits of the 'two-keels-to-one' standard. It did not, however, result in a public policy commitment by the leadership on the lines envisaged by party activists. 'I think the matter will wait until we meet in October', Selborne had written to Law on 4 September. In the event, it waited a good deal longer. An official handbook for party canvassers, published in late 1912, contained no reference to the 'two-keels-to-one' in its section dealing with naval questions.[59] No declaration of policy was forthcoming from the Opposition front bench in the debates of March and July 1913. A full year after his discussions with colleagues, in August 1913, Selborne was writing airily to a journalist: 'I do not think there will be any difficulty in the Unionist party adhering to the Two Keels to One Standard.'[60] Yet the party would still not have done so publicly when war broke out in August 1914. In the Navy Estimates debate of March 1914 Lee again resorted to the now lame argument that policy-making was 'not our business'.[61]

What had happened? The answer is twofold. On the one hand, Law and Lansdowne were too preoccupied with other issues, notably Ireland and Lloyd George's land campaign, to devote attention to a change in naval policy whose advantages could seem more apparent than real. After all, as Selborne admitted, the difference between 'two-keels-to-one' and the government's 60 per cent standard was a mere two or three ships. What then was the point of pushing it? The possibility that an election might occur at any time was a further disincentive to policy initiatives. Law showed a determination to avoid encumbering the party programme unnecessarily which bore a striking resemblance to Balfour's 'general rule of Opposition'. Clarifying party policy necessarily presented hostages to fortune, in this case a financial hostage. Churchill had alleged that the measures demanded by the Opposition would increase the Navy Estimates by up to £50 million; he jeered that 'such a crazy expenditure would form a very proper counterpart to the Tariff Reform finance by which the money would be supplied'.[62] The £50 million figure was a deliberate flight of exaggerated fancy on Churchill's part, but there is reason to suppose that Law was influenced by the financial implications of adopting a new naval standard. Recognizing that a future Unionist government would have to spend heavily on national defence, Law told Salisbury in May 1912 that 'it would be simply impossible for us to do otherwise than raise the additional money at once by a Tariff Reform Budget'.[63] Defence policy was therefore tied in with the divisive question of fiscal policy. The issue of whether or not an incoming Unionist gov-ernment would propose food duties continued to generate controversy within Unionist ranks in 1912 and 1913 and stretched Law's authority as leader to its limit.[64] It is hardly surprising therefore that Law should avoid action in the defence debate which would aggravate his and his party's difficulties.

As important as wider political considerations in explaining the Opposition's stance on the 'two-keels-to-one' is the fact that, for all Lee's rhetorical complaints across the floor of the House, Liberal policy under Churchill gave the Unionists less cause for concern than at any time since 1906. The First Lord's 'masculine handling of our naval policy' defused that pressure for active opposition which had built up in 1909–10.[65] The fact that only a handful of Opposition MPs were pre-sent in the Chamber for Lee's major speech on the Estimates in March 1913, and the concentration of speakers on detailed technical issues, symbolized the return of the Navy to calmer political waters.[66] While it would be wrong to suggest that Lee's denunciations of Churchill sig-nified nothing, they did contain a generous helping of 'sound and fury'. Churchill's fertile rhetoric infuriated the waspish Lee – 'if only perora-tions were Dreadnoughts, then he would indeed have provided us with an invincible Armada' – who was ambitious and cannot have enjoyed 'shadowing' a younger man who had entered Parliament in the same year (1900) and reaped a rich reward for political apostasy. In 1912 Walter Long told Churchill in the Commons that the Opposition would support him against any attempt by the Liberal Left to reduce arma-ments.[67] In fact, the drum of retrenchment was banged but fitfully and weakly in 1912 and 1913. It was only in 1914, when Lloyd George challenged the Navy Estimates, that memories of 1906–9 revived. Then the Opposition were as good as Long's word. The care taken by the Unionist front bench to support Churchill in his Cabinet struggle over the 1914–15 Estimates confirms their broad acceptance of his policy. The Opposition Chief Whip, Lord Edmund Talbot, was apprehen-sive about the possibility of Unionist MPs unwittingly abetting Lloyd George.[68] Selborne consulted Balfour, an old hand at such games. 'It is difficult to know what to do', he wrote on 5 January 1914. 'If [Lloyd] George & the Suicide Club triumph in the Cabinet, we shall not then be able to affect the result, the Government will not change their policy because of our remonstrances & the mischief will have been done'.[69] Not believing that Churchill would be much helped by a premature Opposition agitation, Balfour characteristically counselled caution and advised Selborne to await more definite information.[70] Selborne con-curred, and the appearance of the hugely increased Estimates duly removed all cause for concern.[71] The result of the Cabinet compromise and the Opposition's favourable response was that the Estimates went through 'on oiled castors, with hardly a murmur of protest'.[72] A cartoon in *Punch* depicted Churchill, dressed as a Jack Tar and holding a bundle marked 'Navy Estimates', ringed by an adoring chorus of bonneted Tory maidens crooning 'You've made me love you. I didn't want to do it.'

The benign attitude of the frontbench towards the First Lord had its counterpart on the back benches.[73] But there was a contrary current. Churchill's conduct of policy could not satisfy or silence a group of inveterate critics led by Lord Charles Beresford, now berthed on the Opposition back benches as MP for Portsmouth.[74] At the root of Beresford's enmity lay Churchill's intimate friendship with Fisher. The 'strange brand of infatuation' between these two flawed geniuses dated from their first meeting at Biarritz in 1907 and would weather many storms, including their explosive quarrel over the Dardanelles campaign in May 1915.[75] 'Unable to resist each other for long at close range', they made a powerful but highly combustible combination of temperament, talent and energy.[76] Once at the Admiralty, Churchill briefly contemplated recalling Fisher as First Sea Lord but determined instead to look to him for informal advice on policy; he also appointed him chairman of the important Royal Commission on Oil Supply and Engines which sat in 1913–14.[77] To punish Churchill for the return to the Admiralty of

'A Sea-Change', cartoon from *Punch*, 14 January 1914.

Fisher – 'the root of all evil and the foundation of all our weakness' – Beresford put himself at the head of the grumbling campaign on the Opposition benches.[78] It was not so much Churchill's policy that fuelled this campaign, as his methods which, it was alleged, were doing great damage to the morale of the service. Churchill's vigorously intervention-ist style of administration led to bruising collisions with naval officers, who regarded him as an interfering ignoramus. Like Fisher, Churchill was no respecter of niceties and protocol and this brought him odium in a service which, for all Fisher's efforts, remained as stiffly traditional as an Eton collar. 'C[hurchill]. very foolishly travels round the coast holding reviews and inspections & so forth without reference to Naval opinion and regulation', wrote an informed critic: 'He is also much addicted to sending for junior officers & discussing with them the proceedings of their superiors.'[79] It was this last 'breach of discipline' which most incensed Churchill's naval critics, who deemed it subversive of discipline and hierarchy. Imitating Beresford's example, disgruntled naval officers fed their complaints to attentive parliamentarians and journalists. A picture was built up outside the Navy of Churchill, reckless and amateurish, treating Lords of the Admiralty 'like clerks at the Board of Trade'.[80] Churchill's acrimonious replacement in 1912 of the First Sea Lord, Sir Francis Bridgeman, 'a crusted Tory' of impeccable connections, was taken as conclusive evidence for the prosecution and provoked a press and parliamentary row.[81] In general, throughout the period to 1914 the First Lord was continually obliged to defend himself from partisan and personalized sniping from the Opposition back benches. Bad-tempered exchanges between Churchill and Beresford, who constantly interrupted each other's speeches, were a staple feature of the Navy debates of 1912–14. To read Beresford's parliamentary speeches – long-winded, opinionated and pettish – is to risk becoming an instinctive Fisherite; not for nothing did Garvin dub Beresford 'the great dirigible . . . the biggest of all recorded gas-bags'.[82]

The back bench snipers were helped by the fact that Churchill's belligerent reaction to Ulster resistance to Home Rule – culminating in his dispatch of the Third Battle Squadron to Lamlash in April 1914 – made him an object of 'peculiar hatred' to Unionists.[83] His naval assailants could count on a cheer from many who had no real quarrel with his policy at the Admiralty. But this favourable context did not bring them the patronage of the Unionist front bench. Although they did nothing to call off the baying wolves, the Opposition leadership chose not to pitch into the continuing squabbles of the so-called Band of Brothers. Apart from a sharp attack by Law on Churchill's 'brutal' treatment of Bridgeman during the adjournment debate on 20 December 1912, and occasional jibing from Lee, they avoided the personal issue and stuck firmly to policy.[84] Selborne squashed any suggestion that the

Opposition should press Asquith for an inquiry into Churchill's administration.[85] The most sympathetic response that Beresford's faction received was from Walter Long, who warned Law in May 1912 that 'the best men *in* the Navy regard W.C. & all his works with profound suspicion & grave misgiving: they look to us', he continued, 'to see through W.C.'s trickery & be ready to fall upon his misdeeds'.[86] But Long went no further than verbal support. Beresford despaired at the inaction of the front bench and complained at length and bitterly about the way in which the Opposition leaders were ignoring him.[87] Sandars, who was a confidant of Bridgeman and whose animus towards Churchill deepened during 1912, lamented what he called the 'decided tendency among men to give undue credit to Churchill' and 'to fall down in admiration of his type written harangue in the H of Commons'.[88] Even in 1914, when condemning Churchill in the language of the lynch mob for his inflammatory speeches on Ulster, Law and his colleagues did not seek to extend the arena of conflict to his administration of the Navy. Their support for his 1914–15 Estimates stood out sharply against a background of unprecedented partisan strife and an atmosphere of imminent civil war in Ireland. How could Unionists complain about the apathy of public opinion on the Ulster issue, asked Beresford pointedly, when 'the people at one date hear the Leaders of the Opposition proclaim the Cabinet as traitors, felons, and guilty of corrupt practices, and a few weeks afterwards the same men state that one of these traitors, (Mr Churchill), is . . . a "genuine patriot"'.[89] Their failure to turn the party leadership against Churchill is another example of the relative impotence of the hard men on the Unionist back benches, the noisy Radical Right. But an opportunity for revenge was eventually to present itself, as will be explained in the next chapter.

Coming Clean On Compulsion

'Efficiency is his great motto', wrote Gwynne of Bonar Law in November 1911: 'By his standard Haldane will be examined and found woefully wanting'.[90] True to form, in the course of his first major speech as leader at the Albert Hall in January 1912, Law fiercely attacked Haldane, of whom he said; 'Neither his merits nor his difficulties should conceal from us the extent of his failure.'[91] If Unionists generally enjoyed the 'new and cutting thrust' which Law gave to the party on the platform, Unionist critics of Haldane were delighted by the cogency and vigour with which he called attention to deficiencies in both the Regular Army and the Territorials. To some extent Law's bruising treatment of Haldane's policy must be seen as a conscious effort to satisfy his party's belligerent mood. But it also reflected that very real sense of pessimism about the outlook in Europe which was described in Chapter 12.

From Agadir onwards the prospect of British involvement in a continental war shaped the military policy of the Unionist party. The Unionists were unaware that in August 1911 the government had decided in principle to send only four of the six divisions of the expeditionary force to France if war came, keeping two divisions at home.[92] They believed erroneously that the entire force had been on the verge of dispatch to the Continent. This was a source of profound concern to them. Haldane had always insisted that the expeditionary force would be retained at home for six months after the outbreak of war, during which time the Territorials could be embodied and trained to assume the burden of home defence. From the outset, therefore, there was a tension at the heart of Haldane's reforms between the role of the first-line army, rapid deployment overseas, and the needs of the Territorial Force. Arthur Lee had identified this flaw in the House of Commons in February 1907, enquiring sarcastically how Haldane was going to persuade the enemy to wait until the Territorial Force had emerged from its 'chrysalis stage'.[93] The Opposition had not pressed the point, because at that date their vision of future war was imperial rather than European. As Balfour had insisted in the Militia debate, in a war with Russia Britain would enjoy a six months' period of grace before the borders of India were actively threatened. Once war in Europe became a possibility, however, no such interval could be expected. 'It all depends which comes first', Repington wrote in 1910, 'India or Germany'.[94] The future of Europe would be decided within weeks, if not days, on the Franco-German frontier. If the expeditionary force were to go – and Unionists believed it must – it would have to go at once.

Lee described the resulting dilemma as 'eminently Gilbertian' but took it far more seriously.[95] If the dictates of continental strategy were met, and the expeditionary force sent, within days of the outbreak of war the defence of Britain would depend upon the untrained, under-strength and artillery-less Territorial Force. The fact that the mobilization of the expeditionary force would depend on its deficiencies in officers and horses first being met, and that those deficiencies could only be met from the Territorial Force, aggravated matters. It was possible that, in such circumstances, public fear of invasion might compel the Navy to concentrate in home waters and so prevent it adopting an offensive strategy. But if the dictates of continental strategy were ignored, and the expeditionary force kept at home until the Territorials were judged fit, France might go under the jackboot with dire consequences for Europe and the British Empire. Coupled with the fitness of the Regular Army for continental war – a sobering visit to the German army manoeuvres in Saxony in 1912 provided Lee with material for a worrying comparison – this potentially agonizing choice was to be the principal theme of the Opposition's case in Parliament between 1911 and 1914.[96] Lee and

Wyndham endeavoured to force an acknowledgement from the government that Britain lacked the military means to ensure simultaneously her own security and her strategic interests in Europe. They concentrated on exposing the deficiencies in Britain's land forces in the hope of building a climate of opinion in which the government would have no alternative but strong action. This was the easy part; with the strength of the Territorial Force in July 1913 some 62,000 below its establishment, and recruitment to the Regular Army and Special Reserve declining rapidly, there was ample evidence on which to base a bleak diagnosis. The hard part was prescribing a cure.

Despite the strength of compulsionist feeling within the party and the clamour for a new military policy, during his first six months as leader Law made no attempt to give his colleagues and supporters a lead. The confusion bequeathed by Balfour persisted. While in private Law pleaded 'the pressure of other topics', above all the campaign against Home Rule, in public he concentrated on criticizing existing shortcomings in the Regular Army.[97] It was easier to denounce the inferiority of British army rifles compared to German (as Law did with gusto at the Albert Hall in January 1912) than to articulate a definite Opposition policy. The political caution which determined Law's handling of 'two-keels-to-one' was naturally heightened in his handling of the far more problematic army issue. But the issue could not be avoided indefinitely. In July 1912, just as Selborne was attempting to clarify Opposition naval policy, Law and Lansdowne agreed to a suggestion (probably from Midleton) that a frontbench committee should inquire into the 'Condition of the Land Forces'. The leaders' acquiescence owed something to the general expectation that an election would not be long delayed. Lansdowne suggested that the party leadership needed 'to clear our minds, so that if a general election were to come upon us we should sing the same kind of song and have something fairly definite to propose'.[98] A straightforward question had to be answered: 'what line [are we] to take as to compulsory service or compulsory training?' To Lansdowne, whose sympathy for compulsion has already been mentioned, it was the 'political' rather than the 'military' aspect of the case that demanded consideration. The brief given to the Committee by Law and Lansdowne was:

> To consider the existing deficiencies in strength of the Land Forces and the means and cost of bringing the fighting strength of the Forces up to the Establishments laid down by the War Office.[99]

The Committee was composed of Salisbury, Wyndham, Lee and Midleton. If the names were familiar, their task was not; for the first time since 1905 the military policy of the party was to be formulated collectively. The Committee met during the autumn and its report was signed on 4 February 1913. The report, which detailed the current shortfall in the various military establishments, demonstrates the extent to which the Unionist vision of the next war had shifted decisively from the Oxus to the Meuse.[100] 'For the public safety', the Committee advocated restoring the cuts in the Regular Army made by Haldane in 1906–7, offering inducements to officer recruitment, and taking measures to enlarge the Special Reserve. The combined cost of such measures it estimated at £1.4 million. In an attached note, Lee expressed his personal view that these proposals must be regarded as no more than the minimum required to make the expeditionary force viable. As far as the Territorial Force was concerned, the Committee concluded that any further increase of expenditure would be 'undesirable and wasteful' since the force was unfit for the service required of it. The Committee's unanimous verdict was that 'efficient Home Defence' could not be secured without the adoption of compulsory training for the Territorials.

However, the Committee did not propose that this, the programme of the NSL, should be adopted as party policy. It pointed out instead that 'any proposal to institute Compulsory Service, if made by one political party would almost certainly lead to . . . defeat at the polls'. While opposition to compulsion within Unionist ranks may have been undermined since 1905, the belief that compulsion was anathema to the public had not. Even those who believed most fervently in the merits of compulsion did not dissent; 'If you pin the label of conscription to the party you run the risk of keeping them out of office for years', warned Repington.[101] In a year when the fate of the Union and with it Law's beloved Ulster hung in the balance, and with a 'Home Rule' election seeming inevitable, the political argument for avoiding policy initiatives of any kind – let alone contentious ones – was overwhelming. In a note appended to the full Committee's report Wyndham expressed the decidedly Balfourian view that it was 'unwise for the Opposition to "air alternative policies" or "frame hypothetical estimates"'. There was a further danger that adopting compulsory training for the Territorials would divide the party. Lord Curzon, a vice-president of the NSL and a prominent member of the Opposition in the Lords, admitted in April 1913 that the party still contained a divergence of views on the compulsion issue and claimed only (and weakly) that it was 'steadily moving in the direction of a belief that some form of compulsion is required'.[102] It was not just a matter of alienating loyal Unionist Territorials, of whom there were many; Salisbury argued that the Unionist party as a whole could 'only assimilate change gradually' and that the advocacy of such 'a sweeping change' would be repugnant to a large and influential proportion of its supporters.[103] The Salisbury Committee's collective sense of political realities thus outweighed the compulsionist sentiment of its individual members. In Balfour's case, political caution and personal conviction had coincided on the compulsion issue and were hard to disentangle; in the case of the

Salisbury Committee the two were distinct but in conflict. Conviction lost and in 1913 the decisive influence of purely political considerations in the compulsion debate stands out in sharper relief than at any time since 1905.

If compulsion was to come at all then, it could only be as the result of an agreement between the parties. Noting that Salisbury and a number of other Unionists had recently been invited to join yet another War Office investigation into the condition of the Special Reserve, the Committee suggested that 'a similar advance with regard to the Territorial Force, if proceeding from the Government and shown to be due to their sense of the public danger, might be a first step to a concordat which would take the whole question of Compulsion out of the arena of party'. The objective of the Opposition in Parliament must be to induce the government to take that step.

The target of the Opposition's efforts was to be Colonel Jack Seely, who had succeeded Haldane at the War Office in June 1912. Previously Haldane's Under-Secretary, Seely was a former Unionist MP whose defection to the Liberals over Tariff Reform had not severed his amicable ties with George Wyndham and other leading Tories.[104] While not held in any great esteem by his former colleagues, he was regarded as like-minded on defence matters and reciprocated, sending papers to Wyndham and Balfour among others.[105] Soon after his arrival at the War Office in June 1912 Midleton and Wyndham signified the Opposition's willingness to work with Seely by offering to 'smooth the passage' of the Army Estimates in July.[106] It was at Midleton's suggestion that the cross-bench Special Reserve Committee was set up in February 1913.[107] In the course of his contacts with Midleton and others Seely had acknowledged the parlous state of the Territorial Force and made noises sympathetic to compulsion.[108] In public his defence of the Force lacked vigour and conviction, and his speeches hinted at a lack of faith in the capacity of the voluntary system to revivify the force. He repeatedly acknowledged 'the desirability of having a large number fully trained to arms' and agreed that military drill, by expanding lungs and cultivating 'the spirit of obedience', could do much for 'national well-being'.[109] In July 1912 Seely attributed the impracticability of compulsory training to the fact that 'no great party in the State shows the least sign . . . of taking it up'.[110] This was the talk of a covert compulsionist. Behind the scenes the Secretary of State was proving susceptible to the persuasive Irish brogue of the Director of Military Training, General Sir Henry Wilson, who was sedulously building support for compulsion within the General Staff. A fierce critic of Haldane – whom his diaries routinely describe as 'that old ass' – Wilson was determined that Britain should assist France against Germany in the European war he thought inevitable.[111] She could only do so, he argued, if the Territorial Force were raised and trained compulsorily; only then could the Regular Army finally be freed from the shackles of home defence and only then could it be sustained in the field against a continental enemy. Under Wilson's adroit chiselling, the War Office consensus in favour of voluntarism began to crack. The General Staff wanted '2 years compulsion in barracks & an army of half a million to fight in Europe', wrote an informed observer in December 1912.[112] The Opposition knew this from Wilson who was an Ulsterman, a Unionist and an aggressive critic of Asquith's government – 'What a Cabinet of Cowards, Blackguards & Fools'.[113] He had been introduced to Law in June 1912 by a mutual friend, Sir Charles Hunter, and they met regularly thereafter. In 1912 and 1913 Law frequently invited Wilson to brief him on military topics and also arranged for him to meet Balfour, with whom he argued out the invasion issue over lunch in April 1913.[114] Other Unionists in contact with Wilson were Walter Long and Arthur Lee; in late 1912 Lee and Wilson were in cahoots with Milner and others over a plan to mount a new press campaign in favour of compulsion.[115] Together with Seely's parliamentary utterances, Wilson's assurances that the Secretary of State was 'coming to heel' on the compulsion issue lent credence to the possibility of an initiative coming from the Horse Guards.[116]

More impressive still were indications from pressmen such as Gwynne and Sir George Riddell, as well as from Henry Wilson, that David Lloyd George and Winston Churchill viewed the necessities of the military situation similarly. In the autumn of 1910 Lloyd George had indicated to Balfour and other Unionists his willingness to accept some form of compulsion as part of a coalition agreement between the major parties.[117] While not reverting to the full coalition plan, in the autumn of 1912 the Chancellor did return to the idea of compulsion.[118] 'L.G. has stated more than once that he rather favours some form of compulsory service', noted Riddell in April 1913.[119] Concern over the European situation explains his interest. He regarded compulsion as potentially a 'great safeguard of peace' and believed that Britain ought to have 'a million men on call'.[120] However, as he had in 1910, Lloyd George stuck consistently to the view that compulsion could not be introduced by a single party 'except in some great national emergency'.[121] Like his opponents, he saw unilateral action in the matter as a recipe for disaster at the polls. Early in 1913 H.A. Gwynne reported to Austen Chamberlain that the Chancellor had been 'nibbling' at the suggestion of informal talks with the Opposition on the military issue.[122] Churchill, who had not lost his enthusiasm for the grand design of uniting 'sensible men in both parties' in a new political grouping, was also known to be attracted to a 'concordat' with the Unionists on compulsion.[123] When he and Lloyd George said as much to Henry Wilson at the Carlton Club in November 1912, Wilson rapidly reported their views to Law.[124] By March 1913

Churchill was openly proclaiming that 'he could not see his way to oppose a scheme for National Service' and intended an early initiative.[125] It seemed, therefore, that there was fertile ground for an Opposition overture to Seely on the compulsion issue. Indirect corroboration came in the form of rumours on the Liberal benches that the government planned to break with the voluntary principle. There were noisy protests in the Liberal press in the spring of 1913 against what the *Nation* called 'a covert conspiracy to militarize this country, and to undermine the civil liberties of its people'.[126]

It was against this backdrop that in early 1913 the Opposition front bench attempted to demolish Seely's claim that compulsory training was 'out of the range of practical politics' by offering privately 'to confer with and support the Government, publicly or privately, for the adoption of measures to bring the Forces . . . up to strength'.[127] It was Midleton who approached Seely, and in his memoirs Midleton claims that his overture was favourably received. He further claims that it was agreed with Seely that the Opposition should take the opportunity of a Lords debate on the Territorial Force in February 1913 to extend a 'golden bridge' to the government. As in 1907 and 1909, therefore, the army debate was subject to frontbench orchestration.

The Opposition's initiative during the debate on 10 February took the specific form of an offer to support the government in introducing compulsory drill and military training in schools. This, Midleton and Lansdowne argued, would provide a reserve of 'half-manufactured soldiers' on which the Territorial Force could draw in peacetime and the expeditionary force in war. Although falling short of the NSL's demand for compulsory training for the Territorials, such a measure would constitute a step in the right direction; it would not only improve the existing home defence situation but also make the eventual introduction of compulsory service both easier and cheaper. 'Cadet training' was not a novel idea. As was shown in Chapter 4, in the autumn of 1905 the Balfour government had briefly considered promoting rifle shooting in schools.[128] Though not followed through at that time, the idea attracted growing interest thereafter both as a solution to the country's lack of trained men and 'on grounds of social discipline'.[129] In the debate in February 1913 Midleton pointed out the advantages to the 'physical and moral health of the younger generation' and offered the Social Darwinistic sentiment that nations stood to gain much 'by striking some rather hard note of national sacrifice'.[130] Drill and rudimentary military training might be considered a reasonable return for the state to expect on its investment in the education and medical care of the young, he argued.

In view of the political caution of the Salisbury Committee it may seem curious that it should recommend and the Opposition then so openly propose a policy which amounted to 'militarizing' the nation's children. Of all the shapes and forms in which compulsion might be introduced, cadet training might be thought to be the one most likely to generate an emotive and passionate resistance. When a much narrower proposal to provide public funds for cadet corps had been brought forward by Haldane in 1907, the Labour party had been outraged; Ramsay Macdonald warned of 'poison[ing] the springs of politics at their very source'.[131] Yet Unionists did not see it in this way. After all, Edwardian society was already characterized by a range of quasi-martial youth organizations – lads' drill brigades, miniature rifle clubs, cadet corps, the Boy Scouts *et al.* 'Playing soldiers' was an established feature of recreational and associational life through boyhood and into adolescence. To make such activities compulsory was a radical innovation but one which would build on an existing framework of voluntary activity. Besides, since W.E.Forster's Education Act of 1870 the British education system had come to rest on compulsion; children had no choice over attending school or over what they learned once there. As Lansdowne put it, 'assuming that you have the right to insist upon teaching a lad the three Rs, you also have a perfect right to teach him how to hold himself and to submit to discipline'.[132] This analogy was drawn by Roberts, too.[133] With the Liberal government listing among its achievements the introduction of compulsory medical inspection and school meals for children, it might be argued that schools were the *obvious* place to introduce compulsory training since education was an area of life in which the voluntary principle had already been qualified. Whatever their assumptions or reasoning, it is highly significant that supporters of cadet training were to be found even among those Unionists who objected to compulsory adult training on grounds of either principle or politics. Thus Salisbury advised Milner in 1908 that the NSL would 'do well to concentrate their efforts upon children, & leave adults alone . . . '.[134] Even Balfour expressed interest in seeing 'something done at secondary schools and at the Universities to encourage such training'.[135] Other firm adherents to the cause by 1913 included Midleton, Lansdowne, Curzon and Lee. In 1905 Walter Long, then President of the Local Government Board, had vetoed the idea of military training in schools, but in 1913, as a member of the National Defence Association, he too fully supported the idea.[136] In short, cadet training was the issue on which the broadest consensus of favourable opinion was to be found among senior Unionists.

Unfortunately, for all Seely's sympathetic statements, during the debate on 10 February the government failed to respond positively to the Opposition's initiative. Lord Crewe virtually ignored the cadet training issue and concentrated instead on refuting the case for applying compulsion to adult males.[137] Undaunted the Unionists returned to the charge in April. During the debate on the Army Annual Bill they again called for the government to adopt cadet training; Lord Curzon formally proposed a round-table conference of 'responsible leaders of both Parties' to take the matter forward.[138] This was an idea which had been floated by Henry Wilson in conversation with Walter Long in July 1912; 'I pointed out', recorded Wilson in his diary, 'that the hands of the Unionists are very clean in this matter, that they have never made a party business of it, & that in fact the whole of the County Associations [of the T.F.] are run by them'.[139] Nothing had come of the plan on that occasion and for six months thereafter the question of a Unionist initiative on compulsion was shelved as expectations mounted that Seely would himself soon act.[140] The April 1913 debate laid such hopes finally to rest. Haldane, now Lord Chancellor but keeping a watching brief on the War Office, deliberately diverted debate from the narrow issue of cadet training and into an acrimonious exchange on the broader principle of compulsion.[141] Ignoring Midleton's protest that the Opposition had 'carefully excluded' the wider compulsion issue from the February debate, the former Secretary of State for War insisted on representing the Opposition's action as an attempt to force compulsory service on the government. Midleton's outrage shows how much he and his colleagues feared being tarred with the brush of compulsion as preached by the NSL. It also shows what a hostage to political fortune their cadet training proposal had been; keen to put a stop to Roberts' 'mischief', Haldane was unlikely to recognize the distinction between one form of compulsion and another.[142] The tone and temper of the debate deteriorated further as Haldane implied that Unionist criticism of the Territorials was itself a major factor in the decline and demoralization of the Force. Curzon angrily reminded Haldane that the Territorial organization had been built on the support of Unionist 'county magnates' and compared the support Haldane had received from his opponents in 1907 and since with the indifference or hostility of his own party.

Thus Haldane, himself the beneficiary of similar manoeuvres in June 1907 and July 1909, had wrecked a cross-bench initiative to bring the parties together on the army question. His heavy-handed intervention during the debate – Curzon later called it 'a triumph of circumlocution unequalled in the Lord Chancellor's long experience of such oratorical feats' – infuriated the Opposition who had been misled by Seely – whether deliberately or unwittingly is not clear – into thinking that the government were prepared to contemplate action on the question of cadet training.[143] The fact was that, however personally amenable, Seely lacked influence in the Cabinet. Lloyd George, who might have made a difference, had lost his nerve in the face of unrelenting press and backbench hostility to the conscriptionists; he had too much at stake in his land campaign to risk a political crisis. As Charles Masterman observed to Riddell, the slightest softening towards compulsion would split the Liberal party from top to bottom.[144] When the less inhibited Churchill forced a debate on the matter in Cabinet he encountered unyielding opposition.[145]

Although the Unionist front bench in the Lords continued to advocate cadet training from time to time, and although the round-table idea was resurrected by Midleton and Curzon in Parliament in March 1914, the bipartisan route to compulsion was impassable from the spring of 1913.[146] The most important legacy of their abortive round-table initiative was the formal identification of the Opposition with the cause of compulsion. Since 1905 Roberts had been trying unsuccessfully to pin the label of compulsion on the Unionist leadership; in 1913 they pinned it on themselves. Their action was imitated beyond Westminster. Unionist candidates in by-elections during 1913 showed 'a greater readiness . . . to let it be known that they favoured compulsion'.[147] The very situation which the round-table idea had been intended to avoid had come about; the Liberals now enjoyed sole tenancy of the tabernacle of voluntarism. The *Westminster Gazette* hailed the debate as marking 'another step forward in the conversion of the Tory party to compulsory militarism'.[148] It seemed inevitable that the Unionist leadership would now pay a political price for lowering its guard in February and April 1913. Law and Lansdowne attempted to limit the damage by offering no encouragement to compulsionist candidates. Lansdowne admitted publicly that public opinion was not 'ripe' for national service.[149] He and his colleagues carefully avoided association with various backbench compulsionist bills introduced in the House of Lords in 1913 and 1914; on one such occasion in June 1913 Salisbury resorted to the argument used by Arthur Lee over the 'two-keels-to-one', namely that it was not the business of an Opposition to 'express confident opinions as to . . . precise policy'.[150] The front bench deliberately preserved their distance from the NSL. It was fortunate for them in this respect that the struggle for the Union was channelling the energies of Unionist militants away from defence issues. The fact that Milner and Roberts were deeply involved in efforts on the mainland to support Carson's Ulster resistance deprived the compulsionist cause of active leadership. In October 1913, when Roberts was confessing to thinking only of Home Rule, Milner was writing that it was 'neither possible or desirable to distract public opinion from the Ulster crisis'.[151] On the other hand, the official Opposition's arm's-length attitude towards the NSL sat awkwardly with their continued support for compulsory cadet training. Unionist policy seemed contradictory and confused. Moreover, the distinction between compelling children to train in arms and compelling adults was not one that Liberal propagandists chose to respect; 'As long as the Tory Party sought to lure their countrymen into the deserts of Protection and Conscription', said one, 'so long would they remain political outcasts in their native land'.[152]

The irony is that those Unionist candidates who openly espoused compulsion in 1913 did their cause no harm.[153] Pro-compulsion Unionists were returned in by-elections at Kendal, Altrincham and Newmarket. How is one to explain this unexpected turn of events? Obviously, it can be argued that by-elections are idiosyncratic and a very different picture would have emerged had the Unionists attempted to carry the banner of compulsion into the altogether more bruising *mêlée* of a general election. Perhaps compulsionists were favoured by the absorption of public opinion with the Ulster crisis? However, other hypotheses suggest themselves. Could it be that the entrenched view of Britain as a country innately opposed to conscription was no more than a tenacious myth? *The Times* suggested in April 1913 that 'while it [compulsion] would be strenuously and conscientiously resisted by a not inconsiderable section of the Liberal Party . . . it would be quietly and just as conscientiously accepted by the people as a whole'.[154] Winston Churchill also thought that, however unpopular, if compulsion were made law it would be accepted.[155] It is also possible that public opinion had genuinely shifted and that politicians had missed the signs; they were perhaps unduly intimidated by the raucous voices of those who tended to 'shudder at a military procession going through the streets as Mephistopheles shuddered when he heard the church bells'.[156] Exploring this question further is beyond the scope of this work; arguably the evidence does not exist from which to assemble a satisfactory answer. Yet the simple fact remains that national service was 'never more of an issue' than in 1913–14 and that the association of the Unionist party with 'conscription' did not have the damaging consequences which had been predicted and which its leaders had tried so hard and so long to avoid.[157]

Plus Ça Change . . .

On Balfour's resignation as leader in 1911 many Unionists had anticipated 'tremendous possibilities' in the field of defence.[158] The adoption of the 'two-keels-to-one' and of compulsion seemed a foregone conclusion. However, by 1914 neither had found its way on to the party platform. Apart from the significant departure of cadet training, little had changed since Law's accession. This situation reflects on Law as leader. Because he held it to be alien to the Opposition's role, and because he feared electoral liabilities, he shrank from formulating policy out of office. In this his attitude had proved indistinguishable from Balfour's. Indeed, in Law's case the primacy of politics stands out more clearly because, unlike Balfour, he personally believed in the merits of the policies he refused to adopt; in 1912 he was described by Henry

Wilson as being 'absolutely clear' on the need for compulsion.[159] For all the frequency with which he invited Wilson's views and expressed agreement with them, Law did remarkably little to further them practically. In this respect, therefore, one can point to a definite continuity in Unionist policy before and after November 1911; the lack of a clear lead on defence policy from the party leader. Balfour had frequently been denounced by Maxse and others for his 'philosophic detachment'; in 1913 we find exactly the same words being applied as critically to Law.[160] But it must be said that Law's 'detachment' can largely be explained by the compelling grip on him of the crisis in Ireland.

In short, where historians have conventionally emphasized the differences of style and policy between Law and his predecessor, in the field of defence it is the similarities which strike one most forcibly. A further parallel may be drawn. As we saw in earlier chapters, for various reasons the period 1905 to 1911 saw a marked element of non-partisanship in Opposition defence policy of which Haldane and Fisher were principal beneficiaries. This chapter has identified a similar theme in Opposition policy between 1912 and 1914. The Navy debate in that period was characterized by consistent Opposition support for Churchill's policy, the reluctance of the Unionist leadership to pitch into internal service disputes contributing further to a relatively uncontentious climate in naval affairs. In the army debate, the Opposition's attempt to reach a constructive accommodation with Seely and their advocacy of round-table talks contradict the assertion that with Law's accession the Army became a 'straight party matter'.[161] The behaviour of the front bench might instead be thought to justify the claim of the *Unionist Workers' Handbook* of 1912 that:

> The Unionist party recognizes the difficulty of the problem, and does not want to make a party question of the army.[162]

This obvious continuity with the Balfour period does not square easily with Law's historical reputation. He is usually seen as introducing into Unionist politics an aggressive partisanship absent in the Balfour era. He was elected to give the party a 'new and cutting thrust', the argument runs, and restored its unity by means of a 'ritualistic opposition' to Liberal policy.[163] Whatever its applicability to the Irish question or to the Marconi scandal, it will be evident that this interpretation does not hold good for the defence debate, where the Unionists pursued what amounted to a 'constructive' opposition.[164] Midleton pledged rhetorically that 'national safety shall not be put behind the exigencies of different parties' but considerations of policy rather than principle lay behind the Opposition's readiness to cooperate with the government in 1912–13.[165] Persuaded that Europe was an open powder magazine liable to explode at any moment, they wished to see Britain's defences strengthened ahead of a war in which (as they thought) her survival would be at stake.[166] Unable to force the government to take action, they had to rely on encouragement and offers of assistance; their sense that belligerence and partisanship could achieve nothing and might be counter-productive reminds one strongly of Balfour's conduct of the Navy debate after 1906. The rigours of Law's 'New Style' – Asquith dubbed him 'spitfire' – can too easily distract attention from a persistent strand of non-partisanship woven into the rough skein of Edwardian politics.

CHAPTER 14

Epilogue: War and Office 1914–15

British politics in 1914 was dominated by the brooding spectre of civil war in Ireland. With negotiations over Home Rule deadlocked and the rhetoric of Ulster resistance becoming daily more defiant and uncompromising, the rival Unionist and Nationalist communities continued to arm themselves in anticipation of a final political breakdown.[1] The murder of the Austrian Archduke Franz Ferdinand by a Serbian nationalist at Sarajevo in Bosnia on 28 June did not immediately divert the attention of British politicians from the Irish crisis; it was only with news of the Austrian ultimatum to Serbia on July 24 that the gravity of the European situation began to dawn. Then, wrote Churchill, 'the parishes of Fermanagh and Tyrone faded back into the mists and squalls of Ireland, and a strange light began immediately, but by perceptible gradations, to fall and grow upon the map of Europe'.[2] As the European crisis unfolded in the last week of July divisions emerged within the Liberal Cabinet over the question of British intervention. In the event, by deferring any decision over military intervention until 3 August when Germany's aggressive intentions towards neutral Belgium had become clear, the Prime Minister was able to carry his colleagues with him.[3] For ministers fearful of embroilment in a continental war, Britain's duty to protect Belgian neutrality under the Treaty of London of 1839 proved a more compelling and acceptable *casus belli* than the considerations of political and strategic interest which dictated Grey's policy of support for France. There were only a handful of resignations, none of which proved damaging.

During the last week of July, Bonar Law went daily to Grey's room at the House of Commons to be briefed on diplomatic developments. In his memoirs Grey recalls the Unionist leader telling him that 'it was not easy to be sure what the opinion of the whole of his party was'. Law apparently doubted whether the Unionist rank and file would be unanimous or overwhelmingly in favour of war, unless Belgian neutrality were invaded.[4] As far as the attitude of the Opposition leadership was concerned, there was no such uncertainty or reservation. Although

Selborne described himself on 3 August as 'full of misery and fear' and
hopeful that England might be 'spared from joining in', his view was
untypical.[5] From the first there was a solid consensus among Law's
colleagues in favour of Britain aligning herself with France and Russia.
Frontbench Unionists were alarmed by rumours reaching them (from
Churchill among others) of the division of opinion within the
government.[6] As on so many occasions in the defence debate since 1906,
they attempted to strengthen the hands of the 'sound' men in the
Cabinet, in this case by indicating their willingness to support a policy
of intervention. On Saturday 1 August, the day on which Germany
declared war on Russia, Law, Lansdowne and Balfour, meeting at
Lansdowne House, sent the Prime Minister a message offering to meet
him to discuss the crisis. The following day, at Austen Chamberlain's
prompting, a further letter bearing Law's signature was dispatched to
Downing Street.

> Dear Mr Asquith,
>   Lord Lansdowne and I feel it our duty to inform you that, in our
> opinion, as well as that of all the colleagues whom we have been able
> to consult, any hesitation now in supporting France and Russia would
> be fatal to the honour and to the future security of the United
> Kingdom, and we offer H.M. Government the assurance of the united
> support of the Opposition in all measures required by England's
> intervention in the war.[7]

There is a clear, if unremarked, parallel between the conduct of the
Opposition leaders in August 1914 and Balfour's action during the
Agadir crisis of 1911, when he pledged full Opposition support for
the government if war broke out over Germany's challenge to France
in Morocco.[8] On both occasions the Unionists behaved as a self-
consciously 'patriotic Opposition'. On both occasions their object was to
counteract perceived divisions within Liberal ranks. It has been argued,
with justice, that Law's letter of 2 August did not have the decisive effect
on the government that its authors subsequently claimed; it was the
violation of Belgian neutrality that stiffened the resolve of wavering
Liberal ministers, not fears that their hesitancy could bring about a war
coalition.[9] But the letter is nonetheless significant in that it not only
confirms the Unionists' unquestioning acceptance of the *entente* but also
reveals their belief that Britain was 'honour' bound to support France,
something the Liberal government consistently denied.[10] The Unionists'
assertion that Britain's 'future security' demanded intervention alongside
France confirms the point made in an earlier chapter that they saw the
prevention of German hegemony in Europe as an imperative British
interest; a second Sedan would sound the death-knell of the British
Empire.

Like their Liberal counterparts, the Unionist leadership believed that Britain would wage a war of limited liability.[11] They did not envisage the total war of 1916-18 or the vast human and industrial resources which Britain would be called on to mobilize. To them, Britain's contribution would be primarily naval and financial; the decision on land would be secured by the French and Russian armies, with the British Expeditionary Force being little more than a token presence.[12] Yet for all their reliance on 'sea pressure and the Russian advance', they were in no doubt that the expeditionary force must go. When on 4 August it emerged that the government had not yet decided on the dispatch of the force, a further conclave of Opposition leaders resulted in Balfour writing to Haldane to urge on him the 'almost overwhelming reasons at this moment for giving all the aid we can to France by land as well as by sea'.[13] Echoing the views of Henry Wilson and the General Staff, Balfour insisted that Britain must do all in her power to ensure that Germany was stalemated in the west, so that the might of the Russian Army could be brought to bear on her in the east. The Unionists' support for the immediate dispatch of the expeditionary force was entirely consistent with views they had expressed in the army debates since 1911. It is interesting, however, that in his letter to Haldane, Balfour pressed only for the dispatch of four of the six Regular divisions of the expeditionary force to the Continent; he assumed that the state of the Territorials required that two divisions be retained for home defence. In this Balfour was respecting the conclusions of the CID on invasion. But he was also implicitly acknowledging that his colleagues had been right since 1911 to insist on the link between the weakness of the Territorials and Britain's capacity for intervention in a European war.

The nature of the naval and military forces Britain had available for war in the summer of 1914 was determined by many factors – from financial constraints and innovations in technology to public opinion and disagreements within the Liberal party. But, as this book has tried to show, it was also influenced by the activities of Unionist politicians in Opposition since 1906. The Unionists' contribution to the state of the Royal Navy in 1914 was twofold. First, their support for Sir John Fisher was of critical importance in sustaining Fisher at the Admiralty and so ensuring the success of his radical programme of naval modernization. Balfour had done much to ensure that when the King's ships put to sea at the end of July 1914 it was to fight a war with means and by methods which bore Fisher's brutal but inspired stamp. Second, the superiority of the Royal Navy to the German High Seas Fleet in 1914 could also be said to owe in some measure to the Unionists; they had not only provided a strong counterbalance to the retrenchment enthusiasms of the Liberal Left since 1906, but also, by keeping the German challenge in the public eye, had made it difficult for the Liberal government not to respond in kind to each advance of German construction. The Unionists' contribution to the state of the Army in 1914 was also twofold. First, they had helped shape and subsequently consolidate the framework of military organization which was in place in 1914 and for which Haldane has wrongly taken exclusive credit; here again Balfour's individual role was of particular significance, here again it has been unremarked. Second, by avoiding identification with the cause of compulsion the Unionists had helped keep the issue off the political agenda before 1914; thus an obvious remedy had been ruled out for the flaws which had become apparent in 'Mr Haldane's army' by 1911 and Britain entered the war as the only belligerent wedded to the voluntary system.

The war ground on through the late autumn of 1914 and the casualty lists lengthened. Christmas came and went with no prospect of the victory which had seemed so easy six months before. As the New Year opened the War Council, a small ministerial committee set up by Asquith in November to take stock of the changing nature of the war, was busy exploring ways of breaking the deadlock on the western front. Simultaneously interest grew in the idea of 'knocking the props' away from Germany by opening up new theatres of war in southern Europe.[14] In January momentum began to build behind a plan to force the Dardanelles Straits, seize the Gallipoli peninsula, and force Germany's newest and most decrepit ally, Turkey, from the war.[15] Throughout this period men continued to flock to recruiting offices:

> Those long uneven lines
> Standing as patiently
> As if they were stretched outside
> The Oval or Villa Park
> . . . moustached archaic faces
> Grinning as if it were all
> An August Bank Holiday lark.[16]

Roberts had been premature in writing the obituary of the voluntary system. The success of the enlistment campaign launched by Lord Kitchener, that imperial hero-turned-poster whom Asquith had appointed to the War Office on the outbreak of war, marked the apogee of the voluntary system in Britain:

> Never such innocence
> Never before or since
> As changed itself to past
> Without a word . . .[17]

While the 'short war' illusion dissolved in the mire and blood of Flanders, the Unionist leadership lived up to their pledge of patriotic support for the government. From August a party truce was in place. With parliamentary life more or less suspended, the energies of leading members of the Opposition were channelled into various areas of the war effort. From the beginning of the war a pattern of frontbench cooperation evolved which might be seen as a continuation of the element of bipartisanship which had characterized defence policy in the pre-war period. Law and Lansdowne received Foreign and War Office telegrams and these were read out at meetings of the Shadow Cabinet; from March 1915 they also received copies of War Council papers. Austen Chamberlain accepted Lloyd George's invitation to sit on a Treasury Committee.[18] Balfour was invited by Asquith to join the newly formed War Council in November, a remarkable tribute to the high regard in which his strategic judgement was held by his opponents and to the cross-bench status in defence matters he had acquired since his resignation from the Unionist leadership in 1911.[19] All this time the Unionist party organization in the country was harnessed to the recruitment drive; in December the Chief Whip, Lord Edmund Talbot, was awarded a Privy Councillorship in recognition of his efforts in placing the party machinery at the disposal of the War Office.

During the spring of 1915, however, the Opposition grew increasingly frustrated by the government's management of the war. The government's assurances about munitions production and supply were contradicted by gloomy reports reaching Law and his colleagues from sources with the Army in France; military failures at Festubert and Neuve Chapelle brought Unionist grievances to a head.[20] At the same time, opinion among senior Unionists was strengthening in favour of 'a system of compulsory organization' of manpower; this they believed necessary not only to sustain the flow of manpower for the Army in France, but also to limit the damage being done to industrial production by the indiscriminate voluntary enlistment of skilled workers.[21] As a means of mobilizing the nation for the struggle against 'Prussian militarism' rather than of patching up the Territorials, and with normal political rules suspended in wartime, the case for compulsion could now be advanced with impunity. Disaffection on the Unionist back benches, marshalled by a newly-established 'Unionist Business Committee', added to the pressure on the leadership to take issue with the government. Meeting at Lansdowne House on 14 May, the Shadow Cabinet decided to press the government for a more energetic prosecution of the war. Their aim was to force a change in war policy, not to bring the Asquith ministry down; Law thought it impossible to form a Unionist government which would command Liberal support and he shared his colleagues' distaste for the idea of coalition.[22]

In the end the Opposition's *démarche* coincided with a crisis at the Admiralty. In November Fisher had returned as First Sea Lord, with a brief to inject vigour and purpose into the naval war effort. With the British Grand Fleet under its Commander-in-Chief Jellicoe lurking at

Scapa Flow out of the reach of U-boats and the German High Seas Fleet declining to sortie to destruction, the naval war was as much a stalemate as the conflict on the Western Front.[23] A string of losses, including the destruction of Admiral Cradock's squadron at Coronel off Chile at the beginning of November, fuelled public disillusionment. Churchill's exploits at Antwerp in October, when he attempted to organize the defence of the beleaguered Belgian port, added to a widespread sense that the Admiralty lacked a steady hand at the tiller. Convinced of the need 'to break some crockery' to restore confidence in the Navy and himself, Churchill turned to his old accomplice, Fisher, and together they began 'meditating fearsome plans of a highly aggressive kind'.[24] But, though it bore early fruit in the victorious Battle of the Falkland Islands in December, the partnership was to prove short-lived. Having initially argued strongly for operations at the Dardanelles, by May 1915 Fisher was bitterly opposed to their continuation; he had come to regard them as a serious drain on Britain's naval strength in the North Sea. By this stage the First Sea Lord, now seventy-four years old, had also tired of working in harness with the brilliant, demanding and headstrong Churchill. His decision to resign over the Dardanelles, coinciding as it did with the Opposition's demand for a new direction in the war effort, created a situation from which Asquith saw coalition as the only way out.[25]

'Suddenly the Ministerial edifice has crumbled', wrote Curzon on 18 May 1915, 'kicked over by old Jack Fisher'.[26] After a decade in Opposition, the Unionist party had returned to office, where it would remain until 1922. It is ironic that the principal agent of this change in the party's fortunes was Fisher, a figure whom so many Unionists loved to hate. In the fraught distribution of offices that followed Asquith's offer of coalition there were two notable Liberal victims: Haldane and Churchill. During the early months of the war Haldane had suffered violent abuse at the hands of the Tory press. His education at Göttingen university, interest in German philosophy and frequent pre-war visits to Germany were seized on to justify malicious accusations of pro-German sympathies. His record at the War Office was loudly condemned, particularly his reduction of the Regular Army.[27] Maxse and his kind were exacting their revenge. Recognizing the hostility to Haldane within his party, Law demanded and secured his exclusion from the new government. As we have seen, Haldane's career as an army reformer had owed much to the cooperation of one Unionist leader; now another had delivered him the *coup de grâce*. Haldane was not alone on the political tumbril. The coming of the coalition had given Churchill's inveterate Unionist critics an opportunity to punish him for his pre-war antics as both Radical tribune and pugnacious First Lord. Law came under irresistible back-bench pressure to demand from Asquith Churchill's removal from the

Admiralty and he made no attempt to head off the baying wolves. Churchill's meagre credit with Law and his colleagues had been dissipated by Antwerp, Coronel and the Dardanelles. 'He seems to have an entirely unbalanced mind', wrote the Unionist leader, 'which is a real danger at a time like this . . . '.[28] Churchill escaped political execution but was condemned instead to internal exile; he stayed in the government but was demoted to the Duchy of Lancaster. Beresford and others exulted. Churchill's successor as First Lord of the Admiralty was none other than Balfour. Having so long watched Admiralty affairs from the outside, Balfour now found himself on the inside, no longer warning of naval war with Germany but waging it. There was no challenge for which he was better prepared. It would have made a splendid ending for this book had Fisher remained at the Admiralty in May 1915, serving as Balfour's First Sea Lord. But this 'dream ticket' was not to be; not only because Fisher actually refused to serve with Balfour, whose support for the Dardanelles campaign he deplored, but also because his impetuous act of resignation had convinced Asquith that he was no longer fit for his post.[29] While Balfour's career was entering a dramatic new phase which would take him from the Admiralty to the Foreign Office in 1916 and thence to a distinguished place among the peacemakers at Versailles, 'Jacky' was doomed to retirement and his rose garden – this time for good.

NOTES

Chapter 1   Introduction

1.   Notable works include: P. Thompson, *Socialists, Liberals and Labour* (London, 1967); P.F. Clarke, *Lancashire and the New Liberalism* (London, 1971); H.V. Emy, *Liberals, Radicals and Social Politics 1892–1914* (London, 1973); M. Petter 'The Progressive Alliance', *History* 58, 192 (1973) 45–59; P.F. Clarke, 'The electoral position of the Liberal and Labour Parties 1910–14', *English Historical Review* 90 (1975) 828–36 and 'The Progressive Movement in England', *Transactions of the Royal Historical Society*, 5th ser., 24 (1974) 159–81; R.I. McKibbin, 'James Ramsay Macdonald and the problem of the independence of the Labour Party 1910–1914', *Journal of Modern History* 42, 2 (1970) 216–5.

2.   Two more recent contributions are: K. Laybourn and J. Reynolds, *Liberalism and the Rise of Labour 1890–1918* (London, 1984) and G. Bernstein, *Liberalism and Liberal Politics in Edwardian England* (London, 1986); for a helpful summary of the debate, see M. Bentley, *The Climax of Liberal Politics: British Liberalism in Theory and Practice 1868–1918* (London, 1987) pp.138–45.

3.   The Unionist party is the name given by contemporaries and historians to the alliance forged after 1886 between the Conservative party and those Liberals who broke with their party over Gladstone's policy of Home Rule for Ireland.

4.   R. Blake, *The Conservative Party from Peel to Churchill* (London, 1970); D. Southgate (ed.) *The Conservative Leadership 1832–1932* (London, 1974); Lord Butler (ed.) *The Conservatives: A History from their Origins to 1965* (London, 1977); J. Ramsden, *The Age of Balfour and Baldwin 1902–40* (London, 1978).

5.   R. Rempel, *Unionists Divided: Arthur Balfour, Joseph Chamberlain and the Unionist Free Traders* (Newton Abbot, 1972); A. Sykes, *Tariff Reform in British Politics 1903–13* (London, 1979).

6.   G. Dangerfield, *The Strange Death of Liberal England 1910–1914* (New York, 1935).

7.   G. Searle, 'Critics of Edwardian society; the case of the Radical Right', in *The Edwardian Age: Conflict and Stability 1900–1914* ed. A. O'Day (London, 1979) pp.79–96.

8.   G. Searle, 'The revolt from the Right in Edwardian Britain', in *Nationalist and Racialist Movements in Britain and Germany before 1914* ed. P.M. Kennedy and A.J. Nicholls (London, 1981) pp.21–39.

9.   A. Sykes, 'The Radical Right and the crisis of Conservatism before the First World War', *Historical Journal* 26, 3 (1983) 661–76; G. Phillips, 'Lord Willoughby de Broke and the politics of Radical Toryism, 1909–1914', *Journal of British Studies* 20, 1 (1980) 205–24.

10.   E.H.H. Green, 'Radical Conservatives and the electoral genesis of Tariff Reform',

Historical Journal 28, 3 (1985) 667–92; F. Coetzee, 'Pressure groups, Tory businessmen and the aura of political corruption before the First World War', *Historical Journal* 29, 4 (1986) 833–52.

11. Paul Kennedy, 'The pre-war Right in Britain and Germany', in *Nationalist and Racialist Movements* ed. Kennedy and Nicholls, p.2.

12. For one useful study, see J. Ridley, 'The Unionist Social Reform Committee 1911–1914: wets before the deluge', *Historical Journal* 30, 2 (1987) 391–413.

13. Kennedy, 'The pre-war Right', pp.1–20; F. Coetzee and M. Coetzee, 'Rethinking the Radical Right in Germany and Britain before 1914', *Journal of Contemporary History* 21, 4 (1986) 515–37.

14. W. Hamilton, 'The nation and the Navy; methods and organization of British navalist propaganda, 1889–1914' (unpublished London Univ. Ph.D. thesis, 1977); Anne Summers; 'The character of Edwardian nationalism: three popular leagues', in *Nationalist and Racialist Movements* ed. Kennedy and Nicholls, pp.68–87 and 'Militarism in Britain before the Great War', *History Workshop* 2 (1976) 104–23.

15. J.W. Mackail and Guy Wyndham, *Life and Letters of George Wyndham* 2 vols (London, 1925) II, p.571.

16. F. Johnson, *Defence By Committee* (London, 1960); N. D'Ombrain, *War Machinery and High Policy: Defence Administration in Peacetime Britain 1902–1914* (Oxford, 1973); D. French, *British Economic and Strategic Planning 1905–1915* (London, 1982).

17. On the Army, see B. Bond, *The Victorian Army and the Staff College 1854–1914* (London, 1972); J. Gooch, *The Plans of War; the General Staff and British Military Strategy c. 1900–1916* (London, 1974); E. Spiers, *Haldane: An Army Reformer* (Edinburgh, 1981); S. Bidwell and D. Graham, *Fire Power: British Army Weapons and Theories of War 1904–1945* (London, 1982); T. Travers, *The Killing Ground: the British Army, the Western Front and the Emergence of Modern Warfare, 1900–1918* (London, 1987); On the Navy, the most important studies are A.J. Marder, *From The Dreadnought to Scapa Flow. Vol.I The Road to War 1900–1914* (Oxford, 1961); R.F. Mackay, *Fisher of Kilverstone* (Oxford, 1973); J.T. Sumida, *In Defence of Naval Supremacy: Finance, Technology and British Naval Policy 1889–1914* (London, 1989).

18. S.R. Williamson, *The Politics of Grand Strategy: Britain and France Prepare for War 1904–1914* (Cambridge, Mass., 1969); P. Haggie, 'The Royal Navy and war planning in the Fisher era', *Journal of Contemporary History* 8, 3 (1973) 118–32; J. McDermott, 'The revolution in British military thinking from the Boer War to the Moroccan crisis', in *The War Plans of the Great Powers 1880–1914* ed. P.M. Kennedy (London, 1980) pp.99–117; J. Gooch, 'Mr Haldane's Army: military organization and foreign policy in England, 1906–7', in *The Prospect of War: Studies in British Defence Policy 1847–1942* (London, 1981) pp.92–115; A. Offer, *The First World War: An Agrarian Interpretation* (London, 1989).

19. S. Roskill, *Hankey: Man of Secrets Vol.I 1877–1918* (London, 1970); P. Fraser, *Lord Esher: A Political Biography* (London, 1973); Spiers, *Haldane*; Mackay, *Fisher*.

20. A.J.A. Morris, *Radicalism Against War 1906–1914: The Advocacy of Peace and Retrenchment* (London, 1972); also by the same author 'Haldane's Army reforms, 1906–8: the deception of the Radicals', *History* 56, 186 (1971) 17–34; H. Weinroth, 'Left-wing opposition to naval armaments in Britain before 1914', *Journal of Contemporary History* 6, 4 (1971) 93–120; G.S. Jordan, 'Pensions not Dreadnoughts', in *Edwardian Radicalism* ed. A.J.A. Morris (London, 1974) pp.162–79; Bernstein, *Liberalism and Liberal Politics*, pp.166–96.

21. B.E.C. Dugdale, *Arthur James Balfour* 2 vols (London, 1936); K. Young, *Arthur James Balfour: The Happy Life of the Politician, Prime Minister, Statesman and Philosopher 1848–1930* (London, 1963); S. Zebel, *Balfour: A Political Biography* (London, 1973); M. Egremont, *Balfour: A Life of Arthur James Balfour* (London, 1980); R.F. Mackay, *Balfour: Intellectual Statesman* (Oxford, 1985).

22. For a discussion of this point see my unpublished thesis, 'The politics of national defence: Arthur James Balfour and the Navy 1904–1911' (Oxford Univ. D.Phil. thesis, 1987) pp.iii–vii.

Chapter 2   The South African War and Army Reform 1899–1903

1. This paragraph draws on J. Darwin, *Britain, Egypt and the Middle East* (London, 1981) pp.3–10.
2. P.M. Kennedy, *Strategy and Diplomacy 1870–1945* (London, 1983) p.18.
3. A.L. Friedberg, *The Weary Titan: Britain and the Experience of Relative Decline 1895–1905* (Princeton, NJ, 1988).
4. J.A.S. Grenville, *Lord Salisbury and Foreign Policy: the Close of the C19th* (London, 1964); G. Monger, *The End of Isolation: British Foreign Policy 1900–1907* (London, 1963).
5. Esher to Balfour, 16 Aug. 1910, British Library Additional MS [hereafter Add. MS] 49719 fos 153–4.
6. F.W. Perry, *The Colonial Armies* (Manchester, 1990) pp.82–6.
7. M. Yakutiel, 'Treasury control and the South African War 1899–c.1905', (unpublished Oxford Univ. D.Phil. thesis, 1989) p.88.
8. Friedberg, *The Weary Titan*, p.222.
9. Cited by J. McDermott, 'The revolution in British military thinking", p.101.
10. R.J.Q. Adams and P. Poirier, *The Conscription Controversy in Great Britain 1900–18* (London, 1987) pp.24–5.
11. This section is based on K. Jeffery, *The British Army and the Crisis of Empire 1918–22* (Manchester, 1984) pp.2–5.
12. H. Cunningham, *The Volunteer Force: A Social and Political History 1859–1908* (London, 1975).
13. For background, see A.N. Porter, *The Origins of the South African War; Joseph Chamberlain and the Diplomacy of Imperialism 1895–99* (Manchester, 1980); T. Pakenham, *The Boer War* (London, 1979) pp.11–114.
14. John Hay, quoted in W.R. Thayer *John Hay* 2 vols (Boston, Mass., 1908) II, pp.232–3.
15. Monger, *End of Isolation*, pp.12–13.
16. Mackay, *Balfour*, p.159, citing a War Office paper of 28 Feb. 1903; *Parliamentary Debates* [hereafter *Parl. Deb.*] 4th series., 1901, vol. 94, cols 382–3, 16 May.
17. I.F. Clarke, *Voices Prophesying War 1763–1984* (London, 1966) esp. pp.107–61; Gooch, *Prospect of War*, pp.1–15, 'The bolt from the blue'.
18. A. Tucker, 'Politics and the Army in the Unionist government in England, 1900–1905', The Canadian Historical Association, Report of the Annual Meeting (1964) with Historical Papers, p.106.
19. *Parl. Deb.* 4th ser., 1905, cxlvi, cols 67–8, 11 May.
20. M. Brett and Viscount Esher, *Journals and Letters of Reginald Brett Viscount Esher* 4 vols (London 1934–8) I, p.239.
21. Yakutiel, 'Treasury control', 149; Yakutiel's thesis offers a detailed analysis of Treasury policy and the financing of the war.
22. Memorandum by Ritchie, 21 Feb. 1903, Chamberlain Papers, AC 17/59.
23. Earl of Midleton, *Records and Reactions 1856–1939* (London, 1939) p.138.
24. For the various post-war commissions of inquiry, see Sir J. Dunlop, *The Development of the British Army 1899–1914* (London, 1938) pp.146–64.
25. Lansdowne to Balfour, 1 Nov. 1900, Sandars Papers, MS Eng. Hist. c.733 fos 11–12.

26. L.J. Satre, 'St John Brodrick and army reform, 1901–1903', *Journal of British Studies*, 15, 2 (1976) 119.
27. *Ibid.*, pp.119–20.
28. Brodrick to Salisbury 20 Jan. 1901, Salisbury Papers, Hatfield House MSS 3M/B/55.
29. Brodrick to Balfour, 29 Jan. 1900, Balfour Papers, Add. MS 49720, fos 74–5.
30. Balfour to Salisbury, 20 Oct. 1900, Salisbury Papers, Hatfield House MSS 3M/E.
31. Yakutiel, 'Treasury control', p.177.
32. Correlli Barnett, *Britain and Her Army 1509–1970* (London, 1970) p.367.
33. *Parl. Deb.* 4th ser., 1901, xc, 1060.
34. Balfour to Sandars, 23 Mar. 1900, Sandars Papers, MS Eng. Hist. c.731 fos 43–4, and 23 Oct. 1900, *ibid.*, c.732, fos 90–101.
35. Midleton, *Records and Reactions*, p.51; A. Lambert, *Unquiet Souls* (New York, 1984).
36. Brett and Esher, *Journals and Letters* I, p.269.
37. Spiers, *Haldane*, pp.4–5.
38. *Parl. Deb.* 4th ser., 1901, xc, 1063, 8 Mar.
39. Satre, 'St John Brodrick', p.121.
40. *Parl. Deb.* 4th ser., 1901, xc, 1059–60, 1079–80, 8 Mar.
41. Tucker, 'Politics and the Army', p.112.
42. 'Army Estimates 1902–3', 7 Dec. 1901, CAB 37/59/128.
43. Satre, 'St John Brodrick' pp.128–30.
44. I. Beckett, 'H.O. Arnold-Forster and the Volunteers', in *Politicians and Defence* ed. I. Beckett and John Gooch (Manchester, 1981) p.53.
45. *Ibid.*, pp.61–2.
46. Sandars to Arnold-Forster, 2 Jan. 1905 (copy), Balfour Papers, Add. MS 49723 fos 1–9.
47. Beckett, 'Arnold-Forster and the Volunteers', p.60.
48. Cunningham, *Volunteer Force*, p.131.
49. *Parl. Deb.* 4th ser., 1902, civ, 606–62, 6 Mar.
50. Hood to Sandars, 1 Mar. 1903, Sandars Papers, MS Eng. Hist. c.738 fos 185–90.
51. Akers Douglas to Sandars, 10 Nov. 1900, *ibid.*, c.733 fos 32–3.
52. For the Fourth Party, a small ginger group of aristocratic Conservatives hostile to the leadership of Sir Stafford Northcote from 1881 to 1884, see R.F. Foster, *Lord Randolph Churchill: A Political Life* (Oxford, 1981) chapters 3 and 4; Satre, 'St John Brodrick', gives a useful list of the imitative group of 1900–2, p.135, note 100.
53. R.S. Churchill, *Winston Spencer Churchill: Vol. II Young Statesman 1901–1914* (London 1967) pp.17–18.
54. *Ibid.*, p.20.
55. *Ibid.*, p.39.
56. Satre, 'St John Brodrick', p.134.
57. Young, *Arthur James Balfour*, p.229.
58. Hugh Cecil to Balfour, n.d.[July 1902], Sandars Papers, MS Eng. Hist. c.736 fos 7–8; J.E.B. Seely, *Adventure* (London, 1930) pp.96–7.
59. W.S. Hamer, *The British Army: Civil–Military Relations 1885–1905* (Oxford, 1970) pp.201–9.
60. Satre, 'St John Brodrick', p.136.
61. Brodrick to Balfour, 28 Oct. 1900, Sandars Papers, MS Eng. Hist. c.732 fos 121–4.
62. Brodrick to Curzon, 25 Oct. 1901, cited Satre, 'St John Brodrick', p.130.
63. *Ibid.*, p.130.
64. CAB 37/64/15, Memo. of 21 Feb. 1903; Beach had left the Cabinet with Salisbury in July 1902.

65. Hood to Balfour, 25 Feb. 1903, Sandars Papers, MS Eng. Hist. c.738 fos 165–7; *Parl. Deb.*, 4th ser., 1901, cxviii, 515–31, 23 Feb.
66. For the Liberal party's difficulties at this time and its recovery see M. Pugh, *The Making of Modern British Politics 1867–1939* (Oxford, 1982) pp.99–102.
67. Hood to Sandars, 1 Mar. 1903, Sandars Papers, MS Eng. Hist. c.738 fos 185–90.
68. Hood to Balfour, 25 Feb. 1903, *ibid.*, fos 165–7.
69. Memorandum by Hood, n.d. [end Feb. 1903], *ibid.*, fos 180–1.
70. R. Churchill, *Winston Spencer Churchill*, II, pp.32, 47.
71. Quoted in Blake, *From Peel to Churchill*, p.169.
72. W.S. Churchill, *Great Contemporaries* (London, 1937) p.242.
73. A.J. Balfour, *Chapters of Autobiography* (London, 1930) pp.103–11.
74. D. Gillard, *The Struggle for Asia: A Study in British and Russian Imperialism, 1828–1914* (London, 1977); P. Hopkirk, *The Great Game: On Secret Service in High Asia* (London, 1990).
75. *The Times* 18 Nov. 1909, pp.8–9, speech at Nottingham.
76. M. Arnold-Forster, *Hugh Oakley Arnold-Forster 1855–1909: A Memoir* (London, 1910), pp.109–10.
77. Lord Newton, *Retrospection* (London, 1941) p.151; Sandars to Balfour, 20 Nov. 1912, Balfour Papers, Add. MS 49786 fos 35–6.
78. A.J. Marder, *The Anatomy of Sea Power: A History of British Naval Policy in the Pre-Dreadnought Era 1880–1905* (London, 1964) p.59.
79. *Parl. Deb.* 4th ser., 1902, cxii, 835–9, 6 Aug.
80. Mackay, *Balfour*, pp.66–70.
81. Young, *Arthur James Balfour*, p.229.
82. For Balfour's speech, see *Parl. Deb.* 4th ser., 1903, cxviii, 775–88, 24 Feb.; Young, *Arthur James Balfour*, p.229; A. Bigge to Sandars, 25 Feb. 1903, Sandars Papers, MS Eng. Hist. c.738 fos 175–8.
83. Hood to Sandars, 1 Mar. 1903, *ibid.*, fos 185–90.
84. Both were Souls.
85. Cunningham, *Volunteer Force*, p.131.
86. *Ibid.*, p.132.
87. *Parl. Deb.* 4th ser., 1903, cxix, 177–235, 10 Mar.
88. There is a substantial literature on the origins and politics of the Tariff Reform controversy; for a penetrating new treatment, see E.H.H. Green, *The Crisis of Conservatism: The Politics, Economics and Ideology of the British Conservative Party 1880–1914* (forthcoming).
89. L.S. Amery, *My Political Life* 2 vols (London, 1953) I, p.236.
90. Rempel, *Unionists Divided*, chapters 3–8, pp.49–150.
91. Hamer, *British Army* pp.201–10.
92. *Ibid.*, pp.187–9.
93. Brodrick to Balfour, 5 Sept. 1903, Balfour Papers, Add. MS. 49720 fos 215–16 & 9 Sept. 1903, Sandars Papers, MS Eng. Hist. c.741 fos 27–9.
94. Rempel, *Unionists Divided*, pp.55–63.
95. Sir Almeric Fitzroy, *Memories* 2 vols (London, 1925) I, p.271.
96. Dugdale, *Balfour*, I, p.366.
97. Midleton to Selborne, 6 Dec. 1927, Selborne Papers, MS 3 fos 212–13; Dugdale, *Balfour*, I, pp.364–70; Young, *Arthur James Balfour*, pp.223–6; Mackay, *Balfour*, pp.119–23.
98. A.N. Porter, 'Lord Salisbury, foreign policy and domestic finance, 1860–1900', in *Salisbury: The Man and his Policies* ed. R. Blake and H. Cecil (London, 1987) p.175.
99. I.F.W. Beckett, 'Edward Stanhope at the War Office, 1887–1892', *Journal of Strategic Studies* 5, 2 (1982) 278–307.
100. Sir C. Dilke and H. Spenser Wilkinson, *Imperial Defence* (London, 1892).

101. Mackay, *Balfour*, p.157.
102. M. Howard, *The Continental Commitment: The Dilemma of British Defence Policy in the Era of Two World Wars* (London, 1972) p.102.
103. D.R. Gillard, 'Salisbury and the Indian defence problem, 1885–1902', in *Studies in International History* ed. K. Bourne and D.C. Watt (London, 1967), p.238.
104. See Friedberg, *The Weary Titan*, chapter 5, pp.209–78, which offers an admirable analysis; also R.L. Greaves, *Persia and the Defence of India, 1884–1892* (London, 1959); G.J. Alder, *British India's Northern Frontier, 1865–95* (London, 1963); D.S. Richards, *The Savage Frontier* (London, 1990).
105. Gillard, 'Salisbury', p.241.
106. *Ibid.*, pp.236–48.
107. S. Mahajan, 'The defence of India and the end of isolation: a study in the foreign policy of the Conservative government, 1900–5', *Journal of Imperial and Commonwealth History*, 10, 2 (January 1982) 168–193.
108. MSS notes on Balfour's career, Chandos Papers, I/2/31.
109. Mackay, *Balfour*, p.157.
110. For a general picture of Russia's Asian policy, see D. Geyer *Russian Imperialism* (Leamington Spa, 1987); Monger, *End of Isolation*, pp.4, 96–7.
111. E.D. Steele, 'Salisbury at the India Office', in *Salisbury* ed. R. Blake and Cecil, p.128.
112. Balfour to Roberts, 18 Nov. 1905, Roberts Papers 7101/23/8/21.
113. Monger, *End of Isolation*, p.139.
114. Balfour to Hamilton, 9 Mar. 1903 (copy), Balfour Papers, Add. MS 49778 fos 93–4.
115. Memorandum on army reorganization, 24 Feb. 1900, CAB 37/52/27.
116. Selborne to Balfour, 5 Apr. 1903, Balfour Papers, Add. MS. 49707 fos 120–2.
117. Mackay, *Balfour*, p.158.
118. *Parl. Deb.* 4th ser., 1905, cxlvi, 62–84.
119. 'A note on the military needs of the Empire', 19 Dec. 1904, CAB 3/1/28A.
120. Cited by Adams and Poirier, *Conscription Controversy*, p.7.
121. Selborne to Brodrick, 2 June 1905, Selborne Papers 2 fos 53–6.
122. Mackail and Wyndham, *Life and Letters*, II, pp.498–500; for the reason for Wyndham's resignation, see p.53.
123. Hamilton to Curzon, 27 Feb. 1903, Hamilton MSS, cited Monger, *End of Isolation*, p.111.
124. Austen Chamberlain to Balfour, 8 Dec. 1908, Sandars Papers, MS Eng. Hist. c.747 fos 72–5.

Chapter 3 The Politics of Naval Reform 1900–3

1. Cited in P. Kennedy, *The Rise and Fall of British Naval Mastery* (London, 1983), p.210.
2. R. Robinson and J. Gallagher, *Africa and the Victorians: The Official Mind of Imperialism* (London, 1961) pp.339–78.
3. Marder, *Anatomy*, p.335.
4. Speech to the Primrose League, Albert Hall, 4 May 1898; *The Times* 5 May 1898, p.7.
5. Repington to Maxse, 17 Oct. 1907, Maxse Papers 458 f.588.
6. Marder, *Anatomy*, pp.375–80.
7. *Ibid.*, p.380.
8. Hamilton, 'Nation and the Navy'; Marder, *Anatomy*, pp.44–61
9. Marder, *Anatomy*, p.55.

10. *Ibid.*, pp.390–1.
11. Hamilton, 'Nation and the Navy', p.201.
12. Summers, 'The character of Edwardian nationalism', pp.68–87.
13. *Ibid.*, p.69: Marder, *Anatomy*, p.54.
14. Hamilton, 'Nation and the Navy', p.310.
15. *The Times* 25 Oct. 1900, p.6.
16. For example, see Arnold White's comments in *Efficiency and Empire* (London, 1901) pp.278–9.
17. Balfour to Salisbury, 20 Oct. 1900, cited Monger, *End of Isolation*, p.9.
18. Even Balfour was sensitive on this point; Balfour to Salisbury, 23 Oct. 1900 (copy), Sandars Papers, MS Eng. Hist. 730 fos 95–8; David Cecil in *The Cecils of Hatfield House* (London, 1973) p.286, describes Salisbury's daughter Maud Selborne as having 'a head like that of a formidable but good-humoured senator of ancient Rome'.
19. A. Hurd, *Who Goes There?* (London, 1942), p.77.
20. Marder, *Anatomy*, chapter 20, pp.417–26.
21. See chapter 5, pp.69–74.
22. Memorandum by the First Lord on the Navy Estimates 1903–4, Cawdor Papers 290.
23. Mackay, *Fisher*, p.245.
24. Marder, *Anatomy*, p.419.
25. Memorandum on the Mediterranean naval situation, 26 June 1901, Balfour Papers, Add. MS 49722 fos 46–62.
26. Arnold-Forster, *Hugh Oakley Arnold-Forster*, p.177.
27. Marder, *Anatomy*, p.418.
28. *Parl. Deb.* 4th ser., 1901, ciii, Appendix I.
29. *Ibid.*, xcvii, 238, 12 July.
30. Marder, a devoted admirer, describes Fisher as 'one of the most interesting personalities of the twentieth century', *From the Dreadnought*, p.15.
31. Sir R. Bacon, *The Life of Lord Fisher of Kilverstone* 2 vols (London, 1929): Marder, *From the Dreadnought*, I; Mackay, *Fisher*; the most readable life (and a very perceptive one) is R. Hough, *First Sea Lord* (London, 1969).
32. *Fear God and Dread Nought: the Correspondence of Admiral of the Fleet Lord Fisher of Kilverstone* 3 vols (London, 1952–9).
33. Edward VII & George V respectively; Mackay, *Fisher*, p.1.
34. Hough, *First Sea Lord*, pp.185–94, offers a vivid picture.
35. Esther Maynell, cited by Marder, *From the Dreadnought*, I, p.14.
36. Hough, *First Sea Lord*, p.193.
37. Until 1904 the naval members of the Board of Admiralty were known as Naval Lords; in October 1904 they were re-designated Sea Lords. To avoid confusion, the revised designation will be used here.
38. Lord Hankey, *The Supreme Command* 2 vols (London, 1961) I, p.19.
39. Chatfield quoted by Mackay, *Fisher*, p.230.
40. Hough, *First Sea Lord*, pp.127–33.
41. Quoted by Mackay, *Fisher*, p.252.
42. Hurd, *Who Goes There?* pp.77–9.
43. Selborne to Balfour, 26 Dec. 1904, Balfour Papers, Add. MS 49708 fos 40–3.
44. 'Some memories and some reflections in my old age', Selborne Papers 191, p.101.
45. Marder, *Fear God*, I, p.222.
46. Hough, *First Sea Lord*, p.150.
47. Mackay, *Fisher*, pp.274–84.
48. Sir Charles Walker quoted by Mackay, *Fisher*, p.284.
49. Marder, *From the Dreadnought*, I, pp.34–5.
50. Archibald Hurd of the *Daily Telegraph* in Sept. 1903, quoted by Marder, *Anatomy*, p.417.

51. Milner to Selborne, 4 May 1903, Selborne Papers 12 fos 21–4.
52. Wyndham to Balfour, 23 Sept. 1903, Sandars Papers, MS Eng. Hist. c.742 fos 97–101; Arnold-Forster, *Hugh Oakley Arnold-Forster*, p.180.
53. Marder, *Anatomy*, p.425.
54. *The Times*, 26 Feb. 1903, p.8.
55. Arnold-Forster, *Hugh Oakley Arnold-Forster*, p.191.
56. Selborne to Balfour, 24 Sept. 1903, Sandars Papers, MS Eng. Hist. c.743 fos 145–8.
57. Notes by Balfour, July 1902, *ibid.*, c.736 fos 1–2.
58. Marder, *Fear God*, I, p.222.
59. W.S. Churchill, *The World Crisis* 2 vols (London, 1938) I, p.55.
60. Marder, *From the Dreadnought*, I, p.29.
61. *Ibid.*, p.31.
62. Quoted by Hough, *First Sea Lord*, p.157.
63. Arnold-Forster, *Hugh Oakley Arnold-Forster*, pp.191–2.
64. Mackay, *Fisher*, pp.296–7.
65. Selborne to Balfour, 24 Sept. 1903, Sandars Papers, MS Eng. Hist. c.743 fos 145–8.
66. Hough, *First Sea Lord*, p.162.
67. Hamer, *British Army*, pp.231–2.
68. Arnold-Forster to Balfour, 16 Oct. 1903, Balfour Papers, Add. MS 49722 fos 71–6; Arnold-Forster to Sandars, 18 Oct. 1903, Sandars Papers, MS Eng. Hist c.745 f.179; Chamberlain to Balfour, telegram, 25 Sept. 1903, Sandars Papers, MS Eng. Hist. c.743 fos 152–3.
69. Memorandum by Balfour, 14 Oct. 1903, Balfour Papers, Add. MS 49761 fos 120–5.
70. Mackay, *Fisher*, p.262.
71. Chamberlain to Balfour, telegram, 25 Sept. 1903, Sandars Papers, MS Eng. Hist. c.743 fos 152–3.
72. Mackay, *Fisher*, p.295.
73. Selborne to Balfour, 6 Sept. 1903, Balfour Papers, Add. MS 49707 f.141.
74. Arnold-Forster to Balfour, 14 Oct. 1903 (copy), Arnold-Forster Papers, Add. MS 50335.
75. Marder, *Fear God*, I, pp.314–15.
76. See p.25.
77. Quoted by Hough, *First Sea Lord*, pp.158–9.
78. Mackay, *Fisher*, pp.299–303.
79. Balfour to Fisher, 3 Jan. 1904 (copy), Balfour Papers, Add. MS 49710 fos 71–3.
80. Balfour to Selborne, 7 Jan. 1904 (copy), Sandars Papers, MS Eng. Hist c.748 fos 30–1.
81. Fisher to Sandars, 23 Apr. 1904, *ibid.*, fos 100–1.
82. Hough, *First Sea Lord*, pp.163–4.
83. Mackay, *Fisher*, p.289.
84. Fisher to Sandars, 10 June 1904, Balfour Papers, Add. MS 49710 f.141.

Chapter 4   Army Reform and the Militia Issue 1903–5

1. Chamberlain to Selborne, 23 Sept. 1903, Selborne Papers 9 fos 166–7.
2. Selborne to Sandars, 27 Sept. 1903, Sandars Papers, MS Eng. Hist. c.742 fos 217–21.
3. Sandars to Selborne, 21 Sept. 1903, Selborne Papers 1 fos 20–5.
4. Hood to Sandars, 20 Sept. 1903, Sandars Papers, MS Eng. Hist. c.741 fos 31–4 and 27 Sept. 1903, c.742 fos 226–9.

5.   Arnold-Forster to Balfour, 15 June 1897, Balfour Papers, Add. MS 49722 fos 15–19; Hamer, *British Army*, p.228.
6.   Viscount Chilston, *Chief Whip* (London, 1961) pp.312–24; A. Tucker, 'The issue of army reform in the Unionist government 1903–5', *Historical Journal* 9, 1 (1966) 92–3; I.F.W. Beckett, 'Arnold-Forster and the Volunteers', p.50.
7.   Notes on a possible Cabinet reshuffle, July 1902, Sandars Papers, MS Eng. Hist. c.736 fos. 9–62.
8.   Selborne to Balfour, 27 Sept. 1903, *ibid.*, c.742 fos 217–21.
9.   Douglas to Selborne, 21 Sept. 1903, *ibid.*, fos 48–9.
10. Balfour to Arnold-Forster, 4 Oct. 1903 (copy), *ibid.*, c.744 fos 128–9.
11. Chamberlain to Balfour, 19 Sept. 1903, *ibid.*, c.741 fos 7–10.
12. Selborne to Balfour, 27 Sept. 1903, *ibid.*, c.742 fos 217–21.
13. Notes by Balfour, n.d. [c.17 Sept. 1903], *ibid.*, c.743 fos 3–6.
14. Sandars to Balfour, 24 Sept.1903 (copy telegram), *ibid.*, f.117.
15. Douglas to Sandars, 21 Sept. 1903, *ibid.*, c.742 fos 48–9.
16. Balfour to Selborne, 23 Sept. 1903 (copy telegram), Selborne Papers 1 fos 26–7.
17. Balfour to Devonshire, 26 Sept. 1903 (copy), Sandars Papers, MS Eng. Hist. c.742 fos 193–5.
18. Selborne to Sandars, 24 Sept. 1903, *ibid.*, c.741 fos 143–4.
19. Sandars to Selborne, 21 Sept. 1903, *ibid.*, c.742 fos 41–2.
20. The other names mooted were those of Sir George Goldie, former Governor of Nigeria, Lord Cawdor, chairman of the Great Western Railway, and the 11th Duke of Bedford, a prominent Militia colonel.
21. Iwan-Muller to Sandars, 24 Sept. 1903, Sandars Papers, MS Eng. Hist. c.742 fos 151–2.
22. Hamer, *British Army*, pp.224–5.
23. Mackay, *Balfour*, p.161.
24. Balfour to the King, 14 Dec. 1903, cited in Young, *Arthur James Balfour* p.229.
25. Arnold-Forster to Balfour, 8 Dec. 1903, Balfour Papers, Add. MS 49722 fos 91–6.
26. Dunlop, *Development of the British Army*, p.172.
27. Arnold-Forster to Balfour, 8 Dec. 1903, Balfour Papers, Add. MS 49722 fos 91–6.
28. Arnold-Forster to Balfour, 15 June 1897, enclosing 'Memorandum with regard to the condition of the Army and the existing military system', *ibid.*, fos 15–42; H.O. Arnold-Forster, *The War Office, the Army and the Empire* (London, 1900).
29. 'The reforms after the war', notes by Brodrick, September 1903, Balfour Papers, Add. MS 49720 fos 228–35.
30. Arnold-Forster, *Hugh Oakley Arnold-Forster*, pp.237–40.
31. Tucker, 'army reform', p.97.
32. See Chapter 2.
33. Notes by Arnold-Forster on the 'Auxiliary forces', May 1904, Balfour Papers, Add. MS 49722 fos 149–52.
34. Arnold-Forster, *Hugh Oakley Arnold-Forster*, p.285.
35. Fraser, *Lord Esher*, p.110.
36. Arnold-Forster, *Hugh Oakley Arnold-Forster*, p.255.
37. Mackay, *Balfour*, p.160.
38. Fraser, *Lord Esher*, p.113, n.15.
39. Mackay, *Balfour*, pp.160–1.
40. Beckett, 'Arnold-Forster and the Volunteers', p.53.
41. Arnold-Forster to Balfour, 29 Feb. 1904, Balfour Papers, Add. MS 49722 fos 130–3.
42. Balfour to the King, 19 May 1904, CAB 41/29/16.
43. Brett and Esher, *Journals and Letters*, II, p.58.

44. Balfour to the King, 13 July 1904, CAB 41/29/25.
45. Dunlop, *Development of the British Army*, p.177.
46. R.S. Churchill, *Winston S. Churchill. Companion Vol. II 1901–1914* (London, 1967) pp.347–8.
47. *Parl. Deb.* 4th ser., cxxxvi, 1176–215, 27 June 1904.
48. G. Phillips, *The Diehards: Aristocratic Society and Politics in Edwardian England* (Cambridge, Mass., 1979) pp.85–7, 97–8.
49. Beckett, 'Arnold-Forster and the Volunteers', p.53.
50. The Hampshire and Bedford regiments respectively.
51. Cited Beckett, 'Arnold-Forster and the Volunteers', p.53.
52. Brett and Esher, *Journals and Letters*, II, p.320.
53. See Lord Wolmer, MP [later 2nd Earl of Selborne], 'A militia regiment', *The Nineteenth Century* 122 (April 1987), 566–75.
54. Selborne to Arnold-Forster, 7 July 1904, Balfour Papers, Add. MS 49708 f.7.
55. Selborne to Salisbury, 5 May 1904, Salisbury Papers, Hatfield House MSS 4M/55/65–6.
56. Wyndham to Salisbury, 17 June 1904, *ibid.*, 4M/55/71–2; Notes on army reform by Salisbury, *ibid.*, 92–7.
57. Phillips, *The Diehards*, p.58.
58. Wyndham to Salisbury, 17 June 1904, Salisbury Papers, Hatfield House MSS 4M/55/71–2; notes on army reform by Salisbury, *ibid.*, 82–3, 96–7.
59. Fraser, *Lord Esher*, p.128.
60. Arnold-Forster to Salisbury, 10 Oct. 1904, Salisbury Papers, Hatfield House MSS 4M/55/104–5.
61. Arnold-Forster to Selborne, 11 Oct. 1904, Selborne Papers 39 fos 229–30.
62. *Parl. Deb.* 4th ser., cxxxvi, 1477–522, 28 June 1904.
63. Sandars to Balfour, 13 Dec. 1904, Balfour Papers, Add. MS 49762 fos 192–4.
64. Viscount Sydenham of Combe, *My Working Life* (London, 1929) p.192; Memorandum by the Prime Minister, 'Army reorganization' (copy), Selborne Papers 125 fos 120–3.
65. Clarke to Chirol, 14 Sept. 1904, Sydenham Papers, Add. MS 50832 fos 35–8; Gooch, *Prospect of War*, p.84.
66. Arnold-Forster's diary, 28 June 1904, Arnold-Forster Papers, Add. MS 50338.
67. Fraser, *Lord Esher*, p.114.
68. Arnold-Forster's diary, 28 June 1904, Add. MS 50338.
69. For a detailed analysis of the Indian defence issue in 1903–5, see Friedberg, *The Weary Titan*, pp.240–73.
70. Memorandum by the Prime Minister, 'Our present minimum military requirements and proposals for fulfilling them by a reorganization of the Regular Army and Militia', 24 Feb. 1905, CAB 38/8/10.
71. Balfour to Roberts, 20 Nov. 1905, printed in 'Universal training. Correspondence between Mr Balfour and Lord Roberts', Cd. 1233.
72. 'The defence of India', dispatch of Military Dept. Simla to the Secretary of State for India, 13 June 1901, Sandars Papers, MS Eng. Hist. c.747 fos 12–15.
73. *Parl. Deb.* 4th ser, cxlvi, 79.
74. Balfour to Roberts, 18 Nov. 1905, Roberts Papers 7101/23/8/21.
75. 'Demands for reinforcements By the Government of India', printed for the CID, 20 Feb. 1905, CAB 38/8/10.
76. Sandars to Esher, 18 Dec. 1904, Esher Papers, MSS 10/32.
77. See p.25 above.
78. Monger, *End of Isolation*, p.96.
79. 47th meeting of the CID, 22 June 1904, CAB 38/8/10, p.8.

80.   Selborne to Balfour, 5 Apr. 1903, Balfour Papers, Add. MS 49707 fos.120–2.
81.   'Army reorganization', paper by the Prime Minister dated 30 Mar. 1905, printed for the Cabinet 3 Apr. 1905, Selborne Papers 125 fos 120–3.
82.   Arnold-Forster's diary, 29 June 1904, Arnold-Forster Papers, Add. MS 50338.
83.   Brett and Esher, *Journals and Letters*, II, p.55; Balfour to Roberts, 12 July 1904, Roberts Papers 7101/23/8/11.
84.   CAB 4/1/26B, dated 22 June 1904.
85.   Esher to Arnold-Forster, 5 Feb. 1905, Arnold-Forster Papers, Add. MS 50344.
86.   Fraser, *Lord Esher*, p.136.
87.   'Our present minimum military requirements and proposals for fulfilling them by a reorganization of the Regular Army and Militia', 24 Feb. 1905, CAB 38/8/10.
88.   Spiers, *Haldane*, p.4.
89.   'Army reorganization', 30 March 1905, Selborne Papers 125 fos 120–3.
90.   Fraser, *Lord Esher*, p.141.
91.   Arnold-Forster to Selborne, 13 Feb. 1905, Selborne Papers 46 fos 15–16; Fraser, *Lord Esher*, pp.137–8.
92.   Arnold-Forster to Balfour, 5 Apr. 1905, Sandars Papers, MS Eng. Hist. c.749 fos 91–4.
93.   Memorandum by the Secretary of State for War, 9 June 1905, CAB 37/78/106.
94.   Selborne to Brodrick, 3 July 1905, Selborne Papers 2 f.159.
95.   Fitzroy, *Memories*, I, pp.240–1; Sir A. Griffith-Boscawen, *Fourteen Years in Parliament* (London, 1907) p.331.
96.   Unionist suspicions focused on Wyndham's Permanent Under-Secretary, Sir Antony Macdonnell, who was a Catholic; for a recent account of the affair, see T.A. Jackson, *The Ulster Party: Irish Unionists in the House of Commons 1884–1911* (Oxford, 1989) pp.243–83.
97.   *Parl. Deb.* 4th ser., 1905, cxli, 725–52, 21 Feb.
98.   Beckett, 'Arnold-Forster and the Volunteers', pp.60–6.
99.   Salisbury to Selborne, 13 May 1905, Selborne Papers 5 fos 96–101.
100.   Brodrick to Selborne, 12 May 1905, Selborne Papers 2 fos 41–7.
101.   Fraser, *Lord Esher*, p.170.
102.   *Ibid.*, p.169.
103.   Balfour to Roberts, 12 Aug. 1905, Roberts Papers 7101/23/8/19.
104.   'The govt. and the Army', draft article [1905], Spenser Wilkinson Papers, O.T.P. 13/47.
105.   Article in the *Daily Mail*, 17 Dec. 1904, quoted by R. Churchill, *Winston S. Churchill*, II, 86.
106.   Mackay, *Balfour*, p.131.
107.   For fuller accounts of the origins and development of the NSL, see; M.J. Allison, 'The national service issue 1899–1914' (unpublished University of London Ph.D. thesis, 1975); Summers, 'Militarism in Britain', pp.104–123; Adams and Poirier, *Conscription Controversy*; Denis Hayes, *Conscription Conflict* (London, 1949) pp.36–49.
108.   G.R. Searle, *The Quest for National Efficiency: A Study in British Politics and Political Thought 1899–1914* (Oxford, 1971).
109.   Allison, 'National service issue', p.65.
110.   Adams and Poirier, *Conscription Controversy*, p.11.
111.   *Ibid.*, p.19.
112.   See Lloyd George's comment in his Criccieth Memorandum of 1910, quoted by John Grigg, *Lloyd George: The People's Champion 1902–1911* (London, 1978) pp.362–8.
113.   Adams and Poirier, *Conscription Controversy*, p.24; Summers, 'Militarism in Britain', p.114.
114.   E.g. Barnett, *Britain and her Army*, p.367.
115.   Roberts to Esher, 3 June 1909, Esher Papers 5/30.

116. Summers, 'Militarism in Britain', p.113.
117. Adams and Poirier, *Conscription Controversy*, p.17; Allison, 'National service issue', pp.73–85; for Roberts' career in general, see David James, *Lord Roberts* (London, 1954); R.J.Q. Adams, 'Field Marshal Earl Roberts: Army and Empire', in *Studies in Edwardian Conservatism* ed. J.A. Thompson and A. Meiji (London, 1988) pp.41–76.
118. Balfour to Roberts, 12 Aug. 1905, Roberts Papers 7101/23/8/19; Roberts' speech is reprinted in Field Marshal Earl Roberts, *A Nation in Arms* (London, 1907) pp.22–65.
119. Allison, 'National service issue', pp.69–72.
120. Balfour to Roberts, 18 Nov. 1905, Roberts Papers 7101/23/8/21.
121. Roberts was proposing a training period of ten months.
122. Balfour to Knollys, 18 Sept. 1905 (copy), Balfour Papers, Add. MS 49865 fos 39–41.
123. Mackail and Wyndham, *Life and Letters*, II, p.515.

Chapter 5   The Politics of Naval Reform 1903–5

1. Quoted in Monger, *End of Isolation*, p.110.
2. Memorandum of 21 Feb. 1903, Chamberlain Papers, AC17/59.
3. Selborne to Balfour, 28 Oct. 1903, Sandars Papers, MS Eng. Hist. c.745 fos 214–17.
4. An interesting comparison can be made with his approach to the issues of *laisser-faire* raised by the tariff debate: see, for instance, Balfour to Devonshire, 27 Aug. 1903 (copy), Sandars Papers, MS Eng. Hist. c.739 fos 184–98.
5. Monger, *End of Isolation* pp.123–7, 147–55.
6. Note on a memorandum by Selborne, 26 Feb. 1904, Chamberlain Papers AC7/5B.
7. Mackay, *Balfour*, pp.161–2.
8. Selborne to Chamberlain, 9 Feb. 1904, with minutes by Chamberlain and Lansdowne, Selborne Papers 39 fos 115–16.
9. Balfour to the King, 14 Dec. 1903, CAB 41/28/27.
10. For Chamberlain, pp.46–47 above.
11. See p.15 above.
12. *Parl. Deb.* 4th ser., 1904, cxxx, 1302, 29 Feb.
13. Austen Chamberlain to Selborne, 7 May 1904, Selborne Papers 39 fos 147–8; Memorandum by Selborne for the PM, [May] 1904, Selborne Papers 158 fos 191–200; Marder, *Anatomy*, p.486.
14. Sandars to Balfour, 14 Sept. 1904, Balfour Papers, Add. MS 49762 fos 120–22.
15. Chamberlain to Selborne, 3 Sept. 1904, Selborne Papers 39 fos 155–6.
16. Monger, *End of Isolation*, p.167.
17. Selborne to Chamberlain, 22 Mar. 1904 (copy), Selborne Papers 39 fos 133–4.
18. Chamberlain to Selborne, 12 Nov. 1904, *ibid.*, fos 159–65.
19. Sandars to Balfour, 14 Sept. 1904, Balfour Papers, Add. MS 49762 fos 120–2.
20. Chamberlain to Selborne, 12 Nov. 1904, Selborne Papers 39 fos 159–65.
21. Selborne to Chamberlain, 11 Nov. 1904 (copy), *ibid.*, fos 157–58.
22. Beaumont to Noel, 26 June 1904, Noel Papers, NOE/5.
23. Quoted by Mackay, *Fisher*, p.306.
24. Marder, *From The Dreadnought*, I, p.24: Mackay, *Fisher*, p.343.
25. Fisher to Thursfield, 5 July 1903, Thursfield Papers, THU/1.
26. Hough, *First Sea Lord*, p.176.
27. *Ibid.*, p.130.
28. Fisher to Sandars, 29 July 1904, Balfour Papers, Add. MS 49710 fos 150–2.
29. Hough, *First Sea Lord*, p.178.
30. Chamberlain to Selborne, 12 Nov. 1904, Selborne Papers 39 fos 159–65.

31. Balfour to Selborne, 26 Nov. 1904, *ibid.*, fos 35–6.
32. Sandars to Balfour, 14 Sept. 1904, Balfour Papers, Add. MS 49762 fos 120–2.
33. Fisher to Sandars, 30 Jan. 1904, *ibid.*, Add. MS 49710 fos 115–19; Mackay, *Fisher*, pp.305–6.
34. What follows is largely based on Marder, *Anatomy*, pp.483–95 and *From The Dreadnought*, I, pp.36–45.
35. Goschen's words, quoted by C.J. Bartlett, 'The mid-Victorian reappraisal of naval policy', in Bourne & Watt eds, *Studies in International History*, p.205.
36. *Ibid.*, pp.189–208: Bartlett shows how this earlier bout of naval redistribution was also economically motivated.
37. Quoted by Hough, *First Sea Lord*, p.494.
38. For 1903 see Mackay, *Fisher*, p.312.
39. Lee to Selborne, 5 July 1905, Salisbury Papers, Hatfield House MSS 4M/56/80–7.
40. *Parl. Deb.* 4th ser., 1906, clii, 1340, 1 Mar.
41. Chamberlain to Balfour, 23 Sept. 1903, Sandars Papers, MS Eng. Hist. c.742 fos 102–3; Long to Sandars, 23 Sept. 1903, *ibid.*, fos 114–17; Viscount Long of Wraxhall, *Memories* (London, 1923) pp.140–2; Fitzroy, *Memories*, I, pp.240–2.
42. Memorandum by Balfour, 4 Dec. 1905, Balfour Papers, Add. MS 49711 fos 133–4.
43. Quoted by Hurd, *Who Goes There?* pp.79–80.
44. Memorandum of 4 Dec. 1905, Balfour Papers, Add. MS 49711 fos 113–14.
45. Mackay, *Balfour*, pp.62–4.
46. Marder, *Fear God*, II, p.47.
47. B. Drake and M. Cole (eds) *Our Partnership by Beatrice Webb* (London, 1948) pp.248–9.
48. Brodrick to Selborne, 8 Dec. 1905, Selborne Papers 2 fos 120–4; Salisbury to Selborne, 1 Sept 1905, Selborne Papers 5 fos 102–5.
49. A. Clark (ed.), *A Good Innings. The Private Papers of Viscount Lee of Fareham* (London, 1974) p.88.
50. Bridge to Noel, 20 Aug. 1905, Noel Papers 5.
51. Marder, *From The Dreadnought*, I, p.85.
52. *Ibid.*, p.56.
53. A. White, 'The new gunnery', *National Review* 45, 267 (May 1905) 515; Pretyman to Selborne, 5 July 1905, Salisbury Papers, Hatfield House MSS 4M/56/88–93.
54. The 6th Marquess of Londonderry was President of the Board of Education 1902–5 and Lord President of the Council 1903–5.
55. The best example is Capt. Reginald Bacon, Fisher's later biographer; see his *From 1900 Onward* (London, 1940) esp. pp.91–103.
56. Arnold-Forster to Haldane, 18 Dec. 1905, (copy), Arnold-Forster Papers, Add. MS 50353 fos 76–86.
57. *Parl. Deb.* 4th ser., 1906, clvii, 1480–2, 24 May, Arnold-Forster.
58. Cd. 2791, issued 4 Dec. 1905, Admiralty Prints, 'Naval necessities', iii, pp.365–403.
59. Cawdor to Balfour, 29 Oct. 1905, Balfour Papers, Add. MS 49709 fos 8–9.
60. Selborne to Sir A. Douglas, 27 Dec. 1905, Selborne Papers 198 f.137; Pretyman to Fisher, 8 Dec. 1905, Fisher Papers 3/1/1836.
61. G. Kennan, *The Fateful Alliance: France, Russia and the Coming of the First World War* (Manchester, 1984).
62. Memorandum by the First Lord, 17 Jan. 1901, cited Monger, *End of Isolation*, p.10.
63. This section is based on the excellent analysis in Friedberg, *The Weary Titan*, pp.135–208.
64. Sumida, *Naval Supremacy*, p.11.
65. Memorandum on the naval situation in the Mediterranean by H.O.Arnold-Forster, 26 June 1901, Balfour Papers, Add. MS 49722 fos 46–62.

66. I. Nish, *The Anglo-Japanese Alliance* (London, 1966).
67. Friedberg, *The Weary Titan*, pp.161–74.
68. *Ibid.*, p.206.
69. P. Padfield, *The Great Naval Race* (London, 1974) pp.93, 95: also J. Steinberg, *Yesterday's Deterrent: Tirpitz and the Birth of the German Battle Fleet* (London, 1965).
70. Selborne to Beach, 29 Dec. 1900, St Aldwyn MSS PCC/83, cited Monger, *End of Isolation*, p.12.
71. For the Anglo-German talks, see Monger, *End of Isolation*, pp.21–45.
72. Selborne to Balfour, 12 July 1902, Sandars Papers, MS Eng. Hist. c.736 fos 119–20.
73. Memorandum on the Navy Estimates 1903–4, Cawdor Papers 290.
74. Mackay, *Fisher*, pp.236–7.
75. Arnold-Forster's Notes on a Visit to Wilhelmshaven, Aug. 1902, Arnold-Forster Papers, Add. MS 50287.
76. Memoranda by the First Lord, 17 Jan. and 16 Nov. 1901, Cawdor Papers 290; Friedberg, *The Weary Titan*, p.206.
77. Navy Estimates, 1903–4, memorandum by the First Lord, 10 Oct. 1902, Cawdor Papers 290.
78. *Parl. Deb.* 4th ser., 1904, cxxx, 1410–11, 1 Mar., Balfour.
79. Marder, *Anatomy*, p.510.
80. Sumida, *Naval Supremacy*, p.186.
81. Sandars to Balfour, 14 Sept. 1904, Balfour Papers, Add. MS 49762 fos 120–2.
82. Marder, *Fear God*, I, p.321.
83. *Ibid.*
84. *Ibid.*
85. Marder, *Anatomy*, pp.511–12.
86. Archibald Hurd, quoted Friedberg, *The Weary Titan*, p.200.
87. C. Andrew, *Theophile Delcassé and the Making of the Entente Cordiale* (London, 1968) pp.180–215.
88. Monger, *End of Isolation*, pp.185–235.
89. Mackay, *Fisher*, pp.328–9.
90. Memorandum by the First Lord on the Navy Estimates for 1904–5, 26 Feb. 1904, Cawdor Papers 290.
91. Friedberg, *The Weary Titan*, p.191.
92. *Ibid.*, p.203.
93. 'Episodes of the month', *National Review* 45, 265 (March 1905) 28.
94. 'Lord Cawdor's opportunity', *National Review* 45, 268 (June 1905) 598.
95. For an account of the genesis of the Dreadnought, see Marder, *Anatomy*, pp.515–45.
96. Selborne to Baddeley, [?] June 1905, Selborne Papers 46 f.200.
97. Marder, *Anatomy*, p.513.
98. *Parl. Deb.* 4th ser., 1906, cxci, 431, 13 July.
99. E.L. Woodward, *Great Britain and the German Navy* (Oxford, 1935) p.98.

Chapter 6 Into Opposition 1905–6

1. Ramsden, *Age of Balfour*, pp.11–16.
2. John Morley's phrase, quoted by Dunlop, *Development of the British Army*, p.165.
3. Fitzroy, *Memories*, I, pp.268–9.
4. Arnold-Forster to Haldane, 11 Dec. 1905, Haldane Papers 5906 fos 259–60.
5. Spiers, *Haldane*, p.46.
6. B. Semmel, *Liberalism and Naval Strategy* (Boston, 1986) pp.124–8.

7.   H.C.G. Matthew, *The Liberal Imperialists: The Ideas and Politics of a Post-Gladstonian Elite* (Oxford, 1973) pp.215–23.

8.   Drake and Cole (eds), *Our Partnership*, p.283.

9.   *The Times* 22 Dec. 1905, p.7.

10.   Balfour to Devonshire, 27 Oct. 1905, quoted by A.K. Russell, *Liberal Landslide: the General Election of 1906* (Newton Abbot, 1973) pp.31–2.

11.   Memorandum by the First Lord for the Prime Minister, December 1904 (copy), Selborne Papers 158 fos 191–200.

12.   'Episodes of the month', *National Review* 45, 266 (Apr. 1905) 221.

13.   Young, *Arthur James Balfour* pp.232–6; Nish, *Anglo-Japanese* Alliance, pp.298–364.

14.   H. Willmott, 'The Navy Estimates, 1906–1909', (Univ. of Liverpool M.A. thesis, 1970) pp.15–16.

15.   Speech at Glasgow; *The Times* 19 Apr. 1909, p.7.

16.   Balfour to Edward VII, 19 June 1905, quoted by Young, *Arthur James Balfour*, p.236.

17.   Arnold-Forster to French, 2 Dec. 1905 (copy), Arnold-Forster Papers, Add MS 50353 fos 20–3.

18.   Matthew, *Liberal Imperialists*, esp. pp.195–223, 287–96.

19.   Fitzroy, *Memories*, I, pp.269–70; S. Koss, *Lord Haldane: Scapegoat For Liberalism* (New York, 1969) p.34.

20.   S. Koss, *Asquith* (London, 1976) pp.64–74.

21.   Brodrick to Tweedmouth, 21 Jan. 1906, Tweedmouth Papers A/333.

22.   Selborne to Baddeley, 4 Jan. 1906, Selborne Papers 46 f.207.

23.   Baddeley to Sandars, 14 Dec. 1905, Sandars Papers, MS Eng. Hist. c.750 fos 241–2.

24.   Tweedmouth to Cawdor, 14 Dec. 1905, Cawdor Papers, Admiralty Box A.

25.   Drake and Cole (eds) *Our Partnership*, pp.325–6.

26.   Spiers, *Haldane*, pp.43–5.

27.   Sir F. Maurice, *Haldane; The Life of Viscount Haldane of Cloan* 2 vols (London, 1937) I, pp.138–9.

28.   Arnold-Forster to Haldane, 18 Dec. 1905, Haldane Papers 5906 fos 271–80.

29.   Arnold-Forster to Maxse, 27 Dec. 1905, Maxse Papers 453 fos 191–4.

30.   Sydenham, *My Working Life*, p.189; Fraser, *Lord Esher*, p.180.

31.   Brett and Esher, *Journals and Letters*, II, p.132.

32.   Maurice, *Haldane*, I, pp.78–9.

33.   Brett and Esher, *Journals and Letters*, III, p.246.

34.   Fraser, *Lord Esher*, pp.175–79.

35.   *Parl. Deb.* 4th ser., 1907, clxxvi, 1344, Lord Crewe on 26 June.

36.   For fuller accounts, see Monger, *End of Isolation*, pp.236–56; Williamson, *Grand Strategy*, pp.55–88.

37.   See Chapter 12.

38.   Salisbury to Selborne, 19 Jan. 1906, Selborne Papers 5 fos 110–17.

39.   W. Arnstein, 'Edwardian politics: turbulent spring or Indian summer?', in *The Edwardian Age; Conflict or Stability 1900–14* ed. A. O'Day (London, 1979) p.71.

40.   *Parl. Deb.* 4th ser., 1906, clii, 152, 19 Feb.

41.   Russell, *Liberal Landslide*, p.70.

42.   *Parl. Deb.* 4th ser., 1906, clxii, 118, 27 July.

43.   St Aldwyn [Hicks Beach] to Balfour, 25 Jan. 1906, Sandars Papers, MS Eng. Hist. c.751 fos 121–2; Salisbury to Selborne, 19 Jan. 1906, Selborne Papers 5 fos 110–17.

44.   Russell, *Liberal Landslide*, p.69.

45.   Election materials, Jan. 1906, Sandars Papers, MS Eng. Hist. c.751 fos 1–8.

46.   Russell, *Liberal Landslide*, p.92.

Chapter 7   Dreadnoughts and Politics 1906–8

1.   Viscount Haldane of Cloan, *Richard Burdon Haldane: An Autobiography* (London, 1929) pp.182–3.
2.   Sumida, *Naval Supremacy*, p.186 and Appendix, table 3.
3.   *Ibid.*, p.190.
4.   Willmott, 'The Navy Estimates', *passim.*
5.   Woodward, *German Navy*, pp.123–40.
6.   *Parl. Deb.* 4th ser., 1906, clxii, 114–119, 27 July.
7.   Maurice, *Haldane*, I, pp.198–9.
8.   Balfour to Arnold-Forster, 3 Nov. 1906 (copy), Balfour Papers, Add. MS 49723 fos 211–14.
9.   *Parl. Deb.* 4th ser., 1906, clxxi, 293–8.
10.   Austen to Mary Chamberlain, 5 Mar. 1907, Chamberlain Papers, AC4/1/143.
11.   Fisher to Balfour, c.11 Nov. 1906, Balfour Papers, Add. MS 49711 f.209.
12.   Sandars to Balfour, 2 Apr. 1907, *ibid*, Add. MS 49765 fos 34–8; Balfour to Arnold-Forster, 3 Nov. 1906 (copy), *ibid.*, Add. MS 49723 fos 215–18.
13.   Balfour to Farquhar, 14 Nov. 1906 (copy), *ibid.*, Add. MS 49859 fos 110–12.
14.   Austen to Mary Chamberlain, 5 Mar. 1907, Chamberlain Papers, AC4/1/143.
15.   Fisher to Balfour, undated [Nov.1906], Balfour Papers, Add. MS 49711 f.143.
16.   Mackail and Wyndham, *Life and Letters*, II, pp.565–6.
17.   For Balfour and Haldane, see Chapter 8.
18.   'Destroying Britain's naval supremacy', *National Review* xlviii, 283 (Sept. 1906), 38–50.
19.   I am grateful to Dr Alvin Jackson for information from the Wyndham Papers at Eaton Hall, Chester.
20.   Arnold-Forster to Balfour, 2 Nov. 1906, Balfour Papers, Add. MS 49723 fos 211–14.
21.   Austen to Mary Chamberlain, 5 Mar. 1907, Chamberlain Papers, AC4/1/143.
22.   Salisbury to Selborne, 23 June 1906, Selborne Papers 5 fos 138–43.
23.   Arnold-Forster to Balfour, 2 Nov. 1906, Balfour Papers, Add. MS 42973 fos 211–14.
24.   *Parl. Deb.* 4th ser., 1906, clxii, 114–19, 1396.
25.   *Ibid.*, 1907, clxx, 678–9; *The Standard* 6 Mar. 1907, p.7, parliamentary report.
26.   Cawdor to Balfour, 5 Mar. 1907, Balfour Papers, Add. MS 49709 fos 29–30.
27.   Austen to Mary Chamberlain, 5 Mar. 1907, Chamberlain Papers, AC4/1/143.
28.   Marder, *From The Dreadnought*, I, p.136.
29.   See pp.145–47.
30.   See p.72.
31.   Clark (ed.), *A Good Innings*, p.89; Lee to Balfour, 8 Feb. 1905, Balfour Papers, Add. MS 49857 fos 145–6.
32.   *Parl. Deb.* 4th ser., 1908, clxxxv, 418, 2 Mar.
33.   *Ibid.*, 584, 3 Mar.
34.   Wyndham to Balfour, 1 Mar. 1908, Balfour Papers, Add. MS 49806 fos 43–4.
35.   Woodward, *German Navy*, pp.134–40; *Parl. Deb.* 4th ser., clxxix, 987–90.
36.   Morris, *Radicalism Against War*, p.123.
37.   Asquith to Edward VII, 19 Feb. 1908 (copy), CAB 41/31/74.
38.   Fisher to Tweedmouth, 20 Dec. 1907, Tweedmouth Papers B/147a.
39.   *Parl. Deb.* 4th ser., 1908, clxxxv, 399, Robertson on 2 Mar. 908.
40.   *Ibid.*, 419.
41.   *Ibid.*, 1155; it was laid down on 22/7/1907 and launched on 22/3/1908.
42.   *Ibid.*, 1906, clxii, 112, 27 July.

43. Slade to Corbett, 15 Oct. 1907, Corbett Papers, 81/143/13.
44. *Parl. Deb.* 4th ser., 1908, clxxxv, 1180–1, Balfour on 9 Mar.
45. *The Standard* 4 Mar. 1908, p.7.
46. Slade's diary, 7 and 10 Mar. 1908, Slade Papers, MRF/39/3.
47. *Parl. Deb.* 4th ser., clxxxv, 1336–8.
48. Brett and Esher, *Journals and Letters*, II, p.295.
49. Williams, 'Politics of national defence', pp.90–3.
50. Sandars to Esher, 10 Mar. 1908, Esher Papers 5/26.
51. *Parl. Deb.* 4th ser., 1908, clxxxvi, 504; Sandars to Esher, 10 Mar. 1908, Esher Papers 5/26.
52. Williams, 'Politics of national defence', pp.93–5.
53. *Parl. Deb.* 4th ser., 1908, clxxxix, 1172–84.
54. Austen to Mary Chamberlain, 30 June 1908, Chamberlain Papers, AC 4/1/305.
55. Arnold-Forster to Balfour, 28 May 1908, Balfour Papers, Add. MS 49723 fos 252–7.
56. Balfour to Nield (copy), 6 Mar. 1908, *ibid.*, Add. MS 49859 fos 233–4.
57. Fisher to Balfour, 23 Feb. 1908, *ibid.*, Add. MS 49712 fos 34–5.
58. Fisher to Balfour, 29 Nov. 1907, *ibid.*, Add. MS 49712 fos 22–3.
59. Chamberlain to Maxse, 5 Feb. 1908, Maxse Papers 458 fos 649–50.
60. *Parl. Deb.* 4th ser., 1908, clxxxvi, 510.
61. Earl Winterton, *Pre-War* (London, 1932) p.140.
62. Maxse to Garvin, 10 Jan. 1908, Garvin Papers 1 [References to the Garvin papers are to transcripts very kindly made available to me by Prof. A.J.A. Morris].
63. Balfour to Nield, 6 Mar. 1908 (copy), Balfour Papers, Add. MS 49859 fos 233–4.
64. Balfour to Farquhar, 14 Nov. 1906 (copy), *ibid.*, fos 110–12.
65. For fuller accounts see: Morris, *Radicalism Against War*; Weinroth, 'Left wing opposition to naval armaments'.
66. Jordan, 'Pensions not Dreadnoughts'.
67. On Brunner, see S. Koss, *Sir John Brunner: Radical Plutocrat* (Cambridge, 1970).
68. *The Times* 3 Mar. 1908, p.9.
69. See Chapter 9.
70. *Parl. Deb.* 4th ser., 1908, clxxxv, 1181, Balfour on 9 Mar., and clxxxvi, 510, Cawdor on 8 Mar.
71. See pp.79–80.
72. Austen Chamberlain to Maxse, 24 Jan. 1907, Maxse Papers 457 fos 475–6.
73. Gwynne to Marker, 23 Aug. 1906, Marker Papers, Add. MS 52277B fos 175–81.
74. *The Standard* 3 Mar. 1908, p.7.
75. *Parl. Deb.* 4th ser., 1908, clxxxv, 369–82.
76. Wyndham to Balfour, 1 Mar. 1908, Balfour Papers, Add. MS 49806 fos 43–4.
77. Austen to Mary Chamberlain, 2 Mar. 1908, Chamberlain Papers, AC4/1/214; *The Standard* 3 Mar. 1908, p.7.
78. Asquith to Campbell-Bannerman, 30 Dec. 1906, Campbell-Bannerman Papers, Add. MS 41210 fos 273–6; Asquith to Tweedmouth, 21 Nov. 1907 (copy), Tweedmouth Papers, 'Navy Estimates, 1908–9'.
79. J. Grigg, *Lloyd George*, pp.174–5.
80. Asquith to Tweedmouth, 10 July 1906, Tweedmouth Papers, Box A/65.
81. S. McKenna, *Reginald McKenna 1863–1943: A Memoir* (London, 1948) p.65.
82. See p.142.
83. Selborne to Midleton, 25 May 1908, Selborne Papers 3 fos 34–43.
84. Austen to Mary Chamberlain, 2 June 1908, Chamberlain Papers, AC4/1/287.
85. Lansdowne to Salisbury, 8 Oct. 1908, Salisbury Papers, Hatfield House MSS 4M/61/52.
86. Esher's journal, 23 Aug. 1908, Esher Papers 2/11.

87.   Midleton to Selborne, 6 Nov. 1908, Selborne Papers 3 fos 86–90.
88.   *Daily Telegraph* 9 Feb. 1909, p.10.
89.   *The Times* 20 Nov. 1908, p.11.

Chapter 8   The Greatest Army Bill for Centuries

1.   *The Morning Post*, 20 July 1906, p.4, 'The question of the Army'.
2.   Sandars to Balfour, 20 Mar. 1906, Balfour Papers, Add. MS 49764 fos 176–9.
3.   In fact, Haldane's 'Blue Water' loyalties were evident as early as 1900; see Matthew, *Liberal Imperialists*, pp.216–17.
4.   *Parl. Deb.* 4th ser., 1906, cliii, 655–86.
5.   Selborne to Haldane, 5 Mar. 1906, Haldane Papers 5907 fos 32–42; *Parl. Deb.* 4th ser., 1906, cliii, 680–95, 1510–16.
6.   *Parl. Deb.* 4th ser., 1906, cliii, 1455–64.
7.   Haldane to his mother, 16 Mar. 1906, Haldane Papers 5975 fos 119–20.
8.   *Parl. Deb.* 4th ser., 1906, clx, 697, 10 July.
9.   *Ibid.*, 1075–1119.
10.   *Ibid.*, 1157–64, Balfour, and 1119–27, Arnold-Forster.
11.   Balfour to Esher, 6 Oct. 1906 (copy), Balfour Papers, Add. MS 49719 fos 55–6.
12.   Dunlop, *Development of the British Army*, p.261.
13.   'A preliminary memorandum on the present situation', Haldane Papers 5918 f.44.
14.   Spiers, *Haldane*, p.77.
15.   Gooch, *Prospect of War*, p.107.
16.   Viscount Haldane of Cloan, *Before The War* (London, 1920) pp.30–2.
17.   Gooch, *Prospect of War*, pp.107–9.
18.   Spiers, *Haldane*, p.81.
19.   *Ibid.*
20.   See Gooch, *Prospect of War*, pp.100–12, for what follows.
21.   'Military needs of the Empire: supplementary note by the Prime Minister', 19 Dec. 1904, CAB 3/1/28A.
22.   *Parl. Deb.* 4th ser., 1906, cliii, 707, 15 Mar.
23.   *Ibid.*, clx, 1161–3.
24.   Spiers, *Haldane*, pp.85–6.
25.   Sixth Memorandum, 8 Nov. 1906, Esher Papers 16/8.
26.   Even though it did not officially adopt the title until 1921, between 1907 and 1914 the Territorial Force was also commonly referred to as the 'Territorial Army'.
27.   Spiers, *Haldane*, pp.86–88.
28.   Bedford to Arnold White, 20 June 1906, White Papers, WHI/80.
29.   Dunlop, *Development of the British Army*, pp.269–71; Haig's diary, 27 June 1906, Haig Papers 3155 2f.
30.   Note by Esher et al. to the Secretary of State, June 1906, Esher Papers 16/8.
31.   Repington to Marker, 5 July 1906, Marker Papers, Add. MS 52277B fos 72–7; Haig to Ellison, 17 Sept. 1906, Haig Papers 40/q: Ellison's 'Notes on certain letters written at various times by the late Field Marshal Earl Haig to Lieut.-Gen. Sir Gerald Ellison, 11 Sept. 1928', Haig Papers 40/q; for Haig's role, see G. De Groot, *Douglas Haig 1861–1928* (London, 1988) esp. pp.119–23; also the same author's unpublished thesis, 'The prewar life and career of Douglas Haig' (Univ. of Edinburgh, Ph.D., 1983) Chapter 8, pp.270–320.
32.   Haldane's 'Sixth memorandum', 8 Nov. 1906, Esher Papers 16/8.
33.   Clarke to Balfour, 20 Sept. 1906, Balfour Papers, Add. MS 49702 fos 217–20; Peter Fraser's claim (*Lord Esher*, p.195) that Esher 'kept Balfour fully informed of the

evolution of the plan' is not borne out by the facts.
34.   Balfour to Arnold-Forster, 3 Nov. 1906 (copy), Balfour Papers, Add. MS 49723 fos 215–18.
35.   'Memorandum of Events Between 1906 and 1915', April 1916, Haldane Papers 5919 fos 129–30.
36.   Haldane, *Autobiography*, pp.193–4.
37.   *Pace* Maurice, *Haldane*, p.212.
38.   Haldane to Campbell-Bannerman, 9 Jan. 1907, Campbell-Bannerman Papers, Add. MS 41218 fos 177–84.
39.   Esher to Balfour, 9 Jan. 1907, Balfour Papers, Add. MS 49719 fos 59–61.
40.   Sir A. Chamberlain, *Politics From Inside: An Epistolary Chronicle 1906–1914* (London, 1936) p.325.
41.   MS note, Harcourt Papers 439 f.150.
42.   Wyndham to Dilke, 21 Feb. 1907, Dilke Papers, Add. MS 43919 fos 205–6.
43.   *Parl. Deb.* 4th ser., 1907, clxxii, 85.
44.   *Ibid.*, 1620–3.
45.   *The Times* 25 Apr. 1907, p.9: see also, *idem* 10 Apr, p.9.
46.   *Parl. Deb.* 4th ser., 1907, clxxii, 1671, 23 Apr.
47.   *Ibid.*, clxxiv, 1508, 28 May.
48.   *Ibid.*, clxxii, 83–98, Wyndham on 9 Apr.
49.   *Ibid.*, clxx, 294, 28 Feb.
50.   *Ibid.*, clxxii, 91.
51.   *The Times* 27 May 1907, p.3.
52.   Repington to Marker, 6 Aug. 1906, Marker Papers, Add. MS 52277B fos 103–10.
53.   Repington to Haldane, 19 Apr. 1907, Haldane Papers 5907 fos 144–5.
54.   Extract from *The Times* 24 Oct. 1905, Mottistone Papers 1 f.90.
55.   Repington to Marker, 19 July 1906, Marker Papers, Add. MS 52277B fos 86–91.
56.   Repington to Marker, 3 Aug. 1906, *ibid.*, fos 98–102.
57.   Repington to Marker, 15 Aug. 1906, *ibid.*, fos 111–14.
58.   It is significant that the National Defence Association, of which Repington was a leading light, passed a series of timely pro-Militia resolutions at its meeting on 23 April; Note of resolutions, Mottistone Papers 1 fos 160–1.
59.   'The Militia and the Lords', *The Times* 29 Mar. 1907, p.5.
60.   'Principles and progress', *The Times* 8 Apr. 1907, p.6.
61.   *Parl. Deb.* 4th ser., 1907, clxxii, 93, 9 Apr.
62.   *Ibid.*, 1670–86.
63.   Haldane's 'Sixth memorandum', 8 Nov. 1906, Esher Papers 16/8.
64.   Clarke to Balfour, 22 June 1907, Balfour Papers, Add. MS 49702 fos 236–7.
65.   Cd. 3336, 8 Apr. 1907, printed in *The Times* 9 Apr. 1907, p.3.
66.   *The Times* 20 Mar. 1907, p.9.
67.   Austen to Mary Chamberlain, 18 Mar. 1907, Chamberlain Papers, AC4/1/156.
68.   *Parl. Deb.* 4th ser., 1907, clxxii, 83–98.
69.   Haldane to his mother, 24 Apr. 1907, Haldane Papers 5977 fos 94–5.
70.   Brett and Esher, *Journals and Letters*, II, p.225.
71.   Haldane to his mother, 19 Dec. 1906, Haldane Papers 5977 fos 180–1.
72.   Repington to Haldane, 19 Apr. 1907, *ibid.*, 5907 fos 144–5.
73.   *Parl. Deb.* 4th ser., 1907, clxxiii, 1374–80.
74.   *Ibid.*, clxxiv, 1495–1501.
75.   *Ibid.*, clxxiv, 1520, Charles Hobhouse on 28 May.
76.   Clarke to Balfour, 1 Mar. 1907 and 12 Mar. 1907, Balfour Papers, Add. MS 49702 fos 228–30; 231–2.
77.   *Parl. Deb.* 4th ser., 1907, clxxiv, 1509–10.

78.   Haig's diary, 28 May 1907, Haig Papers 3155 2g.
79.   Salisbury to Balfour, 1 June 1907, Balfour Papers, Add. MS 49758 fos 178–81.
80.   Haig's diary, 3 June 1907, Haig Papers 3155 2g.
81.   Balfour to Clarke, 13 June 1907 (copy), Balfour Papers, Add. MS 49702 f.238.
82.   Lansdowne to Balfour, 7 June 1907, Balfour Papers, Add. MS. 49729 fos 296–7.
83.   *Parl. Deb.* 4th ser., 1907, clxxv, 1176–9, Balfour and 1180, Haldane.
84.   Haldane to his mother, 11 June 1907, Haldane Papers 5977 fos 163–4.
85.   'Military reforms. I The first line', *The Times* 21 June 1907, p.15.
86.   Balfour to Clarke, 13 June 1907 (copy), Balfour papers, Add. MS 49702 f.238.
87.   *Parl. Deb.* 4th ser., 1907, clxxvi, 182–7.
88.   *Ibid.*, 187; Memorandum sent by Balfour to the Duke of Bedford, 18 June 1907 (copy), Balfour Papers, Add. MS 49859 fos 152–3.
89.   Haldane to Pringle-Pattison, 11 June 1907 (copy), Haldane Papers 5907 f.168.
90.   *Parl. Deb.* 4th ser., 1907, clxxvi, 533–9.
91.   Cawdor to Balfour, 17 June 1907, Balfour Papers, Add. MS 49709 fos 34–5.
92.   Salisbury to Selborne, 27 June 1907, Selborne Papers 5 fos 170–3.
93.   *Parl. Deb.* 4th ser., 1907, clxxvi, 1273–87, Salisbury, and 1332–43, Lansdowne.
94.   *Ibid.*, 1313–14.
95.   Bedford to Salisbury, 9 Feb. 1907, Salisbury Papers, Hatfield House MSS 4M/MY11/130.
96.   Selborne to Salisbury, 15 Aug. 1907, *ibid.*, 4M/61/8–16.
97.   Brett and Esher, *Journals and Letters*, I, pp.240–1.
98.   Salisbury to Balfour, 4 June 1907, Balfour Papers, Add. MS 19758 fos 178–81.
99.   Esher to Edward VII, 3 July 1907 (copy), Esher Papers 4/2 f.44; Douglas to Esher, 29 June 1907, *ibid.*, 5/22 fos 242–3.
100.   Haig's diary, 4 and 5 July 1907, Haig Papers 3155 2g.
101.   Haldane to his mother, 4 July 1907, Haldane Papers 5978 fos 1–2; *Parl. Deb.* 4th ser., 1907, clxxvii, 1085–90.
102.   Haldane to Selborne, 19 July 1907, Selborne Papers 79 f.22.
103.   *Parl. Deb.* 4th ser., 1907, clxxviii, 554–61; Bedford to White, 30 June 1907, White Papers, WHI/80.
104.   *Parl. Deb.* 4th ser., 1907, clxxviii, 865–70; Haldane to his mother, 18 and 19 July 1907, Haldane Papers 5978 fos 25, 27–8.
105.   *The Times* 19 July 1907, p.9.
106.   Haldane to his mother, 31 July 1907, Haldane Papers 5978 fos 43–4.
107.   Fitzroy, *Memories*, I, p.326.
108.   'Memorandum of events between 1906 and 1915', Haldane Papers 5919 f.130.
109.   Haldane, *Autobiography*, p.195.
110.   *Parl. Deb.* 4th ser., 1907, clxxvii, 1387.
111.   Clarke to Balfour, 12 June 1907, Balfour Papers, Add. MS 49702 fos 236–7.
112.   Brett and Esher, *Journals and Letters*, II, p.240.
113.   Spiers, *Haldane*, pp.11–28: Gooch, *Prospect of War*, pp.94–8.
114.   J.A. Spender, *The Life of the Rt. Hon. Sir Henry Campbell-Bannerman* 2 vols (London 1923) II, p.326.
115.   The quotation is from Fraser, *Lord Esher*, p.196; Peter Simkins is still wider of the mark in claiming that the Bill 'aroused little excitement in the Commons', *Kitchener's Army: The Raising of the New Armies 1914–1916* (Manchester, 1988) p.14.
116.   See the comment of Gilbert Parker, MP, on 5 June, *Parl. Deb.* 4th ser., 1907, clxxv, 1106.
117.   Fraser, *Lord Esher*, p.198.
118.   Repington to Balfour, 3 June 1907, Balfour Papers, Add. MS 49859 fos 138–9.

Chapter 9   The Politics of Naval Reform 1906–10

1.   This chapter is an amended version of my article, 'Arthur James Balfour, Sir John Fisher and the politics of Naval Reform 1904–1910', *Historical Research* 60, 141 (Feb. 1987) 80–99.
2.   Marder, *Fear God*, II, p.67.
3.   *Parl. Deb.* 4th ser., 1906, clvii, 1461–71, 24 May, Bellairs; *ibid.*, clii, 234–43, 6 Mar., Goschen.
4.   *Ibid.*, clvii, 1480, 24 May; the description of Robertson comes from a parliamentary report in *The Standard* 4 Mar. 1908, p.7.
5.   *Ibid.*, clii, 1335–42, 1 Mar.
6.   *Ibid.*, 1365; Marder, *Fear God*, II, pp.68–9.
7.   *Parl. Deb.* 4th ser., 1906, clvii, 1471–7, Lee, and 1480–2, Arnold-Forster.
8.   *Ibid.*, clxii, 294, 30 July.
9.   *Ibid.*, clx, 118, 12 July, Haldane; *ibid.*, clxii, 76, 27 July, Lee.
10.   *Ibid.*, clvii, 1477.
11.   Marder, *Fear God*, II, p.67.
12.   *Ibid.*, p.68.
13.   *Parl. Deb.* 4th ser., 1906, clxii, 67–75, 27 July.
14.   'Episodes of the month', *National Review*, 48, 283 (Sept. 1906) 2–9; 'The reduction of the Navy', *The Morning Post* 28 July 1906, p.6.
15.   Marder, *From The Dreadnought*, II, pp.71–2.
16.   Thursfield to Buckle, 18 Oct. 1906, Times Newspapers Archive; *The Standard* 2 Mar. 1907, p.7.
17.   Maxse to Lady Bathurst, 17 Dec. 1906, Glenesk-Bathurst Papers.
18.   Willmott, 'The Navy Estimates', pp.76–8.
19.   Mackail and Wyndham, *Life and Letters*, II, pp.565–6; Arnold-Forster to Balfour, 2 Nov. 1906, Balfour Papers, Add. MS 49723 fos 211–4.
20.   'The state of the Navy', *The Times* 22 Jan. 1907, p.8.
21.   King-Hall to Esher, 6 Feb. 1908 (copy), Fisher Papers 1/6/287.
22.   Esher's journal, 3 Jan. 1907, Esher Papers 7/20.
23.   Fisher to Thursfield, 25 Dec. 1906, Thursfield Papers Thu/1; John Morley was Secretary of State for India and John Burns President of the Local Government Board.
24.   Lambert to Fisher, 28 Jan. 1907, Fisher Papers 1/5/222.
25.   Willmott, p.88: Fisher to Tweedmouth, 21 Feb. 1907, Tweedmouth Papers B/125.
26.   Dilke to Thursfield, 24 Jan. 1907, Dilke Papers, Add MS 43893, fos 167–9.
27.   Fisher to Tweedmouth, 22 Feb. 1907, Tweedmouth Papers B/125; *The Papers of Admiral Sir John Fisher* ed. P. Kemp, 2 vols (Navy Records Society, London, 1964) I, pp.392–3.
28.   Fisher to Tweedmouth, 22 Feb. 1907, Tweedmouth Papers B/125.
29.   Fisher was informed of Robertson's attitude by the latter's private secretary, L.G. Brock; Fisher to Lambert, 20 Feb. 1907 (copy), Fisher Papers 1/5/229; *The Daily Telegraph*, 1 Mar. 1907, p.10, speech by Tweedmouth at Weymouth.
30.   Marder, *Fear God*, II, p.119.
31.   Grey to Noel, 7 Dec. 1906, Noel Papers, NOE/5.
32.   Fisher to Corbett, 9 March 1907, Corbett Papers 81/143/12.
33.   *Parl. Deb.* 4th ser., 1907, clxxii, 1089. 17 Apr.
34.   *Ibid.*, clxxiii, 294, 25 Apr.
35.   Fisher to Balfour, 2 Feb. 1907, Balfour Papers, Add. MS 49711 f.222.
36.   Fisher to Lambert, 31 Jan. 1907, Fisher Papers 1/5/224.
37.   Marder, *Fear God*, II, pp.151–2.
38.   *Ibid.*, p.118, n.1.
39.   *Parl. Deb.* 4th ser., 1907, clxx, 1037, 7 Mar.

40. Fisher to Balfour, 8 Mar. 1907, Balfour Papers, Add. MS. 49711 fos 223–4.
41. *Parl. Deb.* 4th ser., 1907, clxxii, 1066–99; *The Times* 18 Mar. 1907, p.9.
42. Gwynne to Beresford, 28 May 1907 (copy), Gwynne Papers 16.
43. Balfour to Farquhar, 14 Nov. 1906 (copy), Balfour Papers, Add. MS 49859 fos 110–12; Balfour to Arnold-Forster, 3 Nov. 1906 (copy), *ibid.*, Add. MS 49723 fos 215–18.
44. Dilke to Wilkinson, 19 Feb. 1907, Wilkinson Papers, O.T.P. 13/11/31.
45. Chamberlain to Maxse, 24 Jan 1907, Maxse Papers 457 fos 475–6.
46. Arnold-Forster to Balfour, 2 Nov. 1906, Balfour Papers, Add. MS 49723 fos 211–14.
47. Balfour to Arnold-Forster, 3 Nov. 1906 (copy), *ibid.*, fos 215–18; the Home Fleet had been created by Order-in-Council in October 1906, and had thus not come before Parliament for approval.
48. *Parl. Deb.* 4th ser., 1907, clxx, 1040, 5 Mar.
49. *Ibid.*, 664–72.
50. *The Daily Telegraph* 6 Mar. 1907, p.10.
51. *The Times* 6 March 1907, p.9.
52. *Parl. Deb.* 4th ser., 1907, clxxi, 257–60.
53. Balfour to Arnold-Forster, 3 Nov. 1906 (copy), Balfour Papers, Add. MS 49723 fos 215–18.
54. For a fuller account of the feud than space permits here, see A.J.A. Morris, 'A not so silent service: the final stages of the Fisher-Beresford quarrel and the part played by the press'; *Moirae* 6 (Trinity 1981) 42–81; also *From The Dreadnought*, I, pp.88–104; Hough, *First Sea Lord*, pp.195–245.
55. For Beresford's life and career, see G. Bennett, *Charlie B.: A Biography of Admiral Lord Charles Beresford of Metemmeh and Curraghmore* (London, 1968).
56. Slade to Corbett, 6 July 1907, Corbett Papers 81/143/13.
57. Esher's journal, 19 Jan. 1908, Esher Papers 2/11, for one such comical instance.
58. Mackay, *Fisher*, p.360.
59. Marder, *From The Dreadnought*, I, pp.71–3, 91–2.
60. Beresford to Balfour, 7 Mar. 1908, Balfour Papers, Add. MS 49713 fos 177–83.
61. For Beresford's parliamentary career before 1906, see Bennett, *Charlie B.*, *passim.*
62. Undated memorandum on the Navy by Lord Charles Beresford [1907], Sandars Papers, MS Eng.Hist. c.753 fos 217–20.
63. Beresford to Wilkinson, 6 Feb. 1908, Wilkinson Papers, O.T.P. 13/21/10.
64. Gwynne to Beresford, 3 June 1907 (copy), Gwynne Papers 16.
65. Gwynne to Beresford, 28 May 1907 (copy), *ibid.*
66. Cawdor to Tweedmouth, 1 July 1907 (copy), Cawdor Papers 290.
67. *Parl.Deb.* 4th ser., 1907, clxxvii, 830–2.
68. *Ibid.*, 832–40.
69. Cawdor to Balfour, 24 July 1907, Balfour Papers, Add. MS 49709 fos 36–7.
70. Fisher to Balfour, 8 July 1907, *ibid.*, Add. MS 49711 fos 232–3.
71. Fisher to Cawdor, 18 June 1907, Cawdor Papers 290.
72. 'War arrangements' enclosed in Fisher to Balfour, 8 July 1907, Balfour Papers, Add. MS 49711 fos 259–63.
73. Mackay, *Fisher*, p.374.
74. Gwynne to Beresford, 18 June 1907 (copy), and Beresford to Gwynne, 2 Aug. 1907, Gwynne Papers 16.
75. Cawdor to Balfour, 24 July 1907, Balfour Papers, Add. MS 49709 fos 36–7.
76. Cope-Cornford to Gwynne, 12 Aug. 1907, Gwynne Papers 16.
77. Beresford to Gwynne, 17 Aug. 1907, *ibid.*
78. *Parl. Deb.* 4th ser., 1907, clxxviii, 304–5, 311–12, 15 July, and 1570–3, 24 July.
79. See Chapter 10, pp.145–46.

80. Midleton to Balfour, 16 Dec. 1907, Sandars Papers, MS Eng. Hist. c.754 fos 274–9.
81. Fisher to Tweedmouth, 16 Nov. 1907, Tweedmouth Papers B/146.
82. Marder, *Fear God*, II, p.161.
83. Wilkinson to Grey, 14 Jan. 1908, F.O. 800/112/257–60.
84. Marder, *Fear God*, II, p.161.
85. Undated memorandum by Fisher, 'The proposed inquiry into Admiralty policy' [Jan. 1908], Fisher Papers 8/44/4974.
86. Esher to Messrs. Wyatt and Horton-Smith [joint secretaries of the IML], 22 Jan. 1908 (copy), Fisher MSS. 1/6/278.
87. Beresford to Gwynne, 10 June 1907, Gwynne Papers 16.
88. Marder, *Fear God*, II, p.159.
89. Brett and Esher, *Journals and Letters*, II, pp.280–4; Fisher to Garvin, 7 Feb. 1908, Garvin Papers 1.
90. See the collection of documents in Lloyd George Papers B/2/7a–h.
91. 'The proposed inquiry into Admiralty policy', Fisher Papers 8/44/4974.
92. Undated memorandum by the First Sea Lord, Tweedmouth Papers B/27.
93. Marder, *Fear God*, II, pp.151–2.
94. Sinclair to Campbell-Bannerman, 10 Jan. 1908, Campbell-Bannerman Papers, Add. MS 42130 fos 210–11.
95. Fisher to Lambert, 25 Mar. 1908 (copy), Fisher Papers 1/6/302.
96. Campbell-Bannerman to Asquith, 5 Jan. 1907, Asquith Papers 10 fos 220–1; Fisher to Lambert, 25 Mar. 1908 (copy), Fisher Papers 1/6/302.
97. A.J.A. Morris, *The Scaremongers: The Advocacy of War and Rearmament 1896–1914* (London, 1984) pp.120–1.
98. Balfour to Fisher, 1 Jan. 1908 (copy), Sandars Papers, MS Eng. Hist. c.756 fos 2–7.
99. Marder, *Fear God*, II, p.161.
100. Cawdor to Balfour, 8 Jan. 1908, Sandars Papers, MS Eng. Hist. c.756 fos 48–9.
101. Balfour to Arnold-Forster, 4 Dec. 1907 (copy), Balfour Papers, Add. MS 49723 f.239.
102. Midleton to Balfour, 16 Dec. 1907, Sandars Papers, MS Eng. Hist. c.754 fos 274–9.
103. Balfour to Cawdor, 9 Jan. 1908 (copy), *ibid.*, c.756 fos 50–1.
104. Slade's diary, 24 Jan. 1908, Slade Papers, MRF/39/3.
105. Hough, *First Sea Lord*, p.226; Morris, *Scaremongers*, p.186.
106. Balfour to Arnold-Forster, 4 Dec. 1907 (copy), Balfour Papers, Add. MS 49723 f.239
107. The Tweedmouth Papers (Box J) include a list of letters exchanged by Fisher and Cawdor after 1906, together with a brief description of their contents; the list refers to two letters which relate to this episode but which it has not been possible to trace – Pretyman to Cawdor, 19 Nov. 1907, and Balfour to Cawdor, 22 Nov. 1907.
108. Beresford to Gwynne, 23 Feb. 1908, Gwynne Papers 16.
109. Arnold-Forster's diary, 5 Dec. 1907, Arnold-Forster Papers, Add. MS 50353.
110. Chamberlain to Maxse, 5 Feb. 1908, Maxse Papers 458 fos 649–50.
111. Arnold-Forster to Balfour, 28 Nov. 1907, Balfour Papers, Add. MS 49723 fos 237–8.
112. Sandars to Balfour, 4 May 1908, *ibid.*, Add. MS 49765 fos 138–41.
113. Arnold-Forster's diary, 5 Dec. 1907, Arnold-Forster Papers, Add. MS 50353.
114. Marder, *Fear God*, II, p.165.
115. Brett and Esher, *Journals and Letters*, II, p.280.
116. Bacon, *Fisher*, II, p.46.
117. Marder, *Fear God*, II, p.165.

118. *Ibid.*, pp.176–7.
119. See p.94.
120. Marder, *Fear God*, II, p.151.
121. Lansdowne to Sandars, 19 Aug. 1909, Balfour Papers, Add. MS 49730 fos 1–2.
122. Beresford to Gwynne, 6 June 1907 and 12 June 1907, Gwynne MSS 16.
123. Sykes, *Tariff Reform*, p.132.
124. Memorandum by W.H. Long, 15 Jan. 1909 (copy), Balfour Papers, Add. MS 49777 fos 33–6.
125. Sandars to Balfour, 13 Jan. 1908, *ibid.*, Add. MS 49765 fos 97–8.
126. Maxse to Lady Bathurst, 12 Aug. 1909, Glenesk-Bathurst Papers.
127. Messrs. Wyatt and Horton-Smith to various editors, 27 Oct. 1909 (copy), Fisher Papers 5/17/4271.
128. Esher to Balfour, 16 Aug. 1910, Balfour Papers, Add. MS 49719 fos 153–4; Fisher to Leyland, 17 Oct. 1911, Fisher Papers 3/5/2154.
129. Marder, *From The Dreadnought*, I, pp.186–201.
130. 'The naval inquiry', *The Times* 23 Apr. 1909, p.9.
131. Arnold-Forster's diary, 5 Dec. 1907, Arnold-Forster Papers, Add. MS 50353 fos 117–22.
132. Fiennes to Fisher, 8 Aug. 1910, Fisher Papers 3/4/2077.
133. Hurd, *Who Goes There?* pp.108–9.

Chapter 10   'The Last Word of Voluntary Service' 1907–10

1.   Arnold-Forster, *Hugh Oakley Arnold-Forster*, p.327.
2.   Sandars to Balfour, 2 Apr. 1907, Balfour Papers, Add. MS 49765 fos 34–8.
3.   *Parl. Deb.* 4th ser., 1907, clxxii, 1608, 23 Apr.
4.   Campbell-Bannerman to Haldane, 3 Sept. 1907, Haldane Papers 5907 fos 186–7.
5.   Spiers, *Haldane*, pp.161–5.
6.   Drake and Cole (eds) *Our Partnership*, p.317.
7.   Haldane to his mother, 24 Aug. 1908, Haldane Papers 5980 fos 101–2.
8.   *The 'Saturday' Handbook for Unionist Candidates, Speakers and Workers* ed. Hon. G. Beckett and G. Ellis (London, 1909) p.166.
9.   Salisbury to Selborne, 5 Sept. 1907, Selborne Papers 5 fos 185–8.
10. Salisbury to Balfour, 5 Sept. 1909, Balfour Papers, Add. MS 49758 f.185.
11. Lansdowne to Long, 11 Nov. 1907, Long Papers dep 4766.
12. *Letters of George Wyndham* ed. Guy Wyndham 2 vols (privately printed, Edinburgh 1915) II, pp.274–6; Mackail and Wyndham, *Life and Letters*, II, p.602; for correspondence relating to the War School plan, see Arnold White Papers WHI/190.
13. M. Egremont, *The Cousins* (London, 1977) p.280; also J.A. Thompson, 'George Wyndham: Toryism and Imperialism' in Meiji and Thompson (eds) pp.110–11.
14. *The Times* 31 Mar. 1909, p.12, Sir Foster Cunliffe.
15. Fitzroy, *Memories*, I, p.399; Haldane to Salisbury, 19 June 1910, Salisbury Papers, Hatfield House MSS 4M/68/24 and 20 June 1910, *ibid*, 4M/70/10–12.
16. *Parl. Deb.* 4th ser., 1906, cliii, 658.
17. *Ibid.*, 1907, clxxvi, 539.
18. *Ibid.*, clxxii, 1603.
19. Ewart's diary, 28 Feb. 1907, Ewart Papers RH4/84/2: Balfour to Clarke, 13 June 1907 (copy), Balfour Papers, Add. MS 49702 f.238.
20. Haldane to his mother, [12] June 1907, Haldane Papers 5977 fos 165–6.
21. *The Times* 20 Jan. 1909, p.7.
22. Balfour to Esher, 18 Aug. 1909, Esher Papers 5/31; for two such occasions see

Haldane to his mother, 17 Dec. 1908 and 16 July 1909, Haldane Papers 5980 fos 235–6; 5981 fos 23–4.

23.   Balfour to Clarke, 13 June 1907 (copy), Balfour Papers, Add. MS 49702 f.238.

24.   Draft letter to an unidentified correspondent, 30 June 1908, *ibid.*, Add. MS 49859 fos 253–5.

25.   Selborne to Midleton, 14 Jan. 1908, Selborne Papers 3 fos 1–3.

26.   Balfour to Esher, 2 Sept. 1909, Esher Papers 5/31.

27.   Arnold-Forster's diary, 18 June 1908, Arnold-Forster Papers, Add. MS 50353 fos 125–31; Lansdowne to Balfour, 22 May 1908, Balfour Papers, Add. MS 49729 fos 313–4.

28.   Mackay, *Balfour*, p.21 n.2.

29.   Haldane to Elisabeth Haldane, 14 May 1908, Haldane Papers 6011 f.63.

30.   See Spiers, *Haldane*, pp.67–72, for a full account; also Morris, 'Haldane's army reforms', pp.24–7.

31.   Haldane to Elisabeth Haldane, 7 Feb. 1908, Haldane Papers 6011 f.44.

32.   Esher's diary, 11 July 1908, Esher Papers 2/11.

33.   Haldane to Elisabeth Haldane, 15 July 1908, Haldane Papers 6011 f.71; *The Times*, 13 July 1908, p.10; Chamberlain, *Politics From Inside*, p.127.

34.   Chamberlain, *Politics from Inside*, pp.126–7.

35.   Haldane to his mother, 9 Mar. 1909, Haldane Papers 5981 fos 96–7.

36.   For membership figures, see Summers, 'Militarism in Britain', p.113.

37.   See Chapter 5; Adams and Poirier, *Conscription Controversy*, p.14.

38.   Roberts to Salisbury, 6 July 1909, Salisbury Papers, Hatfield House MSS 4M/60/160–4.

39.   Arnold-Forster's diary, 21 May 1907, Arnold-Forster Papers, Add. MS 50353 fos 106–12.

40.   Morris, *Scaremongers*, Chapters 8 and 12.

41.   Adams and Poirier, *Conscription Controversy*, p.14.

42.   Roberts to Esher, 3 June 1909, Esher Papers 5/30.

43.   *Pace* De Groot, *Douglas Haig*, p.125.

44.   Esher, *Journals and Letters*, II, p.190.

45.   Balfour to Arnold-Forster, 3 Nov. 1906 (copy), Balfour Papers, Add. MS 49723 fos 215–18.

46.   Milner to Garvin, 25 July 1906, Garvin Papers.

47.   Repington to Milner, 17 July 1906, Milner Papers dep 33 fos 104–7.

48.   Haldane to Spender, 26 Feb. 1907, Campbell-Bannerman Papers, Add. MS 46390 f.152.

49.   Cited by Adams and Poirier, *Conscription Controversy*, p.31.

50.   Repington to Garvin, 15 Mar. 1908, Garvin Papers.

51.   Milner to Roberts, 21 June 1908 (copy), Milner Papers dep 16 fos 153–7; Milner to Roberts, 2 Dec. 1907, Roberts Papers 7101/23/45/89.

52.   Garvin to Roberts, 30 Apr. 1908 (copy), Garvin Papers.

53.   Arnold-Forster, *Hugh Oakley Arnold-Forster*, p.345, citing H.O. Arnold-Forster, *Military Needs and Military Policy* (London, 1909).

54.   *Parl. Deb.* 4th ser., 1906, cliii, 665, 8 Mar.

55.   For a summary of the evidence, see 'Notes for Mr Balfour on invasion' (undated), Milner Papers dep 132 fos 71–86.

56.   Correspondence between Repington and Roberts in Roberts Papers 7101/23/62.

57.   C. à C. Repington, *Vestigia* (London, 1919) pp.277–83.

58.   Repington to Maxse, 29 Jan. 1908, Maxse Papers 458 f.637.

59.   Repington to Maxse, 15 Oct. 1907, *ibid.*, f.587.

60.   Adams and Poirier, *Conscription Controversy*, pp.34–9; Morris, *Scaremongers*, Chapter 11.

61. Esher to Edward VII, 29 May 1908 (copy), Sandars Papers, MS Eng. Hist. c.756 fos 151–2.
62. 'Statement made by Mr A.J. Balfour before the SubCommittee on Invasion, Friday 29th May, 1908' (copy), Cawdor Papers Box 290.
63. Adams and Poirier, *Conscription Controversy*, p.35.
64. Arnold-Forster to Balfour, 28 Sept. 1908, Balfour Papers, Add. MS 49723 fos 252–7; Selborne to Midleton, 14 Jan. 1908, Selborne Papers 3 fos 1–3.
65. See Chapter 3.
66. Midleton to Balfour, 16 Dec. 1907, Sandars Papers, MS Eng. Hist. c.754 fos 274–9.
67. A fact of which Balfour had reminded his audience at the CID in May 1908; 'Statement by Mr Balfour', Cawdor Papers Box 290.
68. See Willoughby de Broke to Selborne, 12 Aug. 1911, Selborne Papers 3 fos 31–3, for a comment on M.'s lack of a 'public': defeated in the 1906 general election, Midleton succeeded to his father's peerage before he had found a new seat in the Commons.
69. *Parl. Deb.* 4th ser., 1907, clxxvi, cols 1273–4, Lords, 26 June; Memorandum on Compulsory Service, 28 Aug. 1907, Salisbury Papers, Hatfield MSS 4M/MY/12.
70. Salisbury to Selborne, 20 May 1908, Selborne Papers 5 fos 207–12.
71. Midleton to Selborne, 9 July 1908, *ibid.*, 3 fos 58–61.
72. See above, p.11.
73. Midleton to Roberts, 7 Nov. 1908, Roberts Papers 7101/23/13/401.
74. Curzon to Selborne, 11 May 1908, Selborne Papers 10 fos 151–6; for Curzon's views on compulsion, see the Earl of Ronaldshay, *The Life of Lord Curzon* 3 vols (London, 1928) III, pp.117–20.
75. P. King, *The Viceroy's Fall: How Kitchener Destroyed Curzon* (London, 1986).
76. Newton, *Retrospection*, p.161.
77. *The Times*, 1 July 1909, p.11.
78. See his preface to *The Unionist Workers' Handbook* ed. L.M. Bragge (London, 1912) pp.vii–xx.
79. Newton, *Retrospection*, p.171.
80. Garvin to Roberts, 19 Mar. 1908 (copy), Garvin Papers.
81. Arnold-Forster's diary, 21 May 1907, Arnold-Forster Papers, Add. MS 50353 fos pp.106–12.
82. Chamberlain to Maxse, 5 Feb. 1908, Maxse Papers 458 fos 649–50.
83. *Ibid.*
84. Law to Ware, 8 Sept. 1908 (copy), Law Papers 18/8/10.
85. Repington to Maxse, 19 May 1909, Maxse Papers 459 fos 188–92.
86. Maxse to Strachey, 9 June 1909, Strachey Papers S/10/9/10.
87. Repington to Maxse, 18 May 1909, Maxse Papers 459 fos 177–9.
88. *Parl. Deb.* 5th ser., 1909, ii, 104–6, 8 Mar.
89. See Chapter 11.
90. Brett and Esher, *Journals and Letters*, II, pp.369.
91. Ian Hamilton to Balfour, 12 June 1909, Balfour Papers, Add. MS 49860 fos 103–6.
92. Roberts to Maxse, 2 Sept. 1908, Maxse Papers 458 f.746.
93. Milner to Roberts, 28 Oct. 1908, Roberts Papers 7101/23/45/99.
94. Roberts to Milner, 22 Aug. 1906, Milner Papers dep 16 fos 129–32: Repington to Milner, 17 July 1906, *ibid.*, dep 33 fos 104–7.
95. Roberts to Strachey, 2 May 1909, Strachey Papers S/12/3/37; the naval crisis of 1909 is described in the next chapter.
96. Strachey to Milner, 3 May 1909 (copy), Strachey Papers S/10/11/2.
97. Haldane to Kitchener, 8 July 1909 (copy), Haldane Papers 5908 fos 131–3: Haldane to Balfour, 15 July 1909 (copy), *ibid.*, 6109 f.80.
98. Esher to Maurice Brett, 23 Aug. 1908, Esher Papers 7/21.

99. Haldane to his mother, 2 Nov. 1909, Haldane Papers 5982 fos 177–8.
100. Haldane to his mother, 9 Mar. 1909, *ibid.*, 5981 fos 96–7.
101. *The Times*, 1 Apr. 1909, 'The City and the Navy'.
102. Milner to Balfour, 6 Apr. 1909 (copy), Milner Papers dep 35 fos 169–70; Allison, 'National service issue', pp.146–9; D. Green, 'The Stratford by-Election of May 1909: national defence and party politics', *Moirae* 5 (1980) 92–110.
103. Balfour to Sandars, 12 Apr. 1909, Balfour Papers, Add. MS 49765 fos 217–18.
104. *The Times* 30 Apr. 1909, p.12.
105. Milner to Roberts, 25 Apr. 1909, Roberts Papers 7101/23/45/103.
106. Newton to Strachey, 3 May 1909, Strachey Papers S/11/1/2.
107. Strachey to Milner, 3 May 1909 (copy), *ibid.*, 10/11/2.
108. Allison, 'National service issue', p.151.
109. Milner to Strachey, 17 May 1909, Strachey Papers 10/11/2.
110. Allison, 'National service issue', pp.157–8.
111. Milner to Roberts, 6 July 1909, Roberts Papers 7101/23/45/108.
112. Haldane to his mother, 12 July 1909, Haldane Papers 5982 fos 17–18.
113. Lucas to Esher, 8 July 1909, Esher Papers 5/31.
114. Adams and Poirier, p.41; Haldane to his mother, 14 July 1909, Haldane Papers 5982 f.21.
115. *The Times* 12 July 1909, p.12; see also 'Political notes', p.10.
116. Midleton to Roberts, 25 June 1909, Roberts Papers 7101/23/13/408; Maxse to Strachey, 9 June 1909, Strachey Papers 10/9/10.
117. See Chapter 11.
118. R. Scally, *The Origins of the Lloyd George Coalition; The Politics of Social Imperialism 1900–18* (Princeton, NJ, 1975) p.86.
119. Repington to Maxse, 19 May 1909, Maxse Papers 459 fos 188–92.
120. Newton's letter in *The Times* 12 July 1909, p.12.
121. Haldane to his mother, 15 July 1909, Haldane Papers 5982 fos 23–4.

Chapter 11 Dreadnoughts and Politics 1909–11

1. 'Statement of German construction' by the First Lord, 29 Dec. 1908, Asquith Papers 21 fos 28–38.
2. Marder, *From The Dreadnought*, I, p.152; Woodward, *German Navy*, pp.204–6.
3. Fisher to May, 28 Sept. 1908 (copy), Esher Papers 10/43.
4. B. Murray, *The People's Budget 1909–10* (Oxford, 1980) pp.125–7; N. Blewett, *The Peers, The Parties and the People: The General Elections of 1910* (London, 1972) p.51.
5. L. Masterman, *C.F.G. Masterman: A Biography* (London, 1939) p.123.
6. R. Churchill, *Winston S. Churchill*, II, pp.515–17.
7. Lloyd George to Asquith, 2 Feb. 1909, Asquith Papers 21 fos 61–7; Esher's journal, 12 Feb. 1909, Esher Papers 2/12; Morley to Esher, 21 Feb. 1909, Esher Papers 5/29.
8. Masterman, *C.F.G. Masterman*, p.125.
9. G.M.Trevelyan, *Grey of Fallodon* (London, 1937) pp.213–15.
10. Grey to Asquith, 5 Feb. 1909, Asquith Papers 21 fos 76–7.
11. Esher's journal, 29 Dec. 1908, Esher Papers 2/11; Crewe to Asquith, 7 Feb. 1909 (copy), Lloyd George Papers C/6/11/4.
12. Masterman, *C.F.G. Masterman*, p.125.
13. Churchill, *World Crisis*, II, p.24.
14. J.A. Spender and C. Asquith, *Life of Herbert Henry Asquith, Lord Oxford and Asquith* 2 vols (London, 1932) II, p.254; for a detailed account and analysis of the Cabinet discussions, see Williams, 'Politics of national defence', pp.168–92.
15. Marder, *From The Dreadnought*, I, p.162.

16. Marder, *Fear God*, II, p.228.
17. McKenna, *R. McKenna*, p.65.
18. Undated memorandum by the P.M., Asquith Papers 21 fos 167–70.
19. *British Documents on the Origins of the War 1898–1914. Vol.VI Anglo-German Tension, Armaments and Negotiation 1907–1912* ed. G.P. Gooch and H. Temperley (London, 1930) pp.237–40.
20. Undated memorandum by the Sea Lords, Asquith Papers 21, fos 163–5; Marder, *Fear God*, II, p.228.
21. Haldane to his mother, 24 Feb. 1909, Haldane Papers 5908 fos 88–9.
22. Fisher to Garvin, 26 May 1909, Garvin Papers 3.
23. P.M. Kennedy, *The Rise of the Anglo-German Antagonism 1860–1914* (London, 1980) p.447.
24. Marder, *From The Dreadnought*, I, pp.170–1.
25. Sumida, *Naval Supremacy*, p.187.
26. Murray, *People's Budget*, pp.112–21.
27. Sumida, *Naval Supremacy*, p.189.
28. Williams, 'Politics of national defence', pp.261–2.
29. Sumida, *Naval Supremacy*, p.191.
30. Balfour to Hewins, 17 June 1908 (copy), Balfour Papers, Add. MS 49799 f.173.
31. *German Diplomatic Documents 1871–1914. Vol.III The Growing Antagonism* ed. E. Dugdale (London, 1969) pp.280–2.
32. Kennedy, *Antagonism*, p.405.
33. J. Joll, *Europe since 1870* (London, 1976) pp.172–3.
34. Mackail and Wyndham, *Life and Letters*, II, pp.613–14; also on Wyndham, see W.S. Blunt, *My Diaries* 2 vols (London, 1920) II, pp.249–50.
35. Lady Selborne to Selborne, 16 Sept. 1908, Selborne Papers, Add. MS 3 fos 11–14.
36. Slade's diary, 6 Nov. 1908, Slade Papers MRF/39/3.
37. Young, *Arthur James Balfour*, p.271; Esher's journal, 4 Nov. 1908, Esher Papers 2/12.
38. Balfour to Asquith, 5 Nov. 1908 (copy), Balfour Papers, Add. MS 49692 fos 98–100.
39. Esher's journal, 28 Dec. 1908, Esher Papers 2/12.
40. Selborne to Baddeley, 9 Nov. 1908, Selborne Papers 46 fos 227–9.
41. *The Times* 19 Mar. 1909, p.12.
42. *Parl. Deb.*, 4th ser., 1908, cxcvi, 30.
43. Austen to Mary Chamberlain, 27 Feb. 1909, Chamberlain Papers AC4/1/383.
44. Cawdor to Balfour, 7 Mar. 1909, Sandars Papers, MS Eng. Hist. c.758 fos 90a–90b.
45. E. David, *Inside Asquith's Cabinet; from the Diaries of Edward Hobhouse* (London, 1977) p.76; Marder, *Fear God*, II, p.236.
46. *Parl. Deb.* 4th ser., 1909, ii, 930–44 (McKenna) and 955–63 (Asquith).
47. Austen to Mary Chamberlain, 16 Mar. 1909, Chamberlain Papers AC4/1/400.
48. *The Morning Post* 18 Mar. 1909, p.7, 'At St Stephen's'.
49. *Parl. Deb.*, 4th ser., 1909, ii, 979.
50. Austen to Mary Chamberlain, 18 Mar. 1909, Chamberlain Papers AC4/1/401.
51. *The Observer* 21 Mar. 1909, p.8, 'The week'.
52. Balfour's prediction was in line with the Admiralty's calculations prior to the Grey-Metternich conversations; see p.156.
53. *Parl. Deb.* 4th ser., 1909, ii, 944–55 (Balfour on 16/3/1909), 1075–6 (Lee on 17/3), 1124–33 (Pretyman on 17/3), 1235–42 (Chamberlain on 18/3), 1264–75 (Law on 18/3), 1284–5 (Balfour on 18/3).
54. *Ibid.*, 1090–9 (Macnamara on 17/3), 1287 (McKenna on 18/3).
55. See Chapter 8.

56. Undated memorandum by Sandars, 'Midnight' [15 Mar. 1909], Balfour Papers, Add. MS 49719 fos 76–7.
57. A. Gollin, *The Observer and J.L. Garvin 1908–14: A Study of Great Editorship* (London, 1960) pp.64–76.
58. *Ibid.*, p.74.
59. Esher's journal, 23 Jan. and 23 Aug. 1908, Esher Papers 2/11.
60. Cawdor to Balfour, 7 Mar. 1909, Sandars Papers, MS Eng. Hist. c.758 fos 90a–90b.
61. Austen to Mary Chamberlain, 24 Mar. 1909, Chamberlain Papers AC4/1/404.
62. *The Morning Post* 18 Mar. 1909, p.7, 'Parliamentary notes'; *The Observer* 14 Mar. 1909, p.8, 'The Fleet and the future'.
63. Letter to *The Times*, 27 Mar. 1909, p.14.
64. *The Standard* 23 Mar. 1909, 'Naval defects'.
65. *The Times* 27 Mar. 1909, p.14, 'Political notes'.
66. Esher's journal, 28 Mar. 1909, Esher Papers 7/20.
67. Austen to Mary Chamberlain, 21 and 30 Mar. 1909, Chamberlain Papers AC4/1/402 & 409; Selborne to Baddeley, 24 Apr. 1909, Selborne Papers 46 f.233; Long to Balfour, 26 Apr. 1909, Balfour Papers, Add. MS 49777 fos 44–5.
68. Austen to Mary Chamberlain, 5 Apr. 1909, Chamberlain Papers AC4/1/413.
69. Speech at Brighton, *The Times* 3 Apr. 1909, p.10.
70. Austen to Mary Chamberlain, 21 Mar. 1909, Chamberlain Papers AC4/1/402.
71. Speech by Lyttelton at Kingston, *The Morning Post* 20 Mar. 1909, p.5.
72. *The Times* 29 Mar. 1909, p.11.
73. Asquith to the King, 19 Mar. 1909, CAB 41/32/7.
74. Austen to Mary Chamberlain, 22 Mar. 1909, Chamberlain Papers AC4/1/403.
75. Austen to Mary Chamberlain, 21 Mar. 1909, *ibid.*, AC4/1/402.
76. *The Times* 20 Mar. 1909, p.12.
77. *Ibid.*, p.11, 'The dominating issue'.
78. *Ibid.*, p.9.
79. *Parl. Deb.* 4th ser., 1909, ii, 1503–8.
80. *Ibid.*, 1508–14.
81. *The Observer*, 18 Mar. 1909, p.6, 'From the cross benches'.
82. Long to Balfour, 26 Apr. 1909, Balfour Papers, Add. MS 49777 fos 44–5.
83. Marder, *Fear God*, II, p.235.
84. *The Times* 23 Mar. 1909, p.12.
85. *Ibid.*, 26 Mar. 1909, p.4.
86. *Ibid.*, p.10.
87. Notes on an interview with Bridgeman, Sandars Papers, MS Eng.Hist. c.758 fos 218–19.
88. Clark (ed.), *A Good Innings*, p.101.
89. *Parl. Deb.* 4th ser., 1909, ii, 39–52.
90. *Ibid.*, 52–70.
91. Haldane to Elizabeth Haldane, 30 Mar. 1909, Haldane Papers 5981 fos 132–3.
92. *Parl. Deb.* 4th ser., 1909, ii, 129–34; *The Standard* 23 Mar. 1909, p.4.
93. *The Standard* 31 Mar. 1909, p.6, 'Germany and England'.
94. *Parl. Deb.* 4th ser., 1909, ii, 134–46.
95. MSS notes, Sandars Papers, MS Eng. Hist. c.756 f.1.
96. Cawdor to Sandars, 7 Mar. 1909, *ibid.*, c.758 fos 89–90.
97. G.J. Marcus, 'The Croydon by-election and the naval scare of 1909', *Journal of the Royal United Services Institution* 103, 162 (Nov. 1958) 500–14; Marder, *From The Dreadnought*, I, pp.167–9.
98. Cited Marcus, 'Croydon by-election', p.505.
99. *Parl. Deb.* 4th ser., 1909, ii, 1249, Carlyon Bellairs MP.

100. Hamilton, 'The nation and the Navy', p.342.
101. *The Daily Telegraph* 18 Mar. 1909, p.10–11.
102. Hamilton, 'The nation and the Navy', p.163; H.F. Wyatt and L.G. Horton-Smith [joint-secretaries of the IML], *The Passing of the Great Fleet* (London, 1909).
103. *The Times* 25 Mar. 1909, p.9; Corbett to Fisher, 4 Apr. 1909 (copy), Fisher Papers 1/8/374.
104. Marcus, 'Croydon by-election'.
105. *The Times* 20 Mar. 1909, p.9, and 29 Mar. 1909, p.9; A.J.P. Taylor, 'We want eight and we won't wait', in *Politics in Wartime* (London, 1964) pp.53–6.
106. *The Standard* 23 Mar. 1909, p.4.
107. Cawdor to Sandars, 7 Mar. 1909, Sandars Papers, MS Eng. Hist. c.758 fos 89–90.
108. *The Times* 31 Mar. 1909, p.9, and 1 Apr. 1909, p.10.
109. Balfour to Somerville, 16 July 1909 (copy), Balfour Papers, Add. MS 49860 fos 115–17.
110. *The Times* 8 May 1909, p.10.
111. Marder, *From The Dreadnought*, I, p.169.
112. See Chapter 7.
113. Gwynne to Sandars, 30 Mar. 1909, Balfour Papers, Add. MS 49797 fos 89–90.
114. *The Observer*, 28 Mar. 1909, p.8, 'The Empire – one!'
115. *The Times*, 5 Apr. 1909, p.9, 'The government and the Navy'; for details of the role of Buckle and *The Times* in March 1909, see Williams, 'Politics of national defence', 215 ff.; also S. Koss, *The Rise and Fall of the Political Press in Britain. Vol. II The Twentieth Century* (London, 1984) p.107.
116. Churchill's letter is printed in *The Times* 15 Apr. 1909, p.6; *Parl. Deb.*, 5th ser., 1909, iv, 480.
117. *Ibid.*, 855–99.
118. *Ibid.*, 899–909.
119. *The Times* 28 July 1909, p.12.
120. Beckett and Ellis, *The Saturday Handbook*, p.146.
121. Chamberlain to Spring-Rice, 25 Sept. 1910, Spring Rice Papers 1/7.
122. *The Daily Telegraph* 18 Mar. 1909, pp.10–11.
123. *The Times* 28 July 1909, p.12.
124. Beckett and Ellis, *The Saturday Handbook*, p.146.
125. *The Times* 25 Jan. 1910, p.7, Balfour speaking at Haddington.
126. *Ibid.*, 27 Aug. 1909, p.9, 'Mr Asquith's statement on imperial defence'.
127. *Ibid.*, 18 Nov. 1909, p.9, Balfour at Manchester.
128. *Ibid.*, 13 Jan. 1910, p.7.
129. Balfour to Somerville, 28 Dec. 1909 (copy), Balfour Papers, Add. MS 49860 fos 192–3.
130. *The Times* 11 Jan. 1910, p.6, speech at Wolverhampton.
131. *Ibid.*, 25 Jan. 1910, p.7, Balfour at Haddington.
132. Morris, *Scaremongers*, pp.203–23; Sandars to Garvin, 22 Dec. 1909, Garvin Papers; Sandars to Balfour, 14 Jan. 1910, Balfour Papers, Add. MS 49766 fos 69–70.
133. Balfour to Steel-Maitland, 8 Sept. 1911, Sandars Papers, MS Eng. Hist. c.764 fos 21–4.
134. *The Observer* 19 Dec. 1909, p.8, 'For England or Germany?'
135. Lansdowne to Roberts, 16 Oct. 1910, Roberts Papers 7101/23/34/485.
136. Chamberlain, *Politics from Inside*, p.200.
137. Blewett, *Peers*, pp.128, 134–5; Morris, *Scaremongers*, p.217; see also K. Lunn and R. Thomas, 'Portsmouth dockyard and society 1905–1914' (Undated occasional paper of the School of Social and Historical Studies, Portsmouth Polytechnic); *British Parliamentary Results 1885–1918* ed. F.W.S. Craig (London, 1974) pp.104, 171.
138. *The Times* 6 Jan. 1910, p.6.

139. See Williams, 'Politics of national defence', pp.283–8.
140. *The Times* 28 Jan. 1910, p.7, Churchill at Frome.
141. Brett and Esher, *Journals and Letters*, II, p.441.
142. Blewett, *Peers*, p.139.
143. *The Times* 14 July 1910, p.12, 'Political notes'; Kennedy Jones to Fisher (undated), Fisher Papers 3/3/2016.
144. *The Times* 1 Mar. 1910, p.9.
145. Marder, *From The Dreadnought*, I, p.215.
146. *The Morning Post* 3 Jan. 1910, p.6.
147. *Parl. Deb.* 5th ser., 1910, xxii, 2530, John Dillon on 16 Mar.
148. *Ibid.*, xv, 14 Mar.
149. Asquith to Edward VII, 17 Feb. 1910 (copy), CAB 41/32/48.
150. Marder, *From The Dreadnought*, I, pp.170–1.
151. Memorandum by Grey of 31 Jan. 1910, Asquith Papers 23 fos 64–6.
152. Fisher to Garvin, 22 Jan. 1910, Garvin Papers.
153. Chamberlain, *Politics from Inside*, pp.233–4.
154. *Parl. Deb.* 5th ser., 1910, xv, 201 (Pretyman) and 537–8 (Long).
155. *Ibid.*, 59.
156. Balfour to Yerburgh, 27 Dec. 1909 (copy), Balfour Papers, Add. MS 49860 fos 188–90.
157. *The Times* 25 Nov. 1911, p.10; 26 Nov., p.9; and 28 Nov., p.8.
158. Blewett, *Peers*, p.326.
159. W. Fest, 'Jingoism and xenophobia in the electioneering strategies of British ruling elites before 1914', in Kennedy and Nicholls (eds.) pp.179–80.
160. *The Times* 28 Nov. 1910, p.11, Review of the session.
161. Chamberlain, *Politics From Inside*, p.233.
162. Sandars to Balfour, 7 Mar. 1910, Balfour Papers, Add. MS 49766 fos 152–60.
163. *Parl. Deb.* 5th ser., 1911, xix, 715.
164. Marder, *Fear God*, II, p.333; Esher to Sandars, 8 Aug. 1910 and Esher to Balfour, 16 Aug. 1910, Balfour Papers, Add. MS 49719 fos 151–2 and 153–4.
165. Alick Murray to Lloyd George, 24 Sept. 1910, Lloyd George Papers (Freshford).
166. Chamberlain to Spring Rice, 25 Sept. 1910, Spring Rice Papers 1/11 fos 18–19.
167. Balfour to Northcliffe, 17 Dec. 1910, Northcliffe Papers, Add. MS 62513 f.42.
168. In speeches at Wrexham and Haddington; *The Times* 8 Dec. 1910, p.6, and 15 Dec. 1910, p.6.
169. *Parl. Deb.* 5th ser., 1911, xxii, 16, 20 and 22 Mar.
170. *Ibid.*, xxiii, 71, Lough.
171. *Ibid.*, xv, 532, Walter Long.

Chapter 12   The Crisis of the Voluntary System 1910–11

1.   Roberts to Balfour, 7 Apr. 1909, Balfour Papers, Add. MS 49731 fos 286–90.
2.   See p.7.
3.   Cited in McDermott, 'The revolution in British military thinking', p.101.
4.   Balfour to Roberts, 27 Oct. 1908, Roberts Papers 7101/23/8/26.
5.   Balfour to Esher, 25 May 1908 (copy), Balfour Papers, Add. MS 49719 fos 21–2.
6.   *The Times* 18 Mar. 1909, p.9.
7.   Lucas to Esher, 8 July 1909, Esher Papers 5/31.
8.   Roberts to Rosebery, 13 June 1909, Rosebery Papers 10121 fos 248–9.
9.   Roberts to Balfour, 7 Apr. 1909, Balfour Papers, Add. MS 49731 fos 286–90.
10. Garvin to Northcliffe, 17 Mar. 1909 [incorrectly dated as 28? July 1908], Northcliffe Papers, Add MS 62236 f.113.

11. Fitzroy, *Memories*, I, p.399.
12. Press cutting in Fisher Papers 1/9.
13. Morris, *Scaremongers*, p.216.
14. *The Times* 4 Jan. 1910, p.5.
15. Milner to Roberts, 24 Nov. 1909 (copy), Milner Papers dep 16 f.188.
16. R.G. Verney (Lord Willoughby de Broke) *The Passing Years* (London, 1924) p.252.
17. Roberts to Maxse, 1 Jan. 1910, Maxse Papers 461 f.450.
18. Durand to Roberts, 22 Dec. 1909, Roberts Papers 7101/23/26/61.
19. Gwynne to Long, 13 Sept. 1910, Long Papers, Add. MS 62415.
20. Arnold-Forster's diary, 18 June 1908, Arnold-Forster Papers, Add. MS 50353 fos 125–31.
21. Spiers, *Haldane*, pp.173–4.
22. See Ewart's diary, 11 Aug. 1910, Ewart Papers RH4/84/3.
23. Arnold-Forster to Maxse, 27 Dec. 1905, Maxse Papers 453 fos 191–4.
24. *Parl. Deb.* 5th ser., 1913, 1, 1177, 19 Mar.
25. 'The voluntary principle', *National Review* 56, 331 (Sept. 1910) 41–7.
26. Spiers, *Haldane*, p.175.
27. *Ibid.*, p.174.
28. Drake and Cole (eds) *Our Partnership*, pp.461–2.
29. Summers, 'Militarism in Britain', pp.104–23.
30. Roberts to Garvin, 20 Mar. 1911, Garvin Papers.
31. Maxse to Strachey, 3 June 1910, Strachey Papers 10/9/12.
32. Garvin to Roberts, 5 Mar. 1908 (copy), Garvin Papers 1.
33. Garvin to Repington, 17 Mar. 1908 (copy), Garvin Papers.
34. Haldane to his mother, 27 July 1910, Haldane Papers 5984 fos 41–2.
35. Allison, 'National service issue', p.144.
36. Roberts to Garvin, 17 Aug. 1908, citing an *Observer* article entitled 'The machine and the men', Garvin Papers.
37. Page Croft to Acland Hood, 12 Sept. 1910, Sandars Papers, MS Eng.Hist. c.761 f.67.
38. Esher's journal, 4 Feb. 1910, Esher Papers 7/23.
39. Phillips, *The Diehards*, p.133.
40. Roberts to Percy, 28 Apr. 1911, Roberts Papers 7101/23/125/1.
41. For Long's sensitivity, see Sir C. Petrie, *Walter Long and His Times* (London, 1936) p.148
42. Midleton to Roberts, 23 Mar. 1911, Roberts Papers 7101/23/13/419.
43. Midleton to Milner, 25 Apr. 1910, Milner Papers dep 36 fos 249–50; Midleton to Roberts, 23 Mar. 1910, Roberts Papers 7101/23/13/415; Amery to Roberts, 25 Oct. 1910, *ibid.*, 7101/23/1/22.
44. *Parl. Deb.* 5th ser., 1910, xiv, 1362, 8 Mar.
45. *Ibid.*, xviii, 701–2, 27 June.
46. Wyndham to Roberts, 6 May 1911, Roberts Papers 7101/23/46/164a.
47. Mackail & Wyndham, *Life and Letters*, II, pp.693–4.
48. Lansdowne to Roberts, 4 June 1909, Roberts Papers 7101/23/34/480.
49. Lansdowne to Roberts, 15 Dec. 1909, *ibid.*, 7101/23/34/481.
50. Lansdowne to Salisbury, 13 Apr. 1911, Salisbury Papers, Hatfield House MSS 4M/70/10–12.
51. Long to Balfour, 3 Oct. 1910, Balfour Papers, Add MS 49777 f.70.
52. Long to Blumenfeld, 11 Mar. 1911, Blumenfeld Papers, LONG/W 7.
53. Sandars to Balfour, 10 Sept. 1910, Balfour Papers, Add MS 49766 fos 244–50.
54. Chamberlain to Spring Rice, 25 Sept. 1910, Spring Rice Papers 1/7; Chamberlain, *Politics From Inside*, p.359.
55. Chamberlain to Spring Rice, 25 Sept. 1910, Spring Rice Papers 1/7.

56.   Midleton to Milner, 25 Apr. 1910, Milner Papers dep 36 fos 249–50.
57.   Memorandum on National Service by Lord Midleton (April 1910), *ibid.*, fos 251–4.
58.   Midleton to Roberts, 23 Mar. 1910, Roberts Papers 7101/23/13/415.
59.   For Nicholson's views, see Nicholson to Wilkinson, 22 Oct. 1904, Wilkinson Papers, O.T.P. 13/13/61: for Wilson, see Adams and Poirier, *Conscription Controversy*, pp.25–6; also C.M. Callwell, *Field Marshal Sir Henry Wilson: His Life and Diaries* 2 vols (London, 1927), I.
60.   See pp.153–54.
61.   Midleton to Roberts, 23 Mar. 1911, Roberts Papers 7101/23/13/419.
62.   Roberts to Strachey, 14 Dec. 1911, Strachey Papers 12/3/48.
63.   That the idea was dropped may be due to Milner, who expressed caution; Milner to Midleton, 27 July 1909, Midleton Papers, PRO 30/67/24 fos 1235–42.
64.   Midleton to Milner, 25 Apr. 1910, Milner Papers dep 36 fos 249–50.
65.   Midleton to Roberts, 23 Mar. 1911, Roberts Papers 7101/23/13/419.
66.   Long to Blumenfeld, 11 Mar. 1911, Blumenfeld Papers, LONG/W 7.
67.   Selborne to Oliver, 30 Mar. 1911, Selborne Papers 74 fos 71–4.
68.   Repington to Maxse, 18 May 1909, Maxse Papers 459 fos 177–9.
69.   Ramsden, *Age of Balfour and Baldwin*, pp.36–7.
70.   Roberts to Garvin, 20 Mar. 1911, Garvin Papers.
71.   Sandars to Balfour, 13 Sept. 1910, Balfour Papers, Add. MS 49766 fos 251–3.
72.   Sandars to Balfour, 10 Sept. 1910, *ibid.*, fos 244–50.
73.   Wyndham, *Letters*, pp.395–7.
74.   Balfour to Midleton, 30 Mar. 1911 (copy), Balfour Papers, Add. MS 49721 f.271.
75.   Allison, 'National service issue', pp.119–21.
76.   Balfour to Sandars, 21 Sept. 1911, Sandars Papers, MS Eng.Hist. c.764 fos 56a–59a.
77.   Balfour to Midleton, 30 Mar. 1911 (copy), Balfour Papers, Add. MS 49721 f.271.
78.   Esher to Roberts, 6 June 1909, Roberts Papers 7101/23/29/17.
79.   'Army Estimates, 1910–1911', Memorandum by the Secretary of State for War, Haldane Papers 5908 fos 205–6.
80.   Balfour to Esher, 20 Aug. 1910, Esher Papers 5/39; see also Balfour to Lord Arthur Cecil, 2 June 1911 (copy fragment), Balfour Papers, Add. MS 48961 f.211.
81.   For which efforts, see Spiers, *Haldane*, pp.181–3.
82.   Haldane to his mother, 7 Feb. 1911, Haldane Papers 5985 fos 85–6.
83.   Haldane to Balfour, 3 Mar. 1910 (copy), *ibid.*, 5909 f.11.
84.   Ramsden, *Age of Balfour and Baldwin*, pp.39–42.
85.   R.B. Jones, 'The Conservative party 1906–11' (Oxford Univ. B.Litt. thesis, 1960) pp.125–59.
86.   Maxse to Long, 17 July 1911, Long Papers (Wiltshire County Record Office) WLP 947/478/10.
87.   Maxse to Law, 17 Nov. 1911, Law Papers 24/3/47.
88.   Maxse to Law, 20 May 1912, *ibid.*, 26/3/32.
89.   Haldane to his mother, 14 July 1910, Haldane Papers 5984 fos 21–2.
90.   Roberts to Garvin, 20 Mar. 1911, Garvin Papers.
91.   Lee to Bonar Law, 21 Jan. 1912, Law Papers 25/1/46.
92.   Balcarres to Sandars, 15 Sept. 1911, Sandars Papers, MS Eng. Hist. c.764 fos 43–4.
93.   Phillips, *The Diehards*, 142–7.
94.   'Recommendations made by the Provisional Committee of the Halsbury Club in respect of its organisation and purposes', undated memorandum [Sept. 1911], Selborne Papers 75 fos 2–3.

95. Chamberlain, *Politics from Inside*, p.358.
96. *Ibid.*, p.360.
97. Selborne to Salisbury, 9 Oct. 1911, Salisbury Papers, Hatfield House MSS 4M/71/43–6; originally a member of the Club, Salisbury soon resigned because he thought its existence divisive; see Salisbury to Selborne, 14 Oct. 1911 (copy), Salisbury Papers, Hatfield House MSS 4M/71/54–5.
98. John Vincent's edition of the diary of the Unionist whip Lord Balcarres offers a vivid first-hand account of these events; *The Crawford Papers* ed. J. Vincent (Manchester, 1984) pp.220–50.
99. Wyndham to Selborne, 16 Aug. 1911, Selborne Papers 74 fos 178–81.
100. Wyndham to Balfour, 28 May 1903, Sandars Papers, MS Eng. Hist. c.738 fos 20–5.
101. Balfour to Law, 22 Jan. 1912, Law Papers 27/4/49.
102. F. Fischer, *War of Illusions: German Policies from 1911 to 1914* (London, 1975) pp.71–94.
103. Grigg, *Lloyd George*, pp.308–9.
104. Williamson, *Grand Strategy*, pp.187–94.
105. Callwell, *Wilson*, I, pp.97–8.
106. K.M. Wilson, *The Policy of the Entente: Essays on the Determinants of British Foreign Policy, 1904–1914* (Cambridge, 1985), esp. pp.54–85.
107. Vincent (ed.) *Crawford Papers*, p.255.
108. Dugdale, *Balfour*, I, p.374.
109. K.M. Wilson, 'The Opposition and the crisis in the Liberal Cabinet over foreign policy in November 1911', *International History Review* 3, 3 (July 1981) 399–413.
110. Balfour to Sandars, 21 Sept. 1911, Sandars Papers, MS Eng. Hist. c.764, fos 56a–59a.
111. Chamberlain, *Politics From Inside*, p.346.
112. Balfour to Churchill, 22 Mar. 1912 (copy), Balfour Papers, Add. MS 49694 fos 75–6.
113. Wilson, *Policy of the Entente*, pp.54–85.
114. *Parl. Deb.* 5th ser., 1912, xl, 1341, L.S. Amery on 4 July.
115. Garvin to Balfour, 10 June 1912, Balfour Papers, Add. MS 49795 f.228.
116. *Parl. Deb.* 5th ser., 1913, l, 1266, 20 Mar.
117. T. Wilson (ed.), *The Political Diaries of C.P. Scott 1911–1928* (London, 1970) p.56.
118. Memorandum of 12 June 1912, FO 800/105.
119. *Parl. Deb.* 5th ser., 1912, xl, 2029–36.
120. *Ibid.*, 1913, xiv, 201–2, 21 Apr.
121. *Ibid.*, 1912, xli, 1444, 25 July.
122. *Ibid.*, xxxv, 210–11, Wyndham on 5 Mar.; 1010, Amery on 12 Mar.
123. For accounts of this episode, see P.G. Halpern, *The Mediterranean Naval Situation 1908–1914* (Cambridge, Mass., 1971) pp.13–46 and Williamson, *Grand Strategy*, pp.264–78; also E.W.R. Lumby (ed.), *Policy and Operations in the Mediterranean 1912–14* (London, Navy Records Society, 1970).
124. *Parl. Deb.* 5th ser., 1912, xl, 2033, 10 July.
125. *Ibid.*, xli, 927, 22 July.
126. *Ibid.*, xii, 298–308, 2 July.
127. *Ibid.*, xii, 332–6.

Chapter 13   New Leader, Old Realities 1911–14

1.   Blunt, *Diaries*, II, p.353.
2.   *The Observer* 27 Dec. 1908, p.4, '1908: a review'.
3.   Garvin to Balfour, 10 June 1912, Balfour Papers, Add. MS 49795 f.228.
4.   Repington, *Vestigia*, p.281.
5.   Printed in *The Times* 20 Oct. 1910, p.7.
6.   Marder, *Fear God*, II, pp.341–2.
7.   R. Churchill, *Winston S. Churchill*, II, p.570.
8.   R. Pound and G. Harmsworth, *Northcliffe* (London, 1959) p.352.
9.   J.A. Spender, *The Public Life* 2 vols (London, 1925) I, p.102.
10.   Corbett to Fisher, 25 Jan. 1910 (copy), Corbett Papers 81/143/12.
11.   *The Times* 18 Nov. 1910, pp.8–9, speech at Nottingham.
12.   Esher, *Journals and Letters*, III, p.69.
13.   *The Times* 21 Oct. 1910, p.8, speech at Llandewi Rhydderch.
14.   Churchill to Balfour, 20 Mar. 1912 and 13 July 1912, Balfour Papers, Add. MS 49694 fos 68, 82–4; Balfour to Seely, 19 Nov. 1912, Mottistone Papers 19 fos 319–20.
15.   Churchill to Balfour, 5 June 1913, Balfour Papers, Add. MS 49694 fos 93–4.
16.   Selborne to Lady Selborne, 24 Apr. 1912, Selborne Papers 102 fos 44–6.
17.   Hankey, *Supreme Command*, I, p.151.
18.   Ramsden, *Age of Balfour and Baldwin*, p.90; Asquith referred to the unsmiling Law as 'Bonar Lisa'.
19.   Gwynne to Beresford, 3 June 1907 (copy), Gwynne Papers 16.
20.   R. Blake, *The Unknown Prime Minister: The Life and Times of Andrew Bonar Law 1858–1923* (London, 1955) pp.71–86.
21.   Chamberlain, *Politics from Inside*, p.527.
22.   Haldane to his mother, 17 Sept. 1912, Haldane Papers 5988 fos 121–2; Egremont, *The Cousins*, pp.281–2.
23.   Blake, *Unknown Prime Minister*, (London, 1955) p.125.
24.   Clark (ed.), *A Good Innings*, p.129.
25.   Haldane, *Autobiography*, pp.229–31; Churchill exchanged offices with McKenna, who went to the Home Office.
26.   Asquith to Haldane, 31 Aug. 1911, Haldane Papers 5909 fos 140–1; for an account of the 23 Aug. meeting see Williamson, *Grand Strategy*, pp.187–92.
27.   Asquith had actually offered Churchill the Admiralty in 1908 but was then declined; Churchill to Asquith, 14 Mar. 1908, Asquith Papers 10 fos 10–15.
28.   Churchill, *World Crisis*, I, p.36.
29.   R. Churchill, *Winston S. Churchill*, II, pp.511–722; Marder, *From The Dreadnought*, I, pp.252–71; S. Roskill, *Churchill and the Admirals* (New York, 1977) pp.19–31; V. Bonham-Carter, *Winston Churchill as I Knew Him* (London, 1965) pp.239–60.
30.   Churchill, *World Crisis*, pp.94–111; Sumida, *Naval Supremacy*, p.193.
31.   Haldane, *Before the War*, pp.56–71; R.B. Langhorne, 'The naval question in Anglo-German relations 1912–14', *Historical Journal* 14, 2 (1971) 359–70.
32.   Woodward, *German Navy*, pp.322–76, 404–28.
33.   *Parl. Deb.*, 5th ser., 1912, xxxv, 1555–6, 18 Mar.
34.   Sumida, *Naval Supremacy*, p.191.
35.   *Ibid.*, Appendix Tables 18–21.
36.   *Ibid.*, Table 3.
37.   Marder, *From The Dreadnought*, I, pp.316–27; the politics of the crisis can be followed in Lord Riddell's *More Pages from My Diary 1908–14* (London, 1934) pp.184–201 and in T. Wilson (ed.) *Scott*, pp.71–81.
38.   Spender to Fisher, 17 Oct. 1911, Fisher Papers 3/5/2155a.
39.   Garvin to Fisher, 25 Oct. 1911, *ibid.*, 3/5/2159.

40. Gwynne to Lady Bathurst, 30 Oct. 1911, Glenesk-Bathurst Papers.
41. Maxse to Law, 17 Nov. 1911, Law Papers 24/3/47.
42. Sandars to Esher, 30 Nov. 1911, Esher Papers 5/38.
43. *Parl. Deb.*, 5th ser., 1912, xxxv, 1549–654, 18 Mar.
44. *Ibid.*, 1574–86.
45. Sandars to Esher, 24 Oct. 1911, Esher Papers 5/38.
46. Goulding to Blumenfeld, 2 Apr. 1912, Blumenfeld Papers WARG/6.
47. See *Parl. Deb.*, 5th ser., 1912, xxxv, 1797–8, for an instance of this; Alan Burgoyne, MP on 19 Mar.
48. *Ibid.*, l, 1889–1906, 27 Mar.; lv, 1489–1503, 17 July; 1914, lix, 1938–54, 17 Mar.
49. For a detailed account of the Dominion Dreadnought issue, see D.C. Gordon, *The Dominion Partnership in Imperial Defence 1870–1914* (Baltimore, 1965); also by the same author, 'The Admiralty and Dominion Navies, 1902–1914', *Journal of Modern History* 33, 4 (1961) 407–22.
50. Churchill to Haldane, 6 May 1912, Haldane Papers 5909 fos 215–16; *Parl. Deb.*, 5th ser., 1913, l, 1892, 27 Mar.
51. *Ibid.*, lv, 1500, Lee, and 1566–77, Pretyman, 17 July.
52. Hurd to Law, 19 Dec. 1911, Law Papers 24/5/145; Lee to Law, 21 Jan. 1912, *ibid.*, 25/1/46.
53. Lee to Law, 21 January 1912, *ibid.*; *The Times* 27 Jan. 1912, p.9.
54. Selborne to Hurd, 12 Aug. 1912, Hurd Papers 1/44.
55. Selborne to Law, Lansdowne and Chamberlain, 29 Aug. 1912 (copy), Selborne papers 79 fos 114–16.
56. Chamberlain to Selborne, 14 and 20 Aug. 1912, *ibid.*, fos 95–6, 107–9.
57. Law to Selborne, 2 Sept. 1912, and Lansdowne to Selborne, 4 Sept. 1912, *ibid.*, fos 113, 117–18.
58. Selborne to Law, 4 Sept. 1912, Law Papers 27/2/4.
59. Bragge, *The Unionist Workers' Handbook*, pp.194–7.
60. Selborne to Hurd, 8 Aug. 1913, Hurd Papers 1/44.
61. *Parl. Deb.*, 1914, lix, 1944, 17 Mar.
62. *Ibid.*, 1486.
63. Law to Salisbury, 3 May 1912, Salisbury Papers, Hatfield House MSS 4M/72/58–62.
64. For accounts see Blake, *Unknown Prime Minister*, pp.105–8 and Ramsden, *Age of Balfour and Baldwin*, pp.73–6.
65. Repington's phrase, cited by R. Churchill, *Winston S. Churchill*, II, p.566.
66. See Keir Hardie's remark in the Commons on 27 Mar. 1913, *Parl. Deb.*, 5th ser., 1913, l, 1906.
67. *Ibid.*, 1912, xli, 1301–2, 24 July.
68. Talbot to Law, 17 Jan. 1914, Law Papers 31/2/48.
69. Selborne to Balfour, 5 Jan. 1914, Balfour Papers, Add. MS 49708 fos 223–4.
70. Balfour to Selborne, 7 Jan. 1914, Selborne Papers 1 fos 139–46.
71. Selborne to Hurd, 17 Feb. 1914, Hurd Papers 1/44.
72. Asquith to Venetia Stanley, 17 Mar. 1914; M. and E. Brock (eds), *H.H. Asquith: Letters to Venetia Stanley* (Oxford, 1982), p.55.
73. *Ibid.*, pp.576–7.
74. On Churchill's appointment to the Admiralty, *Punch* (1 Nov. 1911) had shown him exchanging courtesies with McKenna, who took his place at the Home Office. 'Congratulations, my dear boy', says Churchill smugly; 'You can take over the strike problem'. 'Thanks so much', replies McKenna; 'And you can have Beresford.'
75. Mackay, *Fisher*, p.431; M. Gilbert, *Winston S. Churchill. Vol.III 1914–1916* (London, 1971) pp.417–81.

76. R. Churchill, *Winston S. Churchill*, II, p.586.

77. Churchill, *World Crisis*, pp.56, 103.

78. Beresford to Blumenfeld, 16 Aug. 1912, Blumenfeld Papers APP.2.

79. Sir Francis Hopwood, Civil Lord of the Admiralty 1912–17, cited by R. Churchill, *Winston S. Churchill* II, pp.641–2.

80. J. Ramsden (ed.) *Real Old Tory Politics: The Political Diaries of Robert Sanders, Lord Bayford 1910–1935* (London, 1984) p.54.

81. Fisher to Esher, undated [Feb. 1911], Esher Papers 5/39; for the Bridgeman episode, see R. Churchill, *Winston S. Churchill* II, pp.628–54.

82. Garvin to Fisher, 1 July 1909, Fisher Papers 3/3/1946.

83. R. Rhodes James, *Churchill: a study in failure 1900–1939* (London, 1973) p.64.

84. *Parl. Deb.* 5th ser., 1912, xlv, 1901–7, 20 Dec.

85. Selborne to Law, 4 Sept. 1912, Law Papers 27/2/4.

86. Long to Law, 27 May 1912, *ibid.*, 26/3/41.

87. Beresford to Blumenfeld, 16 Aug. 1912, Blumenfeld Papers APP.2; Almeric Paget to Law, 14 Jan. 1914, Law Papers 31/2/38.

88. Sandars to Maxse, 8 Aug. 1912, Maxse Papers 466 fos 150–1.

89. Beresford to Vesey, 2 Feb. 1914 (copy), Law Papers 31/3/5.

90. Gwynne to Lady Bathurst, 11 Nov. 1911, Glenesk-Bathurst Papers.

91. *The Times* 27 Jan. 1912, p.9.

92. Williamson, *Grand Strategy*, pp.193–4.

93. *Parl. Deb.*, 4th ser., 1907, clxx, 93, 27 Feb.

94. Repington to Esher, 14 Aug. 1910, Esher Papers 5/35.

95. Lee to Law, 21 Jan. 1912, Law Papers 25/1/46.

96. Clark (ed.), *A Good Innings*, pp.121–2.

97. Roberts to Law, 13 Jan. 1912, Law Papers 25/1/26; Garvin to Law, 13 and 15 Mar. 1912, *ibid.*, 25/3/28 and 33.

98. Lansdowne to Law, 6 July 1912, *ibid.*, 26/5/11.

99. Report of the Committee on Condition of Land Forces, 4 Feb. 1913, Law Papers 29/1/14.

100. *Ibid.*

101. Repington to G.Robinson, 11 Dec. 1912, Times Newspapers Archive.

102. *Parl. Deb.* 5th ser., 1913, xiv, 210, 21 Apr.

103. Salisbury to Selborne, 12 Sept. 1911, Selborne Papers 6 fos 116–21.

104. Wyndham to Seely, 16 July 1911, Mottistone Papers 19/9; Seely, *Adventure*, p.148.

105. Balfour to Seely, 19 Nov. 1912, Mottistone Papers 19/319–20; Wyndham, *Letters*, pp.543–4.

106. Seely, *Adventure*, p.143.

107. Midleton to Seely, 15 Nov. 1912, Mottistone Papers 19/317–18; for Salisbury's involvement, see correspondence in Salisbury Papers, Hatfield House MSS 4M/73 & 74.

108. Lansdowne to Law, 18 Jan. 1914, Law Papers 31/2/49.

109. *Parl. Deb.* 5th ser., 1913, l, 1093, 19 Mar.

110. *Ibid.*, 1912, xli, 316, 16 July.

111. Wilson's diary 16 Feb. 1912, Wilson Papers DS/MISC/80/HHW21; 'That old ass Haldane has been doing something stupid in Berlin I feel sure.'

112. Repington to Robinson, 11 Dec. 1912, Times Newspapers Archive.

113. Wilson's diary 11 Mar. 1913, Wilson Papers, DS/MISC/80/HHW22.

114. Wilson's diary 23 and 27 June 1912, 4 Dec. 1912, *ibid.*, DS/MISC/80/HHW21; 16 Apr. 1913, *ibid.*, DS/MISC/80/HHW22.

115. Wilson's diary 14 July (Long) and 21 Nov. (Lee) 1912, *ibid.*, DS/MISC/80/HHW21.

116. Wilson's diary 5 Nov. 1912, *ibid.*

117. Grigg, *Lloyd George*, pp.264–76.
118. Callwell, *Wilson*, I, pp.118–19.
119. Riddell, *More Pages*, p.140.
120. *Ibid.*, p.98.
121. *Ibid.*, p.94.
122. Chamberlain, *Politics from Inside*, p.522.
123. *Ibid.*, p.576.
124. Wilson's diary 5 Nov. 1912, Wilson Papers DS/MISC/80/HHW21.
125. Riddell, *More Pages*, p.130.
126. *The Nation*, 19 Apr. 1913, cited by A. Havighurst, *Radical Journalist: H.W. Massingham 1860–1924* (Cambridge, 1974) p.221.
127. *Parl. Deb.* 5th ser., 1912, xl, 1391–406, Seely on 4 July; Memorandum by Midleton [1915?], PRO 30/67/25.
128. See above, p.57.
129. Repington to Robinson, 11 Dec. 1912, Times Newspapers Archive.
130. *Parl. Deb.* 5th ser., 1913, xiii, 906.
131. *Parl. Deb.* 4th ser., 1907, clxxii, 1600, 23 Apr.
132. *Ibid.*, 5th ser., 1913, xiii, 940–7.
133. Esher to Roberts, 6 June 1909, Roberts Papers 7101/23/29/17.
134. Salisbury to Selborne, 20 May 1908, Selborne Papers 5 fos 207–12.
135. Balfour to Knollys, 18 Sept. 1905 (copy), Balfour Papers, Add. MS 49685 fos 39–41.
136. Allison, 'National service issue', p.212.
137. *Parl. Deb.* 5th ser., 1913, xiii, 1002–11.
138. *Ibid.*, xiv, 209–10.
139. Wilson's diary 14 July 1912, Wilson Papers DS/MISC/80/HHW21.
140. It may be significant that Wilson dined with Law and Midleton on 10 April 1913, just three days before the Lords debate in which the Opposition put forward the round-table proposal; Wilson's diary, 10 Apr. 1913, Wilson Papers, DS/MISC/80/HHW22.
141. *Parl. Deb.* 5th ser., 1913, xiv, 180–92.
142. Haldane to his mother, 28 and 29 Nov. 1912, Haldane Papers 5988 fos 207–10.
143. Midleton, *Records and Reactions*, pp.283–4; *Parl. Deb.* 5th ser., 1913, xiii, 895–908.
144. Riddell, *More Pages*, p.140.
145. *Ibid.*, p.142.
146. *Parl. Deb.* 5th ser., 1914, xv, 551–6, Midleton, and 585–92, Curzon, 18 and 19 Mar.
147. Allison, 'National service issue', p.221.
148. *The Westminster Gazette*, 3 May 1913, cited in Ronaldshay, *Curzon*, III, p.121.
149. *Parl. Deb.* 5th ser., 1914, xv, 590, 19 Mar.
150. *Ibid.*, 1913, xiv, 502–3, 2 June, Visct. Galway's motion; see the debate on Lord W. de Broke's motion, *ibid.*, 1914, xv, 461–99, 518–608, 12, 18 and 19 Mar.
151. Roberts to Milner, 28 Oct. 1913 and Milner to Roberts, 30 Oct 1913 (copy), Milner Papers dep 16 fos 209–10, 211.
152. Percy Illingworth, Liberal chief whip, in a speech quoted by Earl Denbigh in the House of Lords on 21 Apr. 1913; *Parl. Deb.* 5th ser., 1913, xiv, 197.
153. Allison, 'National service issue', p.221.
154. *The Times* 19 Apr. 1913, p.9.
155. Riddell, *More Pages*, p.104.
156. *Parl. Deb.* 5th ser., 1914, xv, 461–7, W. de Broke on 12 March.
157. Allison, 'National service issue', p.138.
158. Gwynne to Lady Bathurst, 8 Nov. 1911, Glenesk-Bathurst Papers.

159. Wilson's diary 26 Oct. 1912, Wilson Papers DS/MISC/80/HHW21.
160. Phillips, *Diehards*, p.122.
161. *Ibid.*, p.99.
162. Bragge, *The Unionist Workers' Handbook*, p.197.
163. J.O. Stubbs, 'The Conservative party and the politics of war 1914–16' (unpublished Oxford Univ. D.Phil. thesis, 1973) p.15.
164. The scandal arose over alleged 'insider trading' by three Liberal ministers, including Lloyd George, in the shares of the American Marconi company; for details, see F. Donaldson, *The Marconi Scandal* (London, 1962); also G.R. Searle, *Corruption in British Politics 1895–1930* (Oxford, 1987) pp.172–200.
165. *Parl. Deb.* 5th ser., 1913, xiii, 908, 10 Feb.
166. Midleton, *Records and Reactions*, pp.283–4.

Chapter 14   Epiloque: War and Office 1914–15

1. For background and an account, see A.T.Q. Stewart, *The Ulster Crisis 1912–14* (London, 1967).
2. Churchill, *World Crisis*, I, p.155.
3. For a masterly recent account, see M.G. Brock, 'Britain enters the war' in *The Coming of the First World War* ed. R.J.W. Evans & H. Pogge von Strandmann (Oxford, 1988) pp.145–78.
4. Viscount Grey of Fallodon, *Twenty Five Years* 2 vols (London, 1925) I, p.337.
5. Selborne to Lady Selborne, 3 Aug. 1914, Selborne Papers 102 fos 148–9.
6. Blake, *Unknown Prime Minister*, p.220.
7. Sir Austen Chamberlain, *Down The Years* (London, 1935) p.99.
8. See Chapter 12.
9. Blake, *Unknown Prime Minister*, pp.223–4.
10. *Ibid.*, p.223.
11. For Liberal attitudes, see D. French, *British Strategy and War Aims 1914–1916* (London, 1986) pp.14–15; also his *British Economic and Strategic Planning 1905–1915* (London, 1982)
12. Selborne to Lady Selborne, 26 Aug. 1914, Selborne Papers 102 fos 158–63.
13. Chamberlain, *Down The Years*, pp.104–5; Balfour to Haldane, 4 Aug. 1914, Haldane Papers 5910 fos 242–48.
14. French, *Strategy and War Aims*, pp.56–77.
15. For the most accurate account of the inception of the Dardanelles campaign see M. Gilbert, *Churchill*, III, chapters 7–10.
16. Lines from Philip Larkin's poem 'MCMXIV', in *The Whitsun Weddings* (London, 1964) p.28.
17. *Ibid.*; Simkins, *Kitchener's Army*, offers an excellent account and analysis.
18. D. Dutton, *Austen Chamberlain: Gentleman in Politics* (Bolton, 1985) pp.114–15.
19. Balfour to Lansdowne, 9 Jan. 1915 (copy), Balfour Papers, Add. MS 49730 fos 272–4; Mackay, *Balfour*, pp.252–3.
20. Long to Law, 1 May 1915, Long Papers 62404.
21. Law to Long, 14 May 1915 (copy), *ibid.*
22. *Ibid.*
23. Fisher described Jellicoe as a man with 'all Nelson's attributes except Lady Hamilton', Marder, *Fear God*, II, p.424; for the naval war, see R. Hough, *The Great War at Sea 1914–1918* (Oxford, 1983) esp. chapter 5, pp.53–68.
24. M. and E. Brock (eds), *Asquith*, pp.314 and 338.
25. There is an interesting, though inconclusive, literature on the origins of the Asquith coalition and, in particular, on Asquith's own motives; see Lord Beaverbrook,

Politicians and the War (London, 1960) pp.94–113; C. Hazlehurst, *Politicians At War: July 1914 to May 1915* (London, 1971) part III; S. Koss, 'The Destruction of Britain's last Liberal government', *Journal of Modern History* 40, 2 (1968) 257–77; M. Pugh, 'Asquith, Bonar Law and the coming of the first coalition', *Historical Journal* 17, 4 (1974) 813–36; P. Fraser, 'British war policy and the crisis of Liberalism in May 1915', *Journal of Modern History* 52, 1 (1982) 1–26.
26.   Ronaldshay, *Curzon*, III, p.125.
27.   Koss, *Lord Haldane*, pp.124–83.
28.   Law to Sir Joseph Larmor, 14 Oct. 1914, cited M. Gilbert, *Winston S. Churchill. Companion Volume III Part 1: August 1914–April 1915* (London, 1972) p.191.
29.   M. Gilbert, *Winston S. Churchill. Companion Volume III Part 2: May 1915– December 1916* (London, 1972) p.915.

BIOGRAPHICAL INDEX

Basic career details, mostly limited to the period before 1914.

ACLAND HOOD, Sir Alexander Fuller (1853–1917)
Educated at Eton & Balliol College, Oxford; Grenadier Guards, 1875–92; served in Egyptian campaign, 1882; succeeded to baronetcy, 1892; Unionist MP for West Somerset, 1892–1911; chief Patronage Sec. to the Treasury, 1902–5; Unionist chief whip, 1902–11; created Baron St Audries, 1911.

AKERS-DOUGLAS, Aretas (1851–1926)
Educated at Eton & University College, Oxford; Conservative MP for East Kent, 1880–85, St Augustine's division, 1885–1911; Opposition whip, 1883; Parlty Sec. to the Treasury, 1885–6, 1886–92; chief Opposition whip, 1892–5; First Commissioner of Works, 1895–1902; Home Sec., 1902–5; Viscount, 1911.

AMERY, Leopold Charles Maurice Stennett (1873–1955)
Educated at Harrow & Balliol College, Oxford; Fellow of All Souls; ardent publicist for imperial causes; journalist & barrister; edited *The Times* history of the South African War, 1900–1909; wrote generally on military affairs; Conservative MP for South Birmingham, 1911–45; staunch tariff reformer; Halsbury Club stalwart, 1911.

ARNOLD-FORSTER, Hugh Oakley (1855–1909)
Grandson of Arnold of Rugby & nephew of Matthew Arnold; educated at Rugby & University College, Oxford; Liberal Unionist MP for W. Belfast, 1892–1906, & Croydon, 1906–1909; Sec. of Imperial Federation League, 1884; writer on naval & military matters; Parlty Sec. to the Adty, 1901–3; Sec. of State for War, 1903–5; advocate of tariff reform.

ASQUITH, Herbert Henry (1852–1928)
Educated at City of London School & Balliol College, Oxford; QC; Liberal MP for E. Fife, 1886–1918, & Paisley, 1920–24; Home Sec., 1892–5; Liberal Imperialist supporter of Lord Rosebery who dissented from party line during Boer War; Chancellor of the Exch., 1905–8; Prime Minister, 1908–16; Earl of Oxford and Asquith, 1925.

BALFOUR, Arthur James (1848–1930)
Educated Eton & Trinity College, Cambridge; nephew of 3rd Marquess of Salisbury; Conservative MP for Hertford, 1874–1885, East Manchester, 1885–1906, City of London, 1906–22; distinguished amateur philosopher; prominent member of social

coterie known as the 'Souls', also of parliamentary 'Fourth Party'; Pres. Local Govt Board, 1885–6; Sec. for Scotland, 1886; Chief Sec. for Ireland, 1887-1891; Leader of the Commons & First Lord of the Treasury, 1891–2, 1895–1902; Prime Minister, 1902–5; Leader of the Opposition, 1905–11; First Lord of the Adty in Asquith coalition of 1915; Foreign Sec., 1916–19; first Earl of Balfour, 1922.

BERESFORD, Admiral Lord Charles William de la Poer (1846–1919)
Entered Navy 1859; took part in bombardment of Alexandria, 1882, & Nile expedition, 1884–5; C.-in-C. Mediterranean 1905, Channel 1907–9; Admiral 1906; feuded violently with Sir John Fisher; Conservative MP for Waterford, 1874–80, East Marylebone, 1885–9, York, 1897–1900; Woolwich, 1902–3, Portsmouth, 1910–16; created Baron, 1916.

BRIDGEMAN, Sir Francis Charles (1848–1929)
Entered Navy, 1862; Flag-Captain in Channel, Mediterranean & at Portsmouth; Rear-Admiral, 1903; C.-in-C. Home fleet, 1907–9, 1911; 2nd Sea Lord, 1910–11; First Sea Lord, 1911–12.

BRODRICK, William St John Fremantle (1856–1942)
Educated at Eton & Balliol College, Oxford; Conservative MP for West Surrey, 1880–85, Guildford, 1885–1906; Financial Sec. to the War Office, 1886–92; U.-Sec. for War, 1895–8, & for Foreign Affairs, 1898–1900; Sec. of State for War, 1900–1903; army reformer; Sec. of State for India, 1903–5; succeeded father as 9th Viscount Midleton, 1907; spokesman for southern Irish Unionism.

CAMPBELL-BANNERMAN, Sir Henry (1836–1908)
Educated at Glasgow University & Trinity College, Cambridge; early career in family business; Liberal MP for Stirling Burghs, 1868–1908; various offices in Gladstone's first & second ministries; Sec. of State for War, 1886, 1892–5; leader of Liberal party in H. of Commons, 1899; denounced Govt's handling of South African War; reunited Liberal party in opposition to tariff reform, 1903–5; Prime Minister from Dec. 1905 until his death in April 1908.

CARDWELL, Edward (1813–1886)
Educated at Winchester & Balliol College, Oxford; MP for Oxford, 1852; 'Peelite' (later Liberal) politician who served in various ministerial posts under Aberdeen, Palmerston & Russell, 1852–66; Sec. of State for War under Gladstone, 1868–74; introduced short service, the army reserve & linked battalion system; notable army reformer who abolished purchase of commissions; created Viscount, 1874.

CAWDOR, 3rd Earl of (1847–1911)
Frederick Archibald Vaughan Campbell; educated at Eton & Christ Church, Oxford; Conservative MP for Carmarthenshire, 1874–85; active Militia officer; chairman, Great Western Railway, 1895–1905; succeeded father, 1898; First Lord of the Adty under Balfour, 1905; Pres. Institute of Naval Architects, 1905.

CHAMBERLAIN, Joseph (1836–1914)
Educated at University College School; reforming mayor of Birmingham, 1873–5; Liberal MP for Birmingham, 1876; member of Gladstone's second cabinet, 1880; combined radical views on domestic policy with vigorous imperialism; split from Liberals over Home Rule, 1886, & allied with Conservatives; entered Salisbury's cabinet as Sec. of State for Colonies, 1895; central role in events surrounding outbreak of South African War, 1899; advocated closer imperial union & saw preferential tariffs as most effective

means; launched tariff reform campaign, Birmingham, May 1903; resigned from Balfour Govt. to evangelize his cause, Sept. 1903; political career cut short by a stroke, 1906.

CHAMBERLAIN, Sir Joseph Austen (1863–1937)
Son of Joseph Chamberlain; educated at Rugby & Trinity College, Cambridge; Liberal Unionist MP for East Worcestershire, 1892–1914; Civil Lord of the Adty, 1895–1900; Fin. Sec. to the Treasury, 1900–1902; Post-master General, 1902–3; Chancellor of the Exch., 1903–5; assumed leadership of the tariff reform cause on his father's retirement in 1906; unsuccessful candidate for the Unionist party leadership in 1911.

CHURCHILL, Winston Spencer Leonard (1874–1965)
Son of Lord Randolph Churchill; educated at Harrow & Sandhurst; saw action as soldier & war correspondent in India, Cuba, the Sudan & South Africa, 1895–1900; escaped from Boer prisoner of war camp, 1899; Conservative MP for Oldham, 1900; joined Liberal party in opposition to tariff reform, 1903; Liberal MP for North-West Manchester, 1906–8, Dundee, 1908–22; Parlty. U.-Sec. for Colonies, 1906–8; Pres. Board of Trade, 1908–10; protagonist, with David Lloyd George, of the 'New Liberalism'; Home Sec., 1910; First Lord of the Adty, 1911–15; blamed for failure of Gallipoli campaign, 1915.

CLARKE, George Sydenham (1848–1933)
Passed first out of Royal Military Academy; gazetted to Royal Engineers, 1868; sec. to Colonial Defence Committee, 1885–92, & to Royal Commission on Navy & Army Admin., 1888–90; Governor of Victoria, 1901–3; member of War Office Reconstitution Cttee. with Sir John Fisher & Lord Esher, 1904; sec. of CID, 1904–7; Governor of Bombay, 1907–13; created Baron Sydenham of Combe, 1913.

COPE-CORNFORD, Leslie (1867–1927)
Journalist & author of works on naval and maritime subjects; naval correspondent of the *Standard* and *Morning Post*.

CORBETT, Sir Julian Stafford (1854–1922)
Educated at Trinity College, Cambridge; barrister & naval historian; works include *Drake & The Tudor Navy* (1898), *England in the Seven Years War* (1907) & *Some Principles of Maritime Strategy* (1911); lecturer, Naval War College, Greenwich, 1902.

CREWE-MILNES, Robert Offley Ashburton (1858–1945)
Son of Baron Houghton; educated at Harrow & Trinity College, Cambridge; succeeded father, 1885; Liberal statesman; Viceroy of Ireland, 1892–5; Lord Pres. of the Council, 1905–8; Lord Privy Seal, 1908–11, 1912–15; Colonial Sec., 1908–10; Sec. of State for India, 1910–15; close colleague of Asquith & Leader of the House of Lords, 1908–14; created Marquess of Crewe, 1911.

CROFT, Henry Page (1881–1947)
Educated at Eton, Shrewsbury, & Trinity Hall, Cambridge; Conservative MP for Christchurch (Bournemouth), 1910–40; strong advocate of tariff reform; founded imperialist 'National Party', 1917–22.

CURZON, George Nathaniel (1859–1925)
Educated at Eton & Balliol College, Oxford; Fellow of All Souls & member of the 'Souls'; lifelong interest in the East where he travelled extensively after 1887 & on which he became a recognized authority; wrote *Russia in Central Asia* (1889), *Persia & the Persian Question* (1892) & *Problems of the Far East* (1894); Conservative MP for Southport,

1886–92; U.-Sec. India Office, 1891; Parlty U.-Sec. for Foreign Affairs, 1895–8; created Baron Curzon of Kedleston, 1898; Viceroy of India, 1899–1905; pursued 'forward policy' in Persian Gulf & partitioned Bengal; resigned over quarrel with Kitchener, Indian C.-in-C.; Chancellor of Oxford, 1907; active in House of Lords, 1907–14; Lord Privy Seal in Asquith coalition, 1915; created Marquess, 1921.

DILKE, Sir Charles Wentworth (1843–1911)
Educated privately & Trinity Hall, Cambridge; lawyer, politician & writer on imperial, military & naval topics; Radical MP for Chelsea, 1868–1886; expressed republican opinions; served in Gladstone's second cabinet, 1880–85, but opposed Home Rule policy; career blighted by divorce scandal, 1885–6; published *Problems of Greater Britain* (1890) & *Imperial Defence* with Spenser Wilkinson (1890); Liberal MP for Forest of Dean, 1892–1911; parliamentary authority on imperial and defence issues.

ESHER, 2nd Viscount (1852–1930)
Reginald Baliol Brett; educated at Eton & Trinity College, Cambridge; Liberal MP for Penryn & Falmouth, 1880–85; member of Queen Victoria's private circle; as Sec., Office of Works, 1895–1902, superintended Victoria's Diamond Jubilee (1897) & funeral (1901), also Edward VII's coronation (1902); took interest in army reform and strategy generally; member of Elgin Commission into preparation for & conduct of South African War, 1902; chairman of War Office Reconstitution Cttee, 1904; member of CID, 1904–14; confidant of Edward VII & A.J. Balfour; *eminence grise* in Edwardian defence circles.

FISHER, Sir John Arbuthnot (1841–1920)
Born Ceylon; entered Navy, 1854; staff of gunnery school, HMS Excellent, 1866–9, 1872–6; pioneer of torpedo development; served in Egypt, 1882; captain of gunnery school, Portsmouth, 1883–6; Director of Ordnance & Torpedoes, 1886–90; Rear-Admiral, 1890; 3rd Sea Lord & Controller, 1892–7; Vice-Admiral, 1896; C.-in-C. North America & West Indies station, 1897; C.-in-C. Mediterranean Fleet, 1899–1902; attended Hague Peace Conference, 1899; 2nd Sea Lord, 1902–3; C.-in-C. Portsmouth, 1903; member of War Office Reconstitution Committee, 1904; First Sea Lord, 1904–10; Admiral of the Fleet, 1905; created Baron Fisher of Kilverstone, 1909; returned to Admiralty as First Sea Lord, 1914; resigned over Dardanelles campaign, May 1915.

GARVIN, James Louis (1868–1947)
Journalist & publicist; edited *Outlook*, 1905–6, *Pall Mall Gazette*, 1912–15, & *Observer*, 1908–42; advocate of military preparedness & supporter of tariff reform; confidant & press champion of Sir John Fisher; influential figure on Edwardian Right.

GWYNNE, Howell Arthur (1865–1950)
Educated at Swansea Grammar School; journalist; Reuters' war correspondent, 1893–1904; editor, *Standard*, 1904–11, & *Morning Post* 1911–37; supported tariff reform; ally of Beresford against Fisher.

GREY, Sir Edward (1862–1933)
Educated at Winchester & Balliol College, Oxford; Liberal MP for Berwick on Tweed, 1885–1916; Under-Sec. Foreign Office, 1892–5; Liberal Imperialist; Foreign Sec., 1905–16; Viscount Grey of Fallodon, 1911; noted ornithologist.

HAIG, Douglas (1861–1928)
Educated at Clifton, Brasenose College, Oxford, & Sandhurst; 7th Hussars, 1885; Staff College, 1896; Sudan campaign, 1898; staff officer then column commander in South

Africa, 1899–1902; Inspector-General of Cavalry in India, 1903–6; Director of Staff Duties, War Office, 1906–9; C. of Staff, India, 1909–11; commander, Aldershot, 1911; commander, First Army Corps, 1914; succeeded Sir John French as C.-in-C., BEF, Dec. 1916; Field Marshal & Earl, 1919.

HALDANE, Richard Burdon (1856–1928)
Educated at Edinburgh Academy, Gottingen & Edinburgh universities; Liberal MP for East Lothian, 1885–1911; lawyer, philosopher & educational reformer; prominent Liberal Imperialist, allied with Asquith & Grey; Sec. of State for War, 1905–12; Lord Chancellor, 1912–15; Viscount, 1911; Lord Chancellor in first Labour government, 1924.

HICKS-BEACH, Sir Michael Edward (1837–1916)
9th baronet; educated at Eton & Christ Church, Oxford; Conservative MP for East Gloucestershire, 1864–85, West Bristol, 1885–1906; served in Disraeli's cabinet, 1876–80, as Chief Sec. for Ireland & Colonial Sec.; Chancellor of the Exch. & Leader of the Commons, 1885–6; Irish Sec., 1886–7; Pres. of the Board of Trade, 1888–92; Chancellor of the Exch., 1895–1902; opponent of tariff reform & high defence spending; created Viscount St Aldwyn, 1906.

KERR, Lord Walter Talbot (1839–1927)
Entered Navy, 1853; Captain, 1872; naval private sec. to First Lord, 1885; Rear-Admiral, 1889; 4th Naval Lord, 1892, & 2nd Naval Lord, 1893–5; commander, Channel squadron, 1895; First Sea Lord, 1899–1904; Admiral of the Fleet, 1904.

KITCHENER, Horatio Herbert (1850–1916)
Educated Royal Military Academy, Woolwich; gazetted Royal Engineers, 1871; attached to French armies on the Loire, 1871; Palestine Exploration Fund, 1874; Gordon relief expedition, 1884–5; Gov.-Gen. of Eastern Sudan, 1886; as Sirdar of Egyptian army successfully reconquered Sudan, annihilating Khalifa's army at Omdurman, 1898; Gov.-Gen. of the Sudan, 1899; chief of staff to Lord Roberts in South Africa, 1899; C.-in-C. South Africa, 1900–1902; as C.-in-C. in India, 1902–9, reformed Indian army; Field Marshal, 1909; British Consul-General in Egypt, 1911; Earl Kitchener of Khartoum and Broome, 1914; Sec. of State for War, 1914–16.

LAMBERT, George (1866–1958)
Devon farmer; Liberal MP for South Molton, 1891–1924, 1929–45; Civil Lord of the Adty, 1905–15; Viscount, 1945.

LANSDOWNE, 5th Marquess of (1845–1927)
Henry Charles Keith Petty-Fitzmaurice; educated at Eton & Balliol College, Oxford; inherited liberal traditions; U.-Sec. for War, 1872–4; U.-Sec. for India, 1880; resigned office in opposition to Gladstone's Irish policy; Gov.- Gen. of Canada, 1883–8; Viceroy of India, 1888–94; with other Liberal Unionists joined Salisbury's cabinet, 1895; lost reputation as Sec. of State for War, 1895–1900; restored reputation as Foreign Sec., 1900–1905; leader of the Unionist party in the House of Lords, 1903–14.

LAW, Andrew Bonar (1858–1923)
Born in New Brunswick; educated at Glasgow High School; iron merchant & bank director; Conservative MP for Glasgow Blackfriars, 1900–6, Dulwich, 1906–10, Bootle, 1911–18; Parlty Sec. to Board of Trade, 1902–5; supporter of tariff reform; succeeded Balfour as leader of the Opposition in the Commons, 1911; led Unionist resistance to Irish Home Rule, 1911–14; Colonial Sec. in Asquith coalition, 1915.

LEE, Arthur Hamilton (1868–1947)
Educated at Cheltenham College & RMA Woolwich; Royal Artillery, 1888; professor at Royal Military College, Kingston, Ontario, 1893–8; military attache, US army in Cuba, 1898; met & befriended Theodore Roosevelt; Conservative MP for Fareham, 1900–18; Civil Lord of the Adty, 1903–5; Opposition spokesman on defence topics, 1906–14; created Viscount Lee of Fareham, 1922.

LLOYD GEORGE, David (1863–1945)
Brought up at Llanystumdwy, Caernarvonshire; lawyer & political radical; Liberal MP for Caernarvon Boroughs, 1890–1945; leading Welsh political figure from 1890s, militant on religious, temperance & educational questions & hostile to English privilege; outspoken opponent of South African War; led Welsh nonconformist opposition to 1902 Education Act; as Pres. of the Board of Trade, 1905–8, & Chancellor of the Exchequer, 1908–15, was a key figure in the 'New Liberalism'; author of 1909 'People's Budget' & prominent in subsequent Liberal campaign against the Lords' veto; moved away from Gladstonianism in his approach to defence & foreign affairs after 1911; tarnished by 'Marconi Scandal', 1913; influential in reconciling grass-roots Liberals to European war in 1914; dynamic force in wartime government; succeeded Asquith as Prime Minister, 1916; created Earl Lloyd George of Dwyfor, 1945.

LONG, Walter Hume (1854–1924)
Educated at Harrow & Christ Church, Oxford; Conservative MP for North Wiltshire, 1880–85, East Wiltshire, 1885–92, Liverpool (West Derby), 1893–1900, South Bristol, 1900–1906, South County Dublin, 1906–10, Midllesex (Strand), 1910–18, St George's Westminster, 1918–21; Pres. of Local Govt Board, 1886–92, 1900–1905; Pres. Board of Agriculture, 1895–1900; Chief Sec. for Ireland, 1905; associated with 'country party' & with Irish Unionism; created Union Defence League, 1907; unsuccessful challenger for Conservative leadership, 1911; Pres. of Local Govt Board in Asquith coalition; created Viscount Long of Wraxall, 1921.

LYTTELTON, Alfred (1857–1913)
Son of 4th Baron Lyttelton; educated at Eton & Trinity College, Cambridge; barrister; first class cricketer & amateur tennis champion; member of the 'Souls' & close friend of A.J. Balfour; Liberal Unionist MP for Leamington, 1895–1906, St George's Hanover Square, 1906–13; Colonial Sec., 1903–5.

MAXSE, Leopold James (1864–1932)
Educated at Harrow & King's College, Cambridge; journalist & publicist; owned & edited the *National Review*, 1893–1932; imperialist and Germanophobe.

MCKENNA, Reginald (1863–1943)
Educated at Trinity Hall, Cambridge; barrister; Liberal MP for North Monmouthshire, 1895–1918; Fin. Sec. to the Treasury, 1905–7; Pres. of the Board of Education, 1907–8; First Lord of the Adty, 1908–11; Home Sec., 1911–15; Chancellor of the Exch. in Asquith coalition, 1915; Chairman, Midland Bank, 1919–43.

MILNER, Alfred (1854–1925)
German-born; educated at Tubingen, King's College, London, & Balliol College, Oxford; Fellow of New College, Oxford, 1876; Inner Temple, 1881; writer, *Pall Mall Gazette*, 1882–5; strong advocate of constructive social policy; co-founder of Toynbee Hall, 1884; Liberal Unionist, 1886; advocate of imperial unity; financial administrator, Egypt, 1889–92; Chairman, Board of Inland Revenue, 1892–7; High Commissioner for South Africa, 1897–1905; supported movements for national service & tariff reform;

K

influential figure with younger 'forward' elements on the Edwardian Right; created Viscount, 1902.

MORLEY, John (1838–1923)

Educated at Cheltenham College & Lincoln College, Oxford; Liberal intellectual & politician; editor of *Fortnightly Review*, 1867–82; biographer of Cobden, Burke, Walpole, Cromwell & Gladstone; Liberal MP for Newcastle, 1883–95, Montrose Burghs, 1896–1908; early political ally of Chamberlain but supported Gladstone over Home Rule; Chief Sec. for Ireland, 1886, 1892–5; reforming Sec. of State for India, 1905–10; resigned from cabinet over decision for war in August 1914; created Viscount Morley of Blackburn, 1908.

NEWTON, 2nd Baron (1857–1942)

Thomas Wodehouse Legh; educated at Eton & Christ Church, Oxford; entered Foreign Office, 1879; Conservative MP, Newton, 1886–98; succeeded father, 1898; active in House of Lords, 1898–1914; co-founder of National Service League; Paymaster-general in Asquith coalition, 1915.

PRETYMAN, Ernest George Pretyman (1858–1931)

Educated at Eton & RMA Woolwich; retired from Royal Artillery, 1889; Hon. Col. 1st Suffolk Volunteer Artillery; Conservative MP for Woodbridge, 1895–1906, Chelmsford, 1908–23; speaker on questions concerning land & taxation; Civil Lord of the Adty, 1900–1903; Parlty & Fin. Sec. to the Adty, 1903–5; Parlty Sec. to the Board of Trade, 1915–16.

REPINGTON, Charles à Court (1858–1925)

Soldier & military writer; Rifle Brigade, 1878; Staff College, 1887; military attache, Brussels & The Hague, 1898; served in South Africa, 1899–1900; military career ended by an indiscreet affair, 1902; military correspondent of *Morning Post*, 1903–4, *The Times*, 1904–18.

RIDDELL, George Allardice (1865–1934)

Trained as solicitor; newspaper proprietor, *News of the World*, 1903–34; golf partner & confidant of Lloyd George & Bonar Law; knighted, 1909; created Baron, 1920.

RITCHIE, Charles Thomson (1836–1906)

Educated at City of London School; joined family firm of jute spinners & manufacturers of London & Dundee; Conservative MP for Tower Hamlets, 1874–85, St George's in the East, 1885–92, Croydon, 1895–1905; Pres. of Local Govt Board, 1886–92; Pres. Board of Trade, 1895–1900; Home Sec., 1900–1902; Chancellor of the Exch., 1902–3; his decision to drop the corn registration duty precipitated Chamberlain's tariff reform campaign; resigned office over fiscal issue, Sept.1903; created Baron Ritchie of Dundee, 1905.

ROBERTS, Frederick Sleigh (1832–1914)

Born Cawnpore; educated at Sandhurst; Bengal artillery, 1851; served Indian Mutiny, 1857–8; awarded Victoria Cross, 1858; Abyssinian expedition, 1868; Quarter-Master-Gen., Indian army, 1875; advocate of 'forward' policy in India; conducted successful pacification of Afghanistan, 1878–9, including famous march from Kabul to Kandahar; C.-in-C. Indian army, 1885–93; Field Marshal, 1895; as C.-in-C. South Africa, 1899–1900, restored British military fortunes; C.-in-C. 1900–5; Pres. of National Service League, 1905–14; Colonel-in-Chief of Indian Expeditionary Force to France, 1914; died at St-Omer; created Earl Roberts of Kabul and Kandahar, 1900.

ROBERTSON, Edmund (1845–1911)
Educated at St Andrew's University & Lincoln College, Oxford; Fellow of Corpus Christi, Oxford; called to the bar, 1872; Lincoln's Inn & Northern Circuit; Public Examiner in Law, Inns of Court; Liberal MP for Dundee, 1885–1908; Civil Lord of the Adty, 1892–5; Parlty Sec. to the Adty, 1905–1908; created Lord Lochee, 1908.

SALISBURY, 3rd Marquess of (1830–1903)
Robert Arthur Talbot Gascoyne-Cecil; uncle of A.J.Balfour; educated at Eton & Christ Church, Oxford; Conservative MP for Stamford, 1853–68; as Lord Robert Cecil, a polemical journalist who contributed numerous articles to *Quarterly Review*, 1860–83; trenchant critic of democracy; Sec. of State for India, 1866–7; resigned from Govt on Disraeli's introduction of household suffrage reform bill, 1867; succeeded father, 1868; Sec. for India, 1874–8; For. Sec., 1874–80; accompanied Disraeli to the Congress of Berlin, 1878; leader of Conservatives in Lords, 1881–5; Prime Minister, 1885, 1886–92, 1895–1902; consolidated Unionist alliance of Conservatives and breakaway Liberals; combined premiership with For. Secretaryship, 1886–1892, 1895–1900; a masterful diplomatist; resigned premiership in July 1902.

WILKINSON, Henry Spenser (1853–1937)
Educated at Owens College, Manchester, & Merton College, Oxford; leader-writer *Manchester Guardian*, 1882–92, & *Morning Post*, 1895–1914; Chichele Professor of military history at Oxford, 1909–23; co-founder of Navy League, 1894; influential writer on military topics; published *The Brain of an Army* (1890) & *The Brain of a Navy* (1895).

WILSON, Henry Hughes (1864–1922)
Ulsterman; commissioned into Militia, 1882; Rifle Brigade, 1884; served in South Africa, 1899–1901; Asst.-Adjutant-Gen., 1903; Commandant Staff College, Camberley, 1907; Director of Military Operations, 1910–14; assisted Lord Roberts' campaign for compulsory service; established close links with French General Staff & pressed for Anglo-French co-operation in a European war; primarily responsible for liaison with French army command, 1914–15; subsequently Chief of Imperial General Staff; Field Marshal, 1919; assassinated by Sinn Fein, 1922.

WILSON, Herbert Wrigley (1866–1940)
Educated at Durham School & Trinity College, Oxford; journalist & writer on naval topics; assistant editor, *Daily Mail*, 1898–1938.

WYNDHAM, George (1863–1913)
Educated at Eton & Sandhurst; Coldstream Guards, 1883; private sec. to A.J. Balfour, 1887; member of the 'Souls'; Conservative MP for Dover, 1889–1913; Parlty. U-Sec. to War Office, 1898; Chief Sec. for Ireland, 1900–5, during which time he passed an important Land Act (1903); active in Cheshire Yeomanry; man of letters.

SALISBURY, 4th Marquess of (1861–1947)
James Edward Hubert Gascoyne-Cecil; eldest son of 3rd Marquess; educated at Eton & University College, Oxford; Conservative MP for Darwen, 1885–92, Rochester, 1893–1903; succeeded father, 1903; commanded 4th Bedfordshire battalion (Militia) in South Africa, 1899–1900; U.-Sec. Foreign Affairs, 1900–1903; Lord Privy Seal, 1903–5; Pres. Board of Trade, 1905; authoritative speaker on military and ecclesiastical issues.

SANDARS, John Satterfield (1853–1934)
Educated at Repton & Magdalen College, Oxford; called to the bar, 1877; private sec. to the Home Sec., Henry Matthews, 1886; stood unsuccessfully as Unionist candidate for

Mid-Derbyshire, 1892; private sec. to A.J. Balfour, 1892–1911; estranged from Balfour over latter's entry into office under Asquith, 1915; keen follower of the Turf.

SEELY, John Edward Bernard (1868–1947)
Educated at Harrow & Trinity College, Cambridge; served in South Africa, 1900–1901; Conservative MP for Isle of Wight, 1900–1904; crossed floor to Liberals over tariff issue, 1904; Liberal MP for Liverpool (Abercromby), 1906–10; Ilkeston, 1910–22; U.-Sec. Colonial Office, 1908–11; U.-Sec. War Office, 1911–12; Sec. of State for War, 1912–14; resigned over so-called 'Curragh mutiny', 1914; commanded Canadian cavalry brigade in France, 1914–18; created Baron Mottistone, 1933.

SELBORNE, 2nd Earl of (1859–1942)
William Waldegrave Palmer; educated at Winchester & University College, Oxford; son-in-law of 3rd Marquess of Salisbury & cousin of A.J. Balfour; Liberal Unionist MP for Petersfield, 1886–92, West Edinburgh, 1892–5; succeeded father, 1895; U.-Sec. for Colonies, 1895–1900; First Lord of the Adty, 1900–1905; as High Commissioner for South Africa, 1905–10, played central role in achievement of South African Union; prominent Unionist peer, 1911–14; President of Board of Agriculture in Asquith coalition, 1915.

SMITH, Frederick Edwin (1872–1930)
Educated in Liverpool & at Wadham College, Oxford; Fellow of Merton College, Oxford, 1896; Grays Inn, 1899; a brilliant advocate whose reputation was made in several celebrated cases; Conservative MP for Liverpool (Walton), 1906–18; acclaimed maiden parliamentary speech, Feb. 1906; aggressive backbench critic of Liberal legislation, 1906–14; prominent on militant right of Conservative party; created Earl Birkenhead, 1922.

THURSFIELD, James Richard (1840–1923)
Fellow of Jesus College, Oxford, 1864–81; historian & writer on naval affairs; naval correspondent of *The Times* from 1881; keen supporter of Sir John Fisher; Knighted 1920.

TWEEDMOUTH, 2nd earl of (1849–1909)
Edward Marjoribanks; educated at Harrow & Christ Church, Oxford; Liberal MP for North Berwickshire, 1880–94; Liberal chief whip under Gladstone, 1892–4; succeeded father, 1894; Lord Privy Seal & Chancellor of the Duchy of Lancaster in Rosebery cabinet, 1894–5; First Lord of the Adty, 1905–8; Lord Pres. of the Council, 1908.

VINCENT, Sir Charles Edward Howard (1849–1908)
Royal Welsh Fusiliers, 1868; published *Elementary Military Geography* (1872); barrister, 1876; student of continental police systems; first director of criminal investigation at Scotland yard, 1878–84; Conservative MP for Central Sheffield, 1885–1908; member of London County Council, 1889–96; knighted, 1896; parliamentary spokesman for Volunteer force.

BIBLIOGRAPHY

Manuscript Sources

Unpublished official papers

Admiralty Papers (Ministry of Defence Naval Library)
Foreign Office Papers (Public Record Office, Kew)
Cabinet Papers (Public Record Office & Bodleian Library microfilms)
Committee of Imperial Defence Papers (Public Record Office & Bodleian Library microfilms))

Unpublished private papers

H.O. Arnold-Forster Papers (British Library)
H.H. Asquith Papers (Bodleian Library)
A.J. Balfour Papers (British Library)
R.D. Blumenfeld Papers (House of Lords Record Office)
Bonar Law Papers (House of Lords Record Office)
G.E. Buckle Papers (Times Newspapers Archive, London)
Sir H.Campbell-Bannerman Papers (British Library)
3rd Earl Cawdor Papers (Carmarthen County Record Office)
Austen Chamberlain Papers (Birmingham University Library)
Chandos [Alfred Lyttelton] Papers (Churchill College, Cambridge)
Sydenham [Sir George Clarke] Papers (British Library)
Leslie Cope-Cornford Papers (National Maritime Museum, Greenwich)
Julian Corbett Papers (National Maritime Museum)
Sir Charles Dilke Papers (British Library)
Lord Esher Papers (Churchill College)
Spencer Ewart Papers (Scottish Record Office)
Lord Fisher Papers (Churchill College)
J.L. Garvin Papers (Transcripts in the possession of Prof. A.J.A. Morris)
David Lloyd George Papers (House of Lords Record Office and Freshford Hall, Avon)
Glenesk-Bathurst [*Morning Post*] Papers (University of Leeds)
Sir Edward Grey Papers (Public Record Office, Kew)
H.A. Gwynne Papers (Bodleian Library)
Douglas Haig Papers (National Library of Scotland)
R.B. Haldane Papers (National Library of Scotland)
Lewis Harcourt Papers (Bodleian Library)
Lionel Horton-Smith Papers (National Maritime Museum)

Archibald Hurd Papers (Churchill College)
Walter Long Papers (British Library and Wiltshire County Record Office, Trowbridge)
Raymond Marker Papers (British Library)
Leo Maxse Papers (West Sussex Record Office, Chichester)
Reginald McKenna Papers (Churchill College)
Earl Midleton Papers (Public Record Office)
Lord Milner Papers (Bodleian Library)
Mottistone [Jack Seely] Papers (Nuffield College, Oxford)
Gerard Noel Papers (National Maritime Museum)
Northcliffe Papers (British Library)
Field Marshal Earl Roberts Papers (National Army Museum, London)
Earl Rosebery Papers (National Library of Scotland)
4th Marquess of Salisbury Papers (Hatfield House)
Jack Sandars Papers (Bodleian Library)
2nd Earl of Selborne Papers (Bodleian Library)
Edmond Slade Papers (National Maritime Museum)
Sir Cecil Spring Rice Papers (Churchill College)
St Loe Strachey Papers (House of Lords Record Office)
James R. Thursfield Papers (National Maritime Museum)
C.à.C. Repington Papers (Times Newspapers Archive, London)
Earl Tweedmouth Papers (Ministry of Defence Naval Library)
Wargrave Papers [Edward Goulding] (House of Lords Record Office)
Arnold White Papers (National Maritime Museum)
Spenser Wilkinson Papers (All Souls College, Oxford)
Willoughby de Broke Papers (House of Lords Record Office)
Sir Henry Wilson Papers (Imperial War Museum)

Printed Sources

F.W.S. Craig (ed.) *British Parliamentary Election Results 1885–1918* (London, 1974)

Dictionary of National Biography

Dod's Parliamentary Companion

E. Dugdale (ed.) *German Diplomatic Documents 1871–1914. Vol. III The Growing Antagonism* (London, 1969)

G.P. Gooch and H. Temperley (eds) *British Documents on the Origins of the War 1898–1914. vol. VI Anglo-German Tension, Armaments and Negotiation 1907–1912* (HMSO, London, 1930)

M. Stenton and S. Lees (eds) *Who's Who of British Members of Parliament. Vol. II 1886–1918* (Brighton, 1978)

Wyman and Sons' *Parliamentary Debates Official Report* 4th and 5th series

Newspapers and Periodicals

The Times
The Standard
The Daily Telegraph
The Observer
The Morning Post
The National Review

The Nineteenth Century and After
Vanity Fair

Books

R.J.Q. Adams and P. Poirier, *The Conscription Controversy in Great Britain 1900–18* (London, 1987)

G.J. Alder, *British India's Northern Frontier 1865–95* (London, 1963)

L.S. Amery, *My Political Life* 2 vols (London, 1953)

C. Andrew, *Theophile Delcassé and the Making of the Entente Cordiale* (London, 1968)

H.O. Arnold-Forster, *The War Office, the Army and the Empire* (London, 1900)

H.O. Arnold-Forster, *Military Needs and Military Policy* (London, 1909)

M. Arnold-Forster, *Hugh Oakley Arnold-Forster 1855–1909: A Memoir* (London, 1910)

Sir R. Bacon, *The Life of Lord Fisher of Kilverstone* 2 vols (London, 1929)

Sir R. Bacon, *From 1900 Onward* (London, 1940)

A.J. Balfour, *Chapters of Autobiography* (London, 1930)

C. Barnett, *Britain and her Army 1509–1970* (London, 1970)

Lord Beaverbrook, *Politicians and the War* (London, 1960)

Hon. G. Beckett and G. Ellis (eds.) *The 'Saturday' Handbook for Unionist Candidates, Speakers and Workers* (London, 1909)

G. Bennett, *Charlie B.: A Biography of Admiral Lord Charles Beresford of Metemmeh and Curraghmore* (London, 1968)

M. Bentley, *The Climax of Liberal Politics: British Liberalism in Theory and Practice 1868–1918* (London, 1987)

G. Bernstein, *Liberalism and Liberal Politics in Edwardian England* (London, 1986)

S. Bidwell and D. Graham, *Fire Power: British Army Weapons and Theories of War 1904–1945* (London, 1982)

R. Blake, *The Unknown Prime Minister: The Life and Times of Andrew Bonar Law* (London, 1955)

R. Blake, *The Conservative Party from Peel to Churchill* (London, 1970)

N. Blewett, *The Peers, the Parties and the People: The General Elections of 1910* (London, 1972)

W.S. Blunt, *My Diaries* 2 vols (London, 1920)

B. Bond, *The Victorian Army and the Staff College 1854–1914* (London, 1972)

V. Bonham-Carter, *Winston Churchill As I Knew Him* (London, 1965)

L.M. Bragge (ed.) *The Unionist Workers' Handbook* (London, 1912)

M. Brett and Viscount Esher, *Journals and Letters of Reginald Brett Viscount Esher* 4 vols (London, 1934–8)

M.G. Brock and E. Brock (eds), *H.H. Asquith: Letters to Venetia Stanley* (Oxford, 1982)

Lord Butler (ed.) *The Conservatives: A History from their Origins to 1965* (London, 1977)

C. Callwell, *Field Marshal Sir Henry Wilson: His Life and Diaries* 2 vols (London, 1927)

D. Cecil, *The Cecils of Hatfield House* (London, 1973)

Sir A. Chamberlain, *Down the Years* (London, 1935)

Sir A. Chamberlain, *Politics from Inside: An Epistolary Chronicle 1906–1914* (London, 1936)

Viscount Chilston, *Chief Whip* (London, 1961)

R.S. Churchill, *Winston Spencer Churchill. Vol. II Young Statesman 1901–1914* (London, 1967)

R.S. Churchill, *Winston Spencer Churchill. Companion Vol. II 1901–1914* (London, 1967)

W.S. Churchill, *Great Contemporaries* (London, 1937)

W.S. Churchill, *The World Crisis* 2 vols (London, 1938)

A. Clark (ed.) *A Good Innings. The Private Papers of Viscount Lee of Fareham* [Arthur Lee] (London, 1974)

I.F. Clarke, *Voices Prophesying War 1763–1984* (London, 1966)

P.F. Clarke, *Lancashire and the New Liberalism* (London, 1971)

F.W.S. Craig (ed.) *British Parliamentary Election Results 1885–1918* (London, 1974)

H. Cunningham, *The Volunteer Force: A Social and Political History 1859–1908* (London, 1975)

G. Dangerfield, *The Strange Death of Liberal England 1910–1914* (New York, 1935)

J. Darwin, *Britain, Egypt and the Middle East* (London, 1981)

E. David (ed.) *Inside Asquith's Cabinet: from the Diaries of Edward Hobhouse* (London, 1977)

G. De Groot, *Douglas Haig 1861–1928* (London, 1988)

Dictionary of National Biography

Sir C. Dilke and H.S. Wilkinson, *Imperial Defence* (London, 1892)

Dod's Parliamentary Companion

N. D'Ombrain, *War Machinery and High Policy: Defence Administration in Peacetime Britain 1902–1914* (Oxford, 1973)

F. Donaldson, *The Marconi Scandal* (London, 1962)

B. Drake and M. Cole (eds) *Our Partnership by Beatrice Webb* (London, 1948)

B.E.C. Dugdale, *Arthur James Balfour* 2 vols (London, 1936)

E. Dugdale (ed.), *German Diplomatic Documents 1871–1914. Vol. III The Growing Antagonism* (London, 1969)

Sir J. Dunlop, *The Development of the British Army 1899–1914* (London, 1938)

D. Dutton, *Austen Chamberlain: Gentleman in Politics* (Bolton, 1985)

M. Egremont, *The Cousins* (London, 1977)

M. Egremont, *Balfour: A Life of Arthur James Balfour* (London, 1980)

H.V. Emy, *Liberals, Radicals and Social Politics 1892–1914* (London, 1973)

F. Fischer, *War of Illusions: German Policies from 1911 to 1914* (London, 1975)

Sir A. Fitzroy, *Memories* 2 vols (London, 1925)

R.F. Foster, *Lord Randolph Churchill: A Political Life* (Oxford, 1981)

P. Fraser, *Lord Esher: A Political Biography* (London, 1973)

D. French, *British Economic and Strategic Planning 1905–1915* (London, 1982)

D. French, *British Strategy and War Aims 1914–1916* (London, 1986)

A.L. Friedberg, *The Weary Titan: Britain and the Experience of Relative Decline 1895–1905* (Princeton, NJ, 1988)

D. Geyer, *Russian Imperialism* (Leamington Spa, 1987)

M. Gilbert, *Winston S. Churchill. Vol. III 1914–1916* (London, 1971)

M. Gilbert, *Winston S. Churchill. Companion Vol. III Part I: August 1914–April 1915* (London, 1972)

M. Gilbert, *Winston S. Churchill. Companion Vol. III Part 2: May 1915–December 1916* (London, 1972)

D.R. Gillard, *The Struggle for Asia: A Study in British and Russian Imperialism 1828–1914* (London, 1977)

A. Gollin, *The Observer and J.L. Garvin 1908–14: A Study of Great Editorship* (London, 1960)

G.P. Gooch and H. Temperley (eds.) *British Documents on the Origins of the War 1898–1914. Vol. VI Anglo-German Tension, Armaments and Negotiation 1907–1912* (H.M.S.O., London, 1930)

J. Gooch, *The Plans of War: The General Staff and British Military Strategy c. 1900–1916* (London, 1974)

J. Gooch, *The Prospect of War: Studies in British Defence Policy 1847–1942* (London, 1981)

D.C. Gordon, *The Dominion Partnership in Imperial Defence 1870–1914* (Baltimore, MD, 1965)

R.L. Greaves, *Persia and the Defence of India, 1884–1892* (London, 1959)

J.A.S. Grenville, *Lord Salisbury and Foreign Policy: The Close of the C19th* (London, 1964)

Viscount Grey of Fallodon [Sir Edward Grey], *Twenty Five Years* 2 vols (London, 1925)

Sir A. Griffith-Boscawen, *Fourteen Years in Parliament* (London, 1907)

J. Grigg, *Lloyd George: The People's Champion 1902–1911* (London, 1978)

Viscount Haldane of Cloan, *Before The War* (London, 1920)

Viscount Haldane of Cloan, *Richard Burdon Haldane: An Autobiography* (London, 1929)

P.G. Halpern, *The Mediterranean Naval Situation 1908–1914* (Cambridge, Mass., 1971)

W.S. Hamer, *The British Army: Civil–Military Relations 1885–1905* (Oxford, 1970)

Lord Hankey, *The Supreme Command* 2 vols (London, 1961)

A. Havighurst, *Radical Journalist: H.W. Massingham 1860–1924* (Cambridge, 1974)

D. Hayes, *Conscription Conflict* (London, 1949)

C. Hazlehurst, *Politicians At War: July 1914 to May 1915* (London, 1971)

P. Hopkirk, *The Great Game: On Secret Service in High Asia* (London, 1990)

R. Hough, *First Sea Lord* (London, 1969)

R. Hough, *The Great War at Sea 1914–1918* (Oxford, 1983)

M. Howard, *The Continental Commitment: The Dilemma of British Defence Policy in the Era of Two World Wars* (London, 1972)

A. Hurd, *Who Goes There?* (London, 1942)

T.A. Jackson, *The Ulster Party: Irish Unionists in the House of Commons 1884–1911* (Oxford, 1989)

D. James, *Lord Roberts* (London, 1954)

F. Johnson, *Defence by Committee* (London, 1960)

J. Joll, *Europe since 1870* (London, 1976)

P. Kemp (ed.) *The Papers of Admiral Sir John Fisher* 2 vols (Navy Records Society, London, 1964)

G. Kennan, *The Fateful Alliance: France, Russia and the Coming of the First World War* (Manchester, 1984)

P.M. Kennedy, *The Rise of the Anglo-German Antagonism 1860–1914* (London, 1980)

P.M. Kennedy, *The Rise and Fall of British Naval Mastery* (London, 1983)

P.M. Kennedy, *Strategy and Diplomacy 1870–1945* (London, 1983)

P. King, *The Viceroy's Fall: How Kitchener Destroyed Curzon* (London, 1986)

S. Koss, *Lord Haldane: Scapegoat for Liberalism* (New York, 1969)

S. Koss, *Sir John Brunner: Radical Plutocrat* (Cambridge, 1970)

S. Koss, *Asquith* (London, 1976)

S. Koss, *The Rise and Fall of the Political Press in Britain. Vol.II The Twentieth Century* (London, 1984)

A. Lambert, *Unquiet Souls* (New York, 1984)

P. Larkin, *The Whitsun Weddings* (London, 1964)

K. Laybourn and J. Reynolds, *Liberalism and the Rise of Labour 1890–1918* (London, 1984)

Viscount Long of Wraxall [Walter Long], *Memories* (London, 1923)

E.W.R. Lumby (ed.) *Policy and Operations in the Mediterranean 1912–14* (Navy Records Society, London, 1970)

J.W. Mackail and Guy Wyndham, *Life and Letters of George Wyndham* 2 vols (London, 1925)

R.F. Mackay, *Fisher of Kilverstone* (Oxford, 1973)

R.F. Mackay, *Balfour: Intellectual Statesman* (Oxford, 1985)

A.J. Marder (ed.) *Fear God and Dread Nought: the Correspondence of Admiral of the Fleet Lord Fisher of Kilverstone* 3 vols (London, 1952–9)

A.J. Marder, *The Anatomy of Sea Power: A History of British Naval Policy in the Pre-Dreadnought Era 1880–1905* (London, 1964)

A.J. Marder, *From The Dreadnought To Scapa Flow. Vol.I The Road To War 1900–1914* (Oxford, 1961)

L. Masterman, *C.F.G. Masterman: A Biography* (London, 1939)

H.C.G. Matthew, *The Liberal Imperialists: The Ideas and Politics of a Post-Gladstonian Elite* (Oxford, 1973)

Sir F. Maurice, *Haldane: The Life of Viscount Haldane of Cloan* 2 vols (London, 1937)

S. McKenna, *Reginald McKenna 1863–1943: A Memoir* (London, 1948)

Earl of Midleton [W. St John Brodrick], *Records and Reactions 1856–1939* (London, 1939)

G. Monger, *The End of Isolation: British Foreign Policy 1900–1907* (London, 1963)

A.J.A. Morris, *Radicalism Against War 1906–1914: The Advocacy of Peace and Retrenchment* (London, 1972)

A.J.A. Morris, *The Scaremongers: The Advocacy of War and Rearmament 1896–1914* (London, 1984)

B. Murray, *The People's Budget 1909–10* (Oxford, 1980)

Lord Newton, *Retrospection* (London, 1941)

I. Nish, *The Anglo-Japanese Alliance* (London, 1966)

A. Offer, *The First World War: An Agrarian Interpretation* (London, 1989)

P. Padfield, *The Great Naval Race* (London, 1974)

T. Pakenham, *The Boer War* (London, 1979)

F.W. Perry, *The Colonial Armies* (Manchester, 1990)

Sir C. Petrie, *Walter Long and His Times* (London, 1936)

G. Phillips, *The Diehards: Aristocratic Society and Politics in Edwardian England* (Cambridge, Mass., 1979)

A. Porter, *The Origins of the South African War: Joseph Chamberlain and the Diplomacy of Imperialism 1895–99* (Manchester, 1980)

R. Pound and G. Harmsworth, *Northcliffe* (London, 1959)

M. Pugh, *The Making of Modern British Politics 1867–1939* (Oxford, 1982)

J. Ramsden, *The Age of Balfour and Baldwin 1902–1940* (London, 1978)

J. Ramsden (ed.) *Real Old Tory Politics: The Political Diaries of Robert Sanders, Lord Bayford 1910–1935* (London, 1984)

R. Rempel, *Unionists Divided: Arthur Balfour, Joseph Chamberlain and the Unionist Free Traders* (Newton Abbot, 1972)

C. à C. Repington, *Vestigia* (London, 1919)

R. Rhodes James, *Churchill: A Study in Failure 1900–1939* (London, 1973)

D.S. Richards, *The Savage Frontier* (London, 1990)

Lord Riddell [Sir George Riddell], *More Pages from My Diary 1908–14* (London, 1934)

Earl Roberts, *A Nation in Arms* (London, 1907)

R. Robinson and J. Gallagher, *Africa and the Victorians: The Official Mind Of Imperialism* (London, 1961)

Earl of Ronaldshay, *The Life of Lord Curzon* 3 vols (London, 1928)

S. Roskill, *Hankey: Man of Secrets. Vol.I 1877–1918* (London, 1970)

S. Roskill, *Churchill and the Admirals* (New York, 1977)

A.K. Russell, *Liberal Landslide; The General Election of 1906* (Newton Abbot, 1973)

R. Scally, *The Origins of the Lloyd George Coalition: The Politics of Social Imperialism 1900–18* (Princeton, NJ, 1975)

G.R. Searle, *The Quest for National Efficiency: A Study in British Politics and Political Thought 1899–1914* (Oxford, 1971)

G.R. Searle, *Corruption in British Politics 1895–1930* (Oxford, 1987)

J.E.B. Seely, *Adventure* (London, 1930)

B. Semmel, *Liberalism and Naval Strategy* (Boston, 1986)

P. Simkins, *Kitchener's Army: The Raising of the New Armies 1914–1916* (Manchester, 1988)

D. Southgate (ed.) *The Conservative Leadership 1832–1932* (London, 1974)

J.A. Spender, *The Life of the Rt. Hon. Sir Henry Campbell-Bannerman* 2 vols (London, 1923)

J.A. Spender, *The Public Life* 2 vols (London, 1925)

J.A. Spender and C. Asquith, *Life of Herbert Henry Asquith, Lord Oxford and Asquith* 2 vols (London, 1932)

E. Spiers, *Haldane: An Army Reformer* (Edinburgh, 1981)

J. Steinberg, *Yesterday's Deterrent: Tirpitz and the Birth of the German Battle Fleet* (London, 1965)

M. Stenton & S. Lees (eds.) *Who's Who of British Members of Parliament. Vol.II 1886–1918* (Brighton, 1978)

A.T.Q. Stewart, *The Ulster Crisis 1912–14* (London, 1967)

J.T. Sumida, *In Defence of Naval Supremacy: Finance, Technology and British Naval Policy 1889–1914* (London, 1989)

Viscount Sydenham of Combe [Sir George Clarke], *My Working Life* (London, 1929)

A. Sykes, *Tariff Reform in British Politics 1903–13* (London, 1979)

W.R. Thayer, *John Hay* 2 vols (Boston, Mass., 1908)

P. Thompson, *Socialists, Liberals and Labour* (London, 1967)

T. Travers, *The Killing Ground: The British Army, the Western Front and the Emergence of Modern Warfare 1900–1918* (London, 1987)

G.M. Trevelyan, *Grey of Fallodon* (London, 1937)

R.G. Verney [Lord Willoughby de Broke], *The Passing Years* (London, 1924)

J. Vincent (ed.) *The Crawford Papers* (Manchester, 1984)

A. White, *Efficiency and Empire* (London, 1901)

S.R. Williamson, *The Politics of Grand Strategy: Britain and France Prepare for War 1904–1914* (Cambridge, Mass., 1969)

K.M. Wilson, *The Policy of the Entente: Essays on the Determinants of British Foreign Policy, 1904–1914* (Cambridge, 1985)

T. Wilson (ed.) *The Political Diaries of C.P. Scott 1911–1928* (London, 1970)

Earl Winterton [Edward Turnour], *Pre-War* (London, 1932)

E.L. Woodward, *Great Britain and the German Navy* (Oxford, 1935)

H.F. Wyatt and L.G. Horton-Smith, *The Passing of the Great Fleet* (London, 1909)

Wyman and Sons' Parliamentary Debates Official Report, 4th and 5th series

G. Wyndham (ed.), *Letters of George Wyndham* 2 vols privately printed, (Edinburgh, 1915)

K. Young, *Arthur James Balfour: The Happy Life of the Politician, Prime Minister, Statesman and Philosopher 1848–1930* (London, 1963)

S. Zebel, *Balfour: A Political Biography* (London, 1973)

Articles, Essays and Theses

R.J.Q. Adams, 'Field Marshal Earl Roberts: Army and Empire', in *Studies in Edwardian Conservatism* ed. J.A. Thompson and A. Meiji (London, 1988) pp.41–76

M.J. Allison, 'The national service issue 1899–1914', London University Ph.D. thesis, 1975

W. Arnstein, 'Edwardian politics: turbulent spring or Indian summer?', in *The Edwardian Age: Conflict and Stability 1900–14* ed. A. O'Day (London, 1979) pp.60–78

C.J. Bartlett, 'The mid-Victorian reappraisal of naval policy', in *Studies in International History* ed. K. Bourne and D.C. Watt (London, 1967) pp.189–208

I.F.W. Beckett, 'H.O. Arnold-Forster and the Volunteers', in *Politicians and Defence: Studies in the Formulation of British Defence Policy* ed. I.F.W. Beckett and J. Gooch (Manchester, 1981) pp.47–68

I.F.W. Beckett, 'Edward Stanhope at the War Office, 1887–1892', *Journal of Strategic Studies* 5, 2 (1982) 278–307

M.G. Brock, 'Britain enters the war' in *The Coming of the First World War* ed. R.J.W. Evans and H. Pogge von Strandmann (Oxford, 1988) pp.145–78

P.F. Clarke, 'The Progressive Movement in England', *Transactions of the Royal Historical Society* 5th series, 24 (1974) 159–81.

P.F. Clarke, 'The electoral position of the Liberal and Labour parties 1910–14', *English Historical Review* 90 (1975) 828–36.

F. Coetzee, 'Pressure groups, Tory businessmen and the aura of political corruption before the First World War', *Historical Journal* 29, 4 (1986) 833–52

F. Coetzee and M. Coetzee, 'Rethinking the Radical Right in Germany and Britain before 1914', *Journal of Contemporary History* 21, 4 (1986) 515–37

G. De Groot, 'The prewar life and career of Douglas Haig', Edinburgh University Ph.D. thesis, 1983

Lord Esher, 'The voluntary principle', *National Review* 56, 331 (September 1910) 41–7

W. Fest, 'Jingoism and xenophobia in the electioneering strategies of British ruling elites before 1914', in *Nationalist and Racialist Movements in Britain and Germany before 1914* ed. P.M. Kennedy and A.J. Nicholls (London, 1981) pp.171–89

P. Fraser, 'British war policy and the crisis of Liberalism in May 1915', *Journal of Modern History* 52, 1 (1982) 1–26

D.R. Gillard, 'Salisbury and the Indian defence problem, 1885–1902', in *Studies in International History* ed. K. Bourne and D.C. Watt (London, 1967) pp.236–48

D.C. Gordon, 'The Admiralty and Dominion Navies 1902–1914', *Journal of Modern History* 33, 4 (1961) 407–22

D. Green, 'The Stratford by-election, May 1909: national defence and party politics', *Moirae* 5 (1980) 92–110

E.H.H. Green, 'Radical Conservatives and the electoral genesis of Tariff Reform', *Historical Journal* 28, 3 (1985) 667–92

P. Haggie, 'The Royal Navy and war planning in the Fisher era', *Journal of Contemporary History* 8, 3 (1973) 118–32

W. Hamilton, 'The nation and the Navy; methods and organization of British navalist propaganda, 1889–1914', London University Ph.D. thesis, 1977

R.B. Jones, 'The Conservative Party 1906–11', Oxford University B.Litt. thesis, 1960

G.S. Jordan, 'Pensions not Dreadnoughts' in *Edwardian Radicalism* ed. A.J.A. Morris (London, 1974) pp.162–79

P.M. Kennedy, 'The pre-war Right in Britain and Germany', in *Nationalist and Racialist Movements in Britain and Germany before 1914* ed. P.M. Kennedy and A.J. Nicholls (London, 1981) pp.1–20

S. Koss, 'The destruction of Britain's last Liberal government', *Journal of Modern History* 40, 2 (1968) 257–77

R.B. Langhorne, 'The naval question in Anglo-German relations 1912–14', *Historical Journal* 14, 2 (1971) 359–70

K. Lunn and R. Thomas, 'Portsmouth dockyard and society 1905–1914', undated occasional paper of the School of Social and Historical Studies, Portsmouth Polytechnic

S. Mahajan, 'The defence of India and the end of isolation: a study in the foreign policy of the Conservative government, 1900–5', *Journal of Imperial and Commonwealth History* 10, 2 (Jan. 1982) 168–93

G. Marcus, 'The Croydon by-election and the naval scare of 1909', *Journal of the Royal United Services Institution* 103, 162 (Nov. 1958) 500–14

J. McDermott, 'The revolution in British military thinking from the Boer War to the Moroccan crisis', in *The War Plans of the Great Powers 1880–1914* ed. P.M. Kennedy (London, 1980) pp.99–117

R. McKibbin, 'James Ramsay Macdonald and the problem of the independence of the Labour Party 1910–1914', *Journal of Modern History* 42, 2 (1970) 216–35

A.J.A. Morris, 'Haldane's army reforms, 1906–8: the deception of the Radicals', *History* 56, 186 (1971) 17–34

A.J.A. Morris, 'A not so silent service: the final stages of the Fisher-Beresford quarrel and the part played by the press', *Moirae* 6 (Trinity 1981) 42–81

M. Petter, 'The Progressive Alliance', *History* 58, 192 (1973) 45–59

G. Phillips, 'Lord Willoughby de Broke and the politics of Radical Toryism 1909–1914', *Journal of British Studies* 20, 1 (1980) 205–24

A.N. Porter, 'Lord Salisbury, foreign policy and domestic finance, 1860–1900' in *Salisbury: The Man and His Policies* ed. R. Blake and H. Cecil (London, 1987) pp.148–84

M. Pugh, 'Asquith, Bonar Law and the coming of the first coalition', *Historical Journal* 17, 4 (1974) 813–36

J. Ridley, 'The Unionist Social Reform Committee 1911–1914: wets before the deluge', *Historical Journal* 30, 2 (1987) 391–413.

L.J. Satre, 'St John Brodrick and army reform, 1901–1903', *Journal of British Studies* 15, 2 (1976) 117–39

G.R. Searle, 'Critics of Edwardian society; the case of the Radical Right', in *The Edwardian Age: Conflict and Stability 1900–1914* ed. A. O'Day (London, 1979) pp.79–96

G.R. Searle, 'The revolt from the Right in Edwardian Britain', in *Nationalist and Racialist Movements in Britain and Germany before 1914* ed. P.M. Kennedy and A.J. Nicholls (London, 1981) pp.21–39

E.D. Steele, 'Salisbury at the India Office', in *Salisbury: The Man and His Policies* ed. R. Blake and H. Cecil (London, 1987) pp.116–47

J. Stubbs, 'The Conservative Party and the politics of war 1914–16', Oxford University D.Phil. thesis, 1973

A. Summers, 'Militarism in Britain before the Great War', *History Workshop* 2 (1976) 104–23

A. Summers, 'The character of Edwardian nationalism: three popular leagues' in *Nationalist and Racialist Movements in Britain and Germany before 1914* ed. P.M. Kennedy and A.J. Nicholls (London, 1981) pp.68–87

A. Sykes, 'The Radical Right and the crisis of Conservatism before the First World War', *Historical Journal* 26, 3 (1983) 661–76

A.J.P. Taylor, 'We want eight and we won't wait', in *Politics in Wartime* (London, 1964) pp.53–6

J.A. Thompson, 'George Wyndham: Toryism and Imperialism', in *Studies in Edwardian Conservatism* ed. J.A. Thompson and A. Meiji (London, 1988) pp.105–28

A. Tucker, 'Politics and the Army in the Unionist government in England, 1900–1905', The Canadian Historical Association, Report of the Annual Meeting (1964) with Historical Papers, pp.105–19

A. Tucker, 'The issue of army reform in the Unionist government 1903–5', *Historical Journal* 9, 1 (1966) 90–100

H. Weinroth, 'Left-wing opposition to naval armaments in Britain before 1914', *Journal of Contemporary History* 6, 4 (1971) 93–120

A. White, 'The new gunnery', *National Review* 45, 267, (May 1905) 515–21

R.H. Williams, 'The politics of national defence: Arthur James Balfour and the Navy 1904–1911', Oxford University D.Phil. thesis, 1987

R.H. Williams, 'Arthur James Balfour, Sir John Fisher and the politics of naval reform 1904–1910', *Historical Research* 60, 141 (1987) 80–99

H. Willmott, 'The Navy Estimates, 1906–1909', University of Liverpool M.A. thesis, 1970

H.W. Wilson, 'Lord Cawdor's opportunity', *National Review* 45, 268 (June 1905) 597–610

H.W. Wilson, 'Destroying Britain's naval supremacy', *National Review* 48, 283 (Sept. 1906) 38–50

K.M. Wilson, 'The Opposition and the crisis in the Liberal Cabinet over foreign policy in November 1911', *International History Review* 3, 3 (July 1981) 399–413

Lord Wolmer, 'A militia regiment', *The Nineteenth Century* 122 (Apr. 1987) 566–75

M. Yakutiel, 'Treasury control and the South African War 1899–c.1905', Oxford University D.Phil. thesis, 1989

INDEX